BUSINESS REPLY CARD

FIRST CLASS MAIL   PERMIT NO. 08078   CAMBRIDGE, MA

POSTAGE WILL BE PAID BY ADDRESSEE

___THE___
AMERICAN
PROSPECT

NEW PROSPECT, P.O. Box 383080
CAMBRIDGE, MA 02238-9810

NO POSTAGE
NECESSARY
IF MAILED
IN THE
UNITED STATES

BUSINESS REPLY CARD

FIRST CLASS MAIL   PERMIT NO. 08078   CAMBRIDGE, MA

POSTAGE WILL BE PAID BY ADDRESSEE

___THE___
AMERICAN
PROSPECT

NEW PROSPECT, P.O. Box 383080
CAMBRIDGE, MA 02238-9810

REQUIRED READING

Don't let your liberal education end here. Continue it by subscribing to THE AMERICAN PROSPECT, the liberal journal of policy and politics. Winner of the 1994 Alternative Press Award for "Best Magazine," THE AMERICAN PROSPECT is a timeless resource for authoritative commentary and unconventional insight.

Don't miss out on another issue. Subscribe now — and send one to a friend. Students pay only $15 a year.

SUBSCRIPTION FORM

CHR1

Yes, please enter my subscription to THE AMERICAN PROSPECT
❑ One Year ($25)   ❑ Two Years ($40)   ❑ Student ($15—payment must be enclosed)
Foreign subscribers add $9 per year; make all checks payable in U.S. dollars.

NAME_____

ADDRESS_____

_____

_____

❑ My check is enclosed ❑ Please bill me ❑ Please charge my Mastercard or Visa

NUMBER_____ EXP. DATE_____

SIGNATURE_____

GIFT SUBSCRIPTION FORM

CHR1G

Please send a gift subscription to THE AMERICAN PROSPECT to a current non-subscriber.
❑ One Year ($18)   ❑ Two Years ($30)   ❑ Student ($15)   ❑ Library($20—special offer)
Foreign subscribers add $9 per year; make all checks payable in U.S. dollars.

NAME_____ SEND MY GIFT TO_____

ADDRESS_____ ADDRESS_____

_____ _____

_____ _____

❑ My check is enclosed ❑ Please bill me ❑ Please charge my Mastercard or Visa

NUMBER_____ EXP. DATE_____

SIGNATURE_____

THE AMERICAN PROSPECT READER IN AMERICAN POLITICS

Forthcoming

The American Prospect Reader in Political Economy
edited by Robert Kuttner

The American Prospect Reader in Public Policy
edited by Deborah A. Stone

The American Prospect
Reader in American Politics

Edited by

Walter Dean Burnham
*The University of Texas
at Austin*

Chatham House Publishers, Inc.
Chatham, New Jersey

The American Prospect Reader in American Politics

Chatham House Publishers, Inc.
Box One, Chatham, New Jersey 07928

Publisher: Edward Artinian
Cover design: Lawrence Ratzkin
Production supervisor: Katharine Miller
Composition: Bang, Motley, Olufsen
Printing and binding: R.R. Donnelley & Sons, Co.

Library of Congress Cataloging-in-Publication Data

The American prospect reader in American politics / edited by
    Walter Dean Burnham

        p.   cm.
    ISBN 1-56643-012-7
    1. United States—Politics and government.   I. Burnham, Walter
    Dean.   II. American prospect.
    JK21.A467   1995
    320.973'09'049—dc20   94-23157
                                                                   CIP

Manufactured in the United States of America
10 9 8 7 6 5 4 3 2 1

Contents

Introduction

WALTER DEAN BURNHAM   American Politics in the   1
1990s

Part One: Foundations

[1] STEPHEN HOLMES   The Liberal Idea   17
[2] PAUL STARR   Liberalism after Socialism   38
[3] ROBERT KUTTNER   Liberalism, Socialism, and   52
Democracy
[4] ROBERT D. PUTNAM   The Prosperous Community: 61
Social Capital and Public Life
[5] DEBORAH A. STONE   Race, Gender, and the Supreme   73
Court
[6] RANDALL KENNEDY   Lani Guinier's Constitution   86
[7] WALTER DELLINGER   Should We Compromise on   101
Abortion?
[8] LESLIE EPSTEIN   Civility and Its Discontents   111
[9] BENJAMIN R. BARBER   The Reconstruction of Rights   121

Part Two: Linkage—The Publics around Government

[10] RICHARD M. VALELLY   Vanishing Voters   137
[11] STANLEY B. GREENBERG   Reconstructing the Demo-   151
cratic Vision
[12] JEFF FAUX   The Myth of the New Democrat   162

[13A] WILL MARSHALL   Friend or Faux?   174

[13B] JEFF FAUX   The Evasion of Politics   180

[14] WALTER DEAN BURNHAM   The Politics of Repudiation   187
1992: Edging toward Upheaval

[15] MARSHALL GANZ   Voters in the Cross Hairs   204

[16] BRUCE ACKERMAN   Crediting the Voters: A New   218
Beginning for Campaign Finance

[17] JAMES S. FISHKIN   Talk of the Tube: How to Get   232
Teledemocracy Right

[18] KAREN PAGET   Citizen Organizing: Many Move-   240
ments, No Majority

[19] JOHN B. JUDIS   The Pressure Elite: Inside the   256
Narrow World of Advocacy Group Politics

Part Three: Institutions

[20] RICHARD M. VALELLY   Divided They Govern   279

[21] ROBERT KUTTNER   Congress without Cohabitation: 294
The Democrats' Morning-After

[22] NELSON W. POLSBY   Constitutional Mischief: What's   309
Wrong with Term Limitations

[23] RICHARD E. NEUSTADT   A Memo on Presidential   315
Transition

[24] PAUL STARR   Can Government Work?   326

[25] LAURENCE E. LYNN, JR.   Government Lite   343

[26] JONATHAN S. COHN   Damaged Goods: Before Rein-   354
venting Government, Clinton Needs to Repair It

[27] CASS R. SUNSTEIN   Constitutional Politics and the   364
Conservative Court

[28A] GENE B. SPERLING   Does the Supreme Court Matter?   378

[28B] CASS R. SUNSTEIN   Cass R. Sunstein Responds   385

[29] RANDALL KENNEDY   The Political Court   389

THE CONTRIBUTORS   393

Introduction

WALTER DEAN BURNHAM

American Politics in the 1990s

I

The American Prospect was launched in 1990, the tenth year of the Reagan-Bush era, to provide a forum for liberal alternative ideas about politics, government, and (political) economics. At the time of its founding, there was no particular reason for assuming that the conservative era was likely to come to an end any time soon. George Bush was running for re-election. With Desert Shield/Desert Storm boosting the president's approval ratings to nearly 90 percent, who could imagine that Bush was destined not merely to lose, but to suffer one of the truly great electoral routs ever experienced by an incumbent seeking a second term? Certainly not the putative heavy hitters in the Democratic Party's leadership councils of the time: like the guests invited to the king's wedding feast, each found his excuses for not attending the great nomination show of 1992. The rest, as they say, is history, and is briefly analyzed in an essay of mine included in this volume.

Bill Clinton's was a famous victory, but it is much too early in his administration to form any judgment as to what good came of it all. That some good has come of it already is obvious, not only in significant policy changes but in some quite sweeping transformations in the public debate: it really does matter who occupies the White House and its bully pulpit. Moreover, contingency—or in common parlance what we call luck—has been working on Clinton's behalf. Presidential success is greatly helped by having the right man in place at the right time, and it grows daily more clear that the American economy is moving into a recovery/growth mode after close to five years of stagnation. With a restructured, downsized economy marked by durable problems of job creation, this rising economic tide may be less likely than those in the past to lift all boats; but if sustained, it will very probably lift Bill Clinton's. Perhaps he will be reelected in 1996, perhaps not. It is hardly possible to

1

form any opinion about this as yet, but it is not too early to attempt the task of placing Clinton and his initiatives "in political time." Doing so, it is hoped, may provide some basis for judgment and reflection on where we are and whither we seem to be going, even though the picture painted will not be one of unalloyed joy from the liberal point of view.

II

We begin with some basics derived from Government 101 courses. The Constitution was deliberately designed as a power centrifuge and to ensure that any really large-scale or comprehensive transformations in public policy require conditions of abnormally broad, deep, and lasting public support. Thus, for example, the Civil War policy revolution of the 1860s, which went far beyond the war and its "Southern question," was made politically possible because, after secession, Republicans usually enjoyed majorities of three-quarters or more in both houses of Congress. The equally comprehensive changes in government's role and public policy linked to the New Deal likewise required a huge and general social trauma (the Great Depression) and again majorities of three-quarters for the innovating party in both houses of Congress. When the latter condition disappeared after 1938, New Deal innovation was abruptly terminated by the conservative coalition. One can also point to a different "abnormal"—and this time very long-lasting—consensus that produced far-reaching institutional and policy consequences. This was the "antitotalitarian," very promptly turning into the Cold War liberal, foreign policy consensus that lasted nearly half a century. This war, as Randolph Bourne remarked of World War I, was the health of the state in general and, in this case, of the presidency in particular. Its disappearance along with the USSR itself after 1989 was a cardinal condition for the election of Bill Clinton in 1992. But, as reflection on the Constitution as a bundle of rules that fragment power would have made it possible to predict, the disappearance of the Manichean struggle with godless communism also implied a swing of the internal American power balance away from the presidency and toward Congress. Every time one hears of another military base closing down, one is also witnessing a disappearance of a small bit of presidential power.

The 1992 election was fought in an atmosphere of vast public disgust with a political system widely regarded in the country as having been hijacked by establishment politicians, Beltway bandits, and other insiders cutting deals at the public's expense and ignoring mushrooming domestic needs: hence Ross Perot's 18.9 percent of the vote. Perot's entry meant that, at the end of the day, Clinton won with only 43 percent of the total vote, a figure not very different from the 1968–1988 mean for Democratic presidential candidates. In a similar multiple-race context, 1912, Woodrow Wilson had won with even less. But then, because the insurgent Theodore Roosevelt was not a "lone ranger" like Perot but had a party that fielded numerous congressional candidates, the minority Democratic Party of the time emerged with a huge majority in the House of Representatives and a comfortable one in the Senate. The policy innovations of 1913–1914 rested squarely on that fact.

Ultimately, no matter how much the public may have been dissatisfied with the gridlock and divided-government dynamics of the current degenerate regime order, overall social and economic conditions were simply not in the same league as those of 1932, nor was the political crisis remotely as immense as in the 1860s. Bush's loss in 1992 was—characteristically for our times—a very personal one. Republicans held their own in the Senate, gained 10 seats in the House, and made gains in state and local contests that continued to roll in during the 1993 off-year elections. There was a huge influx of congressional newcomers, 92 of them, the largest in many decades. But, unlike the "classes" of 1946, 1974, and 1980, these newcomers, entering in proportions very close to those of re-elected incumbents, tended to fit right into the mainstreams of their legislative parties, making few waves.

What all this adds up to is the ongoing politics of a country about half of whose voters for the first time live in suburbs. Since at least the 1960s, it has been characteristic of this public that it is ideologically hostile to "big government," while demanding the services that only big government can provide. Systematically miseducated by politicians both before and after the Reaganite transformation of 1980 that one can have governmentally facilitated consumption without paying its economic cost, this public prefers to have its cake and eat it too; to have, for example, universal health care coverage with no increases in my taxes, thank you, to pay for it. Only some general systemwide catastrophe might work for a time to override this deep contradiction, but fortunately none has arisen in two generations and none seems imminent.

The existence of "too many Republicans" in the 103rd Congress is one reflection of the balance of forces these underlying realities produce. It has concretely meant a series of absolutely minimal victories for Clinton in 1993 (notably on the budget) and has clearly forecast the deepest sort of trouble for his health care proposals in 1994.

Let us try to put the situation in a nutshell. Beginning with the constitutional rule bundle, American politics in "normal" times is dominated by negative feedback processes (the more you put in to innovate, the less you get per unit as groups with interests opposite to your own mobilize against you). This makes the system extremely conservative and resistant to change, particularly to anything that looks like comprehensive change. The Clinton initiative involves a policy area whose overall price tag is about $1 trillion, or some 17 percent of the national economy. In sheer size, it is the largest effort at comprehensive policy change since the New Deal—if we except, perhaps, Truman's Fair Deal health coverage proposals of 1949. And these, we may remember, got exactly nowhere in an 81st Congress, similar in its partisan distribution to the present one.

The key to success, if there is one, lies in energizing a strong and lopsided public opinion as a counterweight to interest-group influence. Success in this kind of endeavor requires simplicity in program and intense and persistent focus on the issue through every available publicity medium. With luck, one can thus trigger a positive feedback situation (every unit of input produces amplified, spillover, and above all mobilizing effects that can decisively alter the political balance by redefining the identity and number of serious players in a particular policy game). The partisan opposition will always be there, in season and out, as will the interest groups whose reason for being is bound up in keeping change as close to zero as the overall political situation will allow. Presidents, on the other hand, have lots of things to distract them, and the so-called bully pulpit is no real substitute for simplicity of program and permanently organized groups out there capable of mounting a sustained propaganda campaign that is competitive with the other side's.*

But the whole thrust of our current political order is hostile, culturally and operationally, to mobilizing masses of people behind a cause. Demobilization is more the order of the day, and both liberals and conservatives have contributed to it: a prime underlying reason for the bitter public reaction to established politics in 1992.

The bully pulpit is helpful, indeed essential for moving a president's program. But its use is only a necessary, not a sufficient, condition for suc-

---

* Something perhaps similar, if expressed in the purely religious language of sixteenth-century England, can be detected in a sermon preached by Hugh Latimer in 1548 against the gross deficiencies of the established clergy: "And now I would ask a strange question: who is the most diligentist bishop and prelate in all England that passeth all the rest in doing his office? I can tell for I know him who it is: I know him well.... It is the devil. He is the most diligent preacher of all other; he is never out of his diocese; he is never from his cure; ye shall never find him unoccupied; he is ever in his parish; he keepeth residence at all times; ye shall never find him out of the way, call for him when you will, he is ever at home; the diligentist preacher in all the realm; he is ever at his plough; no lording nor loitering can hinder him; he is ever applying his business, ye shall never find him idle, I warrant you." G.R. Elton, *The Tudor Constitution* (Cambridge: Cambridge University Press 1960), 327. In the language of a twentieth-century secular political scientist such as E.E. Schattschneider, we could say that what Latimer was complaining about was a "structurally induced mobilization of bias."

cess. If mobilization of large numbers of ordinary people is needed, organized structures for doing that must be in place or must be created: structures we have conveniently called political parties. But our age is one
whose chief defining political characteristic is that parties, at least as mass
mobilizers, are really not there any more. Current turnout rates, including
those of 1992, give us a good sociological profile—an extreme inequality of
voting input along class lines—that gives us some sense of the scope of our
modern politics of mass demobilization. The insurance company advertisements against the Clinton health care plan in 1993 and 1994 have brilliantly
played to the sociological realities of this selectively demobilized political
order. They aim squarely at a relatively affluent, broadly based white
middle class, many or most of whose members are relatively satisfied with
their current health care programs and are concerned that (1) their taxes
will rise and/or (2) the quality and choice they think they get now will be
compromised if the Clinton program is adopted.

III

The underlying point of the previous discussion is that it is difficult to
make bricks with insufficient straw. No general and acute domestic crisis
exists that might force action on a liberal, pro-statist agenda. There are
grossly inadequate presidential party (Democratic) majorities in Congress for moving such a reform program, which fact reflects (among
other things) this lack of general crisis. Moreover, since more than purely
rhetorical reform costs a lot of money, such an effort is in any case very
severely constrained by the debt-deficit problem inherited from the Reagan-Bush era. Even as economic recovery develops—itself paradoxically
undercutting any pressure for large-scale policy change—the economy
remains studded with problems, especially job-creation problems, that
make it politically very difficult to propose raising taxes to pay for new
initiatives or, in fact, to call proposed taxes by their right names.

To this must be added the underlying reality of American middle-
class politicians in the late twentieth century. Survey studies repeatedly
show that American anti-state ideology remains very much in the ascendant, as it has through most of our political history. But at the same
time, it also shows that the same public tends to prefer various divisible
benefits and policy outputs that only big government can provide. To
that should be added a general tendency for Americans to want expensive things but not to support tax increases to pay for them. The Reagan-
Bush "synthesis" rested fundamentally on giving and getting something
for nothing or, perhaps more precisely, on stimulating consumption that
was substantially greater than its productive support base. Out of the
vortex of these forces came the dominant structural pattern of politics be-

tween 1969 and 1993; divided government, with a middle-class public's ideological conservatism reflected in Republican control of the presidency and its operational liberalism reflected in Democratic control of Congress; and, of course, the set of decisions and nondecisions that produced a quadrupling of the national debt. The miseducation of the public during those years was as colossal as the debt was ultimately to become.

This "political time" created the opportunity space for Bill Clinton's election to the presidency, as the economy soured, corporations downsized, and angst grew in the leafy reaches of Montgomery County, Pennsylvania, and the sunlit coast of San Diego County, California. But political time also surrounds Clinton and his administration, giving the president opportunities but also probable limits on what he can expect to accomplish during his term.

If we view his leadership up to this point in some such terms as outlined here, some features of it may be more sharply defined than they have been in many journalistic accounts. In general, Clinton stands somewhere to the left of the modal opinion center of this era, but also on a number of issues—the North American Free Trade Agreement (NAFTA) being the most notorious—to the right of his congressional party. Possessed of apparently inexhaustible energy, Bill Clinton has prevailed on issue after issue by an extraordinary outpouring of executive effort. At times he almost seems a one-man band. Yet these frenetic bursts of activity are ultimately driven by the inadequacy of his political resources on Capitol Hill: not merely the presence of "too many Republicans," but the glaring extent to which leading archons of his own party in the Senate have repeatedly gone into business' for themselves and against his interests and policies. A remarkable ad hoc quality has also emerged: pure reliance on Democrats to get his budget enacted, alliance with Republican leaders (and rank and file) against Democrats in the NAFTA struggle, and what will almost certainly be a "mixed grill" coalition on health care, with considerable Republican input at the end of the day. The presidential coopting of traditional Republican themes on welfare and crime in Clinton's 1994 State of the Union address is matched by a budget proclaiming the elimination of more than a hundred federal programs and by evident presidential pride in the reduction of the budget deficit to its lowest share of the GDP since the 1970s. These themes have been duly noted by Republicans worried about losing control of "their" issues and by Democratic liberals in Congress who are plainly unhappy with these initiatives.

One could go on, including a discussion of the Lani Guinier affair and the curious lapse of a year before a successor nominee for the Civil Rights Division of the Justice Department was finally selected. But this suffices for the moment. I am less concerned with taking sides on any of these initiatives (for most or all of which a case could be made) than in thinking about their deeper implications. If Bill Clinton often seems to resemble the man on the flying trapeze, there are personal, strategic, and structural reasons for it all.

The post-1968 era has been one of normal Republican control of the executive. It is somewhat oversimplistic but, I think still true to say that the Republican Party is much more *monocolore* conservative than its Democratic rival is liberal. The Republicans come relatively close to being a genuine political party by comparative standards; the Democrats are more of a holding company of diverse and often warring interests. This asymmetry extends to quite different levels of cohesion not only among party activists and at conventions but in their electorates. The ultimate reason for this is teased out from comparative inquiry. The social stresses and unequal outcomes in advanced capitalist democracies everywhere produce fairly congruent structures of political oppositions in the electoral/policy market. Almost everywhere but in the United States, this produces an array extending from hard-to-moderate Right, to moderate-to-hard Left; and typically the vast majority is mobilized to come to the polls. In the United States, where social democracy has never been an "OK concept" in the mainstream political culture, we find instead three large groupings. The first, the Republicans, correspond very well on the whole to parties of the Right elsewhere. The second, the Democrats, find themselves in the intrinsically difficult position of representing interests that elsewhere would have their own parties of the Center and the Left: hence one reason for the much greater heterogeneity of the Democrats' electoral base and their greater failure to deliver it in presidential elections. The third component, of course, is the "party of nonvoters," more than 80 million of them in the 1992 election. While nonvoting is found at all levels of society, it is chiefly concentrated toward the bottom; its relative incidence and fluctuation from election to election form the outer limit of a political system thoroughly based on the relatively better off in general and of the Democratic Party in particular.

In a culture so hostile to social democratic ideas and movements, there are other consequences. One of them is that politicians on the Left end of the spectrum are usually very careful to use nomenclature for what they are proposing (and occasionally enacting) that leads away from recognition of the social democratic impulse underlying their efforts. Language that is euphuistic if not downright evasive becomes common currency. Another consequence is that while the system as a whole has a stable anchor on the Right, the situation at the Center and the Left is typically much more fluid and less well defined.

President Clinton recognizes quite clearly that if we are to deal as a country with our larger economic problems in the longer run, the state will have to play a much more important coordinating and facilitating role than would be tolerable to Reagan-Bush orthodoxy. Clinton is also personally committed to the view that government is not exclusively a necessary evil at best, but that it can be a significant force for ameliorating the public condition. On the other hand, there is a great deal of the "New Democrat" in him. He has seemed to spend some considerable effort to distance himself publicly from core Democratic activist constituencies that are also unpopular with the white middle-class center at which he is aiming. He is, in short, a man of the Center in a highly polarized interest-group and partisan world. As such, he inevitably reflects the Center's internal contradictions and limitations, just as his virtuoso performances in forging highly diverse and often supremely narrow majorities demonstrate that he can navigate the multiple shoals and crosscurrents in the stream he is traversing.

There is an Italian political term for this sort of thing: *trasformismo*. Developed to describe a modal political tendency in Italian politics before World War I, and turned into an art form by such skilled coalition manipulators like Giovanni Giolitti, *trasformismo* is the practice of staying on top by turning your winning coalitions inside out as need arises. It has its links with politics in France under the Third Republic, in which a "Left" majority produced by voters in the last election was rather prominently dissipated within the Chamber of Deputies itself and something like the status quo was restored. Frenetic and dramatic activity at the political Center is complemented by considerable substantive immobility, and collective-agenda problems—along with more fundamental steering problems generally—tend to mount over time.

IV

On occasion, time really does run out. Both examples cited previously perished as a consequence of involvement in a world war. Surely, there is no chance of anything of the sort affecting the United States now that the Soviet Union has disappeared and America is the only world superpower? Of course not. But this brings us to the foreign policy dimension of American politics in the contemporary world, one that seems only too likely to have its own non-Soviet dangers during the 1990s.

It is no secret that President Clinton has much less interest in world politics than in the domestic arena or that his "team" in the defense/foreign policy field is notably weaker (at least so far) than the domestic policy "team" is. Changes are rung repeatedly by spokesmen and allies that Clinton was elected to deal with domestic problems. And there is certainly no doubt that foreign and defense policy was less salient in 1992 than in any other election since 1936: one reason, among others, why a

Clinton victory was possible at all. But it is not 1936, much as we could will it otherwise, and Francis Fukuyama to the contrary, history has not come to an end and is not likely to. One is reminded of a parable in the New Testament, that most penetrating of commentaries on human nature: A demon was expelled from a man, wandered desert places looking for a new home, did not find one, and returned. Seeing that the home was now empty, he brought back seven companions, each worse than he was, to fill the void. With the Evil Empire only a memory, virulent nationalism and religious fundamentalism seem poised to make their home in various empty dwellings, starting perhaps with the next Russian presidential election. We may be in a temporary lull between the threat system of the past half century and a newer one that may prove far less stable. Long before the end of this decade, we will know.

Several different aspects of this uncertain world setting lie in wait for President Clinton. The first is the virtually overt alliance between the military and the Republican Party that has emerged in recent years. The second is the abundant potential for becoming "trapped" in open-ended commitments costing American lives and presidential support; yesterday, Somalia; tomorrow, Bosnia? And the third brings us back to the Constitution again.

The military-Republican alliance and its development have had much to do in the longer run with the effects of the takeover of the Democratic Party by anti-Vietnam war forces under George McGovern 20 years ago; and to a lesser extent, the era of being "in the doghouse" following defeat in Vietnam and especially under Jimmy Carter. Since then, Republicans have typically held the "high ground" as far as imperial policy is concerned, an important strategic asset in winning presidential elections as late as 1988. Bill Clinton had, of course, been able to arrange things so that he did not have to serve in the Vietnam war, something that many thousands of others could and did do. His first initiative, revising the existing policy concerning homosexuals in the military, touched off a firestorm of protest in military circles and among their allies, including Senate Armed Services Committee Chairman Sam Nunn (D-Ga.). And reports have circulated about the unfriendly treatment of senior military leaders when they have visited the White House. Finally, budget decisions have proposed cuts in military spending that go far beyond George Bush's level of comfort. How important this will be in the long run remains to be seen. But it is clear, first, that historically we have never had the level of the American military's political opposition to a commander in chief that now exists, and there is something worrying in this development. Second, this unsatisfactory relationship, given the right circumstances of international military involvement, may prove an Achilles' heel for the political future of the administration as a whole.

This might especially surface if the United States becomes involved, say, in a years-long struggle in the Balkans. Here, as elsewhere, the general rule of such open-ended involvements, with American casualties, has been that they can topple presidencies. It is not difficult to see why President Clinton has been so reluctant to cross this Rubicon in Bosnia, particularly after having been burned in Somalia. Enough has been said to create a widening impression that the credibility of NATO and of Clinton personally have become at risk—an obvious factor in the February 1994 ultimatum to the Bosnian Serbs surrounding Sarajevo. At best, the road ahead will seem far more confusing than usual: the half-century bipolarity between the rival superpowers provided a definition of, and public support for, very expensive defense that is no longer available. As in the past, a Democratic president is disproportionately vulnerable to attack for not maintaining control when things take an ugly turn in world politics: More than any other single factor, Jimmy Carter's presidency was sunk by such developments.

The third aspect of world politics, as we have said, is linked to the Constitution as a power centrifuge with very great in-built properties of dynamic equilibrium. Cutting the size of the military-industrial complex in the 1990s is not in principle a partisan issue: debates between Republicans and Democrats are not over whether to cut, say, by the standards of the late 1980s, but by how much. There is, however, one basic paradox in all this. It can be most succinctly expressed by noting that every time a military base is closed, a small fragment of presidential power disappears with it. Overall, our history supports the view that war is the health of the state, and the institutional health of the presidency in particular. The pre-1940 situation was one in which acute conflict was rare and was coupled with great but temporary bursts of state-building and in the relative institutional importance of the presidency vis-à-vis its congressional rivals. Since then, until just a few years ago, the Cold War—a kind of war, after all, which, heated up twice into significant uses of American military power—tilted the power balance, it seemed permanently, away from Congress and toward the presidency.

While we cannot know what lies just over the horizon, it seems unlikely that conditions in the near future will support the enhanced presidential role in American politics that seemed not so long ago to be a permanent feature of "the modern presidency" and recent American politics generally. If this is so, it suggests that Bill Clinton may be the first of a number of institutionally diminished presidents, and Congress's role will acquire proportionately greater importance as the constitutional dynamic equilibrium moves somewhat closer to its traditional balance. Rhetorical "cheerleading" and bully pulpit exercises may somewhat conceal this drift for a time, but the drift continues nevertheless.

V

It may seem to the reader that the foregoing amounts to a counsel of despair insofar as liberals and the liberal agenda are concerned. In reality, nothing is further from the truth. What we have tried to do here is to present a realistic view of the contexts of leadership and of policy delivery in a Democratic administration existing at a specific moment in "political time." If this moment, as I think, is not particularly favorable to the realization of grandiose and integrated objectives, it is well to take this context into account in order not to be unduly disappointed when events fail to live up to predictions. The sociologist Max Weber had it exactly right when he observed that politics is the slow boring of hard boards. If one becomes dissatisfied with our current version of *trasformismo* and what it produces, at least we can appreciate why the present balance of political forces is such that this seems the dominant, and perhaps the only, alternative to outright conservative rule. Of course, the balancing act can be taken too far: leaders of organized labor claimed that it was in the NAFTA struggle. It is also a mistake for leaders to assume that deep-seated historic interests within a major party have nowhere else to go and thus can be discounted in the struggle for dominance over the soft middle of the road. But we need not dwell further on these issues. With a very different cast of characters in the executive high command than George Bush's team, with ample opportunities to make judicial appointments of very different orientation from those of the preceding twelve years, and with what has already been accomplished in public policy, liberals will have made real gains of their own. This is a different political world from that which saw the birth of *The American Prospect* in 1990.

Stephen Skowronek closes his magisterial new book, *The Politics Presidents Make* (Cambridge, Mass.: Harvard University Press, 1993), by concluding that secular trends over recent decades in the growth of the state have increasingly acted to impose outer limits on the capacity of presidents to orchestrate genuine politics of reconstruction. This "thickening" of the state parallels arguments made elsewhere (e.g., Frank Baumgartner and Bryan Jones, *Agendas and Instability in American Politics* [Chicago: University of Chicago Press, 1993]) that the radical growth and polarization of interest-group activity since the 1960s has significantly undermined the leverage of the presidency in the achievement of policy transformation. From Skowronek's point of view, the situation suggests the emergence of a dominant presidential stance. This is the politics of preemption, in which the president operates, as it were, outside traditional partisan alignments and commitments. This is a risky strategy indeed, as such diverse historic figures as John Tyler, Andrew Johnson, and Richard Nixon found to their cost. If there is such a movement toward a politics of "perpetual preemption" in the White House, this development would imply that the fragmentation of American politics has now reached the point where the presidency as an institution has become isolated to a degree not seen since Andrew Jackson's elevation in 1828. Preemptors, in Skowronek's vision, have historically been unusual, what he calls the "wild cards" among presidents. If most or all presidents henceforth become "wild cards," the perennial American governing problem cannot but become more acute than ever. Be all this as it may, one has to say that, thus far, Clinton has been acting out a role that looks very like the one Skowronek assigns to presidents now and in the immediate future.

Perhaps all this is so, but one can think of another line of explanation.

As is pretty well known, my own analyses of "political time" have strongly suggested an embedded tension between stasis-prone politics-as-usual and the political effects of dynamic and uneven development of society and economy. Out of this tension comes that remarkable punctuated equilibrium-event sequence, the critical realignment. According to this model, such realignments have broken through the inertia and conservatism of the political system at strikingly regular intervals throughout American history, culminating (thus far) in the New Deal realignment of the 1930s and the "interregnum-state" realignment of the period centering on the 1968 election. But the tensions and dynamics involved extend beyond megaevents such as realignments. They include (and have included since at least the late 1830s) midpoint crises. These mini upheavals occur halfway between one huge realigning "peak" and the next, that is, halfway through the lifetime of a given regime order that occupies a particular stretch of "political time." There was such a midpoint mini upheaval around 1875 in the Civil War era or system, another around 1913 (intimately connected with the Progressive movement) in the "system of 1896," and another around 1951, halfway in the lifetime of the fifth, or New Deal, system.

Such "midlife crises" are genetically akin to critical realignments and arise ultimately from the same root causes embedded in what James Madison once called "our feudal constitution" coexisting with the world's most dynamic private sector. But instead of overthrowing and replacing a whole regime order, as realignments do, these events only modify this still-robust order. One is faintly reminded of Karl Marx's assertion that no social formation is replaced until it has reached impasse and decay, that is, has exhausted all the possibilities inherent in the way it is put together and functions. Historically, it would seem that these midpoint punctuations of change subdivide ongoing regime orders: before they occur, the order is consolidated and maintained; afterward, it tends increasingly toward decay, and eventual overthrow a half-generation later.

Each regime order has its unique time- and context-defined charac-

teristics, as does each critical realignment and each midpoint stress moment. The boxes must thus be filled in with concrete empirical information, a task we can hardly begin to attempt here. It is enough to say on
this occasion that the realignment of the late 1960s produced an unprecedented political regime of disarticulation and eclipse of traditional partisan channels that once tended to bond rulers and ruled together: what I
call the "interregnum state." Thus, one of its chief features has been a
"normal" state of divided government. Another has been a remarkable
speedup in the displacement of proposed "political formulas" or "public
philosophies" whose purpose it is to legitimate what is going on in government and to regulate political traffic. The electoral foundations of the
New Deal order were shattered in the 1968–1972 period, but in policy it
lingered on until Ronald Reagan's election in 1980. Then it achieved full
repudiation, to be replaced by an attempted Reaganite synthesis not
merely in the policy domain but in "public philosophy" as well. But this
in turn achieved bankruptcy within a dozen years instead of (as historically) over about 30 to 40 years. So far, at least, no plausible successor has
been developed, though clearly many around President Clinton have
been attempting to organize one. Such efforts seem to project a stress on
redeveloping the state as a significant, legitimate, and proactive player in
managing economic revitalization through achieving social harmony:
business, labor, consumers, and government all working, for example, to
minimize the socially disruptive consequences at home of universal free
trade and pursuing indicative, coordinated, policies for remaining economically competitive in an increasingly integrated world economy.

Whether anything will come of such efforts remains to be seen. For
what it is worth, the model discussed above "predicted" the emergence
of a midpoint crisis in the present (sixth) regime order sometime around
1989. Granted that reality is messier and tends to work out more slowly
than any change model can do (particularly a priori), it is reasonable
enough to say that 1992 qualifies as a "midpoint crisis" election, very
much like an election with which it is sometimes compared (third-party
protest and all): 1912. Yet if the analysis is valid, it implies that the interregnum state is not likely to be dissolved or replaced but rather
recalibrated: The conditions supporting it have not in fact ceased to be
robust. The deadlock embedded in it, as I have suggested earlier, is ultimately rooted in the ambiguities and contradictions of middle-class politics. These are unlikely to change very dramatically unless or until a very
severe and generally widespread socioeconomic crisis, something far exceeding the real discontents and stresses of the 1989–1992 period,
emerges. (For what it is worth, the model "predicts" the next realigning
upheaval as occurring around 2004 or 2008. Stay tuned.)

Coming back to Skowronek's argument, it certainly would not seem reasonable to view George Bush as a presidential preemptor. Instead, he was a pretty classic third-term understudy, attempting to carry on the basic policies and commitments developed in the innovative Reagan regime. If Bill Clinton seems to reflect a presidential *trasformismo* style (or if one prefers, that of presidential preemption), this would appear to fit the logic of his particular situation in this moment of political time. Activist, committed to a positive governmental presence that negates the attempted orthodox public philosophy of the Reagan-Bush era, he also has (and cultivates) a strikingly asymmetric relationship with the core groups, interests and values of Democratic Party leaders, activists, and bedrock constituencies. Unlike Woodrow Wilson in 1913–1916, Clinton lacks the power base in Congress to work as much of his will as he would wish. And, while the president and the First Lady may call for ideological deescalation and pragmatic, bipartisan problem solving in such a vast and contentious policy area as health care, such efforts are unlikely to be successful. This is not only because of the obvious incentives of out-party politicians, it is because the entire political society —particularly in Washington—has become increasingly dominated by the mobilization and proliferation of ideologically polarized interest groups. Moreover, their level of ideological polarization appears to be rising. This development, as much as or more than anything else, has given the interregnum state its particular political balance and seems to make it (for the moment, at least) virtually indestructible. Politics in the 1990s has already seen the passing of the Reaganite synthesis into the discard, very soon after it had emerged on the ruins of late New Deal interest-group liberalism. If there is a certain sense of disorientation among the public, one can hardly be surprised, for at the moment, there is no policy/public philosophy synthesis. Bill Clinton and his team may yet produce one; and nothing I have said here in any way implies any prediction one way or the other about the prospects for his success in the 1996 campaign. At the moment, however, it is hard to see where, how, and through what means the rather acute American governing problem of today will be mitigated very much in the foreseeable future. In all this, the role of a journal such as *The American Prospect* becomes more rather than less significant. Defining who we are and what we should be as a political society is a central feature of today's and tomorrow's political agenda. The vacuum calls to us; it creates an incentive for us to fill it with something positive, humane, and, of course, realistic. The challenge is no mean one.

Part One
Foundations

[1]

Stephen Holmes

The Liberal Idea

Liberalism looms prominent in contemporary debates—in this journal and elsewhere. But the term, however ubiquitous, remains elusive. By some, it is treated with cruel derision; by others, with breathtaking sanctimoniousness. A few writers, such as Alasdair MacIntyre or Christopher Lasch, finger liberalism as the source of all our miseries; others, such as Milton Friedman, preach that our most painful problems would be solved if we returned to liberalism in a pure and uncorrupted form. Some argue that the United States is a radiant monument to the liberal ideas of its Founders. Others retort that our society has evolved in unexpected ways and that stale eighteenth-century principles have become largely irrelevant to twentieth-century problems. Such postures are exhilarating. But they do not help us understand what liberalism was or how it has changed.

One claim about liberalism, common in textbooks, is that a major discontinuity divides classical from twentieth-century liberals—James Madison from Franklin Roosevelt, Adam Smith from John Maynard Keynes. Both left and right seem to agree about this purported reversal in theory and practice. Contemporary welfare programs, conservatives assure us, represent a betrayal of the liberal legacy. And progressives in principle agree: we would never have implemented Social Security and a progressive income tax if we had not turned our backs on the devil-take-the-hindmost attitude of eighteenth-century liberals.

But is this true? What is liberalism? What was it in the seventeenth and eighteenth centuries? Was its original promise fulfilled or betrayed? Have American liberals, following Roosevelt, simply misappropriated a term that originally meant the opposite of what it has come to mean today?

"Liberalism" is not a vague *Zeitgeist* or the outlook of modern man, but a clearly identifiable cluster of principles and institutional choices endorsed by specific politicians and popular movements. The early history of liberalism, in fact, cannot be detached from the political history, in the seventeenth and eighteenth centuries, of England and Scotland, the Netherlands, the United States, and France. Liberal principles were clearly expressed not just in theoretical texts but in the English Habeas Corpus Act, Bill of Rights, and Act of Toleration (1679, 1688–89), and the first Ten Amendments to the American Constitution and the *Déclaration de les droits de l'homme* (both of 1789). Some liberal politicians, such as the Federalists, succeeded brilliantly; others, such as their contemporaries, the French Feuillants, just as dramatically failed.

The political theorists who most cogently defended liberal aspirations—Milton, Spinoza, Locke, Montesquieu, Hume, Voltaire, Blackstone, Smith, Kant, Madison, and J.S. Mill—were deeply immersed in contemporary controversies. Each spent his life responding to local challenges, agitating for specific reforms, struggling with circumscribed problems. They faced different enemies and allied themselves with different social forces. Their epistemologies and metaphysical beliefs were sometimes diametrically opposed. None can be fully understood if plucked ahistorically from his political and intellectual context and forced to march in a syllabus-like parade of liberal greats.

The positions they defended, nevertheless, tend to converge. Their common liberalism—for we might as well call it that—has nothing whatsoever to do (as their critics say) with "atomistic" individualism or a hostility to the common good. So what did it involve? Liberals are sometimes said to advocate "the priority of liberty." While not totally false, this catchphrase is needlessly telegraphic. A list of the basic components of liberalism would have to include, at a bare minimum, religious toleration, freedom of discussion, personal security, free elections, constitutional government, and economic progress. But much more was and is involved.

Most liberals were both anticlerical and antimilitaristic, for instance. They were also opposed, in varying degrees, to hereditary monopolies, especially to the privileges of a few "great" families who owned large tracts of land. They scorned ties of vassalage and peonage and aimed to universalize the condition of personal independence. Most believed in the value of literacy and secular education for all, a fairer system of taxation, and the legitimacy of social mobility within and across generations. They welcomed immigration and freedom of movement in general. They supported the right to divorce. They opposed legal disabilities on religious minorities (so long as national security was not at stake). They endorsed the freedom to establish churches and to preach.

Legitimate authority, they argued, is based on popular consent, not on divine right or dynastic succession. They therefore defended not merely electoral politics but also the right of rebellion in some form. They advocated political pluralism and government by public discussion among provisionally elected and publicly accountable representatives. They hoped that bloody confrontation between armed factions could be, to some extent, replaced by rational bargaining and debate. They proposed a constant widening of the suffrage, more or less in tandem with the expansion of literacy, the relaxation of religious orthodoxy, and the abatement of religious passions. They also favored an independent judiciary, as well as laws that were clearly framed, publicly proclaimed, and fairly enforced. They prescribed the abolition of torture and savage punishments, legal checks on the police, guarantees both against retroactive legislation and arbitrary imprisonment, and jury trials in criminal cases. They tended to conceive punishment as a means of deterrence rather than a form of revenge. They advocated civilian control of the military. And they admired science or free inquiry as a deepening of human understanding, not merely as an instrument for mastering nature.

They were devoted not only to legal equality, but also to equality of economic opportunity. They were more distressed by poverty and personal dependency, however, than by inequality of income or wealth. Thus, they urged a wide and rapid diffusion of private property. They believed that contracts should be enforced. They favored the abolition of domestic customs barriers, free entry into trades and occupations, and the freedom to exchange goods and services. In other words, they had a generally welcoming attitude toward commercial society. They looked favorably on commercialism because they believed that economic competition would create (among other things) enough general prosperity to improve the lives of even the poorest members of the community. Adam Smith defended free trade, for example, on the grounds that it would increase the welfare of "the lowest ranks of the people" and work "for the benefit of the poor and the indigent."

This cluster of moral principles and most-favored practices provides the best starting point for an understanding of the liberal tradition. By an inversion and simplification, we can convert this unwieldy catalogue into a shorter list of liberalism's most disliked institutions and regimes. Four classically illiberal arrangements leap to the eye: autocracy, aristocracy, theocracy, and collective ownership. (Today we might add ethnocracy.)

In an autocratic regime, a single faction, party, or clique monopolizes power, the press is censored or superintended by the government; individuals can be imprisoned for long periods without legal recourse; the secret police are given enormous discretion to liquidate "unreliables" and enforce political subservience; the ordinary police are poorly monitored and controlled; the economy is centrally managed; criticism of political rulers is forbidden and, therefore, government is likely to be capricious, oppressive, corrupt, and grossly misinformed. In an aristocracy, access to privilege is determined almost wholly by pedigree; landownership is the key to life; a closed oligarchy monopolizes political power; and social mobility within and across generations is minimal. In a fundamentalist theocracy or clerical authoritarian regime, bigotry is rewarded, innovation is sacrificed to indoctrination, intellectual exchange is quashed, deviations punished, orthodoxy enforced.

All three regimes are patently illiberal. None stirs much sympathy in the West. Outrage is expressed whenever their vestiges are discovered in liberal societies today. Remedies are proposed and sometimes applied. To the extent that autocracy, aristocracy, and theocracy are decried, liberal rhetoric, at least, has triumphed.

It is different with communism and the principle of economic leveling on which it is purportedly built. The socialist tradition, despite its trumpeted embrace of "progress," has assiduously cultivated and kept alive an archaic inequality taboo, inherited, it seems, from subsistence economies of the distant past. (The archaic roots of communism may partly explain the extraordinary contagiousness of authoritarian socialism in underdeveloped countries where traces of a premodern communalist ethos remain strong.)

What characterizes liberalism, by contrast, is its unembarrassed repudiation of ancient and Christian prohibitions on inequality of resources. While adamantly opposed to any sort of caste system, liberalism is notoriously tolerant of disparities in income and wealth. Liberals are intensely concerned about poverty and economic dependency, about absolute levels of well-being (including a "bottom floor" of decent subsistence) as well as economically entrenched relations of mastery and control. Liberals did not, however, view inequality of wealth itself, apart from problems of dependency and poverty, as an unacceptable social evil.

Critics often assert that liberal acquiescence in economic inequality stems from a profound belief that superior talents "deserve" superior rewards. But that is a dubious claim. Liberals accepted inequality of resources, in fact, because they saw it as an inevitable side effect of a productive economy. They viewed the inequality taboo as an expression of irrational envy, it is true. But they rejected it primarily because they saw it as an infallible formula for reproducing scarcity and exacerbating dependency. As Alexis de Tocqueville said in 1848: "Socialism wants equality in poverty and slavery." Collective ownership is not only economically inefficient; it also destroys the independent resources on which political opposition is based.

In these pages, I do not offer a concise definition of liberalism. Without identifying liberalism's essence, I nevertheless sketch out a set of claims that are broadly characteristic of liberal political thought, including what I consider to be its three "core norms." I examine the basic contours of the liberal idea by looking sequentially at five concepts: the state, interests, rights, democracy, and welfare.

State Power

Liberalism is classically defined as an attempt to limit the power of the state for the sake of individual freedom. Liberals, it is true, were obsessed with curbing political tyranny. Their driving concern, many historians have argued, was to prevent hypertrophic government from oppressing individuals and groups. The essence of liberalism, from this perspective, lay in techniques for taming absolute power.

There are good reasons for emphasizing the antipower ethos within the liberal tradition. Liberals have a better grasp of economic realities than socialists and Marxists. But the most obvious superiority of liberal over Marxist thought stems from liberalism's persistent concern for —and Marxism's infamous blindness to—abuses of accumulated political power.

In fact, the antityrannical strand has always been, and remains today, a vital element within liberal thought. But it is not the whole story. To identify liberalism with a crusade to restrict state power is inadequate. For one thing, liberal states have, since the very beginning, proved breathtakingly powerful. The twentieth century provides some outstanding examples of the superiority of liberalism over autocracy from purely military and administrative perspectives. It is enlightening to reread, after the events of 1989, the speeches that Solzhenitsyn delivered in the United States during the 1970s. There he tells us that the West—infected by the spirit of liberalism—is becoming weaker and weaker, while the Soviet Union is moving with doom-like inevitability toward world domination. Many people made the same error about fascism in the 1930s. Liberal states are stronger than those awed by authoritarian power believe.

The dramatic story of nineteenth-century Britain is another case in point. The age of free trade and the industrial revolution, of course, was simultaneously the age of the British Empire. Shockingly enough, a small island off the northwest coast of Europe gained mastery over a third of the globe. The classic country of political liberalism did not display state weakness in any obvious sense. Liberal politics, in fact, seems to have been accompanied by a startling increase in the capacity of the state to mobilize resources for collective purposes.

This was already clear in the early eighteenth century. In the first great wave of liberal propaganda, Voltaire and Montesquieu praised England not only for its liberties, but also for its power—for the number of ships in its harbors. Oppression, they both argued, weakens a state. Intolerance deepens sectarian conflict and drives useful citizens abroad. Censorship blocks the flow of information vital for the governance of a large nation. Cruel and excessive punishments crush the spirit of ordinary citizens, depriving the government of their active collaboration. Heavy-handed regulations of trade decrease the private wealth that might be tapped for the public treasury. A liberal polity is much better situated than a tyrannical one for enlisting citizen cooperation in the pursuit of common objectives. Voltaire, and even Montesquieu, identified liberalism with a welcome magnification (along some dimensions) of state power.

This line of reasoning makes perfect sense. It is implausible, after all, to view liberal rights as naturally incompatible with political power, as if such rights flourish only when the state withers away. Authority and liberty are interdependent, not simply opposed. As Kant, among others, made clear, rights (including property rights) are defined and enforced by the state. Referring to "natural rights," Emile Durkheim convincingly wrote that "the State creates these rights, gives them an institutional form, and makes them into realities." To violate liberal rights is to disobey the liberal state. In a sovereignless condition, rights can be imagined but not experienced. In a society with a weak state, such as Lebanon for the past decade, rights themselves are weak or underenforced. Statelessness means rightlessness, as the story of migrating Kurds, Vietnamese and Caribbean boat people, and many others should by now have made abundantly clear.

The positive correlation between individual rights and state capacities is an important theme in the history of liberal thought. An emblematic figure in this regard is Pierre Bayle, one of the originators of the liberal defense of religious toleration. Bayle was a theorist of toleration. But he was also an "absolutist," that is, an advocate of increasing the powers of the crown or centralized state. The logic of his position may seem anomalous to those who understand liberalism as vehemently antistatist. But the Baylean linkage of liberal rights to sovereignty is actually quite straightforward. Only a powerful central state can protect individual rights against local strongmen and religious majorities. Only a powerful state can defend the weak against the strong. In France, to be more specific, only a powerful state could resist the pressure of ecclesiastics to persecute the Protestant minority. (Bayle was a Protestant.) Historians of liberalism, as I said, tend to repeat that liberalism was born in protest against state power. This is an accurate but one-sided picture. Bayle's tolerationism was born in protest against a lack of state power. His liberalism was most lucidly displayed in his plea to extend the protection of the secular state to a beleaguered sect.

Libertarian rhetoric about "getting the government off our backs" makes the positive correlation between individual rights and state power difficult to comprehend. Better guidance comes from classic liberals, who insisted that, when organized constitutionally, liberty and authority can be mutually reinforcing. Consider David Hume's famous essay, "Of Commerce." In this classic defense of liberal political economy, Hume argues that Britain should deregulate commercial and industrial life and welcome the accumulation of private wealth, because such a system will increase the resources "to which the public may lay claim." An autocratic government, intent upon controlling all economic life, will decrease the stock of private wealth and thereby indirectly undermine its own power. It is a lesson that the leaders of the Soviet Union have absorbed only today.

Not private property alone, but all typically liberal institutions were partly justified because they strengthened the state's capacity to govern and solve collective problems. Consider, by way of illustration, one of the most fundamental institutions of liberal constitutionalism: freedom of discussion. We might justify freedom of speech by arguing that the sphere of individual liberty must be maximally expanded while the sphere of state power must be contracted to a proportional degree. But liberals thought about free discussion in another way. Immanuel Kant, for example, argued that a government could not stifle freedom of the press because, by so doing, it would lose access to vital information and undermine its own capacity to govern.

Early modern theorists of absolutism, such as Jean Bodin, were the first to focus attention clearly on the advantages of liberty for the power of the state. In his *Six Books of the Republic* (1576), Bodin provided a series of extremely influential *raison d'état* arguments for constitutional limits on governmental power. Limited power is more powerful than unlimited power. That is the master thought of his great treatise and his principal legacy to the liberal tradition. Consider the following example. One of the most acute problems any ruler will face is control of his own officials. How will the king know what his agents are doing, especially in remote regions of the kingdom? Are they exceeding his commands? Are they taking bribes to enforce his laws selectively? How can such information travel from the periphery of a large kingdom to the center? How can a ruler monitor the activities of his "staff" without creating another "staff" whose activity would also be suspect and need monitoring? How can the king hear anything his inner circle of advisors do not want him to hear? Bodin's answer to all these questions is that if a king wants to learn promptly about the misdeeds of his own agents, he ought to create an assembly where representatives from the entire kingdom can come together and complain openly under a grant of immunity. Freedom of speech in a national assembly is an indispensable tool in the modern "art of governance."

What can we learn by looking at preliberal arguments for typically liberal political institutions? We can learn to question the conventional interpretation of classical liberal theory as ardently antistatist. Liberals were not anarchists. They were opposed to capricious and oppressive authority, not to authority in general. They embraced state power as a means both to prevent anarchy and to enforce impartial laws (against the grain of human partiality). Because they assumed that political rulers will themselves be human, and therefore partial and potentially unjust, they also devised institutional machinery to contain authority within legal channels. The constitutionalizing of authority is antiauthoritarian. But it does not imply a weakening or crippling of the state.

As the countries of Eastern Europe struggle to establish constitutional democracies in difficult circumstances today, we should ask ourselves again how the United States managed to stabilize a liberal-republican regime at the end of the eighteenth century. The endurance of the Constitution written at Philadelphia in 1787 was not foreordained. The members of the Constituent Assembly in Paris in 1791, whose ideals were not radically distant from those of the American Founders, produced a respectable liberal constitution that guttered to a swift and miserable end. Why did the Americans succeed and the French fail? There are many reasons, of course, stemming from the different political, religious, economic, demographic, and military situations of the two countries. But one neglected reason deserves to be pointed out. Unlike their French contemporaries, the American Founders wrote our Constitution after a period of frustration with the weakness of central government. They aimed, therefore, not only to prevent tyranny, but also to create a sturdy government with the capacity to govern effectively and "promote the general Welfare." This devotion to governmental effectiveness was virtually absent at the French Constituent Assembly of 1791. The desire simultaneously to limit and reinforce the state resulted, in the American case, in a constitutional regime that was neither tyrannical nor weak.

When granting powers to the government, the American Founders looked for guidance to the great European liberals. What powers should government be assigned, from a liberal point of view? These powers were not trivial. The power to defend the country from foreign invasion is usually mentioned first. But what should be the domestic powers of a liberal state? Liberals, for one thing, expected the government to provide security from private as well as public violence. In other words, they sought to create not only a police force, but also the mechanisms for monitoring and controlling the police. The liberal state was also expected to define property rights and enforce property law, contract law, and trespass law. No rules for the inheritance or conveyance of property existed in the state of nature; they had to be created by political means.

Civil society, therefore, was society "civilized" by the state. The state imposed civilization on society, among other ways, by constantly breaking up spontaneous economic and social monopolies.

But the power of the liberal state did not stop here. Constitutional government also had a significant allocative role. It had to make available judicial institutions for private litigation. It had to deliver fair procedures in criminal cases, allowing a reasonable defense for the accused. It had to provide poor relief. And, of course, it had to provide a whole series of public goods: canals, highways, safe water, street lights, sewers. State-help was conceived as providing the preconditions for self-help. This idea was nowhere more apparent than in liberal advocacy of subsidized education. Adam Smith, for one, favored a publicly financed system of compulsory elementary education aimed to help the indigent. John Stuart Mill, too, held it to be "the duty of the government" to supply "pecuniary support to elementary schools, such as to render them accessible to all the children of the poor." Far from being a road to serfdom, government intervention was meant to enhance individual autonomy. Publicly financed schooling, as Mill wrote, is "help toward doing without help."

Interests

From a Marxist perspective, the primary liberal right is the right to economic liberty: the right to own property, to make contracts, to enter into business, to buy and sell, to exchange goods and services. But is it true that liberals viewed economic rights as somehow primary or exemplary? According to Max Weber, freedom of conscience was the first and basic liberal right. More generally, liberals embraced religious toleration, freedom of discussion, the right to criticize government officials, and prohibitions against bodily torture for their own sakes—not merely because these practices were good for trade. However important, economic liberty was merely one of the core practices valued by liberals.

This is not to deny the emphasis that many liberals placed on market freedoms and economic self-interest. The role of self-interest in liberal theory, however, has been poorly understood. All too often, commentators assume that liberals who adopt a friendly attitude toward self-interest are advocating some sort of hyperegoistical attitude in which nothing matters but the pursuit of personal gain. This is an overly theatrical view of the liberal tradition.

Liberals are often accused of psychological reductionism. They purportedly believed that human beings are propelled by rational self-interest alone, as if benevolence, love of others, and devotion to the common good were wholly unreal motivations. This accusation is reckless. The truth is that, before the nineteenth century, motivational reductionism was virtually unknown. Most human behavior was understood to spring from irrational passions. Rational choice of action was exceptional. Self-destructive and wasteful conduct was rampant. Most individuals were compulsive or impulsive, hidebound by habit or victimized by passing frenzies. For neo-Stoics, calculating and self-interested behavior was a rare moral ideal. It could be achieved only by a few philosophers after a strenuous process of moral discipline, whereby irrational passions were systematically weakened and purged. It could certainly not be expected from everyone.

Given this cultural background, it is implausible to assume that classical European liberals were motivational reductionists. Their focus on calculating self-interest must be understood in a subtler way. It was not a descriptive claim, first of all, but rather a normative recommendation. We can see this most clearly in the work of the greatest of all preliberal theorists, Thomas Hobbes. If human beings were rational pursuers of their own self-interest, Hobbes reasoned, history would not be an endless chronicle of wasteful butchery and self-destruction. Civil wars are so frequent because some individuals are prepared to risk death for the sake of "higher" ideals such as glory and salvation. To eliminate the destructive violence of civil war, it is crucial to discredit all ideals that tempt individuals to defy death. In Hobbes's ideal society, people would rationally pursue their self-preservation, oblivious to the siren-songs of aristocratic glory and religious redemption. While he favored such a purging of irrational motivations, Hobbes did not believe that most people could be wholly rescued from preposterous habits of mind. He cannot be accused of thinking that human beings were self-disciplined enough to be rational and self-interested in an emphatic sense.

The same is true of the liberals who built upon Hobbes's thought. Montesquieu, for instance, believed that economic growth would discourage irrational and self-destructive behavior. It would weaken the vise-grip of xenophobia and bigotry. It would incite forethought and sharpen people's awareness of the remote consequences of their actions. Neither Montesquieu nor any other liberal however, thought that human beings were programmed at birth to be calculating maximizers of individual well-being.

There is also a moral component to the liberal emphasis on universal self-interest. To say that all individuals are motivated by self-interest is to assert that, from a political perspective, all human beings are fundamentally the same. For political purposes, no individual can claim to have motives that are morally superior to his neighbor's. There are no higher types. Everyone has interests. And one individual's interests are, in principle, as worthy of satisfaction as another's. The right to rule cannot be grounded on natural superiority. All people, including rulers, are driven by self-interest. As a result, constitution-makers must design institutions (such as periodic and competitive elections) to make the interests of rulers coincide with the interests of the ruled. The concept of universal self-interest can thus be said to provide the anthropological foundations for democracy.

The concept of self-interest, in short, contains an implicit reference to some sort of universalistic or egalitarian norm. Moreover, liberals uniformly took an additional step and endorsed the norm of fairness even when it spelled coercive checks on the principle of self-interest.

There is nothing shameful about the pursuit of personal advantage. That concession is a distinctive innovation of the humanism to which all liberals subscribed. Self-interest is not a sign of moral depravity or cowardice (though it does express a novel insouciance toward would-be social "superiors"). Advantage-seeking nevertheless presents an important social problem. Government is necessary, as Locke and the others argued, precisely because individuals are partial to themselves. Liberals worried about self-interest, then, because they were conscious of the damaging effects of human partiality. A self-interested individual will prefer that everyone else obeys the law, while he or she continues to disobey it. Such an arrangement would be in the individual's private interest, but it would also be wrong from a liberal point of view. To benefit from the self-restraint of others, while continuing to benefit from one's own lack of self-restraint, is flagrantly unjust or unfair. Individuals who exempt themselves from otherwise universal constraints implicitly assert, contrary to liberal principles, that they are special, superior, higher types.

Liberalism is a norm-based, not an interest-based, theory. The self-exemption taboo is the first core norm of liberal thought. This norm—the injunction to play by rules which apply equally to all—was most systematically expounded by Kant; but it is unambiguously advanced in the works of all liberal theorists. It would be in the interests of each of us to make an exception of ourselves; we would prefer to free ride on the taxes paid by our neighbors or to break the speed limit whenever convenient while benefiting from the well-monitored driving of others. But we cannot be permitted to do this because self-exemption from generally valid laws would be unfair. For liberals, in short, a norm of fairness overrides the motive of self-interest.

Rights

Classical liberals uniformly believed that rights are specified and maintained by state power. And they saw economic liberty as only one kind

of right, of no greater importance than, say, freedom of speech, the right
to a fair trial, freedom from bodily fear, freedom of conscience, the right
to vote. In "On the Jewish Question," the young Marx accused bourgeois
rights of destroying community. It has never been clear, however, why
limitations on the discretion of armed policemen should be anticommu-
nal. In fact, liberal rights do not protect the atomized individual from society. They protect fragile channels of social communication (such as the
press) from being infiltrated, controlled, and destroyed by political authorities. Authoritarian regimes, based on fear, are much more "atomistic" than liberal societies organized around rights.

One of the greatest obstacles to a fresh understanding of liberal
rights is the tyranny of false polarities. Political theory lives in thrall to a
sequence of binary schemes: individualism versus community, self-interest versus virtue, negative liberty versus positive liberty, limited government versus self-government. Indeed, the history of modern political
theory has recently been reconstructed as a running battle between two
rival traditions: liberalism versus republicanism. Republicanism, it appears, was everything that liberalism was not. Supposedly, republicans
believed in virtue, community, and citizen involvement in politics,
whereas liberals were devoted to base self-interest, personal security,
and private independence. This stylized contrast between liberalism and
republicanism, however, does not provide an accurate picture of the real
alternatives that confronted seventeenth- and eighteenth-century political thought or that confront us today.

One source of the misleading antithesis between liberalism and republicanism seems to be Isaiah Berlin's famous essay on negative and
positive liberty. The faults of this stimulating essay are well-known. For
one thing, Berlin employs the term "positive liberty" in an ambivalent
sense. He uses it to mean both the romantic realization of the real self
and democratic self-government. This is an unfortunate conflation, since
collective self-rule and individual self-fulfillment have no necessary connection with one another.

The second major problem with Berlin's position is his claim that
negative and positive liberty are logically, institutionally, and historically
unrelated: it is easy to have one without the other. This is a perplexing
claim. Political participation has plainly proved to be an indispensable
tool for protecting individuals against capricious, corrupt, and tyrannical
government. That, after all, is the essential meaning of "no taxation without representation." Similarly, the protection of private rights provides a
crucial precondition for "positive liberty" in both of Berlin's senses. If the
police can knock down our doors at midnight and drag away our families to unknown dungeons or graves, our chances for "personal fulfillment" will be drastically reduced, as will our desire to participate ac-

tively in political life. There is no good reason, again, why controls on police misconduct should be considered either undemocratic or unromantic.

The German liberal Alexander Humboldt argued that limited government makes self-realization possible. His contemporary, James Madison, argued that limited government makes collective self-rule possible. Both claims are reasonable and, taken together, provide good grounds for doubting the adequacy of Berlin's scheme. Madison's argument runs as follows. All attempts to organize popular government in the past have failed miserably. Republican regimes seem doomed to collapse into factionalism and anarchy. To escape from the intolerable chaos, some sort of Caesar or Cromwell is inevitably handed absolute power. The constitutional problem was how to thwart this powerful historical pattern. How could the Americans design a popular government that, unlike all other republics throughout history, would have a decent chance to survive?

Liberal rights are democracy-reinforcing. For self-government to endure, Madison reasoned, it must be limited government in a special sense. For the will of the majority to prevail, outvoted minorities must be willing to comply with electoral results. They must not resort to violence whenever they lose an election. To purchase minority compliance, the electoral majority must assure the electoral minority that its most precious values and rights will not be violated. A baseline of universal security, provided to all citizens, will create a willingness among the outvoted to acquiesce peacefully in the decisions of the majority.

Madison's famous sensitivity toward property rights should be seen in this light. While expecting and encouraging a greater diffusion of property ownership, Madison foresaw the maintenance in the United States of an important distinction between the rich and the poor. For a popular government to endure, the mass of poorer citizens must keep the confidence of the wealthy. Without the willing cooperation of the rich, no system as inherently unstable as collective self-rule could possibly last. If property-holders believe that democratic procedures will lead to confiscatory policies, they will not go along. They will sabotage the workings of popular government. The likely outcome is class warfare, anarchy, and the universal call for a dictator-on-horseback.

This line of reasoning may seem excessively cynical. Are property rights merely concessions that the many make to the few in order to purchase their cooperation in the workings of popular government? The impression of cynicism is mitigated, however, once we recall that Madison also assumed an economic rationale for property rights. They are productive, not merely protective; they contribute to overall prosperity, enhancing the well-being of the poorest members of the community.

Madison's argument suggests not only that positive liberty is a nec-

essary precondition for negative liberty, but that negative liberty is a necessary precondition for positive liberty. A market economy alone cannot
guarantee a democratic government or liberal legal institutions. (Germany has notoriously had more or less the same "market system" under
the Kaiser, the Weimar Republic, Hitler, and the Federal Republic.) Without decentralized economic power, however, liberal democracy is very
unlikely, if not wholly unable to survive. Economic liberty is a necessary
but not sufficient condition for the creation and endurance of a liberal-
democratic or liberal republican regime.

Negative liberty does not refer solely to economic freedom. It refers,
even more essentially, to personal security. In a liberal state, individuals
generally assume that, if they obey the law, they will not be harassed,
tortured, or killed by the police. The logical, psychological, and historical
connection between negative and positive liberty becomes even more
persuasive when we take this into account.

Individuals want their private rights protected because, among
other reasons, personal security allows them (1) to exercise their virtues
and realize their potentials, and (2) to participate without inhibition or
fear in public debate and processes of collective self-rule. Liberalism's
critics seldom take the virtue-fostering and democracy-enabling functions of private rights into account. Citizens will not throng voluntarily
to the public square, as I said, if their homes can be ravaged at will by the
police.

Note, finally, that negative liberty makes another crucial contribution to democratic government. Individual rights of religious conscience
and group freedom of worship do not merely protect a nonpolitical (but
still social) sphere. They also help keep a divisive issue off the political
agenda. By privatizing religion in a multidenominational society, liberal
freedom helps make public discussion and majoritarian decision-making
more effective. By securing a "private space" for religious activity, constitutional government encourages citizens to engage in mutual learning
and cooperation on a whole range of non-sacred issues. Separation of
church and state unclutters the democratic agenda and creates an opportunity for collaboration across sectarian lines. Again, because rights are
protective, they can also be productive.

Democracy

The claim by the critics of classical liberalism that it was inherently hostile to democracy is baffling from a historical point of view. First, the only
countries in which the majority of citizens has any chance at all to exercise influence on political decisions are those with liberal-constitution-
alist regimes. Second, the democratization of the suffrage in the West

did not seriously threaten the primary predemocratic liberal gains: religious toleration, freedom of the press, constraints on police misbehavior, freedom of entry into occupations and trades, and so forth. So from whence derives the myth that liberalism and democracy are mutually exclusive?

For one thing, liberals have always viewed political participation as voluntary and part-time. In a large nation densely populated with busy citizens, collective decision-making can occur only in a representative assembly, informed and stimulated by national discussion conducted by means of the free press. Those who identify democracy with direct full-time, obligatory participation in public life, therefore, have traditionally smeared liberals as antidemocrats. Aspiring to an unrealizable ideal, they condemn liberals for the sin of being practical-minded. To be sure, liberals did not look back with nostalgia to the ancient Greek polis. But was their skepticism, in this regard, antidemocratic? On the contrary. While admiring the extraordinary freedom of discussion in the Greek assemblies, liberals did not want to imitate most of the other characteristics of impoverished, slave-holding, militaristic oligarchies that managed to consume themselves in class warfare.

Another common argument for liberalism's antidemocratic bias relies upon the historical debate over the restricted suffrage. Liberals did have doubts and worries about majoritarian politics, and some were legitimate. Mill, for instance, was naturally distressed at the election of Louis Napoleon to the presidency of the Second French Republic by universal manhood suffrage. Nevertheless, despite practical reservations, liberals provided a strong theoretical basis for democratic politics as it eventually developed.

To be free, for liberals, was to obey laws made by oneself or one's representatives. That, in fact, was the second core norm of liberal theory. "Freedom to choose," liberals argued, includes freedom to choose the laws under which all citizens must jointly live. It is not surprising, therefore, that the two main political institutions of every liberal regime are the suffrage and a representative legislature. Citizens are bound to obey only those laws made by those expressly authorized to do so, laws made by legislators whom the electorate can oust from office if it wills. Locke insisted that the legislative power is "but a delegated Power from the People" and that "the Legislative being only a Fiduciary Power to act for certain ends, there remains still in the People a Supream Power to remove or alter the Legislative, when they find the Legislative act contrary to the trust reposed in them."

That is the classic liberal formulation of a right of rebellion. Democratic politics, as we now know it, is but a routinization of this fundamental liberal right. Our legislators are our trustees whom we remove from office when they violate our trust. Madison was simply following his liberal predecessors when he asserted that "a dependence on the people" is "the primary control on government," more important even than the separation of powers.

The third core norm of liberal theory, and one that again reveals the interconnection between liberalism and democracy, is the idea that public disagreement is a creative force. The standard view among preliberal political theorists was that uniformity of belief is necessary for social order. John Milton was one of the first to reject this traditional idea, scorning what he called "obedient unanimity" and "a grosse and conforming stupidity." The creativity of public disagreement is the theme of Milton's *Areopagitica* (1644). This improbable idea had an earlier incarnation, among other places, in a few city-states of ancient Greece. But it was only encoded in the political systems of large nations during the liberal period. It is so radical that not even Rousseau, the father of modern radicalism, accepted it.

Liberal rights, as mentioned, are not only protective. They are also productive. The purpose of freedom of speech, from this perspective, is less the protection of individual autonomy than the production of intelligent political decisions. Participation in "the free market of ideas" does not guarantee self-fulfillment or emotional identification among citizens. Instead, it is a technique designed to enlist the decentralized imagination and knowledge of citizens, to expose errors, and to encourage new proposals. The free market of ideas is an implicitly egalitarian idea, moreover. It assumes that every citizen can, in principle, make a useful contribution to public debate. Milton wrote of "the voice of reason from what quarter soever it be heard speaking." A regime built around free-wheeling debate, finally, can be said to be based on "human nature" in a loose sense. Human beings are animals capable of self-correction. Government-by-discussion is a political embodiment of the elemental human capacity to learn from experience and repair mistakes.

Suppose you wanted to create a political system for a large nation in which the majority would have a chance to influence public policy. What would you do? You would certainly avoid giving excessive power to urban mobs, who never represent more than a slim minority of the population. The only technique available to you would be electoral politics of some sort. Liberal universalism implies that every individual's vote should count the same. The only morally justified decision-making rule in liberal politics, therefore, is majoritarianism.

Liberal polities, however, while based on free and periodic elections, have all instituted a variety of restraints on majority rule. How can these limits be reconciled with a commitment to democracy?

Liberal limits on the power of electoral majorities have basically five justifications. The first three follow directly from the majority principle itself. First, the present majority must not be allowed to deprive future majorities of the right to correct earlier mistakes. Second, the present majority needs the willing cooperation of outvoted minorities, whose personal rights must therefore be protected. Third, without freedom of debate, shielded from majority censorship and bullying, elites will capture power and ensconce themselves beyond criticism, eventually confiscating the majority's own power.

Finally, there are two powerful nonmajoritarian principles at work behind liberal limitations on majority rule. One is the norm of fairness. Majorities cannot be allowed to apply laws selectively or unequally. The second is the idea that political decisions will be more intelligent if produced by a process of wide-open debate and subjected (even after they are made) to an ongoing process of criticism. The majority cannot silence its critics, even if it would love to do so. This prohibition insures that its decisions are more thoughtful and informed than they otherwise would be. The latter restrictions are indeed antimajoritarian. But they are not antidemocratic if "democracy" includes—as it surely does—both equality before the law and government by discussion.

One additional point needs to be made about majority rule. Both conservatives and radicals enjoy citing the passage in *The Federalist Papers* where Madison writes that "the people in its collective capacity" should have no role in political life. This phrase has always seemed oddly dissonant with other passages where Madison insists that the constitution being framed will create a "popular government." The solution to this paradox lies in the nature of majoritarian politics. As I mentioned, the only way to give power to the majority is through elections. To allow "the people" to act collectively, like the Roman mobs, is to disenfranchise the majority. Only when the people act individually as voters, rather than collectively as a mob, can some influence of the majority over the long haul be secured.

The problem with this arrangement, of course, is that the power wielded by voters on election day is relatively feeble. To make popular participation compatible with majority rule, liberalism makes it dangerously weak. What, then, can be done to increase the marginal leverage that a majority exerts through popular elections?

To this problem, liberals provided a classic solution: the separation of powers. The separation of powers was a liberal application of the old maxim: divide and rule. Traditionally, the *divide et impera* strategy had been employed by tyrants against their restive subjects. Liberals boldly turned this technique into a tool that the people could use against their rulers. By introducing internal divisions within government, liberals did not simply want to prevent tyranny. They were trying to create a regime that was relatively easy to influence from the outside. A "balance" is not stable. On the contrary, it can be upset by a grain of sand. Thus, a multi-branch and multi-level government provides a sensitive barometer for registering changes in public opinion, electorally expressed. This analysis, brilliantly advanced by Hamilton in *The Federalist*, number 28, suggests again that liberalism and democracy, far from being enemies or rivals, are mutually reinforcing.

Welfare

Transfer programs presuppose the continued existence of private property. Only a robust market economy, relying on individual incentives, can produce a surplus worth distributing by political means. In fact, welfare measures were originally proposed by liberals to improve liberal economies and enhance their chances of survival. Such policies were not designed to create equality of resources but only a "bottom floor" under which the indigent would not be allowed to fall. This is why communists, who favored collective ownership, were consistently opposed to welfare. They despised the incipient welfare state because they saw it as hostile to collectivism—as irredeemably liberal.

The historical relation between eighteenth-century rights and modern welfare entitlements is somewhat obscure. But the case for some sort of continuity between the two is quite strong. Spinoza's assertion that "the care of the poor is incumbent on the whole of society" is echoed by every major liberal theorist. One of the key liberal values, moreover, was security. True, this concept originally referred primarily to protection from violence. But as the resources of liberal societies expanded enormously, it was only natural for the concept of security to be gradually stretched to include unemployment insurance and other programs of "social security."

The government should protect citizens from force and fraud, libertarians argue, but it should take no "positive" action. Individuals should not be pampered by the nanny-state. This way of conceiving our constitutional system is inadequate. All liberal rights, including those enshrined in the first Ten Amendments, are exercised on the basis of resources furnished by the state. The government alone is in a position to define and enforce property rights, for example. And what other institution can provide citizens with a sense of physical security? (The social contract, according to Locke, required individuals to surrender the right of violent self-defense to the state.) In a liberal society, self-help always depends upon state help. There is nothing at all illiberal then, about the idea of an entitlement. Liberal citizens are entitled to a fair trial and to a high school education, for example. Do libertarians doubt this? The widely endorsed plan to give vouchers to every school-age child is illuminating in this regard. In the public discussion about vouchers, all sides on the ideological spectrum plainly accept the liberal state's duty to provide a minimum level of resources to all citizens. Entitlements to affirmative state action, then, are a staple of the liberal tradition. The controversy begins only when we ask: what sort of help, and how much, should the government provide? This is a proper topic for political debate, a debate that cannot be peremptorily closed by the assertion that our liberal Constitution forbids the government to provide individuals with resources of any kind.

Liberalism is individualistic. Liberals believe that individuals should be rewarded for achievement and merit. In no liberal society, however, are benefits and burdens allocated wholly on the basis of individual desert. Many of society's delights are purchased by means of inherited resources while its headaches fall disproportionately on those who are born without. The current rate of black infant mortality is only the most shocking example of a nonindividualistic pattern in the allocation of social goods. The decisiveness of inherited resources in all modern societies, in fact, presents a huge dilemma for liberals. We cannot justify the vastly unequal distribution of inherited resources (including parental attention) on individualistic grounds. No infant deserves either to be reared in luxury or to shiver undernourished and poorly clothed in a dangerous and drug-ridden tenement. Liberals will argue, of course, that inheritable property is indispensable for maintaining the prestige and cohesion of the family (the best environment we know for the socialization of individuals). They will also point out that the right to bequeath is itself a form of liberty, that it provides an incentive for industriousness and savings, and so forth.

But liberal inheritance law remains a radical concession to an institution that is not truly individualistic at all. Thus, liberals have naturally sought to redeem individualism by providing some life-enabling means to children who are born (through no conceivable fault of their own) without inherited resources. Child nutrition programs, according to this line of reasoning, are redistributive and yet wholly individualistic. They are attempts not to create a society of equals, but simply to compensate in a modest way for a maldistribution of inherited resources, difficult to justify on liberal grounds.

Liberalism is also universalistic. No individual has, by nature, greater entitlements than another. Human equality extends across class, ethnic, racial, and religious lines. It also extends, and for the same reason, across borders. Why should someone starve because he or she happens to live on the wrong side of a political frontier? Can this be "justified" within a liberal framework? No. There is no moral reason for such grim fate. But there is, alas, brute necessity.

Liberals have succeeded in realizing some of their ideals. But they were able to do so only because they willingly compromised with the realities of national sovereignty. Liberal rights are meaningful only within the confines of a liberal state, only where there exists a rights-enforcing power. To the extent that no enforcing power operates between states or across borders, liberal rights are futile.

So, liberals reason in the following manner. It is morally obligatory to secure a "bottom floor" of subsistence to all humanity. Unfortunately, it is unrealistic to attempt domestic-scale redistributions across borders, not only because of scarce resources, but also because of the location of sovereign power. Hence, although we may urge benevolence toward the poor beyond our borders, enforceable welfare rights will remain limited to co-nationals.

Contrast this argument to communitarian thinking about welfare. Communitarians argue that we owe special attention to co-nationals, not on practical considerations, but on grounds of solidarity: We are morally obliged to love our countrymen and to prefer them to foreigners. A liberal would demur.

Being practical, of course, liberals are willing to compromise with human passions. If a sense of "common identity" makes inhabitants of Scarsdale accept income transfers that benefit inhabitants of Harlem, there is nothing objectionable in that. A sense of shared nationality does seem to mobilize support for economic redistributions. (European countries with higher degrees of ethnic homogeneity are more successful in winning electoral support for transfer programs than welfare advocates in the ethnic crazy-quilt of the United States.) Such communitarian considerations may be very useful strategically. They do not, however, provide a moral reason for redistribution from a liberal point of view.

Liberal Discontent

The classical liberals were reformers and social critics. They were not hand-holders and flag-wavers for established regimes. Today, no liberal in the United States would advocate a wholesale remaking of our constitutional, legal, and economic system. But neither can a liberal heir of Locke and Mill ignore the painfully illiberal features of our society. In many places, urban violence makes a mockery of the promise to protect every citizen from physical fear. The homeless are deprived of the elementary security a liberal regime owes to all. Decaying schools represent a national betrayal of liberalism's pledge to the next generation. The steady increase of children living in poverty conflicts rudely with a liberal commitment to equal opportunity. The rising costs of litigation have thrown into doubt the principle of equal access to the law. Rising campaign expenditures suggest that economic inequality is being converted directly into political inequality, against all liberal norms. And how can liberals accept the continuing marginalization of women from positions where political and economic influence is wielded? Finally, black Americans still live to an appalling extent as a stigmatized caste. Infant mortality, poverty, unemployment, school and housing segregation, and reduced access to health care all indicate that social resources are being allocated according to skin color, not along individualistic lines.

A reconstruction of the liberal tradition cannot provide recipes for solving stubborn problems such as these. But it can help us understand why they are problems from a liberal point of view. And it can embolden us to reaffirm today the aims that liberals have traditionally pursued. Those aims are difficult to realize, but not utopian. A liberal nation is a nation that keeps them steadily in sight.

[2]

Paul Starr

Liberalism after
Socialism

Over the past century, many reformers and critics in the West have believed that liberal democratic capitalism was evolving, inexorably and appropriately, toward a socialist, planned economy. Liberalism even in its modern form has seemed to them transitional and incomplete, outdated in its individualism, unsatisfying in its conception of the good life and the good society, inadequate to the demands of justice. Socialism would take civilization to a higher stage; it would fulfill ideals that liberalism professed but failed to honor, as well as ideals that liberalism failed even to profess.

Those who have taken this view have not necessarily been Marxists. Most have been devoted to movements of reform rather than revolution and sought an alternative system that they hoped would achieve the best of both worlds, preserving the political freedoms of liberal democracy while introducing the economic planning, public ownership, and economic equality of socialism. This is the synthesis that many European socialists and American progressives have held up as an ideal—liberal democracy reconstructed into a benign and democratic socialism, a "third way" between communism and capitalism.

This vision has exerted a wide influence, even among liberals, who have been, I believe, all too ready to accept the critics' indictment of liberalism and give up on the possibilities of their own tradition. Early in the twentieth century, a synthesis of liberalism and socialism understandably seemed exciting, even promising. Around the world, socialist ideas were just beginning to be put into practice. The idea that democracy was advancing from one sphere to the next—from the civil to the political, then to the social and the economic—had an unquestionable appeal. During the 1930s, the Depression graphically demonstrated the havoc the market could wreak; to many, the accomplishments of the

New Deal and of wartime planning in the 1940s demonstrated that socialism would work in practice.

The Cold War and rapid economic growth in the Western economies in the 1950s and 1960s did not put an end to the hopes of a third way. On the contrary, the vision seemed confirmed by the successes of the European social democracies, especially Sweden. In light of the Soviet experience, the democratic Left emphasized its anticommunism. In light of the West's economic growth, it focused its criticism of capitalism on individual alienation, the loss of community, the culture of consumption, racial injustice, and, beginning in the 1970s, environmental problems. Of course, not everyone concerned about these issues had socialism in mind as a solution. But, explicitly or not, many of the critics on the left were pointing in that direction.

Today, this criticism of the limitations of capitalism continues—as it should—but the solution that so many had in mind has lost its plausibility. The socialist economic project, consisting fundamentally of national planning and extensive public ownership, has been thoroughly discredited as a means of economic growth. It has no better reputation as a means of reducing alienation and restoring community. The case for ecosocialism has suffered as well with the growing recognition that communist governments in the East have polluted on a far greater scale than have the capitalist countries of the West.

To the advocates of a third way, it seems a cruel irony and intellectual injustice that democratic socialism should lose its plausibility because of the bankruptcy of Soviet communism. But there are four good reasons why socialism even with a human face no longer looks appealing.

First, the sheer magnitude of the communist collapse has had a devastating impact on evaluations of the performance of command economies. It is now indisputable that communism impoverished the people who lived under it, and it is not clear how or why a more democratically planned socialist economy would do much better—or that such a system is feasible at all.

Second, repeated efforts to reform communism from within, to make it both more responsive and more efficient, came to nought. Once a window of political light opened, those who lived under communism sought to escape altogether. If there is a third way, they have pretty much given up hope of discovering it.

Third, the record of socialism in Africa and Latin America has been equally disastrous. Socialism in the Third World is undergoing as severe a crisis of belief as communism in Eastern Europe and the Soviet Union. This shift reflects not only indigenous experiences, but also the withdrawal of Soviet support, the changing political winds from the West and from international agencies, and the example of East Asia. To be sure, the economic successes of East Asian capitalism are no vindication of laissez faire, but socialism was not their inspiration, either.

Finally, the Western European countries that have had Socialist and Labour parties in power have drifted progressively further away from a commitment to socialism. Soon after World War II, if not before, most Western socialists gave up the goal of replacing capitalism, and instead adopted programs that called for limited nationalization and the extension of welfare state measures first introduced by earlier authoritarian, corporatist, and liberal governments. In recent years, however, Socialist parties have even given up nationalizing industry when in power and threatening to nationalize industry when out; indeed, some nominally Socialist governments have been actively privatizing public enterprises. Where firms have remained under public ownership, as in France, socialists have been operating them on a thoroughly commercial basis. Similarly, either the idea of a planned national economy has been abandoned or planning of limited scope has accommodated the basic contours of capitalism. Although European social democrats have Marxist grandparents on their family tree, they have largely outgrown not just Marxism, but socialism itself, and accepted—wisely, I believe—political ideals and social and economic institutions that have a more liberal character.

As a result, the synthesis of liberalism and socialism that once excited imaginations now seems almost drained of content. Much of what socialism once promised to bring to a synthesis, socialists with the experience of government no longer defend. Yet many who once dreamed of a third way are not ready to accept the economic framework of capitalism, much less capitalist civilization in the larger sense. They continue to hold out the idea of some sort of synthesis or a transcendent socialist alternative to liberalism, often now conceived as a more decentralized economy with a communitarian ethos.

This reluctance to let go of socialism, in the hope of finding some new, untried form in which it can still be defended as an ideal, is, I think, deeply mistaken. Liberals ought to continue striving to reform capitalism—to eradicate poverty, to overcome racism, to protect the integrity of the environment, in short to achieve a variety of humane and democratic objectives. But it is time, I will argue, to give up on the idea of a grand synthesis or a third way, if by that is meant some system mid-way between capitalism and socialism or an alternative altogether "beyond" them. Reform capitalism, yes; replace it, no—just as in the East many have concluded: Reform communism, no; replace it, yes.

There is, moreover, a need for clarity about intellectual premises as well as ultimate political objectives. In opposing evils like racism and poverty, reformers can find the grounds of justification and persuasion in liberal principles. They have no philosophical need to appeal to the socialist tradition, and in the United States no conceivable political rationale for doing so. Indeed, instead of softening or erasing the distinction between liberalism and socialism, as many have long hoped to do, liberals should be redrawing that distinction in their own minds and in public perception. Whatever the party of reform once may have had to learn from the ideas of socialism, it has already absorbed; indeed, some of what it learned, it ought to unlearn. Those who have believed socialism to be a higher stage of liberalism now need to take to heart, not the great vision of socialist theory, but the bitter disappointment of the practice. They need not conclude, however, that the only alternative to a socialist liberalism is a conservative liberalism. There is a liberalism that is serious, realistic, and where necessary even radical about liberal principles. That tradition is waiting for them to invoke and reclaim.

Points of Departure

Before making this argument, I need the help of a few definitions. Perhaps nothing makes it more difficult to talk about liberalism and socialism than the likelihood that different people hear different things in those words. This is a problem, not of loose language, but of a messy world and complex history. A great variety of thinkers, movements, and parties have called themselves liberal and socialist. In different parts of the world, they have evolved in distinctive, even contradictory directions. Since there is no way to establish who holds proper title to the names, the best that we can do is to make clear what each of us means by them.

By "socialist" I mean a party or program that gives highest priority to equality of economic condition and calls for replacing private ownership with public ownership in the sphere of production and substituting some form of public control for the market as the principal mechanism for allocating investment.[1] Socialist programs vary, of course, in how comprehensive a transformation they envision. At the extreme, some have called for, or even tried, eliminating a money economy and private property in all its forms, while others have sought to nationalize only the "commanding heights" of industry.

Let us leave aside the pure communist project of eradicating private

---

1. This last element is a historical latecomer. In the nineteenth century, when the term "socialism" first came into use, its central theme was its criticism of private property; many and various were the proposals for socializing property and the fruits of labor. Socializing investment only became a theme of socialism in the twentieth century, after the Russian Revolution.

property. Socialism in the twentieth century has been mainly about socializing industrial production and investment. The theory has been that
these measures, supplemented by social insurance, socialist education,
and other influences, would eliminate the irrationalities and inequities of
capitalism, producing a world of plenty, an equal and just distribution of
income and life chances, greater social harmony, and a transformation of
the human personality, away from an alienated "possessive individualism" toward a more cooperative spirit.

Some prefer to define socialism solely in terms of one or another of
these aspirations, particularly equality. I believe, however, socialism
ought to be defined in part by the measures that socialists have characteristically called for, rather than solely by the aims that they have hoped
to achieve. The relation between means and results is a hypothesis, and
history has shown it to be a doubtful one. Socialist aspirations, particularly for a classless society, are distinctive, but socialism consists of more
than aspirations. To define socialism now only by its aspirations, rather
than its actual practice, is not just a theoretical choice; it is an evasion of
the burden of socialist experience.

As the concept of socialism is deeply contested, so, too, is the concept of liberalism. Indeed, the problem of definition is, if anything, more
difficult. The key premises of socialism are economic; socialism cannot
be separated from economics. But liberalism can be defined on either an
economic or political basis, and a major question arises as to which has
priority. Here a distinction is helpful. *Economic liberalism* identifies private property and reliance upon the market as the defining elements of
liberalism; in this view, liberalism is joined indissolubly with capitalism
and opposed to socialism. *Political liberalism,* on the other hand, maintains that what is essential to liberalism is the constitutional limitation of
power and guarantee of individual civil and political rights.

In speaking of liberalism, I generally have in mind the political
rather than the economic conception of liberalism. This choice agrees
with current usage in the United States, where economic liberalism is
identified with political conservatism. Political liberalism is also the relevant conception in a discussion of any potential synthesis or reconcilia-
tion between liberalism and socialism. For as the economic liberals have
conceived it, liberalism is antithetical to socialism. They have insisted
that the political institutions of liberal democracy depend upon a free
market economy and private property. Political liberalism, on the other
hand, is open to the possibility that liberal democracy is compatible with
varying economic arrangements. In short, while economic liberalism necessarily excludes socialism, political liberalism does not—at least in principle.

Those who subscribe to what I am calling the political conception of liberalism differ greatly among themselves in how they conceive liberal political principles and what may be derived from them. Of greatest relevance here is that they differ on how universal and how comprehensive a democracy liberalism implies. At the risk of multiplying terms to the point of confusion, I want to call by the name of democratic liberalism the tradition that has been committed to extending democracy more universally and broadening it to wider spheres of social life. Democratic capitalism has a built-in tension between its capitalist and democratic elements; economic liberals favor the former, democratic liberals the latter. From the "new liberalism" of L.T. Hobhouse in late nineteenth- and early twentieth-century Great Britain, through the liberalism of the New Deal and Great Society in the United States, this tradition of democratic liberalism creates the greatest ambiguity about the boundaries of liberalism on the left. When I suggested earlier that European social democracy has evolved into a kind of liberalism, this is the kind I meant.

Ever since their emergence as self-conscious movements and systems of thought in the nineteenth century, liberalism and socialism have been divided in their responses to the other. Some on each side have been polarizers: anxious to insist upon the opposition and incompatibility of the two. In this regard, Leninists and economic liberals have much in common. Others in both camps have been reconcilers, more open-minded and willing to accept lessons from the other side. Of the open-minded, two figures in the history of liberal thought seem to me particularly instructive: John Stuart Mill and John Dewey. I shall take them as exemplars of two different types of liberal receptivity to socialism.

Mill's Wisdom, Dewey's Error

Those who know Mill only from his essay *On Liberty* easily mistake him for a libertarian who believed in the most minimal conception of the state. But one has only to open Mill's other works, particularly his *Principles of Political Economy*, to discover that while he praises laissez faire, Milton Friedman is not his reincarnated spirit. Mill did not deny the state was responsible for welfare and distributive justice; on the contrary, he insisted that the distribution of wealth was in no way dictated by economic necessity, but was rather a social choice, depending on such measures as laws of inheritance. Moreover, far from condemning socialism outright, he saw merit in socialist ideas and accepted the possibility of a fundamental reconstruction of industry with the ownership of firms belonging to those who provided labor rather than those who provided capital. He supported cooperatives and was curious to learn from the experimental communities of his time conceived on socialist principles.

But Mill could not agree with socialists on some fundamentals. He argued that whatever the ownership of the firm, competition was essential. In evaluating the merits of systems of political economy, he believed that the decision would ultimately rest with the system "consistent with the greatest amount of human liberty and spontaneity." And he insisted that judgments of the liberal economy not underestimate what it was capable of achieving in the future. "If . . . ," he wrote in 1852,

> the choice were to be made between Communism with all its chances, and the present state of society with all its sufferings and injustices . . . all the difficulties, great or small, of Communism would be but as dust in the balance.

"But," Mill went on,

> to make the comparison applicable, we must compare Communism at its best, with the regime of individual property, not as it is, but as it might be made. . . . The laws of property have never yet conformed to the principles on which the justification of private property rests. They have made property of things which never ought to be property, and absolute property where only a qualified property ought to exist. They have not held the balance fairly between human beings, but have heaped impediments upon some, to give advantage to others; they have purposely fostered inequalities, and prevented all from starting fair in the race. That all should indeed start on perfectly equal terms is inconsistent with any law of private property; but if as much pains as has been taken to aggravate the inequality of chances arising from the natural working of the principle, had been taken to temper that inequality by every means not subversive of the principle itself; if the tendency of legislation had been to favour the diffusion, instead of concentration of wealth . . . the principle of individual property would have been found to have no necessary connexion with the physical and social evils which almost all Socialist writers assume to be inseparable from it.

Marx once remarked acidly that the eminence of John Stuart Mill in England was due to the flatness of the terrain. But on the central question of the historical possibilities of capitalism, Mill was by far the wiser of the two.

In his emphasis on the potential contribution of socialism at the level of the firm, rather than the economy as a whole, Mill was also, I believe, wiser than my second exemplary liberal, John Dewey. Dewey subscribed to the view that socialism is a higher stage of liberalism and that the great "task before us," to use a favorite phrase of his, is to find a synthesis between liberal political values and socialist economics.

Dewey spelled out the argument in *Liberalism and Social Action*, published in 1935. His understanding of early liberalism reflected Marxist influence; he accepted the premise that liberalism had emerged as the ideology of the rising bourgeoisie. But, unlike the Marxists, Dewey thought if one stripped away the "adventitious" elements that accompanied liberalism at its genesis, enduring values remained, and he particularly identified three: "liberty, the development of the inherent capacities of individuals made possible through liberty, and the central role of free intelligence in inquiry, discussion and expression." The challenge to liberalism, as Dewey saw it, was to recognize that the realization of these values now required a dramatic shift. "The ends," Dewey wrote, "can now be achieved only by reversal of the means to which early liberalism was committed. Organized social planning ... is now the sole method of social action by which liberalism can realize its professed aims. Such planning demands in turn a new conception and logic of freed intelligence as a social force."

This emphasis on intelligence was the core of Dewey's argument and, alas, the core of what was wrong with it. He credited all economic advance to intelligence, nothing to the market. "[T]wo forces, one active, the other resistant and deflecting, ... have produced the social scene in which we live," Dewey wrote. "The active force is ... scientific method and technological application. The opposite force is that of older institutions and the habits that have grown up around them." For Dewey, the institutions of capitalism were the older, resisting force, arresting, deflecting, and corrupting the progressive force of science. Since he saw capitalism as having no positive impact at all, Dewey was unable to see how subjecting the economy to collective control could hinder its development.

Dewey continually spoke about the need for "social control of the economy," but exactly what he wanted is unclear. In *Liberalism and Social Action* he criticized current political life for merely summing up individuals quantitatively, as if intelligence were purely an individual possession; for still depending upon "the method of discussion, with only incidental scientific control"; and for relying upon symbols, which are readily manipulated. "The crisis in democracy," he wrote, "demands the substitution of the intelligence that is exemplified in scientific procedure for the kind of intelligence that is now accepted."

Dewey did not, however, take the model of science to imply a need for technocratic rule because, in his mind, the world of science was a democratic community. Indeed, his primary criticism of socialism was that it was insufficiently committed to democratic practice. Writing to James Farrell in 1948, he asked, "What is Democratic Socialism? I read considerable talk about 'the democratic' as applying to the process of

getting socialism; damn little about it as an adjective applying to socialism when you get it." Robert B. Westbrook, who quotes this and similar
passages in a new intellectual biography of Dewey, sees in Dewey a
guide for a vision of a liberal, socialist, participatory democracy.[2] But to
say that Dewey opposed state socialism, as he did, or was aware of the
danger that planning might lead to domination by experts, is not to establish that he had any solution to the problem. His belief that the
method of intelligence, as embodied in science, could be applied to social
choices reflected a failure to understand the irreducible differences between science and politics. Despite frequent references to planning and
public ownership, Dewey failed to specify how participatory democratic
planning and public ownership would work in practice—for example,
what branches or levels of government would have what powers; how
people were to be represented; or how decisions were to be made on
investments in firms.

This vagueness is not simply a limitation of Dewey's work; it is indicative of the deeper problems in the tradition of democratic socialism.
The theory comes to grief on the hard rock of specifying political arrangements. To condemn bureaucracy is easy; to find means that will actually avoid it is the trick. To favor participation is fine; to find means to
sustain it is another thing. Oscar Wilde's famous remark that the problem with socialism is that it takes too many evenings is not just the view
of the ironic aesthete; it is the basic problem with a theory that is unrealistic about human interests and energies. No matter how participatory in
theory, democratic planning cannot escape the problem of bureaucracy;
democracy creates bureaucracy. As James Q. Wilson points out in his recent book *Bureaucracy*, the demands for democratic access and participation in America are one of the principal reasons why bureaucracy in
America is especially encumbered with rules. To avoid domination by
experts, the experts must be checked, and these checks involve formal
rules controlling their discretion, requiring public disclosure, providing
opportunities for hearings, and so on. If the modern economy were
simple, planning could be simple. But it cannot be simple, and every attempt to make it democratic would make it more complex.

If the economic world were not only simple but stationary, a democratically planned economy might be manageable. Change, however, is
devastating. The reasons for the failure of the planned economy lie fundamentally in its inability to generate innovation or to deal with fundamental shifts in markets and technologies. In theory, socialist governments should be able to set prices in line with marginal costs; the

---

2. *John Dewey and American Democracy* (Ithaca: Cornell University Press,
1991).

socialist planner, as the economist Oskar Lange argued in the 1930s, should be capable of taking into account all costs and consequently be less resistant than the private entrepreneur to technological progress that devalues existing capital investments. But, in practice, the difficulties in securing information and maintaining political legitimacy, as well as the privileges of elites with a stake in protected economic sectors, prevent socialist planners from readily adjusting prices or promoting technical change. The concentration of economic responsibilities on the state makes it difficult to impose the economic cruelties of higher consumer prices, factory shutdowns, occupational displacement, and social dislocation that innovation and growth typically require. Over time, prices typically get drastically out of line with costs; public enterprises become sinkholes of public subsidy; and the planned economy becomes a backwater of development. More democratic economic planning, far from solving these problems, quite likely would aggravate them, since it would be even harder to carry out the changes that development requires.

These difficulties do not necessarily appear in the short term or under conditions of national crisis. That is why command-and-control planning can be successful in wartime or in the initial stages of a revolution, especially if a regime is able to transplant technologies developed elsewhere. But as time wears on, the planned economy's slowness to innovate and its resistance to what Joseph Schumpeter called capitalism's "gales of creative destruction" bring about a long-term deterioration.

I am not suggesting that the human costs of economic and technological change should be of no political concern. On the contrary, cushioning the losses and insecurities of economic upheaval is one of the principal interests of the liberal state, in part to ensure that the costs and benefits of change are fairly distributed and that progress does not founder because of resistance from those who would otherwise be the losers. But it has proved far more advantageous to release the transformative powers of capitalism and spread the gains, than to try to preserve the stakes of the weak in the status quo.

I also do not wish to suggest that the difficulties of economic planning on the command-and-control model extend to every other type of state intervention. The problems arise specifically from micro management of the economy and suppression of the price system. Planning and public ownership, especially when combined, simultaneously suppress information (market signals) and demand continuously replenished information of minute detail. Both the basis for economic decisions and the mechanisms for correcting them are fatally weakened. This is not so of the use of fiscal and monetary instruments in macroeconomic policy. Nor does it apply to social insurance and other income-transfer programs, to government planning in the management of a limited public sector, to planning of public investments in human capital and physical infrastructure, and other areas where the term "planning" merely stands for the making of policy in line with longer-term objectives and projections of trends. Indeed, without national economic planning of the kind envisioned by socialists, we have achieved at least some of the social control of economic life that Dewey and others half a century ago wanted. But we do so—and, in some areas, ought to do more—without the detailed management of finance and industry that the socialist critics of capitalism thought necessary.

Marxists and other socialist critics earlier in this century, and even some today, have repeatedly underestimated the capacities of capitalist democracies for adaptation, stability, redistribution, and growth. But, of course, many defenders of capitalism have thought its requirements to be equally rigid. The tradition represented by Mill, in contrast, saw that capitalism could be drastically altered by law and government and was compatible with radical advances in equality and democratization, including a more just distribution of income, diminished status differences, and an altered hierarchy in the firm. This recognition that capitalism is not governed by iron laws of motion, as Marx believed, but can be modified politically and culturally lies at the foundation of the tradition of democratic liberalism. For Dewey and others to have believed half a century ago that capitalism needed to be transformed into socialism to realize liberal values was perhaps understandable, given what they knew of the two systems. But that was, in a sense, before socialism, at least before we had accumulated much experience of socialism.

The socialist experiment has now been run in many variations. Governments professing socialism have come to power by armed force and exercised dictatorial power; others have come to power through elections and exercised power more democratically. Some regimes, initially totalitarian, have tried to reform themselves from within. Nonetheless, we have yet to see the socialist economic model succeed in practice. It is evidently as hard for human beings to enter the kingdom of socialism as it is for a camel to pass through the eye of a needle. If socialism is so difficult to get right, people are justifiably skeptical of the democratic socialists among us who say that it has yet to be tried.

Now we know what we could not have known when socialism was a theory, and liberalism *after* socialism can never be the same. The task before us is plainly not to synthesize liberal political values with socialist economics. Neither is it to reconceive socialism on a more democratic, decentralized basis; the idea of a decentralized socialism bears even less relevance to economic realities today than the model of central planning whose bad odor socialist theorists are trying to escape. Socialism is simply not our appointed historical destiny. Indeed, the great irony is that while theorists have vexed themselves over the much-anticipated transition from capitalism to socialism, the great task in Eastern Europe and the Soviet Union is the reverse: how to build liberal societies after socialism has done such great damage to their economies, civil life, and even the legitimacy of their states.

Democratic Liberalism

The socialist critique of liberalism and its program for the reconstruction of society had other aspects besides those I have mentioned. To give a full assessment of those arguments, or of communitarianism—which might be thought of as socialism without the embarrassment of socialist economics—is more than I can attempt here. By way of conclusion, let me spell out some elements of a realistic democratic liberalism, as I see it.

Like all versions of political liberalism, democratic liberalism rests on a foundation of constitutionalism and guarantees of individual political and civil liberty. These rights are primary; they take priority over property rights where they come into conflict, and the most fundamental of them cannot be sacrificed or compromised for prudential reasons, except in cases of rare and compelling state interest. Since the capacity to hold leaders accountable is essential to the limitation of power, the protection of liberty requires democracy. And as Dewey properly argued, liberal values require democracy as a thoroughgoing social practice, a way of life. But where Dewey and others were mistaken was in asking too much of democracy, particularly by expecting that the economy as a whole could be directly subjected to democratic rule. "Economic democracy," appealing as a slogan, makes sense only in the immediate environment of the firm, and even there within limits. For the economy as a whole, collective interests require collective political restraint.

The choice is not between "market" and "plan," as so many theorists have put it. For even for those committed to reliance on the market, the question remains, "What market?" Markets do not exist in nature; they are institutions that have a design, based first of all in law. The realistic, democratic alternative to socialist planning lies primarily in the design of markets and other institutions: the shaping of the rules of the game. Banks and other financial institutions, broadcasting stations, school systems, health care services, agriculture—these institutions all require a framework of legal rules that influence what they do, whom they serve, how they are controlled. In the shaping of the framework, not in the active management of those institutions, lies the principal point of liberal influence. To be sure, choices in institutional design are not as grand and inspiring as the great ideological struggle between capitalism and socialism. But those choices are where the big public decisions of our time lie.

Unlike socialism, which has held up an impractical vision of a class-less society and total equality in all spheres, liberalism has a vision of equality that is more restricted, but less likely to be perennially disappointed. Liberalism has often been accused of failing to extend its egalitarian ideals beyond the civil and political spheres. But there is good reason for holding back from organizing the economy according to the same rules as the polity. Political and civil liberty imply political and civil equality: equality before the law, equal rights of political participation. But even the strong, affirmative efforts necessary to create the institutions and conditions for civil and political liberty do not require an equalization of wealth and income or eradication of class differences. In matters of income distribution and material well-being, the objective should be, above all, to eliminate poverty and maintain a minimum floor of decency to enable individuals to carry out their own life plans.

What that floor entails is a distinctly social judgment; it will likely rise over time. Since the support of that floor will be a political decision, policies must be designed to maintain not only the floor, but the political support beneath it. As a result, the evaluation of policies and programs, even from the standpoint of distributive justice, cannot be separated from the overall task of constructing democratic majorities. And that imperative will often mean support for programs that provide universal benefits to all groups, including the middle class as well as the poor and majorities as well as minority groups.

Moreover, the long-term tasks of nation-building and of fostering a common culture and a sense of shared citizenship also strongly argue for public and universal schooling, old-age pensions, and other services that serve an integrative as well as egalitarian purpose. In a few cases, particularly those involving insurance, the universal alternative is also simply more efficient because of endemic market failures.

But the universalism of liberal democratic policies is limited to particular spheres of social life; it is not a stepping stone to generalized equality of economic condition, if only because of the inevitable conflict, which socialists hardly anticipated, between democracy and equality. The level of redistribution required to achieve the socialist vision of a classless society is so vast that it is unlikely ever to command majority support. It is difficult enough, and often impossible, to secure democratic approval even for the more limited equality that liberals favor. This problem must be taken, not as a temporary obstacle arising from false consciousness, but as a permanent problem arising from rational voter hesitations about losses of income and the role of the state.

Where socialism imagined transforming things "private" into things "public," liberalism seeks to maintain the public-private distinction and to enrich the forces of civil society, not in opposition to the state, but in partnership with it. The state has a comparative advantage in performing certain functions; for example, it can collect taxes more reliably and efficiently than can charities raise voluntary contributions. But it is not always best able to produce or deliver the services it finances. Through the devolution of functions to the independent associations and agencies of civil society, liberal policy provides a genuine way to limit governmental bureaucracy. In addition, the cultivation and strengthening of civil society reflects a commitment, not to some mythical idea of a single community, but to the many and various communities that must exist peaceably and tolerantly along with each other in a liberal society.

As I have said nothing about international affairs and foreign policy, about the problems of moral authority, education, and the family, and countless other matters, this can scarcely be counted a general discussion of the problems facing liberalism. What I have tried to argue is that we need to draw, more sharply than we have, the distinction between liberalism and socialism. In everyday American politics, liberalism is now identified with a commitment to expanding public social programs, and this link is partly the cause of the general confusion of liberalism and socialism, which to many people appear to stand for the same thing.

Why American conservatives conflate liberalism and socialism is clear since, in their eyes, any defense of positive government counts as statism. What is less understandable is the confusion of American "progressives"—a term which itself serves to obscure the difference between liberal and socialist positions. "Progressive," now the label of choice on the left, has the function of avoiding any overt ideological commitment and minimizing potential divisions; in some contexts, it has become the contemporary linguistic form of the Popular Front.

But while the house of liberalism in America has many rooms, it should not be allowed to become the last refuge of a defeated and disappointed socialism. When socialism was young and full of fervor, some liberals were understandably infatuated and thought of marrying their political values to socialist economics. But the romance should be over once and for all.

[3]

Robert Kuttner

Liberalism, Socialism, and Democracy

What, if anything can be usefully salvaged from the socialist tradition, now that communism lies in final disgrace? Paul Starr argued in these pages last fall that four developments—the implosion of communism, the collapse of efforts to reform communism from within, the failure of socialism in the Third World, and the shift of European socialists toward liberal policies—should persuade American liberals that socialism ought not to be part of our vision of an ideal society.

What follows is less a rejoinder than a brief for social democracy, as a tradition that loathed communism and may yet enrich liberalism. Social democracy, for at least a century, has been the domesticated form of socialism—a vaccine made of benign cultures that can inoculate against the ravages of both communism and laissez faire.

Social democracy, certainly, is no mechanical third way. As a worldview, it accepts private ownership and parliamentary democracy, yet retains a broadly egalitarian ethic and keeps a weather eye on the nastier tendencies of capitalism. Social democracy does not propose to supplant capitalism, but to tame it. So, in a sense, does liberalism—but the differences are telling.

Like liberalism, social democracy belongs to the tradition of a limited state based on political rights and civil and social liberties; it has no sympathy for either command planning or command politics. In our century, social democrats have also been among the most resistant to dictatorship and the most inventive in demanding that if the state is to be an engine of progress, governments must be both accountable and competent. Social democracy resists extreme inequality but does not advocate absolute equality. Yet social democracy does go somewhat beyond liberalism as generally understood. And it does reflect some constructive influence of democratic socialism, particularly in its insistence that capitalism be understood as a system. It is this virtue that most distinguishes social democracy from liberalism, yet also makes it an important ally of liberalism.

Understanding the dynamics of how capitalism, as a system, tends to intrude on both the democratic polity and on the social viability of a market economy itself is essential to a politically sustainable liberalism. The dilemma is only compounded by the globalization of markets that out-run national polities. In my reading, especially of recent thinkers, I find the best insights on the dilemma of reconciling capitalism and democracy in the work of social democrats and democratic socialists.

Thus, though liberalism and social democracy substantially overlap in their vision of a good society, notably in their policy particulars, this ideological distinction is more than a semantic or sectarian one. These labels, and their resonances, invite careful differentiation. Social democracy is not merely a prodigal mutant of liberalism, now free of its youthful socialist indiscretions. On the contrary, American liberalism is often vulnerable, analytically and politically, precisely because it has not learned more from its social democratic cousins. My purpose here is to persuade the reader that a bigger dose of social democracy would enrich liberalism, not confuse it.

The liberalism of America's Founders was a rather conservative brand of liberalism, one that sought restraint on the passions of the masses as much as it sought limits on the abuses of the state. As industrial capitalism developed, the challenge of building a good society, of assuring ordinary people life, liberty, and the pursuit of happiness, necessarily evolved with the new economic circumstances. The anomalies and cruelties of a market economy came to be as much of a threat to ordinary life and to civil society as the threat of state tyranny. Twentieth-century liberalism, particularly at its New Deal zenith, rejected laissez faire and embraced economic intervention. It nominated the state as the agency of intervention, invoking, in Herbert Croly's famous inversion, "Hamiltonian means for Jeffersonian ends."

At its most potent moments, the liberalism of the Progressive and New Deal eras was indeed influenced by socialism. The progressives were wary of concentrated wealth, for political as well as egalitarian reasons. New Dealers understood that market economics could be at odds with other liberal objectives; that markets needed to be tempered for the sake of economic stability and efficiency, as well as for broader opportunity and distributive justice. The high-water marks of the New Deal, like Roosevelt's little-remembered 1944 Economic Bill of Rights, were nothing if not social democratic.

But these innovations in a time of upheaval left only weak roots, in inhospitable soil. They stopped short of fundamental revision of the liberal creed. Individualist liberalism returned as soon as the storm passed and the sun came back out. As Louis Hartz presciently observed in 1955, Roosevelt lacked either a serious socialist challenge on his left or a convincing conservative challenge on his right, so he resisted ideological revision and sold his reforms as merely pragmatic. Albert Hirschman, writing a quarter-century later, at the dawn of Reaganism, ruefully commented on Hartz's insight, "Today, of course, we can appreciate the high cost of Roosevelt's maneuver. The New Deal reforms ... were never truly consolidated as an integral part of a new economic order or ideology."

To be sure, it is not entirely fair to blame something called "liberalism" for the extreme individualistic tendencies of American society, which make it so difficult for a politically robust liberalism to take root. Nor is it realistic to expect that European social democracy, which grew in a rather different soil, could simply be imported whole and expected to thrive. My point is that liberalism, which today has reverted to one of its conservative moods, is strengthened and not weakened when it learns from social democracy. This is less a brief for a social democratic label—in America the label of choice for our kind of politics is necessarily "liberal"—than a plea for a social democratic sensibility.

Europe's social democrats, developing a welfare state and a Keynesian strategy of economic stabilization roughly in parallel with American liberals, nonetheless had a somewhat different understanding of what they were about. As part socialist and part liberal, they understood the enterprise not just as spreading social benefits or fighting unemployment, but as taming capitalism and as building a durable political constituency to make that enterprise electorally possible. Sometimes they overreached and embraced excessively statist mechanisms. But they understood that attaining some social control over private capital was a necessary part of building a sustainable mixed economy. I am sympathetic to social democracy, not as a bridge to socialism, but as a bridge to a more durable liberalism.

The taming of an economy whose dynamics are fundamentally capitalist is an excruciatingly difficult political and institutional endeavor, for market forces keep relentlessly encroaching on whatever social bargains are made. To grasp that, one needs to think hard about capitalism as a system. Social democrats at least take the exercise seriously; many American liberals seem to be uncomfortable with it. A decade or so ago, when the social democratic compromise began to falter seriously, it was voguish in democratic-left circles to insist that one had to go "beyond social democracy, to democratic socialism." Alternatively, other social democrats retreated into neoliberalism and settled for Keynesian tinkering around the edges. This debate sometimes had the familiar, tedious whine of left-sectarian politics. Yet it also signaled a willingness to think hard about the dynamics of taming capitalism as a system—something all too rare among liberals. Most American liberals, like Roosevelt, still sell their reforms "as merely pragmatic."

Admittedly, American liberalism and European social democracy are under assault from similar forces. These include the globalization of commerce, the fiscal limits of redistribution and macroeconomic management, the oddly conservatizing effects of slow growth, the erosion of trade-union solidarity, the crowding out of civic forces by market forces, and the timeless appeal of radical individualism for society's haves. Superficially, labor and social democratic parties in the west have suffered the same political reverses. Yet they are better bolstered to recover, it seems to me, because they have more systematic understanding of what is taking place.

The social democratic/mixed economy compromise came unstuck in the early 1970s, on both sides of the Atlantic. There followed an era of conservative rule, which attempted to resurrect a purer free market, celebrate individualism and entrepreneurship, pare back the welfare state, and thus rekindle economic growth. The conservative project failed; its diagnosis was mistaken and its remedies flawed. But the collapse of communism is taken as a vindication of the conservative brand of classical liberalism—laissez faire. While there is no mechanical third way, just as there is no "moral equivalence" between the failures of, say, Thatcher and Brezhnev, we liberals nonetheless need to resist the laissez-faire triumphalism that falsely follows from the death of state socialism and remember the systemic flaws in pure capitalism.

There is now an opportunity to revive a center-left. However, the social democratic version of this conversation often tends to be richer than its liberal counterpart. And the liberal version remains vulnerable to a set of fallacies that flow from its connection to classical liberalism. In Europe, the question of how to revive a social market economy—the euphemism of choice for social democracy—in the face of transnational private commerce is a center-stage public debate. In America, the counterpart debate is largely dismissed as merely a subterfuge for economic "protectionism," the latter being a sin defined by the lexicon of classical economic liberalism.

Another concept central to social democracy and almost entirely marginal to American liberalism is the idea of "social solidarity." In the development of the social democratic compromise, two things became clear early on. First, public policy had to create loci in which solidarity values could flourish. Social solidarity means an ethic based on the treatment of people as citizens with equal rights and entitlements, rather than as consumers purchasing commodities in a marketplace based on their private incomes. These oases of solidarity values were necessary as a counterweight to the ethic of radical individualism and the political power of individual and corporate wealth. They include, above all, trade unions, and also universal programs of social income, based on the criterion of citizenship rather than destitution or prior contribution. Second, class mattered immensely. Unless the broad class of nonwealthy wage earners remained in a high state of political mobilization, both solidarity values and the political constituency for the center-left party would melt away.

Now, it is possible to find some version of this conversation in the opus of American liberalism, if one looks hard enough, though this is not primarily what American liberals talk about. Writers who come immediately to mind include Charles E. Lindblom, whose discussion of the disproportionate power of money in a political democracy in *Politics and Markets* is a classic; in this category one would also put Robert Heilbroner and Walter Dean Burnham. But all three, and others like them, are liberals who have been influenced by socialism. Indeed, the most astute writing in the genre tends to come from liberals who have considered themselves of the left, at least long enough to have read some Marx, and are best classed as recovering socialists. Marx himself, as Schumpeter was among the first to distinguish, was a false prophet and an incompetent social architect—but still worth reading as an analyst of capitalism. (Marxists eavesdropping on this discussion will find it hopelessly meliorist, if not downright reactionary, which suggests that our own differences are quite manageable.)

Lindblom's way of looking at politics, appreciated in the academy, has had lamentably little influence on the popular conception of political economy—far less than, say, the lingering influence of neoclassical economics. Politically, the more resonant construct is that of thinkers like Theodore Lowi or Mancur Olson, whose subject is the degradation of pluralism and the eventual gridlock of politics itself. It is a slippery slope to the inference that we'd better just trust markets.

In American discourse, solidarity issues simply don't resonate, even among many liberals. Trade unions, for the most part, get a terrible press. They are seen as just another self-interested pressure group rather than the logical and necessary constituency for a mixed economy. Given the chronic economic insecurity and hence conservatism of wage earners, unions are essential if wage workers are to be the constituents for a broad agenda of social justice rather than quick to blame the systemic failures of capitalism on immigrants, blacks, or Japanese. Conservative liberals tend to desert labor—and even some labor unions tend to desert labor, with devices like a two-tier wage structure, because the labor movement itself partly reflects American individualist rather than solidaristic traditions.

In liberal America, concerns about the political power of concentrated wealth are too easily dismissed as merely the politics of envy rather than a Lindblom-style worry about asymmetry in political power. Because of our weak social democratic tradition, leftish impulses are frequently orphaned or misunderstood. Populism, the inchoate and ideologically amorphous cry for economic justice, often finds a home on the right rather than the liberal left. It is sneered at by enlightened commentators as unseemly class warfare or nativism. Social democracy in contrast is seemly, ritualized, and ultimately a more durable class conflict on behalf of wage earners.

Another contemporary liberal movement with populist overtones is consumerism. But in a political culture with no social democratic idiom, consumer advocates tend to couch their criticism of corporate power as the right of individual consumers not to be overcharged, poisoned, polluted, or otherwise ripped off. This is admirable as far as it goes, but consumerism quintessentially speaks the language of markets, not the idiom of social solidarity. It stops just short of a systematic critique of a market economy, and it doesn't connect as fully as it might to other progressive constituencies. In the absence of a social democratic context, the consumerist critique sometimes even overreaches by seeming viscerally and unreasonably anti-corporate per se (but wait, don't we need corporations to provide jobs?)—rather than an effort to tame corporations and turn them to public purposes, in the manner of European social market corporatism.

Social class is seldom an explicit part of the American political conversation. And attempts to inject discussions about some of the uglier systematic tendencies of capitalism itself are characteristically rejected by many liberals as tendentious and childishly radical. Indeed, my social democratic friends keep insisting that their critiques of particular market failures—in health care, housing, transit, financial speculative excess, environmental pillage, and so on—be anchored in a systemic critique of captalism. This formulation invariably elicits a weary wince from my liberal friends, who see the reference to "capitalism" as merely an archaic left-wing rhetorical flourish rather than a necessary analytical frame.

The liberal resistance to social democratic insight also helps explain why our form of liberalism is so chronically vulnerable to the tendency to flake off into neo-conservatism. Many liberals in the 1980s joined conservatives in exaggerating the potential of deregulation and privatization, and in the false logic of sacrificing equity to growth. Conversely, the liberalism of the 1960s was too ready to target the poor as a separate population, rather than anchoring anti-poverty in a broad, solidaristic agenda. And when the anti-poverty crusade produced a backlash, some liberals abandoned the poor entirely as a political albatross. Social democracy is a good antidote to liberal fragmentation.

Take the issue of the budget deficit. The obsession with deficits and savings rates is now being argued—by Brookings-style liberals—as if Keynes had never lived. For example, the claim advanced by Charles Schultze in the 1990 Brookings volume on economic choices that "the United States" was on a "decade-long consumption binge" is a compositional fallacy that no social democrat could ever make. This formulation ignores the fact that during the 1980s the real incomes of more than 70 percent of Americans dropped. Who is to be the constituency for a politics of budget balance uber alles? On what kind of pre-Keynesian economics is it based? But this is precisely the legacy of conservative liberalism, which is to ignore questions of social class and the relationship of wealth to political power, and to seek technical solutions.

Conservative liberalism tends to be uncomfortable with "the passions," preferring a politics based on cool, rational, secular self-interest and institutional invention. With the Constitutional Founders, liberalism mistrusts mass movements, which it fears as potentially despotic. While the liberal tradition has good reason to worry about the tyranny of majorities, in modern industrial capitalism mass movements are often indispensable if the power of wealth is to be offset by the power of people. Without mass movements, occasionally even impolite ones, energizing civic life—the labor movement, the women's movement, and the civil rights movement come to mind—we are left with a bloodless, cerebral, and feeble politics.

Take the issue of universalism in social entitlement, one of *The American Prospect*'s favorite causes. Many liberals, particularly the "neo" sort, conceive of paying Social Security pensions to the middle class as fiscally irresponsible and socially odd, since society obviously has more deserving cases who could use the money. In the end, the neo-liberals shrug and conclude that this must be mere "bribery" of the middle class. The most convincing defenders of universalism understand its logic in terms of class alliance and wage-earner solidarity. Not coincidentally, William Julius Wilson and Theda Skocpol—and your faithful essayist—are all self-described social democrats.

Take the issue of health care. Market-influenced conservative liberals make the mistake of imagining that some yet-to-be invented system of consumer choice may somehow allow society to offer universal health care while using market mechanisms to discipline providers. But this is delusional, for any universal entitlement is no longer operating in market-land. It can use some "market-like" devices, but to be efficient it requires universal rules specified by government. Moreover, the more opportunity there is for the well-to-do to opt out, the more the constituency for a solidaristic approach tends to erode. It might help if we admitted George Bush's charge that providing health care on the basis of to each according to his needs is, well, a wee bit socialist. Likewise free public education. The need to counteract capitalism's relentless "commodification" of human life is a socialist insight.

It is true that nearly every social democratic policy invention can be found somewhere outside the socialist tradition. Free public education was invented in Massachusetts, in the 1660s, nearly two hundred years before Marx. And, as we all know, social insurance was invented by Otto von Bismarck. Yet Bismarck championed social insurance largely because the rising Social Democratic Party was beginning to capture the affection of Germany's industrial workers, whose allegiance Bismarck wanted for the Prussian crown. And in this century, it is fair to say that labor and social democratic parties have done a better job than either conservatives or liberals at both extending and defending social entitlement.

This brings me back to political and ideological history. Liberalism is partly an ideal type—a philosophical construct with knowable boundaries. But the liberalism that has existed in historic time has been rather more supple, fluid, and evolutionary. The "New Liberalism" of Hobhouse in Britain of a century ago, the radical liberalism of Lloyd George, and of course the New Deal liberalism of FDR indeed created ambiguities about the boundaries between liberal and "left." But didn't liberalism grow stronger precisely when it was receptive to the influence of democratic socialism?

Some left-liberals, such as John Dewey, thought liberalism might lead to democratic socialism. Others, such as John Stuart Mill, were receptive to socialist ideas at the level of the firm, but not the entire economy; and, on balance, Mill considered himself an anti-socialist. However, while Mill can be revered as a buried treasure of democratic liberal theory, the evolution of modern liberalism and social democracy did not proceed mainly via Mill, but via Roosevelt and Reuther, Keynes and Attlee, Palme, Brandt, Mitterrand, et al., with a strong assist from the labor movement. As for Dewey, just as there is no Manichean wall between liberalism and social democracy, we cannot fairly divide Dewey into the educational prophet whom we admire and the soft-headed philosopher who was naive about socialism. His views on universal public education were not unrelated to his receptivity to socialist ideals.

Social democracy has been around since the schism within German Marxism over a century ago. In the postwar era, social democracy pulled back even further from its socialist ancestry and became more clearly allied with the liberal tradition. But it preserved basic insights and instincts having to do with the limits of marketization, the virtue of social solidarity, the need for social limits if not controls upon private capital, and a comprehension of the relations between class, money, and political power in a market society.

At bottom, the common goal of the editors of this journal is to repair and reclaim American liberalism. My own personal heroes in the field of political economy—Keynes, Polanyi, Joan Robinson, Galbraith, Hirschman, Heilbroner, Lindblom, Dean Burnham, Irving Howe, and the late, sainted Mike Harrington are all people of liberal spirit who blurred the bounds between liberalism and socialism somewhat, and by so doing served to push liberalism outward. Our task today is to do the same, and particularly to infuse decent social and economic policy with a durable politics. By all means, let us define clear boundaries between a liberal society and either a command economy or a dictatorship. But in doing this we should not just make room for social democracy on our side of the line, but also cherish it.

[4]

ROBERT D. PUTNAM

The Prosperous Community: Social Capital and Public Life

Your corn is ripe today; mine will be so tomorrow. 'Tis profitable for us both, that I should labour with you today, and that you should aid me tomorrow. I have no kindness for you, and know you have as little for me. I will not, therefore, take any pains upon your account; and should I labour with you upon my own account, in expectation of a return, I know I should be disappointed, and that I should in vain depend upon your gratitude. Here then I leave you to labour alone; you treat me in the same manner. The seasons change; and both of us lose our harvests for want of mutual confidence and security.

— David Hume

The predicament of the farmers in Hume's parable is all too familiar in communities and nations around the world:

- Parents in communities everywhere want better educational opportunities for their children, but collaborative efforts to improve public schools falter.
- Residents of American ghettos share an interest in safer streets, but collective action to control crime fails.
- Poor farmers in the Third World need more effective irrigation and marketing schemes, but cooperation to these ends proves fragile.
- Global warming threatens livelihoods from Manhattan to Mauritius, but joint action to forestall this shared risk founders.

Failure to cooperate for mutual benefit does not necessarily signal ignorance or irrationality or even malevolence, as philosophers since Hobbes have underscored. Hume's farmers were not dumb, or crazy, or evil; they were trapped. Social scientists have lately analyzed this fundamental predicament in a variety of guises: the tragedy of the commons; the logic of collective action; public goods; the prisoners' dilemma. In all these situations, as in Hume's rustic anecdote, everyone would be better off if everyone could cooperate. In the absence of coordination and credible mutual commitment, however, everyone defects, ruefully but rationally, confirming one another's melancholy expectations.

How can such dilemmas of collective action be overcome, short of creating some Hobbesian Leviathan? Social scientists in several disciplines have recently suggested a novel diagnosis of this problem, a diagnosis resting on the concept of *social capital*. By analogy with notions of physical capital and human capital—tools and training that enhance individual productivity—"social capital" refers to features of social organization, such as networks, norms, and trust, that facilitate coordination and cooperation for mutual benefit. Social capital enhances the benefits of investment in physical and human capital.

Working together is easier in a community blessed with a substantial stock of social capital. This insight turns out to have powerful practical implications for many issues on the American national agenda—for how we might overcome the poverty and violence of South Central Los Angeles, or revitalize industry in the Rust Belt, or nurture the fledgling democracies of the former Soviet empire and the erstwhile Third World. Before spelling out these implications, however, let me illustrate the importance of social capital by recounting an investigation that several colleagues and I have conducted over the last two decades on the seemingly arcane subject of regional government in Italy.

Lessons from an Italian Experiment

Beginning in 1970, Italians established a nationwide set of potentially powerful regional governments. These 20 new institutions were virtually identical in form, but the social, economic, political, and cultural contexts in which they were implanted differed dramatically, ranging from the preindustrial to the postindustrial, from the devoutly Catholic to the ardently Communist, from the inertly feudal to the frenetically modern. Just as a botanist might investigate plant development by measuring the growth of genetically identical seeds sown in different plots, we sought to understand government performance by studying how these new institutions evolved in their diverse settings.

As we expected, some of the new governments proved to be dismal failures—inefficient, lethargic, and corrupt. Others have been remarkably successful, however, creating innovative day care programs and job-training centers, promoting investment and economic development, pioneering environmental standards and family clinics—managing the public's business efficiently and satisfying their constituents.

What could account for these stark differences in quality of government? Some seemingly obvious answers turned out to be irrelevant. Government organization is too similar from region to region for that to explain the contrasts in performance. Party politics or ideology makes little difference. Affluence and prosperity have no direct effect. Social stability or political harmony or population movements are not the key. None of these factors is correlated with good government as we had anticipated. Instead, the best predictor is one that Alexis de Tocqueville might have expected. Strong traditions of civic engagement—voter turnout, newspaper readership, membership in choral societies and literary circles, Lions Clubs, and soccer clubs—are the hallmarks of a successful region.

Some regions of Italy, such as Emilia-Romagna and Tuscany, have many active community organizations. Citizens in these regions are engaged by public issues, not by patronage. They trust one another to act fairly and obey the law. Leaders in these communities are relatively honest and committed to equality. Social and political networks are organized horizontally, not hierarchically. These "civic communities" value solidarity, civic participation, and integrity. And here democracy works.

At the other pole are "uncivic" regions, like Calabria and Sicily, aptly characterized by the French term *incivisme*. The very concept of citizenship is stunted there. Engagement in social and cultural associations is meager. From the point of view of the inhabitants, public affairs is somebody else's business—*i notabili*, "the bosses," "the politicians"—but not theirs. Laws, almost everyone agrees, are made to be broken, but fearing others' lawlessness, everyone demands sterner discipline. Trapped in these interlocking vicious circles, nearly everyone feels powerless, exploited, and unhappy. It is hardly surprising that representative government here is less effective than in more civic communities.

The historical roots of the civic community are astonishingly deep. Enduring traditions of civic involvement and social solidarity can be traced back nearly a millennium to the eleventh century, when communal republics were established in places like Florence, Bologna, and Genoa, exactly the communities that today enjoy civic engagement and successful government. At the core of this civic heritage are rich networks of organized reciprocity and civic solidarity—guilds, religious fraternities, and tower societies for self-defense in the medieval communes;

cooperatives, mutual aid societies, neighborhood associations, and choral societies in the twentieth century.

These communities did not become civic simply because they were rich. The historical record strongly suggests precisely the opposite: They have become rich because they were civic. The social capital embodied in norms and networks of civic engagement seems to be a precondition for economic development, as well as for effective government. Development economists take note: Civics matters.

How does social capital undergird good government and economic progress? First, networks of civic engagement foster sturdy norms of generalized reciprocity: I'll do this for you now, in the expectation that down the road you or someone else will return the favor. "Social capital is akin to what Tom Wolfe called the 'favor bank' in his novel, *The Bonfire of the Vanities*," notes economist Robert Frank. A society that relies on generalized reciprocity is more efficient than a distrustful society, for the same reason that money is more efficient than barter. Trust lubricates social life.

Networks of civic engagement also facilitate coordination and communication and amplify information about the trustworthiness of other individuals. Students of prisoners' dilemmas and related games report that cooperation is most easily sustained through repeat play. When economic and political dealing is embedded in dense networks of social interaction, incentives for opportunism and malfeasance are reduced. This is why the diamond trade, with its extreme possibilities for fraud, is concentrated within close-knit ethnic enclaves. Dense social ties facilitate gossip and other valuable ways of cultivating reputation—an essential foundation for trust in a complex society.

Finally, networks of civic engagement embody past success at collaboration, which can serve as a cultural template for future collaboration. The civic traditions of north-central Italy provide a historical repertoire of forms of cooperation that, having proved their worth in the past, are available to citizens for addressing new problems of collective action.

Sociologist James Coleman concludes, "Like other forms of capital, social capital is productive, making possible the achievement of certain ends that would not be attainable in its absence. . . . In a farming community . . . where one farmer got his hay baled by another and where farm tools are extensively borrowed and lent, the social capital allows each farmer to get his work done with less physical capital in the form of tools and equipment." Social capital, in short, enables Hume's farmers to surmount their dilemma of collective action.

Stocks of social capital, such as trust, norms, and networks, tend to be self-reinforcing and cumulative. Successful collaboration in one endeavor builds connections and trust—social assets that facilitate future collaboration in other, unrelated tasks. As with conventional capital, those who have social capital tend to accumulate more—them as has, gets. Social capital is what the social philosopher Albert O. Hirschman calls a "moral resource," that is, a resource whose supply increases rather than decreases through use and which (unlike physical capital) becomes depleted if *not* used.

Unlike conventional capital, social capital is a "public good," that is, it is not the private property of those who benefit from it. Like other public goods, from clean air to safe streets, social capital tends to be underprovided by private agents. This means that social capital must often be a by-product of other social activities. Social capital typically consists in ties, norms, and trust transferable from one social setting to another. Members of Florentine choral societies participate because they like to sing, not because their participation strengthens the Tuscan social fabric. But it does.

Social Capital and Economic Development

Social capital is coming to be seen as a vital ingredient in economic development around the world. Scores of studies of rural development have shown that a vigorous network of indigenous grassroots associations can be as essential to growth as physical investment, appropriate technology, or (that nostrum of neoclassical economists) "getting prices right." Political scientist Elinor Ostrom has explored why some cooperative efforts to manage common pool resources, like grazing grounds and water supplies, succeed, while others fail. Existing stocks of social capital are an important part of the story. Conversely, government interventions that neglect or undermine this social infrastructure can go seriously awry.

Studies of the rapidly growing economies of East Asia almost always emphasize the importance of dense social networks, so that these economies are sometimes said to represent a new brand of "network capitalism." These networks, often based on the extended family or on close-knit ethnic communities like the overseas Chinese, foster trust, lower transaction costs, and speed information and innovation. Social capital can be transmuted, so to speak, into financial capital: In novelist Amy Tan's *Joy Luck Club*, a group of mah-jong-playing friends evolves into a joint investment association. China's extraordinary economic growth over the last decade has depended less on formal institutions than on *guanxi* (personal connections) to underpin contracts and to channel savings and investment.

Social capital, we are discovering, is also important in the development of advanced Western economies. Economic sociologist Mark

Granovetter has pointed out that economic transactions like contracting or job searches are more efficient when they are embedded in social networks. It is no accident that one of the pervasive stratagems of ambitious yuppies is "networking." Studies of highly efficient, highly flexible "industrial districts" (a term coined by Alfred Marshall, one of the founders of modern economics) emphasize networks of collaboration among workers and small entrepreneurs. Such concentrations of social capital, far from being paleo-industrial anachronisms, fuel ultra-modern industries from the high tech of Silicon Valley to the high fashion of Benetton. Even in mainstream economics the so-called "new growth theory" pays more attention to social structure (the "externalities of human capital") than do conventional neoclassical models. Robert Lucas, a founder of "rational expectations" economics, acknowledges that "human capital accumulation is a fundamentally *social* activity, involving *groups* of people in a way that has no counterpart in the accumulation of physical capital."

The social capital approach can help us formulate new strategies for development. For example, current proposals for strengthening market economies and democratic institutions in the formerly Communist lands of Eurasia center almost exclusively on deficiencies in financial and human capital (thus calling for loans and technical assistance). However, the deficiencies in social capital in these countries are at least as alarming. Where are the efforts to encourage "social capital formation"? Exporting PTAs or Kiwanis clubs may seem a bit far-fetched, but how about patiently reconstructing those shards of indigenous civic associations that have survived decades of totalitarian rule.

Historian S. Frederick Starr, for example, has drawn attention to important fragments of civil society—from philanthropic agencies to chess clubs—that persist from Russia's "usable past." (Such community associations provide especially valuable social capital when they cross ethnic or other cleavage lines.)

Closer to home, Bill Clinton's proposals for job-training schemes and industrial extension agencies invite attention to social capital. The objective should not be merely an assembly-line injection of booster shots of technical expertise and work-related skills into individual firms and workers. Rather, such programs could provide a matchless opportunity to create productive new linkages among community groups, schools, employers, and workers, without creating costly new bureaucracies. Why not experiment with modest subsidies for training programs that bring together firms, educational institutions, and community associations in innovative local partnerships? The latent effects of such programs on social capital accumulation could prove even more powerful than the direct effects on technical productivity.

Conversely, when considering the effects of economic reconversion on communities, we must weigh the risks of destroying social capital. Precisely because social capital is a public good, the costs of closing factories and destroying communities go beyond the personal trauma borne by individuals. Worse yet, some government programs themselves, such as urban renewal and public housing projects, have heedlessly ravaged existing social networks. The fact that these collective costs are not well measured by our current accounting schemes does not mean that they are not real. Shred enough of the social fabric and we all pay.

Social Capital and America's Ills

Fifty-one deaths and $1 billion in property damage in Los Angeles last year [1992] put urban decay back on the American agenda. Yet if the ills are clear, the prescription is not. Even those most sympathetic to the plight of America's ghettos are not persuaded that simply reviving the social programs dismantled in the last decade or so will solve the problems. The erosion of social capital is an essential and under-appreciated part of the diagnosis.

Although most poor Americans do not reside in the inner city, there is something qualitatively different about the social and economic isolation experienced by the chronically poor blacks and Latinos who do. Joblessness, inadequate education, and poor health clearly truncate the opportunities of ghetto residents. Yet so do profound deficiencies in social capital.

Part of the problem facing blacks and Latinos in the inner city is that they lack "connections" in the most literal sense. Job-seekers in the ghetto have little access, for example, to conventional job referral networks. Labor economists Anne Case and Lawrence Katz have shown that, regardless of race, inner-city youth living in neighborhoods blessed with high levels of civic engagement are more likely to finish school, have a job, and avoid drugs and crime, controlling for the individual characteristics of the youth. That is, of two identical youths, the one unfortunate enough to live in a neighborhood whose social capital has eroded is more likely to end up hooked, booked, or dead. Several researchers seem to have found similar neighborhood effects on the incidence of teen pregnancy, among both blacks and whites, again controlling for personal characteristics. Where you live and whom you know —the social capital you can draw on—helps to define who you are and thus to determine your fate.

Racial and class inequalities in access to social capital, if properly measured, may be as great as inequalities in financial and human capital, and no less portentous. Economist Glenn Loury has used the term "social capital" to capture the fundamental fact that racial segregation, coupled with socially inherited differences in community networks and norms, means that individually targeted "equal opportunity" policies may not eliminate racial inequality, even in the long run. Research suggests that the life chances of today's generation depend not only on their parents' social resources, but also on the social resources of their parents' ethnic group. Even workplace integration and upward mobility by successful members of minority groups cannot overcome these persistent effects of inequalities in social capital. William Julius Wilson has described in tragic detail how the exodus of middle-class and working-class families from the ghetto has eroded the social capital available to those left behind. The settlement houses that nurtured sewing clubs and civic activism a century ago, embodying community as much as charity, are now mostly derelict.

It would be a dreadful mistake, of course, to overlook the repositories of social capital within America's minority communities. The neighborhood restaurant eponymously portrayed in Mitchell Duneier's recent *Slim's Table*, for example, nurtures fellowship and intercourse that enable blacks (and whites) in Chicago's South Side to sustain a modicum of collective life. Historically, the black church has been the most bounteous treasure-house of social capital for African Americans. The church provided the organizational infrastructure for political mobilization in the civil rights movement. Recent work on American political participation by political scientist Sidney Verba and his colleagues shows that the church is a uniquely powerful resource for political engagement among blacks—an arena in which to learn about public affairs and hone political skills and make connections.

In tackling the ills of Americas cities, investments in physical capital, financial capital, human capital, and social capital are complementary, not competing alternatives. Investments in jobs and education, for example, will be more effective if they are coupled with reinvigoration of community associations.

Some churches provide job banks and serve as informal credit bureaus, for example, using their reputational capital to vouch for members who may be ex-convicts, former drug addicts, or high school dropouts. In such cases the church does not merely provide referral networks. More fundamentally, wary employers and financial institutions bank on the church's ability to identify parishioners whose formal credentials understate their reliability. At the same time, because these parishioners value their standing in the church, and because the church has put its own reputation on the line, they have an additional incentive to perform. Like conventional capital for conventional borrowers, social capital serves as a kind of collateral for men and women who are excluded from ordinary credit or labor markets. In effect, the participants pledge their social connections, leveraging social capital to improve the efficiency with which markets operate.

The importance of social capital for America's domestic agenda is not limited to minority communities. Take public education, for instance. The success of private schools is attributable, according to James Coleman's massive research, not so much to what happens in the classroom nor to the endowments of individual students, but rather to the greater engagement of parents and community members in private school activities. Educational reformers like child psychologist James Comer seek to improve schooling not merely by "treating" individual children but by deliberately involving parents and others in the educational process. Educational policymakers need to move beyond debates about curriculum and governance to consider the effects of social capital. Indeed, most commonly discussed proposals for "choice" are deeply flawed by their profoundly individualist conception of education. If states and localities are to experiment with voucher systems for education or child care, why not encourage vouchers to be spent in ways that strengthen community organization, not weaken it? Once we recognize the importance of social capital, we ought to be able to design programs that creatively combine individual choice with collective engagement.

Many people today are concerned about revitalizing American democracy. Although discussion of political reform in the United States focuses nowadays on such procedural issues as term limits and campaign financing, some of the ills that afflict the American polity reflect deeper, largely unnoticed social changes.

"Some people say that you usually can trust people. Others say that you must be wary in relations with people. Which is your view?" Responses to this question, posed repeatedly in national surveys for several decades, suggest that social trust in the United States has declined for more than a quarter century. By contrast, American politics benefited from plentiful stocks of social capital in earlier times. Recent historical work on the Progressive Era, for example, has uncovered evidence of the powerful role played by nominally nonpolitical associations (such as women's literary societies) precisely because they provided a dense social network. Is our current predicament the result of a long-term erosion of social capital, such as community engagement and social trust?

Economist Juliet Schorr's discovery of "the unexpected decline of leisure" in America suggests that our generation is less engaged with one another outside the marketplace and thus less prepared to cooperate for shared goals. Mobile, two-career (or one-parent) families often must use the market for child care and other services formerly provided through family and neighborhood networks. Even if market-based services, con-

sidered individually, are of high quality, this deeper social trend is eroding social capital. There are more empty seats at the PTA and in church
pews these days. While celebrating the productive, liberating effects of
fuller equality in the workplace, we must replace the social capital that
this movement has depleted.

Our political parties, once intimately coupled to the capillaries of
community life, have become evanescent confections of pollsters and
media consultants and independent political entrepreneurs—the very
antithesis of social capital. We have too easily accepted a conception of
democracy in which public policy is not the outcome of a collective deliberation about the public interest, but rather a residue of campaign
strategy. The social capital approach, focusing on the indirect effects of
civic norms and networks, is a much-needed corrective to an exclusive
emphasis on the formal institutions of government as an explanation for
our collective discontents. If we are to make our political system more responsive, especially to those who lack connections at the top, we must
nourish grass-roots organization.

Classic liberal social policy is designed to enhance the opportunities
of *individuals*, but if social capital is important, this emphasis is partially
misplaced. Instead we must focus on community development, allowing
space for religious organizations and choral societies and Little Leagues
that may seem to have little to do with politics or economics. Government policies, whatever their intended effects, should be vetted for their
indirect effects on social capital. If, as some suspect, social capital is
fostered more by home ownership than by public or private tenancy,
then we should design housing policy accordingly. Similarly, as Theda
Skocpol has suggested, the direct benefits of national service programs
might be dwarfed by the indirect benefits that could flow from the creation of social networks that cross class and racial lines. In any comprehensive strategy for improving the plight of America's communities, rebuilding social capital is as important as investing in human and physical
capital.

Throughout the Bush administration, community self-reliance—"a
thousand points of light"—too often served as an ideological fig leaf for
an administration that used the thinness of our public wallet as an alibi
for a lack of political will. Conservatives are right to emphasize the value
of intermediary associations, but they misunderstand the potential
synergy between private organization and the government. *Social capital
is not a substitute for effective public policy but rather a prerequisite for it and,
in part, a consequence of it.* Social capital, as our Italian study suggests,
works through and with states and markets, not in place of them. The social capital approach is neither an argument for cultural determinism nor
an excuse to blame the victim.

Wise policy can encourage social capital formation, and social capital itself enhances the effectiveness of government action. From agricultural extension services in the last century to tax exemptions for community organizations in this one, American government has often promoted investments in social capital, and it must renew that effort now. A new administration that is, at long last, more willing to use public power and the public purse for public purpose should not overlook the importance of social connectedness as a vital backdrop for effective policy.

Students of social capital have only begun to address some of the most important questions that this approach to public affairs suggests. What are the actual trends in different forms of civic engagement? Why do communities differ in their stocks of social capital? What *kinds* of civic engagement seem most likely to foster economic growth or community effectiveness? Must specific types of social capital be matched to different public problems? Most important of all, how is social capital created and destroyed? What strategies for building (or rebuilding) social capital are most promising? How can we balance the twin strategies of exploiting existing social capital and creating it afresh? The suggestions scattered throughout this essay are intended to challenge others to even more practical methods of encouraging new social capital formation and leveraging what we have already.

We also need to ask about the negative effects of social capital, for like human and physical capital, social capital can be put to bad purposes. Liberals have often sought to destroy some forms of social capital (from medieval guilds to neighborhood schools) in the name of individual opportunity. We have not always reckoned with the indirect social costs of our policies, but we were often right to be worried about the power of private associations. Social inequalities may be embedded in social capital. Norms and networks that serve some groups may obstruct others, particularly if the norms are discriminatory or the networks socially segregated. Recognizing the importance of social capital in sustaining community life does not exempt us from the need to worry about how that community is defined—who is inside and thus benefits from social capital, and who is outside and does not. Some forms of social capital can impair individual liberties, as critics of communitarianism warn. Many of the Founders' fears about the "mischiefs of faction" apply to social capital. Before toting up the balance sheet for social capital in its various forms, we need to weigh costs as well as benefits. This challenge still awaits.

Progress on the urgent issues facing our country and our world requires ideas that bridge outdated ideological divides. Both liberals and conservatives agree on the importance of social empowerment, as E. J. Dionne recently noted ("The Quest for Community [Again]," *TAP*, Summer 1992). The social capital approach provides a deeper conceptual underpinning for this nominal convergence. Real progress requires not facile verbal agreement, but hard thought and ideas with high fiber content. The social capital approach promises to uncover new ways of combining private social infrastructure with public policies that work, and, in turn, of using wise public policies to revitalize America's stocks of social capital.

[5]

Deborah A. Stone

Race, Gender, and the Supreme Court

The confirmation hearings of Clarence Thomas were a great national Rorschach test. The lesson, some say, is that the United States has made great progress in race relations. Or, is it that racism is alive and well? Some concluded that women gained a new place in politics, so that even an issue as threatening to men as sexual harassment can no longer be swept under the rug. Others learned that women are still not taken seriously by a male power establishment and it doesn't pay to speak up. For a few, the Thomas affair demonstrated the strength and adaptability of our political institutions. For many, it revealed rot at the core.

Whichever interpretations ultimately dominate the nation's collective self-understanding, politics after Thomas will never be the same. The hearings not only changed the way we will frame issues of race and gender, but also the institutional machinery with which we will resolve them. Lost in all the rumbling about race and gender and party politics is the most profound transformation of all: the gradual erosion of the Supreme Court's moral authority as it becomes less a co-equal branch and more explicitly a creature of presidential ideology and policy strategy.

Political analysts of every stripe immediately recognized the nomination as a brilliant maneuver to split the traditional liberal alliance between the civil rights movement and the women's movement. By naming an anti–affirmative-action black man to fill the ninth seat on an otherwise all-white court, Bush forced liberals to choose between black representation on the court or public policy efforts to create opportunity for minorities. By naming an opponent of choice on the abortion issue, he forced liberals to choose between their black constituents, who strongly favored a black replacement for Justice Thurgood Marshall, and their female constituents, who for the most part favored leaving abortion deci-

73

sions in the hands of individual women. In short, liberals had to choose between the potent symbolism of demographic representation and the pragmatic reality of policy substance.

The real comeuppance for liberals is that they will have to stop relying on crude symbols of race and gender, and instead develop policy positions that speak to women and blacks in all their diversity about issues of well-being, work, and family. This means going beyond the civil rights agenda of the sixties, and even the social equality agenda of the seventies and eighties, to a deeper understanding of how discrimination, subjugation, and exclusions work—and work differently—in different social institutions.

Affirmative Inaction

Republicans successfully maneuvered the confirmation process so it became a parable about the dangers of affirmative action as conservatives have portrayed it. Liberals, so the conservative story goes, in their efforts to provide equal opportunity for the disadvantaged, might ignore competence, sacrifice quality, and destroy organizations in the process. The Democrats fell right into the conservative trap and played out the script.

First George Bush, a steadfast opponent of affirmative action who sees quotas lurking everywhere, made a nomination that looked an awful lot like filling a black quota on the Court. He named a black man who had less than a year and a half of judicial experience; lacked any coherent judicial philosophy; and was in all probability willing to lie to get the job, since it is unlikely in the extreme that a lawyer of his generation never discussed *Roe v. Wade*.

Next, Clarence Thomas, who has insisted blacks don't need special consideration, that they should earn their positions the hard way, invoked racism as a special consideration the moment he got into trouble, precisely so he wouldn't have to defend against the harassment charge the hard way. ("I will not get into any discussion about my private life," he said, and Democrats on the Judiciary Committee obliged him. Only a week earlier, he and the White House had peddled his private life as his main qualification for the job.) Even though Thomas is black, and pejorative racial stereotypes about sexuality do exist, does that mean his behavior cannot be examined and held to the standards of the law of the land? Thomas seemed to think so.

Thus, conservatives capitalized on the very brand of affirmative action policy they nominally reject: fixed quotas and lowered standards applied on the basis of skin color. The southern Democrats, too, used Thomas as a cipher; if voting for him would get them kudos from their constituency, they would support him, no questions asked. Sad to say, many liberals participated in this form of deference to skin color, though it is not the brand of affirmative action most would otherwise defend. Hobbled by the Dixiecrats, by their own unwillingness to play hardball politics, by Senator Ted Kennedy's personal troubles, and by a general squeamishness about confronting racial issues head on, liberals on the Judiciary Committee did exactly what many people most fear and resent about affirmative action: They brushed aside the question of the candidate's competence.

Although the American Bar Association rated Thomas as only "minimally qualified" for the Supreme Court, the Judiciary Committee failed to investigate his competence in any serious way. They deferred to him when he insisted he had no opinion on issues of jurisprudence or specific cases, or when he said it would be "inappropriate" or "improper" for him to comment on recent cases. Improper for someone applying for a permanent job on the Supreme Court? When the committee questioned Thomas about legal views he had expressed in speeches, he often replied that his statements weren't really his positions, that they were thoughts of the moment, and that he hadn't really understood the implications of decisions about which he had offered strong opinions. Thomas's strongest defense was that his critics had mistaken mere opportunism for extremism.

The Judiciary Committee largely ignored all these signs of his inability to articulate a coherent position, and assumed instead that he was stonewalling to avoid giving opponents anything to use against him. But it was entirely possible and plausible that Thomas simply didn't know constitutional law and didn't follow the jurisprudential disputes about recent cases of the Supreme Court. No one was willing to push very hard to find out.

The Democrats' great political failure on affirmative action went virtually unnoticed. They allowed the conservatives to act out a bankrupt version of affirmative action, one that ought to get elected representatives into trouble with both black and white voters.

Democrats might have started by forcing Thomas to address his views on affirmative action in the context of his own life. They could have used the Thomas family story to show that access to jobs in the privileged, primary labor market is largely through expensive credentials and personal networks. Lacking these credentials and networks, most of the working poor, like Thomas's sister and mother, participate in a secondary labor market where the jobs are underpaid and carry no pensions, health insurance, unemployment benefits, job security, or pathways to better jobs. Economic security and upward mobility through hard work—the great social backdrop against which affirmative action seems unnecessary—are simply not there for many Americans.

Democrats might have used the hearings to challenge the conservative portrayal of affirmative action as a departure from the "normal" merit-based system of job recruitment, promotion, and pay allocation. They could have asked Thomas whether he supports veterans' preferences and seniority, two major departures from merit in the normal labor market that overwhelmingly disadvantage women and blacks respectively.

They could have shown how the notion of individual achievement used by conservatives to promote Thomas and debunk affirmative action profoundly oppresses women. It labels men like Thomas, supported at every stage of his life by female relatives, as products of their own efforts, while it denigrates women like his sister, who work at taking care of their families, as dependent scroungers.

The hearings were, at bottom, a political default. Many Democrats have come to accept the tacit premise that a president is entitled to his Supreme Court nominees, no matter how scantly qualified, no matter how extreme their views. The Senate was moved to vote down Robert Bork not because of his extreme views, but because of his extreme arrogance. Thomas in the end received forty-eight negative votes rather than the anticipated thirty to thirty-five, only because of the sexual harassment charge. Democratic senators seem to accept that as long as a candidate has no overt prejudices, no criminal record, and—better yet—no record of jurisprudence, controversial or otherwise, they are obliged to vote for him. They seem to accept that if they turn down scholarly right-wing judges, the corollary is that they must vote to confirm mediocre ones.

These assumptions are, of course, preposterous. The Democrats ought to demand that the president's judicial nominees be both judicially distinguished and ideologically moderate, not one or the other. This is, after all, the all-time record era of divided government. It is only reasonable that a president who shares power with a Democratic Senate should not be able to insist on nominees well to his own right—men whom he has been nominating mainly to curry favor with the Republican party's extreme right wing. Bush has no respect for either the Senate's advise-and-consent function or for the Court's stature as an institution. Dwight Eisenhower, who had both, nominated William Brennan—Willam Brennan!—with the full knowledge that he was a liberal Democratic state judge, as well as Earl Warren, a moderately liberal Republican governor.

Supreme Courtship

It was a failure of politics in the first set of hearings—a failure to challenge the candidate's temperament, philosophy, and qualifications—that led indirectly to the bungled attempt in the second set of hearings to challenge the candidate's character. If the hearings united everyone against the idea of sexual harassment, they also exposed profound disagreement over what it is. The term is nowhere mentioned in Title VII of the Civil Rights Act of 1964, but since 1986, the act's prohibition of "discrimination on the basis of sex" has been interpreted by the Supreme Court to include two types of sexual harassment: "Quid pro quo" harassment, when a supervisor or employer makes sexual favors a condition of the job or promotion; and "hostile environment" harassment, when an employer permits unwelcome remarks, pornographic posters, or constant attention to a person's sexuality that interferes with her ability to perform her job.

The treatment of Anita Hill demonstrated one of the inadequacies of formal civil rights law. When a woman comes forward with a sexual harassment claim in 1991, she is protected by a judicial doctrine that recognizes sexual harassment as a civil rights violation. But judicial doctrine is only as good as the way it is interpreted, and sexual harassment, like rape, has mostly been adjudicated from a male point of view which largely ignores realities of gender power.

Hill was verbally battered by older white men who asked her in a hundred ways why she hadn't behaved as they would have in such a situation. Why had she followed Thomas to another job and maintained good relations with him if she found his behavior so unbearable? They simply could not imagine what it is like to try to make it as a young, black woman in a racist, sexist world. As soon as they got close to understanding, they shivered at how the dirty little secrets of their own world of power would look to the American public. Perhaps, as elected politicians, they could imagine all too well what it is like to have to make nice to people you despise but whose support you need. But like Clarence Thomas, they pretended that individuals make their careers by themselves, and so refused to regard Anita Hill's situation from the point of view of someone who needs other people—and knows and admits she needs other people—to get anywhere.

Anita Hill's hearing was a kind of symbolic rape trial. Her virtue and character were challenged, while Thomas's behavior and motives were taken at his word. Her sexuality was examined and pontificated upon by witnesses-turned-pop-psychologists. Witnesses for Thomas were encouraged to speculate on her motivations for fantasizing the events she described. An acquaintance was brought in to testify to her proclivity to see romantic interest where there was none. She even underwent the ritual physical examination familiar to rape victims, this one in the form of a lie-detector test. Though Senator Joseph Biden, the Judiciary Committee's chairman, didn't admit the test as evidence, it is a tribute to the power of the symbolic ritual that her lawyer advised her to take the test, while Bush publicly called it "a stupid idea" for Thomas.

For all the prurient interest that may have made people watch, listen, and read, the motive force for this national exercise was a clash of deep male and female anxieties. For women, it was the anger at being transformed into a raw sexual object and the powerlessness to stop or undo that transformation. For men, it was the fear of false accusation and of prosecution for a crime whose standards are not clear to anyone, least of all themselves.

The hearings, surveys, interviews, and polls dramatized this conflict without moving an inch toward resolving it. We were left with a host of questions. What are the limits of permissible courtship in the workplace? Have the boundaries of the workplace expanded to include the bar around the corner, the restaurant, the apartment near the office, the out-of-town conference hotel? What can a woman reasonably be expected to do to defend herself at the moment? Since sexual harassment, like rape, is usually an offense without witnesses, what will count as evidence? How can a man defend himself against harassment charges besides simply denying them?

For starters, to frame the issue as one of confusion over standards of permissible courtship is to miss the mark. True, harassment often includes activities that in another context would be courtship—asking for a date, making flattering comments, touching, kissing—but context is all the difference. Though the workplace is often the setting for social mixing, the job and particularly the supervisory relationship are not mixers. No woman or man can do his or her job, let alone be perceived as doing it well, while being treated as an object of sexual conquest. What may seem to a man a minor sexual comment, joke, or advance can assault a woman by abruptly shifting her mental focus from work tasks and temporarily casting her out of her work role. That's the mild form. Sexual demands, forced conversations about sex, or unwelcome touches do more than temporarily displace her identity; they suppress it and deny it by making her sexuality more important than her work. This is what women mean when they say harassment is about power, not sex.

This is also why styles of courtship are irrelevant. The issue is not, as Orlando Patterson wrote in *The New York Times*, whether people from different regions, social classes, or ethnic backgrounds have different styles of courtship. According to Patterson, regaling a woman with "Rabelaisian humor" is a normal part of Southern working-class courtship ritual, and Anita Hill, who surely understood that, was "disingenuous" when she displaced Thomas's behavior from its context and brought it into the white, upper-middle class work world of the senators. Patterson concluded that if Thomas had done exactly what Anita Hill said he did, he would be morally justified in lying because she had applied the wrong standards to his behavior and he didn't deserve the "self-destructive and grossly unfair punishment" that telling the truth would bring.

Therein lies the rub. Just whose standards should be applied to the kind of behavior at issue here? Sexual harassment, like rape, is a crime of coercion (though it is not strictly a crime, but a civil rights violation). Harassment is coercing someone into sexual contact they don't want to have and coercing them out of one identity and into another. Only genuine consent can render an activity noncoercive, and therefore the standard of judgment should reflect how the action looks to the weaker party, given the real disparity of power. It is a mockery of the liberal ideal of autonomy to interpret a potentially coercive relationship from the point of view of the person who has the power to coerce. The only just criterion in a harassment case is whether the woman felt she had the freedom to resist, without taking career risks.

Is that unfair to men? Are men supposed to be mind-readers, you ask? Well, yes. Parents, who exercise inordinate physical and psychological control over children, are morally and legally obliged to understand their children's needs, even when their children can't talk. They are not free to abuse children because the children don't protest. In any situation of power, the powerful have a moral obligation to see the world from the point of view of those they govern or control, and to exercise power in the interests of the governed. Just consent is what makes power legitimate instead of tyrannical.

Especially since most harassment takes place in private, with no witnesses, the weaker party needs the protection of a legal standard that says her "no" means "no." She can't enforce her "no." Sometimes, she feels too threatened even to utter her "no." As long as men are in positions of power, the burden is on them to anticipate how their actions affect weaker people. This is the burden that goes with the privilege of power.

There is work to be done to get this standard to prevail in courts as harassment cases are adjudicated, and even more important, in men's heads as they live their daily lives. The women's cause was enormously advanced by the outpouring of tales of harassment following the Hill testimony. Perhaps the next step should be "outing"—telling stories with names attached. The fear of false accusations might just do wonders to get men to feel in their stomachs the vulnerability and powerlessness women live with constantly.

Fair Judging

It is in just such situations, where the points of view of the powerful can obliterate those of the weak, and where objective evidence is difficult if not impossible to obtain, that we most need judges we can trust. We need judges who have the capacity to empathize, to evaluate evidence and arguments from multiple points of view, and to suspend judgment while they move between different points of view. Clarence Thomas showed few of these qualities.

As Ronald Dworkin noted in the *New York Review of Books*, Thomas asserted views in a speech to the Heritage Foundation that would logically require the Supreme Court to outlaw abortions after conception. (In other words, the Supreme Court should not just roll back *Roe v. Wade* so that states may outlaw abortions if they wish, but it should revoke the states' current authority to permit abortions.) If, as he told the Judiciary Committee, he was merely trying to appeal to his conservative audience in that speech, had only skimmed the article whose ideas he endorsed, and had thought the ideas would be interesting "to play around with," then he has a rather cavalier attitude about the responsibilities of a federal judge to develop considered views on issues over which he will exercise great power.

Thomas gave us other glimpses of his cavalierness toward judging. In maintaining he had never discussed *Roe v. Wade*, he was saying he felt no need to engage with the legal community or anyone else about one of the major constitutional and political issues of his era. In endorsing the view that Anita Hill was part of a liberal interest group conspiracy to undo him, he showed a healthy disrespect for evidence. In announcing that he had not watched or listened to any of Anita Hill's testimony, he showed a disdain for the fact-finding process. It is not clear which is the scarier prospect: a Supreme Court justice who thinks abortion should be entirely outlawed, or one who thinks it is proper for a judge to decide without paying much attention to evidence or argument.

Equal Opportunity on Trial

In the background of the Thomas hearings was the paradoxical issue of affirmative action. Was he the ultimate affirmative action hire? Would he do the ideological bidding of his conservative sponsors and be the definitive fifth vote against affirmative action? And is affirmative action worth defending? This was the debate that the Judiciary Committee never quite had, and one that liberals ought to be leading. In the hearings themselves, the Democrats failed to use the confirmation process as a venue to dissect the symbol affirmative action has become, and to defend a coherent affirmative action policy aimed at making formal legal equality a reality.

In the university, ordinarily a bastion of liberal values, the scramble to recruit black university professors from a very small pool of qualified applicants has created a mentality of grudging tokenism in many academic departments and has left a residue of bad feeling among the professorate of both races. Many white college professors feel coerced into hiring colleagues of seemingly lower formal qualification, while many highly qualified blacks resent the presumption that they were hired only because of their race. This dynamic has left some liberal intellectuals particularly skeptical of the whole approach. However, it is wrong to project the college experience onto affirmative action generally. Affirmative action is not simply, or even mostly, for professional elites. The real action is out there in construction, manufacturing, clerical jobs, unionized public-sector jobs, transportation, and the like. It is in these sectors that formal qualifications matter less, yet oddly, minorities and women have been excluded from the better paying manual jobs.

Affirmative action has also been criticized for giving disproportionate help to relatively advantaged blacks, while ignoring masses of poor blacks. But affirmative action was never intended as a means to improve jobs at the lower end; it couldn't possibly do anything to increase pay, benefits, job security, or advancement opportunity in the secondary labor market. Of course, we ought to make bad jobs better through other policies such as minimum wage, tax credits, health insurance, and unemployment insurance; and we ought to make paid employment less hostile to family life.

Liberal leaders need to explain that the working poor are poor and sometimes unemployed because their government and business leaders don't provide a stable economy and a decent safety net, not because unqualified women and members of minority groups are taking their otherwise terrific jobs. But affirmative action shouldn't be blamed for these broader economic failures. Rather, affirmative action was intended and designed to improve access to better jobs and careers, and to do so by altering systemic barriers to entry. In that, it has succeeded.

Liberals need to distinguish between the caricature of affirmative action exploited by the conservatives and the original spirit of affirmative action. They would do well to remind citizens—and themselves—of the social circumstances under which the Johnson administration devised affirmative action and the Supreme Court approved affirmative action in the first place. In 1965, under Executive Order 11246, the administration required federal contractors to take affirmative steps to overcome past patterns of racial exclusion. In 1969 the Nixon administration's pilot "Philadelphia Plan" added the requirement of specific "goals and timetables" to overcome persistent racial exclusion in skilled construction work. In the 1978 *Bakke* case, involving a University of California minority admissions plan, a fragmented Court concluded that minority representation goals could be constitutional. In 1979 the Supreme Court approved a voluntary affirmative action plan adopted by United Steelworkers and Kaiser Aluminum. The company hired only people with prior experience for its skilled crafts positions. On its face, the prior experience requirement was neutral, but since black workers had long been excluded from craft unions, few had any experience in skilled craftsmanship. To address this problem, the union and company created an on-the-job training program for all its employees. Entry into the program was determined by seniority (which again gave white workers an advantage), but half the slots were reserved for black employees, even if they had less seniority than other white applicants.

The Supreme Court's first explicit approval of a court-imposed plan with preferential hiring goals came in 1986, in a case filed against a local union of the Sheet Metal Workers International Association by the Equal Employment Opportunity Commission. The union had barred black workers from its apprenticeship program until 1964, and after that, continued to award apprenticeship positions primarily on the basis of "sponsorship" by current union members. Obviously, the sponsorship requirement, although it never mentioned race, had the effect of keeping out nonwhites. By the time the case reached the Supreme Court, the union had ignored several court orders enjoining it to stop its discriminatory practices and increase its hiring of nonwhites.

Also in 1986, the Court approved a voluntary affirmative action program in a government agency. In this case, the Santa Clara County (California) Transportation Agency was trying to increase the number of ethnic minorities and women in professional, administrative, technical and skilled craft positions. In fact, at the time of this case, there were no women in the 238 skilled craft jobs, although women were 36 percent of the area labor force. Despite the nominal openness of traditionally male jobs to women, deep and long-standing patterns of hostility to women prevented them from seeking these jobs or succeeding in them. So the agency set long-term hiring and promotion goals based on percentages of ethnic minorities and women in the area labor force, but didn't reserve any fixed number of slots for these groups. Instead, its plan called for taking sex and ethnicity into account as additional factors when there were several qualified applicants for a position. On that basis, the agency promoted a woman to the job of road dispatcher, from a pool of seven applicants who were deemed qualified after a first interview. The plan was challenged by a man who had received two points more than she—on an eighty-point scale—in the initial interview. (Think about the validity of a two-point difference in anything so subjective as an interview.) The Court allowed her promotion and the plan to stand, noting approvingly that the agency's plan created no "absolute bar" to men, set no quotas, and used sex and ethnicity criteria only in addition to job-related standards.

These cases established the broad outlines of affirmative action policy. Neither these nor other affirmative action plans approved by the Supreme Court were cases of someone arbitrarily seeking to fill a statistical quota for women or minority workers. They were cases where simply changing the formal rules and nominally opening up jobs and training programs to previously excluded groups was patently insufficient to establish genuine equal opportunity.

Affirmative action is sometimes necessary to enforce formal civil rights. Deeply rooted patterns of racial and gender exclusion, harassment, and discrimination have not been eliminated by one generation of civil rights law. The Supreme Court has approved race-conscious remedies when ostensibly race-neutral selection procedures either deliberately or inadvertently perpetuate the effects of prior discrimination. The Court has shown an increasing preference for race-neutral remedies, but has never said that race-conscious remedies for prior discrimination would be impermissible when race-neutral remedies are ineffective.

There is still plenty of room for this kind of affirmative action, if only liberal leaders dared articulate a rationale. Defensible affirmative action programs do not, as the caricature suggests, put people in skilled positions for which they are not qualified. They put sufficiently qualified people in a position to acquire more skills and knowledge, and to be eligible for further upward mobility genuinely based on their achievement. These programs recognize that when there is a surplus of qualified people for any job or training position, it is permissible to take into account other standards, such as ethnicity or sex, in making a selection from a pool of qualified people. The Supreme Court has consistently endorsed this kind of affirmative action, as long as the plan is temporary and doesn't entirely exclude whites or males from the opportunities.

Of course, an increasingly conservative Court may well pull back from the brand of affirmative action that seeks to broaden minority representation on the job, and narrow permissible affirmative action to cases of individual remedy rather than redresses of social patterns of exclusion. But that is no reason for liberals to give up on the affirmative action ideal, any more than liberals should give up on reproductive rights because the courts have begin to erode the guarantees of *Roe*. As in the case of *Roe*, an increasingly hostile judiciary means precisely that liberals must win their case in the court of public opinion and electoral politics. The tellingly labeled "Civil Rights Restoration Act," opposed by the administration all the way to the signing ceremony in the Rose Garden, illustrates how strong political action can and should counteract backsliding by conservative courts.

Since 1989, attempts to overturn major Supreme Court rulings have been virtually permanently on the congressional agenda. The Thomas hearings brought an almost immediate White House "compromise" on the previously deadlocked civil rights legislation, which, for all its gaps, is a vigorous rejection of a major line of recent Supreme Court interpretation. Congress failed to overturn *Rust v. Sullivan*, the "gag rule" on publicly funded women's health clinics. Ironically, that failure will probably assure that abortion is a prominent issue throughout the 1992 presidential campaign, and therefore a constant reminder of just how far out of touch with the mainstream the Supreme Court has strayed.

Congress and Court in the Dock

By the end of the second round of hearings, nearly everyone had lost sight of the Supreme Court as an institution. The Senate didn't grapple in the slightest with the institutional questions raised by Anita Hill's testimony: In the adjudication of disputes, how should judges assist the weak? How, in other words, is a court to be more like an umpire and less like a hired thug? And getting down to the brass tacks of advice and consent, is Clarence Thomas a man who has any moral sense of how to handle his own power? The Senate failed as a body of public counselors. It behaved instead like a master of television ceremonies and submitted Hill's and Thomas's performances to the national clap-o-meter of a hasty public opinion poll.

Most senators framed the issue as a criminal trial where the decision was guilty or innocent. Senator Biden told *The New York Times*, "In my mind if there is substantial doubt, you resolve that doubt in favor of the accused." Beyond-a-reasonable-doubt is indeed the standard of justice courts apply when they are considering depriving someone of fundamental liberties—sending them to prison, for example. But it is assuredly not the appropriate standard when a legislature is considering elevating someone to a position of great power, from which he can be removed only with tremendous difficulty, and in which he will decide on the liberties of every citizen. Senator Kennedy came close to the point when he said, "In a case of this magnitude, where so much is riding on our decision, the Senate should give the benefit of the doubt to the Supreme Court."

Lacking any standard by which to assess the rightness of political issues, our politicians grab at standards from other spheres of life, such as personal character or criminal trials. The important questions remain unasked: What kind of institution is the Supreme Court? How and to whom is it accountable? What are reasonable criteria by which to evaluate the qualifications of proposed justices? What makes for good judging, and how can the extraordinary power of judges contribute to democracy rather than erode it?

While the legal scholars are still debating whether judges decide by some neutral principles of legal reasoning or are mere mortals exercising power, the public and the politicians know the answer. Nomination politics over the last few years has made that clear to anyone who doesn't remember Franklin Roosevelt's court packing scheme. The last two Presidents have nominated judges with extremist views, and used their appointment powers to gain control of the judicial branch and thereby implement their preferred policies, in open defiance of Congress. Congress and interest groups have responded by playing the same game —though far less adroitly—treating the federal courts, and especially the Supreme Court, as just another political institution to be "won."

Even the Supreme Court, in an otherwise unobjectionable spring 1991 decision holding that elections of state judges are subject to the Voting Rights Act, implied that courts are political bodies. But if judges are to have legitimacy as neutral umpires and if they are to decide conflicts on the basis of higher principles, then they must not be regarded as merely political creatures representative of particular constituencies or current ideological fashions. If courts become merely representative institutions rather than deliberative ones, they risk losing their ability to resolve conflict on the basis of principle rather than raw power, and the rule of law suffers.

The Supreme Court's moral authority may have taken particularly heavy blows with the Thomas appointment, but if so, these losses are only part of a larger trend. Supreme Court nominations are increasingly hard to distinguish from electoral campaigns. Large majorities of Congress have voted on several recent occasions to overturn Supreme Court rulings. Coming at a time when several Supreme Court rulings on civil rights and one on abortion were under siege within Congress, the Thomas hearings only further dramatized that the Court's decisions are the result of a highly politicized selection process, just like the decisions of the other branches of government. It may be harder and harder to sustain popular support for the least democratic branch. Not that anyone will attempt to do away with the Court, but the Court's only real enforcement power resides in its ability to command respect and exert moral suasion.

[6]

RANDALL KENNEDY

Lani Guinier's Constitution

When President Clinton abandoned Lani Guinier, she became the latest in a string of jilted appointees dumped once controversy arose. Guinier, who was nominated as head of the Justice Department's civil rights division, was a respected civil rights lawyer, legal theorist, and Friend of Bill, whom she has known since their days at Yale Law School. Why ultimately did he abandon her nomination? What in her writings as a University of Pennsylvania Law School professor prompted such bitter opposition? Did the president err in nominating her—or withdrawing her nomination? What is the meaning of this affair in the ongoing struggle for the soul of the Democratic Party?

A hard-nosed political calculation best explains why Clinton dumped Guinier: he believed that he stood to lose less by abandoning than supporting her. Other considerations—personal, accidental, and ideological—also played a role. Clinton has shown that, unlike Presidents Reagan and Bush, he has no strong sense of attachment to people whom he exposes to attack. And he felt he was losing his grip on his presidency as a result of setbacks large and small. At the very moment the debate over Guinier became most intense, Clinton was seeking to regain his footing by openly moving rightward, a move best symbolized by his hiring of David Gergen.

Clinton said he changed his mind about Guinier because, upon actually reading her work, he found it at odds with his own views. It probably is true that Clinton disagrees with some of what Guinier has written. But neither that nor the reasons noted above fully explain why he dropped her.

Had opposition to Guinier been limited to conservative Republicans, Clinton surely would have stood by her. But the opposition included the centrist-liberal *New York Times*, New Democrats like Al From of the Democratic Leadership Council, and Neanderthal liberals such as A.M. Rosenthal. Joseph Biden, chairman of the Senate Judiciary Committee, was openly skeptical, and even Edward Kennedy, one of the Senate's most stalwart liberals, distanced himself. Thus in addition to predictable Republican opposition, Guinier faced opposition from important sectors of the Democratic Party. In fact, her only solid base of support was the civil rights establishment including the Congressional Black Caucus (CBC). Clinton does not wish to offend that establishment gratuitously, but he is willing to offend to avoid alienating other allies whom he perceives as more essential to his presidency.

What New Democrats Understood

The Democratic right and center correctly perceived that Lani Guinier's racial politics sharply differ from theirs. At the same time, many of these opponents failed to understand large aspects of her work. I doubt that A.M. Rosenthal actually read and understood Lani Guinier's writings before writing that she stands for "racial polarization" and for "setting black and white politically and legally apart." And both Bill Clinton and Vice President Al Gore sputtered to the verge of incoherence when they were challenged to specify precisely the aspects of Guinier's writings to which they objected.

But this critique cannot be pushed too far. After all, even the most intellectually rigorous observers depend upon secondhand or third-hand information in evaluating policies or politicians. Does one really have to read the collected writings of David Duke before denouncing him? And if some of Guinier's opponents rejected her solely on the basis of what they had heard as opposed to what they knew from personal study, isn't the same true of her supporters? Did members of the Congressional Black Caucus studiously examine her work before announcing their ringing endorsements? For all the ignorance, exaggeration, and misunderstanding that animated the campaign against Guinier, there was an accurate perception that, whatever its particulars, her work reflected a racial politics at odds with that of centrist and conservative liberals, the chief constituency of the New Democrats.

In "Keeping the Faith: Black Voters in the Post-Reagan Era"—the first of the four law review articles that mainly constitute the public record of Guinier's thinking on racial policy—she articulates themes that clearly indicate why many New Democrats (not to mention Republicans) would oppose her nomination as the administration's leading voice on civil rights policy. "Keeping the Faith" harshly criticizes the Reagan administration's racial policies, particularly its slack enforcement of the Voting Rights Act, noting that under the stewardship of William Bradford Reynolds, the Justice Department's civil rights division "had contributed to an increasing sense of isolation among African Americans." While this might anger some conservatives—especially insofar as she describes the newly inaugurated George Bush as "the president of the white electorate"—it alone would not bother Clinton's New Democrat allies, many of whom vaguely perceive the Reagan-Bush racial policies as "divisive."

What would upset these allies, however, is a second aspect of Guinier's writing. She not only condemns the Republicans who "refused to court the black vote at all" but also castigates Democrats. Mainstream Democrats, she writes, have "taken blacks for granted" and "do not accept black Democrats, such as Jesse Jackson, as legitimate party spokespersons." Taking aim at the low priority Michael Dukakis placed on issues of racial justice in his presidential campaign, Guinier writes that "the vision Democrats offered in 1988 hardly mentioned, even indirectly, problems of race, and ... deliberately ignored connections between racism and poverty."

> *Reading Lani Guinier*
>
> "Keeping the Faith: Black Voters in the Post-Reagan Era," *Harvard Civil Rights-Civil Liberties Law Review*, 1989.
>
> "The Triumph of Tokenism: The Voting Rights Act and the Theory of Black Electoral Success," *Michigan Law Review*, 1991.
>
> "No Two Seats: The Elusive Quest for Political Equality," *Virginia Law Review*, 1991.
>
> "The Representation of Minority Interests: The Question of Single-Member Districts," *Cardozo Law Review*, 1993.

"The Democratic Party," she charges, "has responded to racial polarization by distancing itself from black interests." Pursuing and broadening her point, Guinier argues that "Democrats who control both Houses of Congress seem unaware that reciprocity in bargaining requires the active promotion of black interests, not just the occasional subvention and authorization of civil rights enforcement. In other words, black legislative issues can be ghettoized from the Left as well as the Right." She asserts, moreover, that "the Democrats' policy of benign neglect toward African Americans has not gone unnoticed." Arguing that blacks' support for Democrats has far outstripped Democrats' support for blacks, she raises the specter of black withdrawal from the Democratic Party.

This critique plainly marks her as part of the left-wing contingent of the Democratic Party, the sector that would like to elevate the plight of the poor—particularly poor racial minorities—to a higher place in the party's policy priorities, the sector that abhors the quietistic stance on racial matters taken by the Dukakis and Clinton campaigns, the sector that worries that the price it pays for remaining part of the Democratic Party coalition is not worth the benefits it receives, the sector whose politics are more in tune with Jesse Jackson and the *Nation* than Bill Clinton and the *New Republic*.

The antagonism between Guinier's perspective and that of New Democrats was presaged by a brief reference in "Keeping the Faith" to a *New York Times Magazine* article by Joe Califano, who served as Jimmy Carter's secretary of health, education, and welfare. In "Tough Talk for Democrats" (Jan. 8, 1989), Califano articulated a message that has subsequently been pressed by Barney Frank (see *Speaking Frankly*), Thomas B. Edsall (see *Chain Reaction: The Impact of Race, Rights, and Taxes on American Politics*), and Jim Sleeper (see *The Closest of Strangers: Liberalism and the Politics of Race in New York*), institutionalized by the Democratic Leadership Council and the Progressive Policy Institute, and tested in electoral competition by Bill Clinton and Al Gore.

Asserting that "the rebirth of the national Democratic Party does not mean abandoning or even tempering our commitment to social and economic justice," Califano wrote that recapturing the White House would necessitate "enduring the painful labor of asking why so many whites perceive us as the party of blacks and special interests, soft on crime and naive about defense." Observing that "racism haunts the American attic like a malevolent specter, denying peace to anyone who would live in the house," Califano also argued that Democrats must be willing to reexamine well-intentioned policies, singling out busing ("a counterproductive failure") and affirmative action (a policy whose time for justified continuation was "running out").

In her article, Guinier responds to Califano in the way that many on the Democratic left interact with the party's right. "Now," Guinier notes (with what I imagine to be a tone of exasperation), "even progressive political, social and economic analysts have begun discounting or ignoring pervasive vestiges of America's racist heritage."

The Role of Racism

Two other aspects of "Keeping the Faith" underline subjects over which Guinier and New Democrats were bound to clash. One concerns the nature and definition of race relations. New Democrats stress that what appear to be racial differences in outcomes increasingly stem from differences in preparation or training as opposed to current, invidious racial discriminations. Guinier, by contrast, emphasizes the continuity of racism as the all-important force shaping race relations. Blacks, she writes, are "still the pariah group."

Another inevitable clash was over race-based affirmative action. New Democrats tend to be skeptical of the justice and efficacy of affirmative action. By contrast, Guinier seems committed to extending race-based decision making. Consider the following suggestion from "Keeping the Faith":

> The Congress can play an important role in encouraging diversity in the appointment process by withholding its advice and consent until enough nominations have been made to establish a pattern of "affirmative recruitment." For example, the Senate Judiciary Committee should begin evaluating federal judicial nominations with reference to specific goals for increasing non-white nominees. The Committee should decline to consider any nominee until a sufficient number of nominations—such as twenty or thirty—were made so as to enable the Committee to consider not only the individual qualifications of each, but the impact of these twenty or thirty nominations as a totality on the composition of the federal bench.

Thus despite efforts by Guinier and some of her supporters to repackage her into a more "mainstream" candidate, her foes accurately perceived her racial politics as those of the Democratic left wing—precisely the racial politics that New Democrats perceive as an impediment to the party's reconstruction. Acknowledging this does not mean siding with her opponents; it simply means clearing the way for a debate over the substance of contending approaches to racial politics.

The Volatile Matter of Voting Rights

Voting rights is the area of racial politics about which Guinier has written most extensively. Its volatility particularly afflicts the Democratic Party, with its far-flung racial, ethnic, and ideological coalition. During the Reagan-Bush years, voting rights was one of the few areas in which the civil rights establishment largely succeeded in shaping the law to its liking. In 1982, for example, aided by the effort of Guinier, who then worked for the NAACP Legal Defense Fund, the civil rights establishment prevailed over Ronald Reagan's opposition and amended the Voting Rights Act, authorizing courts to prohibit not only electoral schemes that intentionally disadvantage racial minorities but schemes that have the effect of disadvantaging them. Subsequently, the federal judiciary interpreted the amended act generously, offering to racial minority plaintiffs an environment more supportive than in any other area of civil rights law.

Until recently, the leading constitutional decision on the permissible use of race in legislative districting was *United Jewish Organizations (UJO)* v. Carey, decided in 1976, a case whose very title is revealing. In *UJO*, organizations representing a Hasidic community sued the Democratic governor of New York in order to block legislation that purposefully created a jurisdiction with a voting majority of blacks, incidentally reducing the voting strength of a Jewish enclave that was split to make way for the new, predominantly black district. The plaintiffs argued, among other things, that the state's action amounted to creating an unconstitutional "racial quota" in electoral results. Only Chief Justice Warren Burger agreed with them. Dissenting, he denounced the race-conscious redistricting in language that sounds as if it were lifted from debates surrounding the Guinier nomination and other recent controversies:

> The use of a mathematical formula tends to sustain the existence of ghettos by promoting the notion that political clout is to be gained or maintained by marshalling particular racial, ethnic, or religious groups in enclaves.... I cannot square the mechanical racial gerrymandering in this case with the mandate of the Constitution.

The majority of the justices, however, upheld the state's action, solidifying one of the main bases on which black electoral representation at every level has depended for growth.

The political consequence of the race-conscious redistricting at issue in *UJO* was a double-edged sword. On the one hand, the purposeful creation of majority-black districts has significantly enhanced black political power. In 1992, for instance, 13 of the 16 blacks elected to Congress (nearly doubling the ranks of the CBC) represent districts that were created to contain a majority of black voters. But this same strategy has produced a backlash against affirmative race-conscious measures. The hostility to Guinier was itself a vivid example of that backlash.

Three weeks after Clinton's withdrawal of Guinier, the Supreme Court, in *Shaw v. Reno*, sidestepped *UJO*, ruling that under some circumstances whites may properly claim that their "constitutional right to participate in a 'color-blind' electoral process" is violated when state governments purposefully create majority-black congressional districts. Although the precise contours of the Court's ruling are murky, its rhetoric, excoriating so-called reverse-discrimination, spells trouble ahead for race-conscious electoral measures. "It is unsettling," stated Justice Sandra Day O'Connor for a 5–4 majority, "how closely [the plan at issue] resembles the most egregious racial gerrymanders of the past.... A reapportionment plan that includes in one district individuals who belong to the same race, but who are otherwise widely separated by geographical and political boundaries, and who may have little in common with one another but the color of their skin, bears an uncomfortable resemblance to political apartheid."

In this context of judicial reconsideration and political backlash, Guinier's receptivity to other strategies to achieve electoral fairness was ahead of the curve.

What Guinier Believes

According to Guinier, blacks' struggle for racial equality in electoral politics has entered a new phase. Her analysis of the initial two phases is uncontroversial. The first involved securing the right simply to cast a ballot free from openly racist exclusionary laws, economic blackmail, or naked violence. This phase came to an end relatively soon after the passage of the Voting Rights Act of 1965. The second phase involved securing the right of blacks to participate in politics free of covert efforts to dilute the effectiveness of their votes. This phase is not yet wholly past; in some locales, white politicians still deliberately draw district lines to fracture or dilute the voting strength of racial minorities. What goes on today, however, is nothing like the wholesale efforts to negate black power in the late 1960s and early 1970s.

What is controversial about Guinier's writings stems from her discussion of what she views as a third phase of the struggle for racial justice in electoral politics—a phase in which, according to her, racial minorities should demand not simply formal access to electoral opportunities but a fair share of actual power. In an article significantly titled "The Triumph of Tokenism: The Voting Rights Act and the Theory of Black Electoral Success," she concludes that "for those at the bottom, a system that gives everyone an equal chance of having their political preferences [by which she means political representatives] *physically represented* is inadequate. A fair system of political representation would ensure that disadvantaged and stigmatized minority groups also provide mechanisms to have a fair chance to have their policy preferences *satisfied*."

Guinier's conclusion rests upon two arguments. First, merely electing a certain number of blacks to a legislature or some other decision making body is insufficient to satisfy her conception of multi-racial fairness. Even after they gain access to a legislature, blacks can be rendered mere tokens if they are isolated by a white majority of lawmakers who refuse to bargain with them and thus prevent them from delivering substantive benefits to their constituents. Guinier contends that this "resegregation within the walls of a formally integrated legislature" has happened often. Thus instead of hailing the enlarged number of black elected officials since 1965 as a sign of substantial progress, Guinier warns that this development represents "the triumph of tokenism."

From this flows her second argument: fairness requires that the legal system protect the representatives of black communities from having their votes diluted in *legislatures*, just as the 1982 amendments to the Voting Rights Act protect black voters from having their votes diluted in *elections*.

This demand, according to Guinier, is insufficiently addressed by most existing political arrangements, including those that have been established over the past decade under pressure from Congress, courts, and the civil rights division of the Justice Department. To meet statutory requirements, many jurisdictions have created majority-black, single-member districts, *the* remedy of choice of the civil rights establishment. Instead of leaving black communities submerged, their voting strength diluted, in districts dominated by white majorities that constantly negate the electoral choices of blacks (to the extent of discouraging those preferred by blacks from even running for office), race-conscious districting aims to subdivide jurisdictions in such a way as to allow minority voters to express themselves in the selection of a representative primarily accountable to them.

Guinier criticizes race-conscious, single-member districting on several grounds. First, she notes that it offers an incentive to residential racial separatism and, for minorities, penalizes dispersion, which seems especially to hurt Hispanics. As Guinier puts it in one of her most recent articles, "Single member districts improve the prospects of minority representation only to the extent that there is substantial residential segregation at the appropriate geographic scale. Thus, for Latinos who live in barrios that are dispersed throughout a jurisdiction, districting does not capture either their real or potential power."

Second, Guinier observes that race-conscious, single-member districting cannot adequately address the multiracial character of many jurisdictions. "In a jurisdiction with a complicated racial, ethnic, and linguistic mix," she warns, "the redistricting struggle can become a source of conflict between blacks and other minority groups."

Third, Guinier objects that redistricting is done by self-interested political professionals who frequently put the preservation of their own power above all other competing concerns. Guinier makes clear that her distrust is race-neutral, focusing on all political insiders whatever their hue. She argues strongly that single-member, winner-take-all districting corrupts not only the political culture of white communities but also the political culture of racial minority communities. She contends that, as conventionally implemented today, race-conscious districting inhibits political competition in minority communities, making them all too safe for the perpetuation of black political elites who insulate themselves from accountability to their nominal constituents.

Fourth, Guinier objects to the way in which single-member districting, even when race-conscious, buttresses the hegemony of the two-party system, marginalizes third party challengers, and encourages a relentlessly centrist, lowest common denominator style of politics that is hostile to any ideas "outside the mainstream."

Fifth, Guinier complains that race-conscious districting impedes the construction of transracial political coalitions. According to her, the process of darkening districts probably separates from the newly created, majority-black jurisdictions some whites who would vote along the same lines as the black majority, relegating these whites to more conservative jurisdictions. Moreover, insofar as the process of darkening some districts entails whitening others, Guinier maintains that this reform will inevitably make some white legislators less dependent on and less accountable to black voters.

Guinier is mindful of benefits race-conscious districting creates. She recognizes, for instance, that while the creation of "safe" black districts may encourage complacency among incumbents, they at least "enable blacks to get elected and then reelected, leading to positions of seniority and status" in the legislative body. And she certainly prefers race-conscious, single-member districting, with all its drawbacks, to the circumstance that prompted its birth as a remedy: governing bodies devoid of people who represent the expressed preferences of communities of black voters. Guinier argues, though, that we are not limited to these alternatives and recommends pressing on to potentially more open, integrated, and participatory forms of democratic governance.

Two points need to be made here about Guinier's critique. First and foremost, it belies certain damaging claims made against her nomination. Opponents contended that her writings showed her to be a racial separatist, hostile to integration, and rigidly attached to racial districting. This portrayal is false. The entire thrust of Guinier's writing has been to find ways that more fully integrate racial minorities into all of the various organs of American self-government. Second, contrary to the claims of some, Guinier is admirably open-minded, possessing a demonstrable willingness and ability to revise her own deeply held beliefs in the face of countervailing evidence and argument. This is best illustrated by the change in her analysis of race-conscious districting. An omnivorous reader, Guinier has the capacity to recognize good ideas even when they come from people with whom she intensely disagrees.

Minority-Sensitive Representation

But what about Guinier's alternatives to race-conscious districting? Do her theories of electoral representation warrant the condemnation she encountered?

Guinier argues that election procedures should be made more sensitive to the preferences of minority voters—not just racial minorities but minorities of all sorts. She contends that winner-take-all systems give too much power to the prevailing majority, condemning to virtual irrelevance the votes of all others. She does not object to the majority wielding the most power. She objects to the majority wielding a degree of power disproportionate to its share of the electorate, particularly insofar as this accentuates the dominance of racial minorities by the white American majority.

To prevent the monopolization of power by a mere majority, Guinier recommends the sort of proportional or semi-proportional electoral systems used in most democracies around the world. Here it must be said that Guinier (like most social critics) is considerably more comprehensive, detailed, and assured when discussing what she rejects than what she wants. Her writings do not yet present a thorough road map of alternatives. They do offer a clear indication, however, of points of departure.

Guinier argues in favor of two broad reforms. One involves changes in the rules governing the selection of representatives; the second involves changes in the rules governing decision making by representatives. With respect to the first, Guinier recommends the creation of multi-member districts where representatives are chosen by cumulative voting. Under such an arrangement, people can cast multiple votes up to the number of open seats and express the intensity of their preferences by aggregating their votes. A voter could, for instance, cast all of her votes for a single candidate. Guinier champions cumulative voting because, like race-conscious districting, it provides a way of making visible the political preferences of racial minorities, protecting them, to some degree, from having their collective choices diluted by surrounding white majorities.

Consider one of Guinier's hypotheticals: a five-member, at-large city council in a jurisdiction in which blacks constitute 20 percent of the population. Under a cumulative voting arrangement, the black community can, if its members vote strategically, always elect at least one representative wholly accountable to that community of voters. This matches what race-conscious districting accomplishes but avoids the drawbacks mentioned above. For one thing, cumulative voting would counteract current incentives toward racially separated residential patterns, removing the anxiety felt by some minority politicians who fear that residential desegregation will inevitably lessen blacks' potential political power.

The second set of reforms Guinier suggests are changes in the rules governing decision making by representatives. She proposes "supermajoritarian decisionmaking rules" that would "give minority groups an effective veto, thus forcing the majority to bargain with them and include them in any 'winning' coalition." For instance, she argues for rules requiring enough votes that at least some representatives of minority groups would have to assent before a given policy could be implemented. In contexts in which a majority of white representatives consistently refrains from bargaining with the representatives of racial minority groups, Guinier proposes imposing supermajority rules that would *compel* the white representatives to bargain.

On balance, Guinier's writing constitutes an impressive intellectual achievement that should have strengthened, rather than destroyed, the case for confirming her as head of the Justice Department's civil rights division. Still, there are weaknesses in her work that should be mentioned. Two are particularly noteworthy.

First, Guinier's discussion of remedies needs considerable refinement. In suggesting the imposition of supermajority voting rules upon legislatures in which minorities are isolated, she only vaguely defines improper isolation. Guinier writes that the supermajority requirement would be triggered for votes "on issues of importance to the majority" or "critical minority issues." However, she neither offers reasons for the limitations she notes nor guidance for distinguishing "critical minority issues" from those that will be critical to *all* voters. Given the interdependencies at work within our society, such distinctions—white folks' business and colored folks' business—are dubious. Guinier also has failed to distinguish adequately the strengths and weaknesses of alternatives to existing voting and legislative ground rules. Given this, it seems premature for Guinier to recommend cumulative voting over other ideas that may deliver more of the benefits she seeks for historically oppressed minorities.

A second major weakness in Guinier's work is the tendency, shared by many on the left, to use indiscriminately "racism" as an all-purpose condemnation of policies with which she disagrees and to minimize the substantial reforms that have transformed race relations over the past half-century. Guinier helped to feed the public relations attack on her with an op-ed piece that ran in the *Philadelphia Inquirer* in February 1992. In it she castigated a recent Supreme Court decision, *Pressley v. Etowah County.* Likening to a lynching the decision in which a 5–4 majority of the justices resurrected "the rhetoric and the logic of white supremacy," she suggested that racism explains the Court's holding that the Voting Rights Act did not reach certain suspicious actions taken by white commissioners in a Georgia county soon after the election of a black commissioner. The Bush Justice Department argued that the act should have been interpreted to reach the defendant's conduct. A different result could have been—should have been—reached.

But an erroneous decision that has the consequence of hurting the interests of racial minorities is not always attributable to racially selective indifference or malevolence. There is nothing wrong with stigmatizing a decision as racist as long as one can justify making such a serious charge. In her op-ed piece, however, Guinier offered no such justification. Instead, evading the problems posed by the case, she argued as if it were self-evident what the correct decision would have been and as if only a moral flaw could divert anyone from her preferred result. *Pressley*, however, raised a difficult issue of statutory construction, a fact that even some of the strongest backers of the act (and of Lani Guinier) concede. By lodging the accusation of racism somewhat recklessly, Guinier pinches the nerves of those who, with some justice, resent overplaying the "racism card."

This tendency surfaces in her law review articles as well. Allegations of racism or prejudice pop up whenever she describes a situation in which a majority of black voters (or legislators) prefers a given result while a majority of white voters (or legislators) prefers another. She gives too little consideration to variables other than prejudice to explain differences in voting patterns that, while racially correlated, may be animated to a significant degree by other causes, including socioeconomic and ideological differences.

Looming behind patterns of what appear to be racially polarized voting are what Samuel Isaacharoff aptly describes as "fundamental differences in the socioeconomic positions of whites and black Americans." According to him, only 2 of every 100 white households would be adversely affected by a cut in welfare payments, compared with 15 of every 100 black households. At the more affluent end of the socioeconomic spectrum, 53.5 percent of all blacks in professional or managerial positions are employed by government. Only 27.5 percent of whites in similar positions serve the public sector. Hence, as Isaacharoff asks, "Is it any wonder that blacks and whites have hugely different views on the critical political issue of government responsibility to guarantee employment and/or decent standards of living?"

Racially correlated divergences on voting patterns may stem from different causes, thereby justifying different responses. Is it the case, as some contend, that whites would be willing to vote for black candidates if they were more conservative than those who currently dominate the CBC? Or is it that whites shun black candidates regardless of the latter's politics (a scenario that would strongly bolster the claim that current electoral outcomes are illegitimate)? The persuasiveness of Guinier's account, which largely favors the second hypothesis, will always suffer to the extent that she negates by assumption, as opposed to empirical testing, plausible explanations that compete with her own.

While there are grounds for criticizing Guinier's writings, those articulated by many commentators after her nomination revealed the appallingly low intellectual standards in even the upper reaches of the political and journalistic establishments. The central slogan of the attack on her writings—one that was pathetically embraced in the end by President Clinton—was that they are "antidemocratic." This was, and is, absurd—unless one limits the definition of "democracy" to the particular set of rules currently dominant in the United States.

Far from abandoning democracy, Guinier maintains that, in all too many circumstances, too few people have too little say about the rules and rulers that govern them. An adherent to a consensus (as opposed to a simple majoritarian) model of democracy, a self-described "democratic idealist" who unashamedly invokes the 1960s rhetoric of "participatory democracy," a synthesizer of John Stuart Mill, Arend Lijphart, and Fannie Lou Hamer, Guinier favors rules of self-governance that she believes will encourage more participation by a wider array of people.

It became increasingly evident during the controversy over Guinier's nomination that many who felt themselves competent to evaluate her work publicly were not only ignorant of its complexity but ignorant, too, of various strands of democratic thought and practice within the United States and around the world. Some condemned Guinier as if they had never read James Madison and *The Federalist Papers* or considered the obstacles to majoritarianism built into the constitutional structure including the Bill of Rights, bicameral legislatures, and quotas dictating that all states must be represented by two senators regardless of difference in populations—or reflected in customs—like the Senate filibuster—by which minorities compel majorities to take their interests into account.

Some of Guinier's opponents spoke as if they were unaware that some of the very devices that she sought to justify have already been implemented to good effect with the backing of the Reagan and Bush Justice Departments in certain locales where a conjunction of racially polarized voting and ostensibly race-neutral electoral rules have, for years, excluded racial minorities from any decent share of political power. Some of Guinier's critics, moreover, spoke as if there were only one truly democratic way. Pressed to justify withdrawing her nomination, President Clinton remarked that in her writings she had seemed to advocate proportional representation, which he termed "antidemocratic and difficult to defend." But, as an unsigned editorial in the *New Yorker* caustically noted, Clinton's view "will come as news to the good people of Germany, Spain, the Netherlands and Sweden.... Indeed, most of the electorates of continental Europe, including those of the liberated East, elect their legislatures under some form of proportional representation." Moreover, as the *New Yorker* further editorialized:

> P.R., as its advocates call it, is the very opposite of undemocratic. It not only facilitates minority representation but also virtually guarantees majority rule (the majority most often being a legislative coalition). By contrast, single-member-district, winner-take-all systems ... often produce

minority governments.... Bill Clinton, himself, it should be remembered, owes his job to forty-three percent of the voters.

Senate hearings on Guinier's nomination might have facilitated a widely watched, widely debated, public seminar about contending conceptions of democracy, the strengths and weaknesses of various electoral and legislative schemes in the United States and around the world, the means and ends of the Voting Rights Act, and other important issues about which American citizens and their representatives are deplorably ill-informed.

Left Behind

The struggle over Guinier's nomination demonstrated certain strengths of the Right and certain weaknesses of the Left. Tactically, her allies were slow in responding to the attacks mounted initially by the *Wall Street Journal*. I was one of those unresponsive allies. I took too lightly the *Journal's* flailing. I did not think that its criticisms would be so influential with politicians and media bureaucrats beyond right-wing circles. I thought, moreover, that the White House would orchestrate appropriate rebuttals on behalf of its nominee—though, in fact, the White House kept her under enforced wraps while Clinton dithered. Only at the eleventh hour did Guinier's allies stage dramatic, public shows of support. By then it was too late.

There is a more important and more subtle way in which the left wing of American politics helped inadvertently to ease the way for Guinier's defeat. Intellectuals on the left supplied a real basis to fuel the anxieties wrongly loosed upon Guinier by people who should have given her the benefit of the doubt. All too many intellectuals on the left have loudly embraced, or quietly accepted, such notions as the claim that nothing substantial has changed in race relations since slavery, that the very idea of merit is a racist myth, that it is impossible for blacks to be racist, that it is better for orphaned black children to be raised in institutions than for them to be adopted by white adults, that only indifference to racial justice can explain refusals to censor speech hurtful to members of racial minority groups, that only racism can explain opposition to affirmative action.

These views, the people who hold them, the rhetoric with which they are articulated, and the judgments to which they give rise were very much in the minds of at least some of those who opposed Guinier. They associated these views with the Left, associated herewith that community, and, frightened, acted accordingly. This observation neither justifies nor excuses caricatures of Guinier. But the affair should prompt progressives to ask how such caricatures could be believable to a broad range of people. And it highlights the political costs progressives incur from loose rhetoric and bad judgments.

Effectively pursuing a progressive racial politics today requires the skill of a tightrope walker. A weakened Left insists in strident rhetoric that the legal and socioeconomic status of blacks has scarcely improved over the past half-century. At the same time, precisely because of the real progress that has been made, white Americans tend to deny the extent to which America remains a pigmentocracy. This denial is prevalent among New Democrats, who have dramatically demoted the race question on their agenda.

To counterbalance this evasion, some progressives emphasize, indeed exaggerate, the extent to which the United States avoids addressing the wound of racial oppression. But this approach lacks credibility in the face of obvious gains made by minorities. Moreover, as progressives, we should not minimize these successes, for progressives helped bring them about, changing America for the better.

Among the multiple lessons of the Guinier affair are that New Democrats need reminding about the unfinished agenda of racial justice; that progressive Democrats need to remember that legislative and electoral progress requires allies and that allies require civility; and that intellectuals who anticipate appointment to high office should consider that their "intellectual musings," in Senator Biden's phrase, are likely to be taken literally.

In the end, it is hard to resist the conclusion that Guinier was unjustly demonized. She is a committed, decent, and eloquent progressive, a first-rate intellectual, an experienced litigator, and a genuine Democrat. Clinton's abandonment of her remains a blot on his presidency. The ferocious opposition of her enemies and his eventual capitulation deprived the nation of an important debate and a talent that is hard to come by.

Perhaps Clinton's desertion of Guinier will soon be eclipsed by other decisions that are more palatable to the left wing of the Democratic camp. If not, the Left will have to reconsider a subject it briefly broached during the fight over Guinier's nomination: how should progressives discipline an electorally weak president with some liberal tendencies when the alternatives are conservative Republican aspirants for the White House? At some point, progressives must be willing to confront a Democratic president, regardless of the specter posed by the Republicans. It is a sign of Lani Guinier's strength and Bill Clinton's weakness that his abandonment of her brought this question into such sharp relief this past summer. One can hope that it will recede as a question that progressives must seriously ponder.

[7]

WALTER DELLINGER

Should We Compromise on Abortion?

The Supreme Court's 1989 decision in *Webster v. Reproductive Health Services* has turned abortion into a central issue of majoritarian politics: more than half a million Americans have rallied in the nation's capital in the past year [1989] to assert strongly that the right to abortion be upheld or restricted. Many prominent commentators are concluding, however, that the "extremists on both sides" must yield to the quieter voices in favor of moderate solutions and legislative compromise. That view, it seems to me, is profoundly mistaken.

The calls for compromise are appearing with increasing frequency. Historian Fred Siegel, for example, writes in a recent issue of *The Atlantic* that the abortion issue "pits advocates for women's rights against proponents of fetal rights on an issue that cries out for the compromise heartily desired by the vast majority of the American people." Once the "true believers" on each side have exhausted themselves, William Safire writes, the sensible "pro-compromise majority" will step forth to "reject politicians who slavishly follow pro-life or pro-choice fundamentalists." Opinion polls consistently show, says the *New York Times*, a "substantial middle ground in public opinion, an ambivalent majority that is opposed to an unlimited right to abortion but is also convinced that there are situations when abortion should be available." Many argue that pro-choice supporters should not be unduly alarmed by the return of the abortion issue to state legislatures. Following the adoption last fall of Pennsylvania legislation precluding most abortions in public hospitals, requiring a 24-hour waiting period, and making every married woman certify in writing that she had informed her husband about her plans for an abortion, the editors of the *Washington Post* offered a reassuring opinion:

It is our suspicion ... that even if the worst nightmare of the abortion rights groups came true and Roe were overturned entirely, not a single state would move to criminalize abortion. There will be skirmishing around the edges for years on questions such as funding and parental notification. Some legislatures will adopt some restrictions, but then the voters will have the final word. In a number of states, minor changes may be accepted. But basic rights will not be withdrawn.

Not only popular publications have argued that legislative compromise on abortion is inevitable and desirable. The argument that legislatures will (and should) gradually compromise on moderate legislative restrictions received serious scholarly support from the publication two years ago of an ambitious comparative study, *Abortion and Divorce in Western Law*, by Harvard Law Professor Mary Ann Glendon. "Interest in her analysis," *The New York Times* recently reported, "has grown since last summer when the Supreme Court ... at least partially returned legal authority over abortion to state legislatures."

In her complex critique of *Roe v. Wade*, Glendon argues that *Roe* endorsed an "extreme and isolating version of individual liberty" and contrasts that with the more "communitarian" approach she finds in Europe where most countries take a "middle position" of disapproving abortion in principle while permitting it in circumstances deemed by the legislature to constitute good cause. She draws a sharp contrast between the European situation and that of the United States where "to a greater extent than any other country, our courts have shut down the legislative process of bargaining, education, and persuasion on the abortion issue."[1] Arguing that a world without Roe "would not necessarily represent a setback for women," Glendon asserts that it is erroneous to conclude that "no compromise is possible" on abortion. The continental experience, she concludes, "shows that when the legislative process is allowed to operate, political compromise is not only possible but typical."

---

1. Glendon suggests that *Roe v. Wade* "insulated the pregnant woman from the larger society" and that it precluded humane statutory initiatives and supportive communitarian approaches to the problem of abortion and unwanted pregnancy. Nothing in *Roe v. Wade*, however, precluded a woman from choosing to consult her parents, spouse, minister or supportive friends about her decision; nothing in *Roe* precluded government from reducing the number of abortions by making more effective birth control widely available; nothing in *Roe v. Wade* precluded the community from providing the financial support that would make it easier for more women to choose to have more children. What *Roe* foreclosed was not communitarianism, but compulsion.

The Perils of Compromise

The widespread desire that some kind of compromise be found for the divisive abortion issue is understandable: our public law should not appear wholly indifferent to the values that underlie the deeply held moral beliefs of large numbers of Americans. Even though I am naturally inclined to welcome suggestions for ameliorating contentious issues, I want to argue here that proposed "compromise" restrictions on abortion are unacceptable. What is proposed as compromise simply does not satisfy the concerns of those who find abortions morally troublesome. But the "moderate" restrictions in force and those now being introduced do impose real harm on many women and fall with such disproportionate force upon the less fortunate that they offend fundamental principles of equality.

The kinds of abortion legislation being advanced in the sheep's clothing of compromise fail to take into account the social and economic reality of abortion in America. Some "intermediate" restrictions now being proposed are coercive laws that would seriously curtail all women's autonomy. Other proposals would retain access to safe and legal abortion for affluent urban women while compromising away the rights of young, poor, uneducated, and rural women. Many compromise legislative proposals are disguised trades that would enable those who are affluent to retain access to abortion (for now at least) in exchange for "moderate" restrictions that place abortion out of the reach of less fortunate women. It is a devil's bargain, and it must be rejected.

Legislative proposals to regulate abortion fall into these general categories: (1) *access restrictions*, such as mandatory waiting periods, abortion-specific health and safety regulations, and parental or spousal notification and consent requirements; (2) *timing restrictions*, which require that abortions be performed only in the earlier weeks or months of gestation; and (3) *justification requirements*, limiting the reasons that count as acceptable grounds for terminating a pregnancy. Each type carries its own perils.

Restrictions on Access

Requirements that all second trimester abortions be performed either in hospitals or in clinics resembling small hospitals may raise the cost of abortion but do not seem wholly to preclude the exercise of choice. Similarly, a mandatory waiting period (recently enacted in Pennsylvania and now under consideration in several other states) may not seem an undue burden from the perspective of an urban professional woman. But from the perspective of a young pregnant woman, eighteen years old, unmarried and living in rural North Carolina, a different picture emerges. Seemingly innocuous requirements may have devastating consequences. A low-income, eleventh-grade girl struggling to finish high school and prepare herself for life may have limited access to transportation and never, in fact, have traveled out of the rural county where she was born. An unnecessary hospitalization requirement can raise the cost of an abortion from $250 to more than $1,000 and involve a trip of hundreds of miles. A 24- or 48-hour waiting period may necessitate *two* long trips and an overnight stay in a strange and distant city.

To the *Washington Post*, such legislative requirements may seem no more than "skirmishing around the edges," minor impediments in a world of otherwise easy access to "abortion on demand." For much of America, however, the reality is far different. Stephen Wermiel and Michel McQueen report in the *Wall Street Journal* that "abortion is already scarcer and more difficult to obtain in many parts of the country than the existence of a constitutional right implies.... Women in western Missouri who want a second trimester abortion must either drive the 250 miles across the state or cross into Kansas." In North Dakota, Isabel Wilkerson writes in the *New York Times*, "what was always a difficult journey has become even more daunting since the only physician performing abortions in North Dakota retired." In part because of hostile pressure from pro-life activists, "none of the state's 1,200 physicians have stepped forward to fill the void." Eighty-two out of the eighty-seven counties in Minnesota have no readily available abortion provider.

The critical fact is that even seemingly modest restrictions will increase the barriers to access in a system that already makes it extremely difficult for many women to secure abortions. Legislative restrictions can be, and often are, the final straw. The ban on Medicaid funding of abortions for the poor, coupled with a ban on performance of abortions in hospitals receiving public assistance (upheld in the Webster decision), severely curtailed access for many. Unnecessary clinic regulations and mandatory, though medically unnecessary, tests add even more to the cost. If hospitalization is required and public hospitals are barred from participation, only expensive private hospitals, often distant and inaccessible to the poor and the young, will remain.

One of the principal consequences of many abortion access restrictions is that they delay abortion. Delayed abortion creates a greater health risk, especially for teenagers. These delays may be lengthy for many young women, especially those who are poor and less well informed: they may postpone state-mandated parental involvement and avoid as long as possible the alternative of going to court for judicial permission. Or they may find it necessary to delay the abortion while raising funds or seeking transportation to a distant location.

Delay is not the only adverse consequence of the mandatory parental involvement laws now on the books in more than thirty states. As one lower court noted, "Although family relationships benefit from voluntary and open communication, compelling parental notice has an opposite effect. It is almost always disastrous." New York Assemblywoman Gloria Davis notes that even parental involvement laws with judicial bypass provisions lead to "scared, pregnant teenagers being shuffled through an overburdened court system along with drug dealers and other violent criminals, or trying to scrape the money together to travel someplace with less restrictive laws." Evidence in the Minnesota case before the Supreme Court this term showed that some pregnant minors "were so afraid of the [judicial] proceeding that they turned mute in court, were 'wringing wet with perspiration,' and frequently required a sedative. Some vomited and one began to abort spontaneously during the court process." However well-intentioned in theory, parental involvement laws in practice often become a form of state-sponsored child abuse.

That so many abortion access regulations are dysfunctional in practice should not be surprising. Such laws are seldom actually motivated by their ostensible goals of enhancing family relationships or protecting women's health. They are instead intended to prevent as many women as possible from having abortions. At that unstated goal they often succeed. In the four years following the implementation of a two-parent notification law in Minnesota, the birth rate among Minneapolis women aged 15 to 17 rose 38.4 percent.

By pricing and regulating abortion beyond the reach of many women, access restrictions draw a line across society on social and economic grounds. Above that line women continue to have access to safe and legal abortions; below it women are relegated to illegal, dangerous alternatives, or forced into continued pregnancy and childbirth. The more regulations the states impose, the higher the line goes.

Restrictions on Timing

More than 90 percent of all abortions in America now occur within the first twelve weeks of pregnancy. Nonetheless, the pro-life movement has succeeded in making late-stage abortions a prominent public issue, often exemplified by graphic pictures of fetuses aborted at advanced stages of development. Proposed laws that limit the performance of abortions to the earlier months of the gestational period appear to respond to legitimate concerns. Later abortions are more dangerous than earlier abortions. And for many, abortion turns morally problematic as the months change a microscopic fertilized ovum (62 percent of which will spontaneously abort) into a fetus that toward the end of pregnancy fully resembles a human infant.

There is no good reason why as many as 10 percent of American abortions should still take place at so late a stage, especially considering the greater health risks to pregnant women caused by delaying abortion. As Mary Ann Glendon notes, "Unlike partisans on either side, the public seems to believe that there is an important difference between early and late stages of gestation."

Yet there is bitter irony to the pro-life movement's public focus on late abortions. If anyone active on the abortion issue is responsible for the unnecessarily high percentage of late abortions now being performed, it is those who march under the pro-life banner. As a result of *Roe v. Wade*, abortion became not only safer and cheaper, but also far more likely to be performed very early in pregnancy.

Some late abortions will always be necessary as fetal abnormalities are discovered or as threats to a woman's health emerge during pregnancy. More importantly, *the way to prevent late abortions is not to obstruct or delay early abortions.* The women most likely to delay until the second trimester are those who are poor, young, and without access to local, affordable providers. The absence of funding for abortions and the presence of waiting periods, consent requirements, and other needless regulations will push many American abortions into the second trimester. The adoption of a parental notification law in Minnesota, for example, caused the percentage of minors obtaining second-trimester abortions to rise by 26 percent. Adding to these burdens will increase the number of late abortions; eliminating restrictions would reduce the number.

Glendon praised European statutes for setting a gestational time limit for legal abortions. These statutes, however, operate in a wholly different context from ours. Glendon notes that Sweden's cutoff for abortion is eighteen weeks, after which permission from a national board is required. But in Sweden the government does everything possible to ensure that any woman who wants to terminate her pregnancy may readily do so in the first eighteen weeks. A woman who wants to end a pregnancy may go to her well-publicized, accessible, free, neighborhood public health clinic and in complete confidence obtain an abortion. In most of the Western world outside the United States, Janet Maslow Cohen notes, a woman who is legally entitled to an abortion will find that "her government will support her abortion decision in the two most equality-promoting ways that government can—by providing her with the safest procedure available in her society and by helping to pay for it."

To enact in the United States laws that simply prohibit abortions after twelve or eighteen weeks would constitute a strange and cruel response to the issue of late abortions. In this country, legislative deadlines for abortion would co-exist with access regulations designed to prevent women from being able to meet the deadline. No state truly concerned about either the increased maternal health risks or the moral implications of late abortions should consider the coercive step of prohibiting second trimester abortions[2] while simultaneously pursuing policies that cause abortion to be delayed. Bans on funding for abortions, shutting off access to public hospitals, parental consent/judicial bypass laws, and testing requirements all fall into this category. Legislators who are troubled in principle by late abortions should support instead measures ensuring that every woman who wants to terminate a pregnancy can do so as early and as safely as possible.

There are further ironies. Better access to abortion, as noted above, helps prevent late abortion. Better access to *contraception* helps prevent abortion altogether. Yet strong elements in the pro-life movement oppose contraception as well. The United States has fallen far behind other advanced countries in the research and development of birth control choices. According to a 1990 study by the National Academy of Sciences, as many as two million unwanted and unplanned pregnancies occur each year because of contraceptive failure; between one-third and one-half of all abortions in America could be prevented if more birth control options were available. The study states that "the stronger the desire to reduce abortion, the greater should be the investment to develop new methods of contraception."

Former Surgeon General C. Everett Koop has noted, "We are at a very strange place in history, where the people most opposed to abortions are also opposed to the one thing that would stop them, which is contraceptive information."

Most pro-life groups strongly oppose making contraceptives more widely available, arguing that such a step might be seen as condoning adolescent sexuality. They seem to prefer subjecting all women to a coer-

---

2. Third trimester abortions—those near or after the point of fetal viability—are almost always a medical crisis, and usually tragic events. But they do not pose a public policy issue, for a simple reason: no one wants to wait until the third trimester to have an abortion. Only 0.8 percent of all abortions occur after the twenty-first week, almost always for fetal abnormalities, and 99 percent of those few abortions that do occur after the twenty-first week occur before the twenty-fourth week. Nancy Rhoden notes, "Essentially the only defect for which abortion will be performed after week twenty-four is anencephaly. Abortion should be permissible at any time for this defect, because the anencephalic fetus, or infant, is never viable." Mary Ann Glendon's harsh criticism of *Roe* for not requiring every state to forbid or regulate third trimester abortions thus seems way off the mark. It is not clear how government regulators could provide any meaningful assistance in these very rare and tragic circumstances.

cive regime of abortion regulation to the slight risk of marginally encouraging premarital sex. That weighing of values is difficult to justify.

Mandatory Justification Requirements

The last category of legislative restriction on abortion are enactments that would limit the reasons for which a woman may decide to terminate a pregnancy. Such laws affect every woman who seeks an abortion. If, despite their harshness, they seem to have significant public support, it is because of a deep confusion among commentators that erroneously translates widespread personal ambivalence about abortion into a positive prescription for coercive public policy.

Undoubtedly, many Americans personally favor abortion in some circumstances, and personally oppose it in others. A national poll by the *New York Times* showed that while most Americans approved of abortion when a woman's health was seriously endangered (87 percent) and when there was a danger of serious fetal defects (69 percent), majorities also thought that a woman "should not be able to get a legal abortion" when "a single woman did not want to marry the man who made her pregnant" (50 percent opposed, 42 percent in favor) or when "a low-income family could not afford any more children" (49 percent opposed, 43 percent in favor).

It is a fundamental mistake, however, to suppose that these respondents would, upon reflection, favor enacting into their state's code of laws their own personal assessment of when abortion is wrong. Although the literal wording of the above questions called for respondents to state when a "woman should be able to obtain a legal abortion," respondents were likely giving their own personal views of when one "should" or "should not" have an abortion. That interpretation is borne out by the answers given when respondents were directly asked the central public policy question: "If a woman wants to have an abortion and her doctor agrees to it, should she be allowed to have an abortion or not?" Sixty-three percent said that woman should be allowed, and only 24 percent said no. The most plausible reading of the ambiguous polling data is that Americans personally condone or disapprove of abortion for a variety of reasons, but, in the end, prefer to leave the choice to individual women.

Even if a majority of Americans did believe in the abstract that the law should determine what reasons justify an abortion, that majority would likely disappear if more people understood the mechanisms of government regulation required to enforce such a policy. Consider, for example, a law that prohibited abortion when "used as a means of birth control." As Gene B. Sperling and I have written, "The fundamental flaw in these laws is what they would require of every woman who decides to terminate a pregnancy. Potentially, each woman could be subjected to an intrusive and humiliating process of proving to some official committee, or court, that she was using birth control when she became pregnant." Even if only one "reason" for having an abortion were prohibited by law, *every* woman would have to prove to some government board that the prohibited reason was not her reason. In the 1990s and beyond, those hostile to all abortions are likely to seek appointment to committees that would decide these questions. In such a case, choice could be replaced by cross-examination.

The Idaho legislature's widely publicized 1990 anti-abortion legislation, drafted as model legislation by the National Right to Life Committee, attempted a different regulatory mechanism for enforcing the state's view of proper and improper grounds for an abortion. Rather than set up an official screening committee to investigate in advance the reasons for which a woman was seeking an abortion, the Idaho bill would have authorized any county prosecuting attorney, and any man claiming to be the "father of the unborn child" (not even rapists were excluded), to bring suit to enjoin any abortion. In addition to actions for injunction, the bill would have imposed very severe after-the-fact penalties on physicians as the means of enforcing the state's limits on "proper" grounds for an abortion. A physician who performed an abortion where the woman's reasons were not within the narrow categories permitted by the statute could be subject to fines of up to $50,000, plus both treble and punitive damages.

In a clever use of semantics, the bill purported to ban those abortions that were "used or sought as a method of birth control." The bill, however, deemed all abortions to be "for birth control" unless the woman and her physician could prove that her abortion fell within one of three exceedingly narrow exceptions: severe fetal disability; pregnancy by rape or incest; and where "severe or long-lasting physical health damage" to the pregnant woman "would result" from continuation of the pregnancy. (A physical condition that "might" result in severe health damage to the woman would not be sufficient.)

Each of the three exceptions would have been nearly impossible to establish. A woman who had been raped, for example, could be enjoined by a judge from having an abortion unless she and her physician could *prove* (1) that she had reported the incident within seven days; (2) that she was in fact raped; and (3) that her pregnancy *resulted from the rape* and not from some other act of intercourse. The second would often be difficult to prove, the third almost impossible. In light of the severe penalties, and the difficulty of proving in court the existence of one of the narrow exceptions, no reasonable risk-adverse physician would ever have undertaken to perform any abortion in Idaho under this statute.

And what did Professor Glendon say about this measure? In spite of her much heralded prediction of legislative moderation and praise for "compromise" laws on the European model, Professor Glendon offered crucial assistance to the passage of the drastic Idaho bill by writing a letter, widely circulated by Idaho pro-life leaders, stating, "I certainly consider the bill to be constitutional" and noting, "As for the appropriateness of the bill to Idaho circumstances, it is my earnest hope that that decision will be made in Idaho (and remade when and if needed), rather than in Washington."

The fact that Governor Cecil Andrus decided after extensive deliberation to veto the bill has obscured the most important political message of the Idaho saga. Contrary to many sanguine predictions, both houses of an American legislature—after extensive hearings and acting with full knowledge of its consequences—were willing to pass an extreme law that would have essentially prohibited all abortions. The Governor's veto—based upon a preference for a somewhat less drastic bill and a concern that the Supreme Court as presently constituted might have invalidated this extreme version—offers scant comfort for the future.

After Idaho, we know that some state legislatures will not be content with "moderate" restrictions that "merely" foreclose abortion for the most vulnerable women. And even if the line can be held against enactment of the most draconian laws, lesser, "marginal" restrictions severely harm women who are hostage to geography, youth, poverty and inadequate education. For the affluent and the comfortable to sacrifice the right to abortion of the less fortunate would not really be a compromise. It would be a sell-out.

[8]

Leslie Epstein

Civility and Its Discontents

I have set myself a moral puzzle. What would I do if I were a college president and had to decide the fate of a student who had been caught writing racial and ethnic epithets—*niggers back to Africa, Hitler didn't finish the job*—on the doors of, respectively, a black and Jewish classmate, and was suspected of writing *gays suck!* in the entryway of an openly bisexual dorm? Hangdog or defiant, the miscreant is brought before me. In real life I expect my reactions would run something like this: righteousness, rage even, before the door opened, along with a fixed determination to expel the criminal from our midst; and a sudden surge of curiosity, zeal for reformation, and a form of fellow feeling, once the flesh and blood chap appeared on the other side of my desk. That's one good reason why the destiny of others should not be placed in my hands.

To expel or not expel? Even in the abstract, on paper, the question leaves me divided. My emotions boil at the prospect of having to share a campus with such bad apples in it. But my mind, which has its instincts too, raises the flag of caution. I've lived in this democracy long enough to know that the First Amendment ought not to be monkeyed with and that the more absolute its protections the better off all of us are (well not *all:* not those libeled, nor, more to the point, not those threatened on campus). I am a member of the ACLU. I am also a writer, with a writer's concern for minimizing the role of the censor in American life.

Wait a minute: The truth is, my view of censorship is more complicated than that. The worst thing that can happen to any artist is to be shot dead by Stalin. The second worst is to be told that anything goes. I suppose the third worst it to be dragooned, by an NEA grant, into respecting the diversity of one's fellow citizens' beliefs. The point is, if there are no taboos in society, there will be few in the psyche. So much, then, for the disguises, the tricks and sleight of hand, that the public, which shares the magician's repressions, calls art.

How could I favor expulsion, moreover, when I had suffered that fate myself, and more than once, in the fifties? The first occasion was at the Webb School in California, when one of the preppies asked, "What's this?" as the turnips and gruel were plopped on his plate.

"The week's profit," quipped I. Papa Webb wasn't one to tolerate teenage quipsters. Gone. Rusticated. Dismissed. Expelled.

A few years later the same wise guy was standing on York Street, in New Haven, when the mayor came out of Phil's Barber Shop and stepped into Fenn-Feinstein next door. "What's the mayor doing?" asked my current straight man, as His Honor emerged from the doorway and ducked into the entrance of Barrie Shoes. "Wednesday. 2:30," I replied, just loud enough. "Time to collect." This was, remember, the fifties. The next thing I knew I had been thrust up against the side of a car, had handed over my wallet, and been ordered to be at the dean's office the next morning at ten. By eleven, I was no longer a Son of Eli.

Hard to believe? Even those who lived through those days might find it difficult to recall the atmosphere that lingered on campus well after Senator McCarthy's demise. The master of my residential college was a particularly despotic fellow. During my junior year a number of my pals secretly published a mimeographed newspaper, *The Trumbullian*, and at three in the morning shoved them under everyone's door: "Ape Rape in Trumbull Lounge" was the leading headline. Doc Nick, as he was known to his subjects, responded by calling in the FBI. For a week afterward we watched as a crack team of pale young men in dark suits went about dusting for fingerprints and testing our typewriters, as they had recently done for the Hiss trial, for telltale keys.

To return to the tale, both my expulsions had been effected in order to remove from two bastions of Civilization, and Christendom, a threat to what is generally called, especially by those who do the expelling these days, civility. How can one learn, so goes the argument, in a boorish atmosphere, especially when one might be subjected to crude, offensive, even inflammatory remarks? The premise deserves examination. My own feeling is that Miss Manners, and anyone else who thinks the university must be governed by a special code of decorum, have, slightly, but crucially, missed the point. Webb might be a finishing school, but Yale is not. At least not any longer. "When Jews and other scum beyond human ken make Yale fraternities ..." The line is from the famed *Yale Record*, 1917 (and not, as you thought, from the *Dartmouth Review*, 1990), and there was enough of that attitude left forty years later to make our Class of '60, if not quite *Judenrein*, then at least controlled by a quota so strict we could count the total number of blacks and Asians on the fingers of one hand, and which, of course, allowed for no women at all.

Many are the sins hidden behind the cloak of gentility; enough of them were revealed in the decade following my graduation to make me forever suspicious of those who invest much of their energy in attempting to make the tattered garment whole. Oddly enough, the worst of those sins was intellectual sloth. I saw this most clearly at Oxford, not long after my adventures in New Haven. Talk about finishing schools! I know of one student, an Englishman, whose tutor advised him to stay on an extra year, "because you haven't quite got the accent yet." My own tutor, a world renowned figure, used to wave away my fears of Armageddon with the repeated mantra: "Epstein! You Americans and your atom bomb! Have another ale!" So frantic were the dons and dullards about their cultivation being violated by a good hard thought that they had institutionalized the sconce as a means of insuring that no one did much more than dally at tea or punt along the Isis. This is how the OED defines the term:

> At Oxford, a fine of a tankard of ale or the like, imposed by undergraduates on one of their number for some breach of customary rule when dining in hall.

At Merton, the customary rule forbade any conversation about one's studies, about politics, or anything roughly resembling an idea. This left, as topics, the girls at St. Hilda's and cricket.

I can't resist relating how, one night, an uncouth American, Michael Fried, now a distinguished critic of art, thoughtlessly let slip a remark about Marx or Freud. An awful hush fell upon the hall. At high table, the dons froze, their asparagus savories hanging above their mouths. Down at the benches, the undergraduates let the peas roll off their knives. Behind the malefactor a waiter appeared, with the customary bloodshot cheeks and bushy moustache, holding a foaming chalice of ale. Fried, deep in discussion, paid no mind. The ruddy servant—in his white apron he looked the kosher butcher—tapped him on the shoulder and held up the tankard with a grin and a wink. Fried whirled round. "What am I supposed to do with this?" he asked, as if unaware that custom dictated he drink down the contents and order an equal portion for all those at table. "Shove it up your ass?" Thus, on the shores of England, did the sixties arrive.

Universities exist not to inculcate manners or teach propriety but to foster inquiry, pass on the story of what has been best thought and done in the past, and to search for the truth. There is no proof that this teaching and this search can be done only when people are being polite to each other. Indeed, there is much evidence, beginning with Socrates, to suggest that it can be done best when people rub hard, and the wrong way, against each other, ruffling feathers, making sparks.

Does this mean, then, that one student may call another *fag* or *nigger* or *kike?* As a college president I would have no trouble allowing anyone on campus who wished to argue that homosexuality was contrary to nature, that blacks were intellectually inferior to whites, or that the Holocaust never happened. Such visitations are far different than hurled epithets. To the awful arguments one may at least offer arguments of one's own, display one's charts and graphs and statistics, confident that the truth will out. But what argument can one make against a slur—even one that is not anonymous? If anything, an epithet is designed to short-circuit rationality, to inflame feelings, to draw a curtain, the color of boiling blood, across the life of the mind. Further, it is not just the life of the mind that is threatened: behind the word nigger hangs the noose, just as the ovens burn and smoke hovers behind the word kike.

This distinction—between, if you will, inquiry and invective—carries almost enough weight with me to force a decision: If anyone seeks to destroy another's ability to join the intellectual life of the university, that is, to reason freely, to search dispassionately, to think, he ought not to have any role in that community himself. Almost. The strongest voice against passing sentence comes not from civil libertarians (to whose arguments I hope to turn soon) but from a Yale Law School student, himself the recipient of an anonymous letter ("Now you know why we call you niggers"), who recently told the Yale *Herald*, "It infantilizes people of color to say we can't handle people saying mean things about us.... It's much better for people of color to know what people think of us. I'd feel much, much better if people said exactly what they think." Back, for the moment, on the fence.

I began the discussion of this moral puzzle by listing a number of reasons why I am, through intellectual makeup and personal experience, drawn toward a merciful resolution of the dilemma. Not the least of these reasons has to do with the allies I would rather not have should I choose to expel. I am thinking, of course, of the movement whose members—though "movement" and "members" are clearly misnomers—have become the most censorious figures on college campuses. It is the politically correct who call for strict codes to define what is and is not permissible speech and who have exercised the will to enforce them.

Now I want to make it clear at once that if I have problems with the PC crowd, I am no happier with what seems to be the orchestrated campaign of attack against them, a campaign whose sole purpose is to transform the last institution in American life not already controlled by the right. I'm caught, for friends, between people who call for the hide of others; or others, who have suddenly seen the virtue of the Bill of Rights, like Representative Henry Hyde. (The congressman's bill states that "federally assisted institutions cannot discipline students if their spoken or printed views are found to be repugnant, offensive, or emotionally distressing to others on campus." This from a man who voted to force recipients of grants from the National Endowment for the Arts to consider their fellow citizens' beliefs!)

Everyone has a favorite example at Michigan, for instance, a male student is officially proscribed from saying "women just aren't as good in this field as men"—of PC excess. Because I'm trying to keep these remarks as personal as possible, I'll turn to my own town, Brookline, which once had a first-rate school system. Nowadays it has embarked on a "hundred year plan" to do away with what an assistant superintendent of curriculum calls the "traditional" white male perspective. Among the things this plan would eliminate is the "vertical" white male notion of excellence, along with disciplined thinking, logic, and what this same superintendent calls the "incredible abomination" of Black History Month, whose sin is to reinforce privileged ideas of excellence by pointing out "pinnacle people" who are "outstanding exceptions to their group."

A few weeks ago, a good thirty-two years after my undergraduate days, I took part in a panel on censorship at what is probably Yale's most prestigious, and certainly its most open-minded, senior society. The current delegation was there, class of '91, together with representatives of delegations going back almost to the days when the *Record* could speak of subhuman scum. The discussion, as you might imagine, was lively. At one point a contemporary of mine, an artist, told the story of how the curators of a Gauguin exhibition had been lobbied to take down half the paintings because they demonstrated "an exploitative colonialist perspective." An appreciative chuckle went round the room. We codgers elbowed each other. Such an absurdity! Suddenly a member of the current delegation rose from his bench. "I'd like to point out," he said, in a voice that was only slightly shaking, "that no people of color are laughing." True enough. Nor was anyone much below the age of thirty-five.

I hope it isn't necessary for me to say how much I like these students. They are bright, sensitive, idealistic, and—at Yale, anyway—they work every bit as hard as I did in the fifties. They may be bamboozled, but these bits of zaniness are no more indicative of a totalitarian spirit than the knee-jerk liberalism I still feel a twitch of on rainy days. At the same time, there are elements of a kind of conformity that cannot be laughed away. To stick to my current campus, I've been present when a harassment officer browbeat my colleagues who merely grinned and bore it—about how to notice sexist attitudes among its members and how to turn the offenders in to her office. And I know of a department that voted to offer a talented young assistant professor ("enchanting" was the word his students used to describe his teaching) the normal extension of his contract, then reversed itself twenty-four hours later, largely because of his supposed sexism (he had, as an example, observed a lousy performance by a graduate student and suggested that perhaps her advanced pregnancy had created a strain). Kaput career. There's more than a whiff of Peking in the air when professors are forced, as they have been, to recant, or apologize for their opinions, or sent to special classes for reeducation.

Yet even the thought police are not what worries me most about political correctness, or what tie these worries to the subject at hand. Perhaps I can best get at what I mean by reiterating what I told my daughter, who is struggling with these issues herself as a college junior, when she asked me for a one-sentence definition of PC. "Well," I said, perhaps less clumsily than this, "I guess this is a way of seeing society as a system of oppression, and that the interests of its victims ought to dictate our thinking and behavior, to the exclusion of pretty much any other consideration." What I didn't add was that the "other consideration" I had in mind was the very idea of objective reality, stubborn and recalcitrant as the law of gravity; and that it was this reality, with its laws, its truths, and—tricky, this—its values that the university was founded to discover, nurture, and pass on.

Which leads me to note that during that debate at Yale, the most engaged and vociferous students invariably tuned out to be English majors. No surprise there. They were well versed in deconstruction and other reader-response theories, which together have provided the ideological underpinnings of political correctness. Here, from Jane Tompkins, a leading feminist scholar, is a nutshell version of how these students have been taught to approach a text:

> Critics deny that criticism has ... an objective basis because they deny the existence of objective texts and indeed the possibility of objectivity altogether.... The net result of this epistemological revolution is to politicize literature and literary criticism. When discourse is responsible for reality and not merely a reflection of it, then whose discourse prevails makes all the difference.

Literary texts, then, have no inherent meaning or even a claim to existence, apart from the baggage of the culture in which they were written and now are read. Free speech? Value? Objective standards? Timeless verities? Reality itself? Truth becomes simply an opinion, whatever has been ferreted out as the reigning myth; and knowledge is the triumph of one ideology over another. It is this academic version of might makes right, with its inherent nihilism, that has helped me to solve the puzzle I set myself these many paragraphs back.

That is to say, there are two slopes that lead from the heights of academe, one as slippery as the other. The first has, with good reason, preoccupied those concerned with civil liberties: once we begin proscribing some speech, what other restrictions will follow? To what end will we come? We already have the answer: to the harassment code at the University of Connecticut, which forbids "inconsiderate jokes," "misdirected laughter," and "conspicuous exclusion from conversation." Yet even these grotesqueries do not resolve our dilemma. If the City College of New York were to prohibit Leonard Jeffries of its Black Studies Department from saying that blacks are superior to whites because of the melanin in their skins, or silence Michael Levin, a professor of philosophy at the same institution, who believes that blacks are inherently inferior, it would surely be exercising a form of thought control. The trouble is, *not* censoring the kind of racial epithet whose effect is to undermine the very processes of logic is a form of thought control as well.

Perhaps the solution, or at least a legal rationale for a solution, to this dilemma lies as near to hand as my daily newspaper. On page 41 of today's *Boston Globe*, under the headline *Black workers at Maine plant win in bias suit*, is the story of how three black men from the South were recruited to work at the International Paper Co. in Auburn, Maine. Once there they were harassed by "ugly oral racial epithets and graffiti," and by coworkers "in Ku Klux Klan-like garb 'prancing' around their work stations."

The United States District Court ruled that in creating "a hostile and offensive workplace" and by substantially altering the plaintiffs' working conditions, International Paper had violated Maine's human rights act. The three workers were awarded $55,000 each. Now there is similar harassment legislation in every state of the union. Is there any reason why, of all the institutions in America, only those of higher education should be exempt from these statutes? The only response is a truism: that a university, with its special mission and need for forceful debate, and comprehensive points of view, is not a paper mill. It is precisely the role of the university, its vulnerability, and its fate in modern history, that leads me to look at the second, and steeper, of the slippery slopes.

The grease for this chute is applied by that same belief in the relativity of all values that now prevails on so many campuses. Here are the words of one university president:

> Every people in every period must form its life according to its own law and fate, and to this law of its own, scholarship, with all other spheres of life, is also subject.... The idea of humanism, with the teaching of pure human reason and absolute spirit founded upon it, is a philosophical principle of the eighteenth century caused by the conditions of that time. It is in no sense binding upon us as we live under different conditions and under a different fate.

The speaker is Ernst Krick, rector of Frankfort University, and the occasion was the 550th anniversary of the University of Heidelberg in 1936.

At the bottom of this slope lies totalitarianism of one kind or another. The movement of nihilism is both centrifugal and centripetal, moving outward from literary texts—which, since they have no enduring value, are all too easily burned— through discipline after discipline, in ever widening circles until even the obdurate laws of nature herself are subject to challenge. Hence, in the universities of the Third Reich, biology became "National Socialist biology," psychoanalysis became "mongrel psychology," and the theory of relativity was "Jewish physics."

If there are no lasting truths, nothing to be handed down from one generation to another, then the only source of authority shrinks centripetally in narrower and narrower circles until one arrives at the fountainhead of truth, which in the German formula was the Fuehrer. What Hitler set out to destroy was Western Culture and intelligence itself— and not in the name of diversity! On the contrary it was the Fuehrer, who became the only thinker, the sole author, the one biologist, legal expert, psychologist, and knower of nature's secrets.

The Weimar Republic had as many laws against harassment as has, these days, the state of Maine. Dueling societies were banned (and with them the practice of refusing to duel with Jews), as were all remarks tending to incite racial hatred or campus strife. The trouble was, the rules were not enforced—or worse, enforced selectively. The book has yet to be written as to why the right has always felt free ruthlessly to suppress the liberal left, and why the liberal left, and liberalism in general, has stood by, Hamlet-like, unable to repress the forces of the right. (The image of Hamlet is appropriate, since, according to the "mongrel science," the reason he cannot strike Claudius is that his uncle has enacted the very crimes—murdering his father and sleeping with his mother—that he wished, in the depths of his unconscious, to commit himself. The liberal may see, in the nationalist, the racist, and the fanatic, the embodiment of the passions he has smothered in his own breast.)

Hence Hitler, after the beer-hall putsch, was put in a cell with a view and handed a paper and pencil. In the name of academic freedom, Weimar permitted every atrocity, even the assassinations it half-heartedly prosecuted and feebly punished. The result was that, well before Hitler took power, the universities had become such hotbeds of anti-Semitism and ultra-nationalism that the professorate, of all the classes in Germany, became the most devoted followers of his cause.

The fundamental mistake of Weimar Germany, and of liberalism in general, is the belief that, confronted by nihilistic fervor, one may yet count on a triumph of reason. Theodor Mommsen, the great German historian, wore himself out (and lost his job) in the attempt to defend what he called the "legacy of Lessing" against "racial hatred and the fanaticism of the Middle Ages." In the end he came to realize:

> You are mistaken if you believe that anything at all could be achieved by reason. In years past I thought so myself and kept protesting against the monstrous infamy that is anti-Semitism. But it is useless, completely useless. Whatever I or anybody else could tell you are in the last analysis reasons, logical and ethical arguments which no anti-Semite will listen to. They listen only to their own envy and hatred, to the meanest instincts. Nothing else counts for them. They are deaf to reason, right morals. One cannot influence them.

Let us return to that Yale Law School student (his name is Anthony K. Jones) who faced with equanimity and no small amount of courage the prospect of a fellow student calling him nigger. What would he feel, I wonder, when faced by two screaming students? Or four? Eventually he would have to run, as others have before him, a gauntlet. Is there any prospect that, hounded by what Mommsen called "the mob of the streets or the parlors," anything resembling the free exchange of ideas could take place?

I cannot remain, even in my imagination, a university president if I do not believe in certain things—chief among them the belief that reality can be known and its truths both taught and learned. Free speech, far from being an end in itself, is an instrument in a process of discovery. When it impedes or perverts that process—for instance by denying a student the exercise of his intellect or putting him in fear for his body —something must be done.

But what? About that I have come, through however tortuous a route, to a decision. It is perhaps natural that, since my ideas have been divided against themselves, this conclusion should take the form of a paradox. Because the tactics of the civil libertarians, and liberalism in general, are unavailing against men and women seized by nihilistic fervor, I shall have to adopt those that belong to the fervent themselves. I do so not so much to circumscribe those who are politically correct, but to guard against those, like the young man about to be brought before me, who have been provoked to react—in what is always a deadly dance —against them.

Here he comes now. Of course he shall have due process. And we shall have to go into every detail, each aspect of his case. But at bottom it is his unwillingness to engage others as free spirits, his attempt to extinguish reason within them, that dooms him. I shall not attempt to put ideas he does not think into his head or words he does not feel into his mouth: no people's court here! Instead, I shall steel myself against my own nature and ask him to leave the university. Perhaps he might re-apply and, if his self-knowledge has grown, be readmitted (as it hap-pens, I got back into Webb and Yale, although the fifties might have been more forgiving than present times). And in passing this harsh sentence I shall turn, as college presidents like to do, to authority—this time, appro-priately enough, to the man who above all others believed in the imper-ishability of ideas. Punishment, Plato said, is the most salutary thing one can do for a man who has done wrong.

[9]

Benjamin R. Barber

The Reconstruction of Rights

If there is a single theme upon which Americans agree, it is that ours is a regime rooted in rights. Rights are how we enter our political conversation: the chips with which we bargain, the collateral in the social contract. They are the ground of both rebellion and legitimacy, of our inclinations to anarchism and our proclivities toward community.

Without coaching, any American will cry out: "I know my rights!" or "You got no right!" or "What about my rights?" or "Read him his rights!"

Corporations mimic individuals in their devotion to rights as barriers against the public regulation of private profit. The Philip Morris Company recently paid the National Archives $600,000 to associate itself with the Bill of Rights, presumably to promote its view of advertising as a First Amendment right essential to selling tobacco in an age of democratic public health advocacy. Rights are how Americans have always advanced their interests, whether as individual or corporate persons. Some might say (I will do so below) that there is even an element of obsession in the American devotion to rights, that we sometimes risk a rights absolutism as unbalanced in its political effects as the fabled "tyranny of the majority" against which rights are often deployed as the primary defense.

Yet there are good reasons for the focus on rights. The naked self comes to the bargaining table weak and puny; the language of rights clothes it. The naked self extends hardly beyond that bundle of desires and aversions that constitute its raw, prelegitimate wants. Rights carve out a space for it to operate in—call it autonomy or dignity or, in its material incarnation, property. Wants become needs and needs acquire a moral mantle that, as rights claims, cannot be ignored. The hungry man wants to eat; the ravenous man needs to eat; the starving man has a right to eat. Rights turn the facts of want into powerful claims powerful, at least, in civil societies that consider rights rhetoric legitimate.

Even the naked self is perforce a social self, whose claims on others imply reciprocity as well as equality. If, as this suggests, democracy is the form of governance especially suited to the language of rights, it is ironic and troubling to find the language of rights often deployed in a fashion adversarial to democracy. Perhaps this is because democracy is often understood as the rule of the majority, and rights are understood more and more as the private possessions of individuals and thus as necessarily antagonistic to majoritarian democracy. But, as I will suggest, this is to misunderstand both rights and democracy.

The Roots of Rights

America has always been a civil society hospitable to rights. It borrowed its earliest norms from diverse roots: from Puritanism, with its egalitarian version of the rights of a Christian; from the English Dissent tradition, which conceived of rights as a bastion against illegitimate monarchic authority; and from classical republicanism (James Harrington or Montesquieu, for example), where rights were linked to civic virtue and constitutional government. Even in colonial times, American institutions treated government as an artificial contrivance which had to be created; a collectivity to be sure but one instrumental to the religious and secular interests of individuals; one that saw government as originating in consensus and in a contract between all those who were to be citizens or subjects. The Mayflower Compact for example, though scarcely a document concerned with natural rights, saw the Pilgrims "covenant and combine" themselves "together into a civil body politick, for (their) better order and preservation."

But just how democratic was this society, hospitable as it was to rights, or how democratic could it become? The question offers one way of considering whether rights and democracy can cohabit or perhaps even reinforce one another.

On the face of things, and in keeping with the eighteenth-century view, the answer would seem to be not very democratic, at least not at the outset. In the great Founders' debate, both Federalists concerned with strong central government and the sovereignty of the whole over the parts, and Anti-Federalists concerned with the relative autonomy of the states and the sovereignty of the parts over the whole, shared one thing: they both understood the Constitution as a tool of rights. Federalists saw in its governmental powers the explicit political expression of rights; anti-Federalists saw in its provisions a set of rights limiting governmental power.

Historically, these standpoints were both complementary and in tension in just the same way as the social contract theories of Thomas Hobbes and John Locke were complementary and in tension. Hobbes sought to protect individual liberty and security *through* strong government; Locke wanted to protect liberty and property *against* strong government. In the Federalist case, there is a Hobbesian faith in strong contract-based government as a guarantor of rights; in the Anti-Federalist case, there is a Lockean distrust of strong government which understands rights as constraints on government. Both positions conceive of government as an artificial means whose primary object is the preservation of rights that are anterior to politics—that exist in a "natural" or "higher" prepolitical form.

Returning to our question, then, the terms of the Federalist/Anti-Federalist debate would suggest that the American rights tradition in both its Federalist and Anti-Federalist forms had a primarily antidemocratic bias. For the Federalists, the issue was how to insulate the power in which rights were expressed and by which liberty and property were to be safeguarded from popular majorities and private opinion. Madison warned against "an infinity of little jealous clashing commonwealths, the wretched nurseries of unceasing discord" and essayed to design a constitution that would supply republican remedies to treat republican vices (among which democracy was paramount!). These included indirect election of representatives and an expanded compass for civil society; by multiplying the number of factions and groups, their capacity for divisiveness might be attenuated.

For the Anti-Federalists, the aim was to limit government *tout court*. Despite the democratic spirit of the strategy favored by Jefferson calling for the devolution of power, the object remained to check and limit central power as the exercise of a unitary popular sovereignty. Here the Bill of Rights figured as a studied obstacle to centrally organized popular power. Locke had worried about how "polecats and foxes" (ordinary men, quarrelsome and contentious) might protect themselves from the sovereign lion brought in to police their disputes. The Federalists wanted to keep the "people" from riding the lion, believing that only the best men could subdue its power and divert it to their virtuous ends; the Anti-Federalists were less concerned with the rider, hoping rather to imprison the lion itself in a cage of rights. Neither had much trust in the people from whom popular government took its legitimacy. Hamilton is said to have expressly calumnized the people as a great beast, "howling masses" not fit to govern.

Thus, it is hardly a surprise that the Founders managed to create a form of government in many ways antipathetical to any real institutional expression of the popular sovereignty that was its paper premise. Moreover, they wrote a constitution whose letter was self-consciously distrustful of democracy. Popular sovereignty could not for them mean popular rule. The abstract status of sovereign permitted "we the people" to establish a government, but did not license it to participate in the government it had brought forth.

The word "equality" failed to make an appearance in the Constitution's language, and almost every device of government contemplated was aimed not at embodying but at checking popular power. The real democrats (Sam Adams, Patrick Henry, Tom Paine, Jefferson himself) were not present at the Philadelphia Creation, and radical democratic models calling for a unicameral legislature and universal white male suffrage of the kind represented by the Pennsylvania Constitution were given short shrift.

Jefferson had written of the Virginia Constitution: "Try by this as a tally every provision of our constitution and see if it hangs directly on the will of the people."[1] By this measure, the federal Constitution failed —and thus, for the suspicious Founders, succeeded. As Patrick Henry had dryly remarked, as far as he could see the people gave them [the Founders] no power to use their names. Such incipient tendencies to popular government as "democrats, mobocrats and all the other rats," as the slogan had it, might have insinuated into the Constitution were unlikely to survive that document's institutional arrangements. These included the separation of powers with its immobilizing checks and balances, federalism as a forced vertical separation of powers enhanced by the Tenth Amendment, the indirect election of senators and the president which interposed a filter between the people and their servants, judicial review as a check on popular legislation (and in time a warrant for judicial legislation), and the division of popular will into two parts equal and opposed—one represented by the House of Representatives, the other by the presidency.

The two expressly democratic instruments—the House of Representatives and the Amendment Article—were hedged in with restrictions. Limitations on suffrage (standards were a matter for the states to decide at their own discretion within the loose confines of republicanism) left it, in Henry Lee's scathing indictment, "a mere shred or rag of representation." The powers to amend the Constitution detailed in Article V were popular sovereignty's most potent constitutional instrument. But they were made sufficiently complicated and unwieldy to turn the amendment provision into a last and improbable recourse of what would have to be, if they really were going to use it, a wildly dissatisfied and endlessly energetic people. Sixteen amendments in two hundred years (I count the Bill of Rights as part of the original Constitution) does not suggest a very democratic instrument or a very engaged popular sovereign.

---

1. Thomas Jefferson, cited in Richard K. Matthews, *The Radical Politics of Thomas Jefferson* (Lawrence: University Press of Kansas, 1984), 78.

And yet the letter of the Constitution and the intentions of the Framers are only part of the story. America's spirit of democracy is older than the republic. Equality had its ardent advocates then as now, and even where it was contradicted by the Constitution's letter, the democratic spirit found its way into the tenor and the logic of the Constitution. This spirit arises not in opposition to rights but from the political context that gives rights meaning and force.

There is a simple but powerful relationship between rights and democracy: universal rights logically require equality. Rights, as political philosophers say, "entail" the equality of those who claim them; and democracy is the politics of equality. Without democracy, rights are empty words, dependent for their realization on the good will of despots. Rights in their own turn promote and promise emancipation, suffrage, and empowerment. Even Madison recognized that rights without supporting political institutions were so many "parchment barriers" to tyranny (one reason for his early opposition to a separate Bill of Rights). Late in his life (in 1821), like so many Americans who had once feared the people as a rabble, he had come to take a less harsh view of democracy. He would not perhaps have agreed with Louis Hartz that "the majority in America has forever been a puppy dog tethered to a lion's leash," but on the question of the enfranchising of the propertyless, he came to acknowledge, "Under every view of the subject, it seems indispensable that the Mass of Citizens should not be without a voice, in making the laws which they are to obey, in choosing the Magistrates, who are to administer them, and if the only alternative be between an equal and universal right of suffrage for each branch of the government and a containment of the entire right to a part of the citizens, it is better that those having the greater interest at stake namely that of property and persons both, should be deprived of half their share in government; then that those having the lesser interest, that of personal rights only, should be deprived of the whole."[2]

Madison's use of the language of "an equal and universal right of suffrage" just thirty years after a Founding consecrated to limiting both popular suffrage and popular access to government seems startling, but rights language permitted no other evolution. If popular government and laws understood as self-prescribed limitations on private behavior are the real guarantors of liberty, if natural rights are secure only when political rights are guaranteed by popular government, then the right to suffrage turns out to be the keystone of all other rights—a principle increasingly recognized in the real democratic politics of the early nine-

---

2. James Madison (1821), "Note to Speech on the Right to Suffrage," Saul K. Padover, *The Complete Madison* (New York: Harper, 1953), 40.

teenth century and one eventually written explicitly into the Constitution with the Thirteenth, Fourteenth, and Fifteenth Amendments.

I mean here to advance both a logical claim and a historical claim. I want to say rights can be shown theoretically to entail equality and democracy. And at the same time, I want to argue that the actual history of rights talk in America unfolds as an increasingly progressive and democratic story. Philosophically, rights claims are always and necessarily equality claims as well. To say "I have a right" is to posit that I am the equal of others and at the same time to recognize the equality of the persons to whom, on whom, against whom the claim is made. No master ever said to a slave: "Give me my rights!" for rights can be acknowledged only by equals. Likewise, the slave who proclaims "I have the right to be free" says in the same breath "I am your equal," and hence "you are my equal." In a certain sense, in speaking of equal rights one speaks redundantly: rights are equalizers. Individuals may use rights to insulate themselves from others, to wall in their privacy, but their rights claims depend entirely on the proposition that as claimants they are the equal of all others, that no one living in a free and democratic society is privileged because of who they happen to be by virtue of race, gender, religion, and so forth.

More than anything else, this is why a constitution rooted in rights cannot systematically exclude whole classes of persons from citizenship without becoming inherently incoherent and thus unstable. Even where it is antidemocratic in its institutional provisions, it will incline to democratization, tend over time toward greater inclusiveness. This is exactly what happened to the American polity in the course of the nineteenth century. That the Constitution included provisions implicitly recognizing slavery (the three-fifths compromise for example) was a shameful comment on the Founders and perhaps on their motives. Nonetheless, such provisions sat like undigested gruel on the Constitution's rights-lined stomach and were in time regurgitated. This resulted not simply from pressures brought to bear from the outside, but arose from the inherently universalizing character of all rights talk, which pushes against artificial boundaries of every kind and makes inequalities increasingly indigestible.

If rights imply citizenship and citizenship appears as a right—the right to liberty, the right to self-legislation, the right to be included in a civic polity founded on "popular" (that-means-me!) sovereignty—the idea of the citizen will always have an aggressive, liberating, even imperial character, pushing to extend its compass to the very periphery of the universal. In Rome, early modern Europe, and America, it has been expansive in its logic and liberating in its politics. Today as rights continue to press outward, reaching the very edge of our species boundary, we can even speak of "animal rights" or "fetal rights" and still seem to be extending rather than perverting what it means for beings to have rights.

Rights are also linked logically to democracy and equality as a consequence of their essentially social character. Rousseau had already observed in *The Social Contract* that though all justice comes from God, "if we knew how to receive it from on high, we would need neither government nor laws. There is without a doubt a universal justice emanating from reason alone; but to be acknowledged among us, this justice must be reciprocal.... there must be conventions and laws to combine rights with duties and to bring justice back to its object." In a classical nineteenth-century idealist argument, the English political philosopher T.H. Green elaborates Rousseau's argument by insisting "there can be no right without a consciousness of common interest on the part of members of a society. Without this there might be certain powers on the part of individuals, but no recognition of these powers ... and without this recognition or claim to recognition there can be no right."[3] Recognition entails the mutuality of a common language, common conventions, and common consciousness: in other words, civility. Citizens alone possess rights, for as Green said, rights "attach to the individual ... only as a member of a society." Tocqueville is, of course, right to remind us that citizens united as a majority are still capable of abusing the rights of citizens taken one by one. But Green's rejoinder is that the tyranny of the majority may be more a reflection on the inadequacies of democratic processes than the absence of rights.

Democracy as the Realm of Rights

Now if rights entail equality and require a civic context of mutual recognition to be effective, the regime form most compatible with rights is neither decentralized, limited government on the model of the Anti-Federalists, nor screened and filtered representative government on the republican model of the Federalists, but quite simply democracy—defined by universal suffrage and collective self-legislation. For democracy is the rule of equality. Limited government is indifferent to who rules so long as the rulers are constrained. Republican government elicits the consent and accountability but not the participation and judgment of the people, which is why Jefferson sometimes called representative government elective aristocracy. Rights do best, however, where those who claim them are one and the same with those upon whom the claims fall— where sovereign and subject are united in one person: a citizen. Without

---

3. Thomas Hill Green, *Lectures on the Principles of Political Obligation* (London: Longmans, 1941).

citizenship and participation, rights can become a charade. Without responsibility, rights may not always be enforceable. Without empowerment, rights can seem like decorative fictions. A constitution is, after all, a piece of paper, and "parchment barriers" are never much use against lead and steel and chains and guns, although they can be a significant trip-wire against majority assaults on minorities, something the Founders obviously appreciated.

In what may be the world's most effusively rights-oriented constitution, a famous document not only guarantees citizens "freedom of speech," "freedom of the press," "freedom of assembly," and "freedom of street processions and demonstrations," but also offers judges who will be constitutionally "independent and subject only to the law," "separation of church from state," as well as the "right to education," "the right to work," "the right to rest and leisure," "the right to maintenance in old age and also in case of sickness or disability," and, as if these were not enough, equal rights to women "in all spheres of economic, government, cultural, political and other public activity," and finally, guaranteeing what comes before, universal elections in which all citizens have the right to vote, "irrespective of race or nationality, sex, religion, education, domicile, social origin, property status or past activities." This unprecedented fortress of human liberty is the Constitution (Fundamental Law) of the Soviet Union, a nation in which rights have been paper parapets from which no defense of liberties can be undertaken.

As Madison observed in questioning the value of a Bill of Rights detached from the Constitution, "Repeated violations of ... parchment barriers have been committed by overbearing majorities in every state.... Whenever there is an interest and power to do wrong, wrong will generally be done and not less readily by a powerful and interested party than by a powerful and interested prince."[4]

Philosophical argument finds persuasive historical expression in the American setting. Successful popular movements aimed at the emancipation of slaves, the enfranchisement of women, and the remediation of the condition of the native American Indian tribes, as well as the empowerment of the poor, the working class, and others cast aside by the American market, have all had in common a devotion to the language of rights. Indeed, the single most important strategic decision faced by those who felt left out of the American way of life has been whether to mobilize against or in the name of the American Founding, understood as the Declaration of Independence, the Constitution, and the Bill of

---

4. Madison, *The Tree of Liberty: A Documentary History of Rebellion and Political Crime in America*, edited by Nicholas N. Kittrie and Eldon D. Wedlock, Jr. (Baltimore: Johns Hopkins University Press, 1986).

Rights. Movements that have made war on the Constitution, holding that its rights promise no salvation to the powerless, have on the whole failed. Movements that have insisted that the Founding can and must make good on the promise implicit in its universalizing rights rhetoric have succeeded.

In their explicit mimicry of the Founders' language and the citation of great rights jurists like Blackstone, the bold women at Seneca Falls in 1846 captured the logic of "entailment" with their own militant rights claims. "We hold these truths to be self-evident," they asserted, "that all men and women are created equal."[5] And although the radical abolitionists at times seemed to declare war on America itself, one of their most fiery leaders understood the entailments of the American tradition well enough. William Lloyd Garrison burned a copy of the Constitution in Framingham on July 4, 1854, but he nevertheless declared in *The Liberator*, in his *To the Public*, and in impassioned speeches throughout the North, that he "assented to the 'self-evident truth' maintained in the American Declaration of Independence, 'that all men are created equal, and endowed by their Creator with certain inalienable rights—among which are life, liberty and the pursuit of happiness.'" On this foundation, he concluded, he would "strenuously contend for the immediate enfranchisement of our slave population."[6]

Some might say these radicals were trying to drive a wedge between the Declaration and the Constitution, but when John Brown went looking for legitimacy he found it in the Preamble to the Constitution as well as in the Declaration. When he offered the People of the United States a "Provisional Constitution," its preamble read: "Whereas slavery, throughout its entire existence in the United States, is none other than a most barbarous, unprovoked, and unjustifiable war of one portion of its citizens upon another portion ... in utter disregard and violation of those eternal and self-evident truths set forth in our Declaration of Independence, therefore we, citizens of the United States, and the oppressed people (deprived of Rights by Justice Taney) ... do ordain and establish for ourselves the following Provisional Constitution and ordinances, the better to protect our person, property, lives and liberties, and to govern our action."[7]

---

5. See "The Declaration of Sentiments and Resolutions of the First Women's Rights Conference," in Elizabeth Stanton, Susan B. Anthony, and Matilda Joslyn Gage, eds., *History of Woman Suffrage* (New York: Fowler & Wells, 1881), 170–173.

6. William Lloyd Garrison, in Wendell Garrison and Francis Jackson Garrison, *William Lloyd Garrison: 1805–1879* (New York: Arno Press, 1969), 408.

7. Louis Ruchames, *John Brown: The Making of a Revolutionary* (New York: Grosset & Dunlap, 1969), 119–120.

From this perspective, the Civil War and Reconstruction Amendments ending slavery and involuntary servitude and guaranteeing universal male suffrage, due process, and the equal protection of the laws to all citizens were not a reversal of America's constitutional history but the culminating event in the history of the Constitution's rights commitments as they manifested themselves in the practical politics and civic life of the nation. Justice Taney's decision in *Dred Scott* was, by the same token, the last gasp of those trying to stem the floodtide on which rights were sweeping through history. Taney's problem was how to construct rights whose thrust was ineluctably universalizing in narrow, self-limiting terms appropriate to his prejudices. He had to show that "we the people," synonymous with "citizens," could somehow be construed to exclude the Negro race. His decision tortuously avoids the entailments of the idea of citizenship and instead turns on the "historical fact" that Negroes "were at that time considered as a subordinate and inferior class of beings." Taney takes care to avoid a careful examination of what such crucial terms as "person," "citizen," and "right" might entail. For it was precisely against those entailments that he was rather desperately trying to construct an argument.

Even at the time of the Founding there had been powerful opposition to slavery as an embarrassment to the language of the Declaration and the Constitution's Preamble. John Adams and John Jay were vigorously eloquent in their opposition to it (although not at the Convention), and there were a number of statesmen who would sympathize with George Mason's refusal to sign the Constitution because its twenty-year extension of the slave trade was "disgraceful to mankind."

Madison had acknowledged "moral equality of blacks" and in *Federalist No. 54* had allowed that Negroes did "partake" of qualities belonging to persons as well as to property and were thus protected in "life and limb, against the violence of all others." The slave, Madison said elsewhere, "is no less evidently regarded by the law as a member of the society, not as part of irrational creation; as a moral person, not as a mere article of property."[8] It was not so much the moral argument but the logic of what it meant to be a person that is captured by Madison, and it was this logic that created the problems for the hapless Taney.

Are Rights Eroding Democracy?

In our century, the powerful alliance between rights and political emancipation, between the claim to be a person and the right to be a citizen,

---

8. James Madison to Frances Wright, Sept. 1, 1825, from *James Madison, Letters and Other Writings*, vol. 3, 495.

seems in danger of coming unstuck. Increasingly, rights have retreated into the private space won for them by their civic entailments, allowing us to forget that they are secured by and only have meaning for citizens. The communities rights once created are now too often pictured as the enemies of right and the political institutions by which we secure rights are made over into external and alien adversaries as if they had nothing to do with us. The sense of rights as a claim for political participation, and participation and civic responsibility as the foundation of rights, has yielded to peculiarly privatized notions of rights as indisputable possessions of individuals who acquire them by birth or membership in some special subgroup, and must do nothing to enforce them. Such rights exist and are efficacious as long as they are noisily promulgated.

There are multiple reasons for the new take on rights, many of which have little to do with the logic of rights itself and for which rights advocates cannot be blamed. The erosion of viable notions of the public and of a common good and the growth of interest-group liberalism in which private factions and their rights come to count as the only political entities worthy of attention has undermined citizenship and the public rights associated with it. Under conditions of privatization, consumerism, radical individualism, and cultural separatism, rights cease to be regarded as a civic identity to be posited and won, and are instead conceived as a natural identity to be discovered, worn, and enjoyed.

As a consequence, young people are more likely to use rights to make a case about what government owes them than to point to what they themselves might owe to the democratic government that is the guarantor of their rights ("Ask not what your country can do for you ..."). Thus, for example, they may exclaim that the government has "no right" to conscript them into the army, as if it were not their government, as if there could be a democratic government in the absence of their willingness and responsibility to service it—quite literally to constitute it. Many young persons in fact do engage in community service or enlist in the armed services or participate in demonstrations and protests, but as often as not these activities are either seen as "voluntary" (it is a "volunteer army") or as a manifestation of rights and prerogatives held against government and the polity. Civic duties and social responsibilities simply do not come into it.[9]

The changing climate of politics is evident in the vanishing of volunteer fire departments for want of volunteers, and in the growing ungovernability of municipalities that cannot afford liability insurance against disgruntled inhabitants who conceive themselves as dissatisfied

---

9. For a provocative symposium on a "bill of duties" in which this commentator participated, see *Harper's*, February, 1991.

clients rather than as responsible citizens. Fire protection comes to be viewed as a service provided by government to residents rather than a service by, for and of citizens. Where Our Town becomes Their Town, rights can become a knife that severs the bonds of citizens rather than the glue that holds it together. The right to sue is a precious resource against abusive authority; yet democratic responsibility is also a powerful guarantee against abuse. We need both. The litigious citizen expresses his rights as an individual but may be overlooking his responsibilities to the community being sued.

The precarious balance between individual and community which rights properly understood can mediate is upset, and rights are introduced on only one side of the scales, leaving the community hard pressed to advance the public good. Legal philosophers like to say that rights are trumps, which is a poignant way of underscoring the crucial subjugation of democratic government to the liberties of citizens. But there is also a sense in which, as Rousseau once wrote, citizens are trumps: "There can be no patriotism without liberty," Rousseau observes, "no liberty without virtue, no virtue without citizens; create citizens and you will have everything you need; without them you will have nothing but debased slaves from the rulers of the state on downwards."

Rights, after all, belong to individuals as citizens, and citizens belong to communities that therefore also have rights. There is no reason not to use the power of rights as legitimizers of claims in order to advance community goods. Tenants organizing against drug traffickers, victims organizing to secure their rights in a criminal justice system disposed (quite properly) to pay special attention to the rights of criminal defendants, and mothers organizing against drunk drivers (MADD) offer compelling examples of the power of rights-thinking on behalf of the community at large.

The American Civil Liberties Union has been an ardent and valuable advocate of the rights of individuals in our democracy. Yet the ACLU's conception of rights has occasionally veered toward a denial of community that may reflect the breakdown of our sense of common civic purposes as a nation. In recent years, in addition to its healthy concerns with the sanctity of political speech and the right of assembly (both of which are important to the polity and the public good), the ACLU has dug itself into a foxhole from which it can engage in a firefight with democracy. The ACLU has opposed airport security examinations, decried sobriety checkpoints (recently declared constitutional by the Supreme Court in a 6–3 decision), argued against the voluntary fingerprinting of children in areas subject to kidnapping. By making privacy over into a supertrump card in a deck of individual rights that, with respect both to public goods and community rights, is already trump to start with, it places at risk the balance between individual and community that is the prize achievement of the history of rights in America.

In the case of the *Michigan Department of State Police v. Sitz*, a leading argument held that sobriety checkpoints abridged the constitutional rights of Michigan motorists by causing them "fright and surprise" in the course of ninety-second stops that were tantamount to "subjective intrusion upon liberty interests." The liberty interests of other drivers as potential victims of drunken driving usually thought of as belonging to the rights of the community, or the responsibility of the body politic, were not weighed and found wanting; they were ignored. This is a growing problem in a society where the idea of civic community has lost its resonance and interest groups such as the National Rifle Association use rights as a foil for their special pleading.

This unbalancing of the rights equation feeds into the historical mistrust some Americans still feel toward popular government. It threatens to disenfranchise the very citizenry rights were once deployed to empower. The new strategy links a Federalist distrust of popular rule with a form of judicial activism that permits courts not merely to enforce rights but to legislate in their name whenever the "people" are deemed sufficiently deluded or insufficiently energetic. It is not at all clear that rights enforced on an obstinate citizen body rendered passive-aggressive (quiescent but angry) by an encroaching court are really made more secure over the long haul. But it certainly is clear that a "democratic" government that will not permit its citizens to govern themselves when it comes to rights will soon be without either rights or democracy.

It was, of course, an original Federalist strategy aimed at curbing democracy that produced judicial review as a limit on popular legislation. In the Madisonian approach to the balance of power, the judiciary has remained a key instrument in preventing majorities from getting out of hand. Yet as Louis Hartz noticed, the majority has not really gotten out of hand very often in America. Tolerance notwithstanding, at least since *Brown v. Board of Education* (1954), impatient democrats seeking to secure rights that majorities sometimes neglected have allied themselves with courts willing to act as surrogate legislators where the people are found wanting. The "filtration" of the public mind favored by the Founders thus has found a modern incarnation in the not so democratic practices of judicial government.

In the recent Supreme Court case upholding a lower court decision concerning Kansas City (Missouri) school desegregation, the majority ruled in favor of a judicial intervention whose final outcome was the raising of taxes. The case is complicated, and the Missouri court did not itself directly levy taxes, but Justice Anthony Kennedy issued a sobering caution about the logic of the judiciary acting as legislative surrogate when he wrote in dissent: "It is not surprising that imposition of taxes by a [judicial] authority so insulated from public communication or control can lead to deep feelings of frustration, powerlessness and anger on the part of taxpaying citizens." Frustration, powerlessness, and anger have become the currency in which many Americans have paid for the usurping of their political authority in the name of their political rights. Americans need their rights, but they need also to understand the responsibilities their rights entail. If seen solely as private things to be secured by judges rather than public things (*res publica*) to be secured by citizens, rights atrophy.

Democracies do not always do justice. Frequently they do injustice. Yet the remedy for this, as Jefferson noted a long time ago, is not to disempower citizens who have been indiscreet, but to inform their discretion, which may sometimes mean extending rather than circumscribing their power. For power teaches responsibility and responsibility limits power. Like experienced legislators, publics can and do become more discreet and competent overtime. The ravages done by Proposition 13 (which initiated the tax revolt in 1978, limiting state expenditures) have gradually educated the people of California into an appreciation of their civic responsibilities. In the spring of 1990, quite on their own, and without the mandate of a court, they approved a referendum raising taxes. What America most needs just now are not more interventionist courts but more interventionist schools; not lessons in the rights of private persons but lessons in the responsibilities of public citizens; not a new view of the Bill of Rights, but a new view of the Constitution as the democratic source of all rights.

Madison might have had a better understanding of rights than the advocates of a separate Bill of Amendments when he argued for including rights in the substantive text of the constitution. For by placing them there, where they would be read in context rather than isolating them in a document that might make them seem a natural possession of passive private persons, their civic and social nature as part and parcel of the fabric of democratic republicanism might have been crystal clear.

On this two hundredth birthday of the Bill of Rights, we need to learn for ourselves what the first seventy-five years of American history, culminating in the Civil War, taught our ancestors in a still young America: that rights stand with, not against, democracy and if the two do not progress together, they do not progress at all.

Part Two

Linkage — The Publics around Government

[10]

RICHARD M. VALELLY

Vanishing Voters

Electoral participation is vital to political democracy. Yet in the past quarter century our rate of voting participation has dropped sharply and shows no signs of rebounding. In 1988 just 50.2 percent of voting-age adults voted for President, down from 62.8 percent in 1960. Voting for lesser offices, chronically lower than presidential voting, has fallen dramatically as well. In 1986 only 33.4 percent of the voting-age population participated in House elections. The last time half the eligible population cast ballots in House elections in a presidential year was 1972.

WORKS DISCUSSED IN THIS ESSAY:

Paul R. Abramson and John H. Aldrich, "The Decline of Electoral Participation in America," *American Political Science Review* 76 (September, 1982): 502–521.

Walter Dean Burnham, "The Turnout Problem," in A. James Reichley, ed., *Elections American-Style* (Brookings, 1987).

Walter Dean Burnham, "The Eclipse of the Democratic Party," *democracy*, July 1982.

Walter Dean Burnham, *The Current Crisis in American Politics* (Oxford University Press, 1982).

Thomas Ferguson and Joel Rogers, *Right Turn: The Decline of the Democrats and the Future of American Politics* (Hill and Wang, 1987).

Paul Kleppner, *Who Voted? The Dynamics of Electoral Turnout, 1870–1980* (Praeger, 1982).

Michael E. McGerr, *The Decline of Popular Politics: The American North, 1865–1928* (Oxford University Press, 1986).

Frances Fox Piven and Richard A. Cloward, *Why Americans Don't Vote* (Pantheon Books, 1989).

E.E. Schattschneider, *The Semisovereign People: A Realist's View of Democracy in America* (The Dryden Press, 1975).

Ruy A. Teixeira, *Why Americans Don't Vote: Turnout Decline in the United States 1960–1984* (Greenwood Press, 1987).

Raymond E. Wolfinger and Steven J. Rosenstone, *Who Votes?* (Yale University Press, 1980).

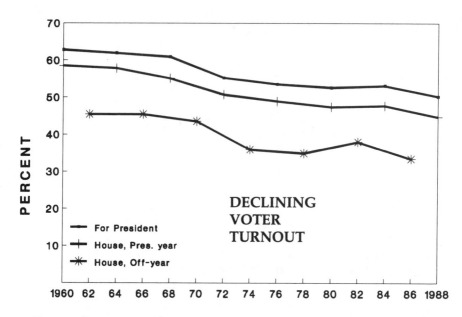

Sources: U.S. Bureau of Census, *Statistical Abstract of the United States: 1989* (109th edition) (Washington, D.C.: 1989), 258. Norman J. Ornstein, Thomas Mann, Michael J. Malbin, *Vital Statistics on Congress* (Washington, D.C.: CQ Press, 1989), 46.

Turnout in 1988 came startlingly close to the depressed levels of 1920 and 1924, the all-time lows for the twentieth century, when a majority of the voting-age population did not vote. If present trends continue, in 1992 a majority of voting-age adults will again sit out the presidential election. Yet unlike the early 1920s, when turnout rates dropped after the Nineteenth Amendment expanded the electorate to include women, no abrupt event in the current electoral era explains the nonparticipation of half the citizenry.

Scholars do not agree on why voting participation has dropped so sharply since 1960. Several popular theories suggest different remedies —or in some cases no remedy. There is, however, one well established fact. Though nonvoting has spread through all social classes, in our time the poor, the uneducated, and the young are least likely to vote. E.E. Schattschneider, a leading American political scientist in the 1950s and 1960s, presciently suggested in his classic essay, *The Semisovereign People*, that those who vote in America may constitute "the largest, most broadly-based, ruling oligarchy in the world." That ironic characterization still aptly describes American politics.

Explaining Voting Decline

Ruy Teixeira's *Why Americans Don't Vote*, the work of Paul Abramson and John Aldrich, and Raymond Wolfinger and Steven J. Rosenstone's *Who Votes?* exemplify one leading school of thought. They explain the propensity to vote mainly in terms of voter traits, such as income, occupation, education, and partisanship. A rather different, more conspicuously historical and structural approach, can be found in Walter Dean Burnham's work. Burnham and those influenced by him, such as Paul Kleppner and the historian Michael McGerr, argue that the dynamics of turnout decline since 1960 are linked to the overall path of party and electoral change since the late 1890s. A variation on this view, exemplified by Frances Fox Piven and Richard Cloward's *Why Americans Don't Vote*, embellishes Burnham's approach to argue that low turnout since 1960 results from explicit political efforts to keep poorer, less educated, and minority voters out of politics.

Others writing in this broad tradition hold that turnout has fallen, particularly among lower-class voters, because the Democrats have moved to the right, abandoning their working-class and poor constituencies as they have become more like Republicans. For these constituencies, party politics now only offers "echoes," not "choices," according to Thomas Ferguson and Joel Rogers, among others. However, as I argue, important differences between the parties persisted, but the policies adopted by Democrats in the sixties weakened their ties to their historic constituencies and thus depressed turnout of their potential base.

Many political scientists of diverse schools now see a microeconomic cost-benefit calculus in the decision to vote. Voting, while easy, does cost time and may require some sacrifice of income or leisure. Sorting out the candidates and issues also takes time and energy; these are "information costs." Yet the individual benefits of voting are nearly zero, since the actual contribution of a single vote to a policy outcome is obviously extremely small. A strictly rational view would predict zero turnout, since if each person precisely calculated his or her costs and benefits, no one would vote. Of course, in crude form this insight borders on the tautological: if someone does not bother to vote, the cost must not be worth the benefit. But when married to an analysis of voter traits, the cost-benefit view can be illuminating, since certain traits help voters to pay the "costs of participation." And when incorporated into historical-structural interpretations, the cost-benefit perspective shows that the evolution of electoral politics has periodically changed the individual logic of voting.

The "Voter Traits" Approach

In *Who Votes?* Wolfinger and Rosenstone refined a standard proposition, namely, that "haves" are more likely to vote than "have-nots." They found that the most potent predictor of voting was not income or occupational status but education. The more their years of schooling, the more likely Americans are to vote. By contrast, past a certain threshold level, income has no impact on turnout. (While occupational status has a more powerful effect, it is nowhere near as great as the effect of education.) Education appears to be so powerful a predictor because it promotes civic-mindedness and better enables citizens to follow politics and navigate the complexity of voter registration.

Plausible as these propositions were, they also posed a puzzle. Because the population has become better educated, turnout should have risen since 1960. Also, outside the South the average presidential turnout from 1840 to 1896 was about fourteen percentage points higher than average presidential turnout from 1900 to 1984, yet twentieth-century Americans are better educated.

A version of the "voter traits" approach, exemplified by the work of Teixeira, resolves the puzzle. This approach links turnout to changes in attitudes, such as depth of partisanship and sense of political efficacy. Teixeira proposes that recent turnout decline reflects a crisis in the "system of the 1950s," when the relatively strong partisan identities created in the 1930s and 1940s still persisted. In those years, voters had a high sense of political efficacy and consequently were willing to pay the costs of participation.

Political parties in the United States, unlike most advanced industrial democracies, do not work hard to mobilize voters. Compared to Europeans, few Americans are formal party members. America is unique in the registration burdens it places on voters. Nonetheless, the relatively strong partisan identities left over from the New Deal and a correspondingly high sense of political efficacy compensated for these obstacles to participation and helped to produce the modern turnout peak that occurred in 1960.

Since 1960, though, voters have lost their previous sense of partisan identity and political efficacy. The American population has become more mobile, more single, and on average younger, all voter traits that tend to lower turnout. But Americans have also become better educated and more prosperous, which should increase turnout. In 1960, for instance, about half the voting age population had less than a high school education; by 1980 only 26 percent fit into that category, and the number with 16 or more years of education had nearly doubled. So changing demographic traits could not fully explain turnout decline; changing attitudes, according to Teixeira, were the key.

Teixeira reports that in 1960 only about 15 percent of the voting age population reported agreeing with two standard statements used in surveys: "People like me don't have any say about what the government does" and "I don't think public officials care much what people like me think." By 1980 about 32 percent of the population agreed with both statements, while the proportion who disagreed dropped from 61 to 34 percent. The percentage reporting strong partisanship dropped from 36 to 26 percent.

Teixeira proposes that these attitudinal changes resulted in large part from the turmoil of American politics since 1960 and, to a degree, from the rising influence of the broadcast media. John F. Kennedy's assassination, the Warren Commission, the Chicago riot of 1968, George Wallace's third-party run in 1968, the assassinations of Robert Kennedy and Martin Luther King, Jr., Vietnam, Watergate, Vice President Agnew's difficulties with the law, President Nixon's resignation, Ford's pardon, Carter's ineptitude—these events apparently left voters skeptical and uncertain, without strong partisan identities or a sense of political efficacy. Increasingly, media campaign professionals took control of the interpretation of events, and while television became more important, the percentage of Americans who read newspapers declined. Watching TV does not appear to be a perfect substitute for reading. When people read less, they are more likely to find politics confusing. The net result of all these changes was lower turnout.

The strength of Teixeira's analysis is conceptual and methodological. He takes into account the demographic approach of Wolfinger and Rosenstone and the work of others, such as Abramson and Aldrich, who emphasize voter attitudes. In this new synthesis, political disorientation resulting from turmoil and from a decline in campaign newspaper reading overwhelmed the "upgrading" effect of demographic changes, such as greater education. The idea that turnout decline since 1960 reflects the erosion of an earlier "system," the system of the 1950s, is a coherent way to make sense out of the diverse demographic, electoral, and political facts of the last three decades.

The Rise of Strong Parties

But where did Teixeira's "system of the 1950s" come from? Why did political parties evolve into organizations that did not work hard to mobilize voters? What were the origins of personal registration and other electoral practices that increase the "costs of participation"?

Burnham and his school trace the collapse in turnout since 1960 to a long historical shift in electoral politics. By the mid-nineteenth century, the professional party politicians who began to revolutionize American politics in the 1820s were producing an average presidential turnout of 74 percent, up from 25 percent at the beginning of the century, when the electorate was much more limited. That achievement was all the more remarkable in light of rapid population growth. Turnout in nonpresidential elections was also very high, apparently averaging about 68 percent. Through torchlight parades, festivities, and marching companies, party professionals created a politics that made partisanship the crucial determinant of an adult's political identity. During political campaigns they involved entire communities of men, women, and children in a continuous, public display of partisanship.

The Civil War—in part a war between the Democratic and Republican parties—only deepened the hold of partisanship. In post-bellum decades partisan identity was so strong and deep in Northeastern and Midwestern states that political independence in an adult male was widely considered effeminate. A wildly partisan press reinforced such attitudes. As Kleppner argues, ethnicity and small-town and religious values also reinforced partisanship, since parties, at the state level, often consciously sought to appeal to different religious and ethnic groups by staging legislative quarrels over temperance, parochial education, and Sunday closing laws. Not surprisingly, presidential turnout reached record highs during these decades, between 78 and 82 percent, even as the voting age population expanded.

While there was vote fraud, most analysts do not believe it was so widespread from 1840 to 1896 as to account fully for the difference between nineteenth- and twentieth-century presidential turnout. Indeed, since parties were competitive, they had strong incentives to monitor each other and to keep fraud to a minimum.

Reform and Retrenchment

By the 1890s three key groups came to see this highly participatory political system as dangerous. Because American electoral democracy so effectively mobilized ordinary people, it had always potentially threatened concentrations of wealth. That potential threat became more palpable at the end of the nineteenth century as disaffected economic groups, such as the Knights of Labor and farmers' alliances, turned to electoral politics, culminating in the Populism of the 1890s.

To antiparty reformers and to Protestant, middle-class Americans, the ubiquity of patronage and the emphasis on spectacle and display also seemed a threat to rational government. They wanted to reduce the role of parties and rely more on disinterested, nonpartisan administration to cope with the strains of urban life, industrial disorder, and immigration.

Finally, to conservative Southerners, a vigorous, unfettered party politics endangered the stability of the South's social hierarchies. From 1868 to 1892 both white and black presidential turnout in the South was at least as high as it is now and probably higher, despite violence and other efforts to restrict turnout. The Populist strategy of building a class-based, cross-racial coalition of poor farmers threatened conservative Democrats and their economic allies.

Through gradual changes on a number of fronts, the groups that were dissatisfied with high participation prevailed. In the pivotal 1896 election, the Democrats embraced some of the Populist rhetoric but lost the White House for nearly two decades. The ensuing realignment left the Democrats strong inside the South, but Republicans strong in every other region, and as a result created enough regional one-party dominance to reduce popular interest in politics, particularly state and local elections. The reduced stimulus of less party competition weakened the hold of what Kleppner calls "party norms" on the electorate. Turnout dropped.

The elections of 1896 also set the stage for attacks on earlier electoral traditions. The sway of the two parties in their different regions made it easier to change the rules of electoral politics. In the South, after the collapse of Populism, Bourbon Democrats were free to revive white supremacist violence and to push blacks out of politics. But the new rules they imposed, including poll taxes and literacy tests, excluded poor whites as well.

Outside the South, new rules also made participation more costly. Legislatures established personal registration during workdays. At that time workers had neither an eight-hour day nor an hour off for lunch. Between 1900 and 1930 the percentage of counties outside the South with personal registration jumped 72 percent, according to Kleppner. Nor did legislatures require registration opportunities to be fairly distributed by neighborhood. As Piven and Cloward stress, personal registration depressed worker presence in politics, so that rational politicians increasingly directed their appeals to middle-class concerns. In turn, the absence of populist or collectivist appeals continued to discourage worker involvement in politics until the New Deal.

One-party politics in the states also heightened the attractiveness of Progressive reforms aimed at weakening parties further. These new provisions for referenda, recalls, party primaries, and nonpartisan elections changed the previous partisan simplicity of politics. They also, if unintentionally, raised the "information costs" of political involvement.

McGerr convincingly argues that politics became more culturally distant from ordinary voters. Party politics once physically involved "the people" in floats, parades, and public gatherings lasting for days of political song and speech. But the new style was more remote. It was an "advertised politics," consciously modeled on mass marketing techniques. In their private worlds, voters would presumably ponder their choices as voter-consumers. The press also changed. Now nonpartisan papers responsibly arrayed facts about politics before a passive electorate.

These changes created a new political context for voting. The handful of Northeastern and Midwestern states and cities where political machines remained had diminishing influence. The machines were isolated remnants of the nineteenth-century system. The addition in 1920 of millions of relatively apolitical female voters sharply depressed presidential turnout to roughly 49 percent in 1920 and 1924. However, the drama of the 1928 Smith-Hoover contest, followed by the New Deal, rekindled political passions, bringing presidential turnout up over 62 percent in 1940. But the New Deal left intact the Southern regime, the registration rules obstructing participation, and a lower level of partisanship in the population as a whole.

Nonetheless, from the 1940s to the early 1960s, the parties again resembled the "team" parties of the nineteenth century. The alliance between Democrats and organized labor's political action committees introduced a new approach at the national level to the mobilization of voters. But since the early 1960s, the Democratic-labor alliance has been undermined by labor's growing weakness, and "advertised politics" has become increasingly dominant. While serious issue differences between the parties persist, campaigns are obsessively organized around the promotion of a candidate's persona, constant fund-raising, the development of campaign momentum by paid consultants, and the use of broadcast media. Paradoxically, the permanent campaign, in Sidney Blumenthal's phrase, has demobilized the electorate.

The work of Burnham, Kleppner, McGerr, Piven and Cloward, and others thus casts a searching light on the larger historical conditions that explain why postwar American voters would respond to confusing political events and to television by losing their sense of partisanship and political efficacy. The party identification and sense of efficacy that characterized the "system of the 1950s" now look relatively fragile. After all, the Civil War, the turmoil of the post-bellum decades, and the Compromise of 1877, when Democrats and Republicans brokered a presidential election behind closed doors, did not shock Americans into weaker partisanship and political disorientation.

Ideology and Democratic Decline

Do conflicts over issues and ideology have anything to do with the collapse in turnout since 1960? Burnham and many working in his tradition argue that since the New Deal, and especially since the 1970s, the Democrats have moved to the right, abandoning both working-class and middle-class Americans concerned about corporate power and government provision of economic security. In response, these people have stopped voting, or they have never started when they have come of voting age. In "The Turnout Problem" and "The Eclipse of the Democratic Party," Burnham explains the move to the right as the result of the inherent instability of a center-left party in a weakly politicized market society. In *Right Turn*, Ferguson and Rogers emphasize pressure from business on the Democrats to move to the right to lower the cost to business of welfare-state measures in the face of international competition.

Yet, as voters recognize, the philosophies of the two parties are different. The Democratic Party did not turn less liberal; it embraced a different version of liberalism that has demobilized its potential electorate. Ira Katznelson and Margaret Weir argue that the Keynesian approach adopted during the Kennedy-Johnson era, which emphasized market-led growth rather than political alleviation of unemployment through increased public spending, and the Great Society, which conceived poverty as a residual, largely racial problem in an otherwise healthy economy, undercut a potential class-based alliance among black and white voters. Democrats targeted social policies on the supposed few unable to get into the mainstream education, labor, and housing markets because of poverty or racial discrimination.

This renewed emphasis on welfare policy departed from the approach of Roosevelt and Truman. Rather than offering protections to the majority, the Democrats now seemed chiefly concerned about the minority below the poverty line. Much of the increased nonvoting may simply result from the Democrats' letting down their historic working- and middle-class constituencies, not by moving right, but by substituting a new approach to welfare for the old one. The Democrats fumbled their chance to rebuild their majority coalition.[1]

The Democrats might not have suffered politically if the economy had continued to perform well. But when inflation, the deficit, and competitiveness emerged as issues in the 1970s and 1980s, the Democrats could no longer present their social policies as essential for prosperity. Rather, they have presented them as moral imperatives but fiscal luxuries. Such policies were affordable in an expansive era, but not in times of austerity. The Democrats have forgotten how to attract key constituencies by making arguments other than "compassion." Consequently, they

---

1. Margaret Weir, "The Federal Government and Unemployment: The Frustration of Policy Innovation from the New Deal to the Great Society," in Margaret Weir, Ann Shola Orloff, Theda Skocpol, eds., *The Politics of Social Policy in the United States* (Princeton University Press, 1988); Ira Katznelson, "Was the Great Society a Lost Opportunity?" in Steven Fraser and Gary Gerstle, eds., *The Rise and Fall of the New Deal Order: 1930–1980* (Princeton University Press, 1989).

have proved unable to resist calls for less government, budget-balancing, and deregulation. Fighting to retain the social policies they created has seemed irresponsible at worst and backward-looking at best, if not impolitic in the face of a tax revolt.

The Democrats' party organization has deepened their difficulty in developing new policies that might rebuild their historic constituencies. The national Democrats are now a fairly cohesive legislative party. They have organized themselves around their congressional power, particularly in the House, establishing caucus government and a firm grip on the committees. But to be a legislative party requires congressional Democrats to get reelected, and to do that they need "permanent," well-funded campaigns and predictable electoral bases. These imperatives make it risky and difficult to adopt new approaches to social and macroeconomic policy. The permanent congressional campaign absorbs time and energy and compromises policy commitments. Building a war chest primarily from well-heeled donors to scare away potential challengers is not an activity that encourages deep reflection on social change.

Implications

Can the turnout decline be reversed? Some observers think it cannot, except under very unlikely conditions. Others are more optimistic and activist. The "voter traits" approach implies that raising turnout may be virtually impossible, especially if the attitudes Teixeira describes have taken on a life of their own. The continuing turnout depression in the last decade, after the political turmoil of the 1960s and 1970s subsided, gives little basis for optimism. The historical-structural approach is also discouraging. The evolution of electoral politics may have permanently reduced the participatory potential of American electoral politics. Party politics, nineteenth-century style, is clearly impossible. In the present context, rational politicians will not agree to give up their candidate-centered approach to elections and submit themselves to the discipline of an inner circle of national party leaders. Social democratic politics, approximated by the Democrats' alliance with the CIO between 1936 and 1948 and the AFL-CIO in the 1950s and 1960s, appears unlikely. Many Democrats now see labor as too weak to be much good to them; political professionals now widely regard Mondale's alliance with labor in 1984 as a major cause of his resounding defeat.

The Piven and Cloward approach, with its emphasis on the demobilizing consequences of personal registration, does offer a clear prescription: scrap all personal registration and other unwarranted barriers to voting. Approaches that emphasize the effect of the Democratic

Party's moderation also suggest a simple solution: go left. Yet there are good reasons for doubting that these ideas would have much net impact.

Piven and Cloward have tried to carry out a strategy based on their understanding of the causes of low participation. They have founded the Human/SERVE Campaign (Human Service Employees' Registration and Voter Education Campaign) to push for simpler registration procedures and to offer registration assistance to clients at welfare offices, motor vehicle bureaus, and other public agencies. Proposed federal legislation would encourage "mail-in" registration and require the states to provide "motor voter" registration (enabling citizens to register to vote when obtaining or renewing a driver's license).[2] The total, five-year cost of this reform, according to an estimate from the Congressional Budget Office would run between $215 million and $250 million.

Currently, several states and the District of Columbia have strong forms of motor-voter registration, combining the two kinds of registration on the same form or containing a "prompt question" on a motor vehicle form that triggers voter registration assistance by the registry clerk. About twenty other states are actively considering similar programs.

The Human/SERVE campaign for registration reform presumes that once registered, people are very likely to vote. About 80 to 85 percent of registrants vote, Piven and Cloward believe. Some data, however, suggest that voting by registrants is down 15 percent since 1960. But Piven and Cloward make a convincing case that this apparent drop in registrant voting results from failures by state election officials to purge registrants who have moved or died. Census surveys continue to show a strong link between registration and voting. So getting rid of legal obstacles to voting should significantly increase turnout, just as Piven and Cloward claim. The increase might be as high as 11 percent of the eligible electorate, or about 20 million voters.[3]

Easing registration procedures is surely one step toward fixing the turnout problem. But changes in other national policies are necessary as well to alter the sense of inefficacy and alienation that undergirds nonvoting. Voting turnout might increase if we pursued a new generation of policies that fostered a sense of civic membership. Universal worker training and retraining opportunities might restore a link between the citizen as worker and the citizen as voter. Improved primary

---

2. As this article went to press, the House of Representatives passed a motor-voter registration bill, but the bill faced uncertain prospects in the Senate.

3. Frances Fox Piven and Richard A. Cloward, "Government Statistics and Conflicting Explanations of Nonvoting," *PS: Political Science & Politics* 12 (September 1989): 580–588. See Burnham, "The Turnout Problem," for other estimates, which tend to be lower than 11 percent.

and secondary schools would help restore voter confidence in public institutions generally. I am not offering a policy platform, only emphasizing that policy ideas should be weighed for their contribution to rebuilding the sense of civic efficacy that invites participation in politics. Registration reform alone, if Teixeira is right, will not motivate people to vote.

Nonvoters' policy preferences are, moreover, a slippery question. Piven and Cloward want registration reform not for aesthetic reasons; they have a political agenda. They want to bring poor people back into politics to move the Democratic Party to the left. Yet their critics, including Teixeira, have convincingly pointed out that even extraordinarily high turnout rates among poor, Hispanic, and black adults eligible to vote would not have won the 1988 election for Dukakis and Bentsen.[4]

Teixeira argues that the broad, downward trend of nonvoting is not limited to the poor; it is far more widespread. To be sure, this point is irrelevant to the Piven and Cloward strategy. Simply winning elections for the Democrats is not their goal. They want to change the agenda of public debate and get the parties to disagree over social and economic policy in new ways. Such change, in turn, would open up American politics to previously foreclosed possibilities. In such a context, turnout rates might surpass those of the 1930s and 1950s.

Implicitly, though, Piven and Cloward are assuming that nonvoters are likely to be farther to the left than voters and more likely to vote Democratic—if Democrats begin responding to economic needs of current nonparticipants. Surveys do not show strong policy differences, however, between voters and nonvoters. Nonvoters, on balance, are only mildly pro-Democratic. There may well be serious measurement error in surveys of nonvoters. Nonvoters who cooperate with surveys are probably not typical of the larger population of nonvoters, who are cynical and politically alienated. But this survey evidence cannot yet be dismissed. It has striking implications, as well, for the position that turnout will increase if the Democratic Party moves left or if it develops a different approach to social policy. Nonvoters do not secretly have intense partisanship, held in reserve until some change in the political agenda or some invitation to participate unlocks their passions. They do not vote in part because they lack strong political affiliations. Partisanship among the nonvoters would have to be constructed, and that will be difficult.

---

4. See Ruy A. Teixeira, "Registration and Turnout," *Public Opinion*, January/February 1989, 12–13, 56–58. The Democratic Leadership Council has also implicitly criticized the Piven-Cloward approach. See William A. Galston, "Rebuilding a Presidential Majority," *The Mainstream Democrat*, September/October 1989, 10–13.

The Future of Nonvoting

If the past is a guide, transforming our participatory structure will require a debate about turnout. Years of intense debate about the political functions of parties preceded the last, great transformation of party politics. Between the 1870s and the 1900s, such magazines as the *Nation*, the *Atlantic Monthly*, and *Harper's Weekly* discussed the dangers of strong party politics. The editors of large newspapers grew hostile to parties as they responded to the emergence of local reform organizations, such as the City Reform Club established in New York City in 1882 by Theodore Roosevelt. A rising class of social scientists and academic leaders, gathered into professional organizations, also attacked parties. In time, too, military officers (who had organized themselves into their own special associations) turned against strong parties, seeing them as obstacles to the professionalization of the armed services. The hostility to democracy that informed much of this late nineteenth century debate now seems offensive. Yet we live, ironically, in a world created in part by such public argument against the old electoral regime.

There will be no contemporary debate if the collapse in turnout since 1960 is taken lightly. We cannot say, as some have, that nonvoting reflects complacency and even contentment among the population. As Piven and Cloward drily remark, "no one has satisfactorily explained why 'the politics of happiness' is so consistently concentrated among the least well off." Others say that nonvoting prevents fascism and demagoguery, yet there is no tradition in America of caesarist politicians succeeding on a national scale. Finally, certain writers insist nonvoting is healthy because high levels of participation overload democratic government. This argument appeals to those who see the general public as made up of grabby people willing to bankrupt government with insatiable demands. But some of the grabby people are those with the power to abuse deposit insurance or to alter the tax code to their benefit. Broader electoral participation would curb such self-seeking demands on our scarce public resources. In the end, it is awfully hard to contend that nonvoting is good for democracy.

The "party of voters" would do well to appreciate its self-interest in bridging the divide that separates it from the "party of nonvoters." While turnout has dropped, the demands on government have grown in this century. If democratic government is to take on the tasks demanded of it, it needs to seek out the voices and the votes of people who now feel they simply do not count.

As in the past, the expansion of participation can help to turn the subjects of administration into citizens capable of self-government. It can create a hardy sense of membership in a political community. Our electoral politics now fails to realize the empowering possibilities of democratic life. We need to recreate the popular ownership of electoral politics that we once had—indeed, that America pioneered. Otherwise, the likely low turnout in the 1990 and 1992 elections will be accepted as routine, and America will increasingly look like Schattschneider's "broadly-based oligarchy."

[11]

Stanley B. Greenberg

Reconstructing the Democratic Vision

The Democrats ended the 1988 election demoralized. Late in October, Michael Dukakis, facing almost certain defeat, stood at railside in Bakersfield, California and made his confession. He was a liberal after all: a liberal in the tradition of Franklin D. Roosevelt, Harry S. Truman and John F. Kennedy, one who "knows you have to pay your bills." He did not elaborate. He did not articulate any set of principles, offered no special perspective, and invoked no deeply resonant historical experience. The public was left, by default, with Lee Atwater's savage caricature: a Democratic Party short on patriotism, weak on defense, soft on criminals and minorities, indifferent to work, values, and family, and, inexplicably, infatuated with taxes.

Among major demographic groups, the Democratic coalition could now depend reliably on only Jewish, African-American, and Hispanic voters. In 1988 both Catholic and union households split their votes evenly between the parties; in both 1984 and 1988 native Southern whites gave two-thirds of their votes to the Republicans. The Democratic advantage in party identification, which hovered at 17 to 18 points for nearly the entire period from 1952 to 1980, sank to 7 or 8 points in the late Reagan years (1984 to 1988) and has perhaps disappeared entirely, according to some surveys.

Looking back at Democratic losses, conservative Democratic analysts conclude, reasonably, that Democratic nominees have proved "unacceptably liberal." The public has lost confidence in Democratic nominees who adhere to a "liberal fundamentalism" and have "lost touch with the American people." The answer proposed by the Democratic Leadership Council, which includes Senators Sam Nunn and Charles Robb, is greater credibility on military and foreign policy, closer alignment with mainstream values of responsibility and hard work, a "progressive" economic message of "upward mobility and individual effort," and a recasting of themes and programs to "bring support from a sustainable majority."*

The Enigma of Public Opinion

Alongside the liberal Democrats' demoralization and the conservative Democrats' critique, however, are a lot of contradictory "facts" that have no place to go. The public favors increased government spending in many area, antidrug programs, Medicare, cancer and AIDS research, day care programs, and Social Security—and wants new spending priorities focused, above all, on domestic investment. Populist impulses remain very strong. Voters want tougher regulation of corporate polluters and insurance companies and higher taxes for wealthy individuals and corporations. Public anxiety centers increasingly on lagging purchasing power, growing inequality, threats to the family and children, rising health care costs, corporate excesses, and America's declining economic position in the world.

Those "facts" remain unexplained and without context because the historic models that could give them meaning—the New Deal and Great Society—have fallen into disrepute. The values and ideas associated with the New Deal and the Great Society still float about in the public discourse, but they are no longer embedded in a common historic experience or a convincing story. Only when new models and ideas gain currency will Democrats be able to take advantage of popular impulses that favor equity, populism, and national effort.

The Democrats do still benefit from a residual, positive image as the party of ordinary people. Voters today distinguish roughly between a party of the people and a party of the rich and powerful. Despite the alienated affection of recent years, they side instinctively with the Democrats on such issues as the environment, insurance rates, tax fairness, energy, and utilities, which pit ordinary citizens against concentrated private power. Lee Atwater seems to understand the divide, even if Democrats are confused about it. As Atwater told William Greider: "Simply put there is constantly a war going on between the two parties for the populist vote. The populist vote is always the swing vote. . . . The Democrats have always got to nail the Republicans as the party of the fat cats, the party of the upper class and privilege. And the Democrats will maintain that they're the party of the common man. The Republicans, of

---

* William Galston and Elaine Kamarck, *The Politics of Evasion* (Washington: Progressive Policy Institute, September 1989).

course, argue that the Democrats are the party of the liberal elites who're not in touch with the mainstream of the country."

The Shrinking Coalition

The New Deal once told a story that gave political meaning to the facts. Against the backdrop of the Great Depression and in the face of a hostile world, that story energized public and collective effort. It honored working people and stood with them against corporate power. It provided social insurance against the prospect of adversity. It championed a Keynesian economic model that united rising public expenditure and rising personal incomes, and it sought a secure future by promoting American leadership in the world.

Keynesian assumptions conveniently served the particular interests of Democrats' electoral base as well as the national interest in stable economic growth. The Democrats could serve simultaneously as a party of the people and a party of the nation. But the high inflation, slow growth, and rising tax rates of the 1970s, followed by the high budget deficits of the 1980s, broke voter confidence in the model and its assumptions. Stimulating demand through government spending now looked profligate, more of a special favor to beneficiaries than an effort to meet the needs of society as a whole. Middle-class voters doubted that the model served their interests.

The New Deal model also crashed on the rocks of America's challenged international position, evident in the defeat in Vietnam and the emergence of competing economic powers, particularly Japan. The assurance of economic security for American workers was linked to an expansive view of American power. That view seemed confirmed by World War II and the world that emerged from it. John F. Kennedy, the last Democratic President to articulate that vision, conveyed an image of America as a leader among nations, rich but generous and respected. However, after the humiliations in Vietnam and Iran, the Democratic Party lost its ability to project that image and thereby lost some of its hold on the loyalty of America's working and middle classes.

Great Society liberalism was forged in a decade of historic upheavals. Innovative and optimistic, it advanced new concepts of justice and altruism that associated the Democrats with advancing civil rights and fighting poverty. But liberalism emerged from this period with a narrowed image of its constituencies. The beneficiaries of liberal initiative no longer appeared to be the broad working population, but rather the poor. And, for many, that meant blacks. Public spending, once conceived as furthering the broad economic interests of the working population, now seemed like a narrow response to special needs and special claims against the coalition.

A Closer Look at Public Opinion

The defeat of national Democratic candidates and the decomposition of Democratic models coexist with public attitudes that contradict the supposed new realities. The voters favor new national priorities; they are restive about the excesses of private power and are open to a broader governmental role in society. A 1989 ABC/*Washington Post* survey, for example, found that voters want to increase spending on drug programs (76 percent of those polled), Medicare (72 percent), and Medicaid (61 percent), cancer research (68 percent) and AIDS research (66 percent), day care programs (61 percent), and Social Security (58 percent). On the other hand there is little interest in increased military spending (18 percent). Warren Miller, a political analyst, points out the paradox: "The shift toward the Republicans occurred in the face of generally increasing support for liberal policies."

Those vague voter preferences, however, lack intellectual or political grounding. Few political leaders try to integrate them into a coherent framework because of the widespread and poorly examined belief that the public's mood is conservative. In the absence of intellectual or political leadership, these "facts" lose significance for voters, social critics, and politicians alike. Voters lose confidence in their own preferences, giving into their worries about taxes and their skepticism about governmental performance. Nonetheless, their concerns about the future persist, as do their inclinations to use public means to effect solutions.

1988: The Contradictions

George Bush's "kinder, gentler" rhetoric reflected a calculated reading of the public mood. Even as voters scorned Michael Dukakis—many because he was "too liberal"—a large majority still wanted the next President to pursue a liberal agenda and a populist course. My own election-eve survey found that 65 percent of respondents gave top priority to making sure the "wealthy and the big corporations pay their fair share of taxes." Sixty percent supported "imposing stricter environmental regulations on corporations" that "produce toxic wastes." Voters wanted a President who would expand the provision of broad-based social welfare services: helping the poor and homeless (49 percent top priority), protecting American jobs from foreign competition by tougher trade laws

(47 percent), and providing long-term health care and health insurance for everyone (44 percent).

The conservative dominance rests on a benign and simple economic vision—rosy economic indicators, strong job growth, slow inflation, incentives for new investment, and above all, low taxes. But in America today, the ordinary voter sees a middle class that carries a disproportionate load for society and that faces increasing economic obstacles. The burden and inequity is immediately evident in the realm of taxes: "rich people and corporations not carrying their share of the tax burden" (72 percent see this as an extremely or very serious problem) as well as the "amount of taxes paid by the average person" (64 percent). But the middle class faces a broad range of economic pressures: "middle-class families having a harder and harder time making ends meet" (71 percent) and "young families unable to keep up with the rising cost of housing and other needs" (62 percent).

The voters believe that a rising foreign economic presence is a growing threat to the country. Nearly three-quarters identify, as very or extremely serious, "foreign investors buying up American companies and land." About two-thirds express similar concerns about "foreign competition for American industry and jobs," "the loss of America's lead in technology," and "America's trade imbalance with foreign countries."

The uncertainty about the future is reflected in the public's view of the external world, where virtually all historic assumptions have been turned on their head. As a result of the shift in relations with the Soviet Union, just 4 percent cite Soviet aggression as a top threat. New threats now loom larger, particularly drug trafficking (identified by 37 percent of those polled), terrorism (10 percent), nuclear proliferation (12 percent), the economic power of foreign countries (9 percent) and destructive environmental practices (5 percent).

In the new world order, few voters see America as the leading nation: it now shares leadership in such critical areas as economic strength and high technology. Concerned that America's problems are going unaddressed, many voters seem ready to respond to national leadership that calls for increased spending for domestic investment and much tougher environmental regulation (68 percent). Seventy-six percent favor increased taxes on upper-income households and corporations "to help finance new initiatives."

Voters seem eager for a mobilization and unity of energies. There is nearly universal support (88 percent) for a proposal to "call together business and civic leaders from all over the country to identify emerging problems and set national goals." Voters like the idea of a "national economic plan that helps direct private sector investment to areas important to America's economic position in the world" (79 percent). They want government to play a larger role "developing and capturing new technologies for American industry" (79 percent). Americans, it seems, are looking for stronger national leadership that would seem to give the country more active control over its own economic future.

The public's receptiveness to new national priorities and activist leadership remains, for popular commentary, a perplexing set of facts largely ignored for want of an explanation. The conservative Democratic discourse is silent on these currents, preferring to save the party by moving to the right. Even the dominant forces in the Democratic Party, while supporting a liberal policy agenda, have lost confidence in the Democrats' economic message and general principles and thus are uncertain what to do. They know that they are standing uneasily on the shoulders of political coalitions and historical models that cannot support them any longer. Many are tempted to draw the lesson that the American people reject a "class warfare political argument" and want instead "leadership that argues for economic growth strategies," as an article in the *New York Times* concluded after the Democrats lost the 1989 vote on a capital gains cut in the House of Representatives.

In the absence of a convincing Democratic story that makes sense of the facts, voters have turned increasingly to the Republicans in one vital area after another. Voters now express greater confidence in the Republicans to promote growth and prosperity (43 to 33 percent) and control inflation (55 to 27 percent). Since World War II, Democrats have not won the Presidency unless they have enjoyed an advantage of at least 15 points in public opinion on the issue of keeping the country prosperous. Recently, Democrats have watched their advantage on that key issue decline from parity in late 1987 to a 21-point deficit in the summer of 1989.

The absence of any Democratic advantage concerning trade is particularly troubling. America's declining economic position in the world is an issue made to order for the Democrats. Yet the Republicans enjoy a small advantage on dealing with foreign imports (40 to 34 percent), despite the Democratic initiatives in the Congress and the absence of any discernible Republican policy. The Democrats, in fact, offer divided counsel on the trade question, finding unity only on tactical responses like 60-day notification of plant closings, rather than on serious economic principles. It is hardly surprising that the public does not know where to place trade on the partisan and ideological spectrum.

These facts are a signal to Democrats: begin building new intellectual and political models that will explain and legitimate the public's still inchoate affinity for greater equity, broad social welfare, checks on concentrated power, and an affirmative role for government. Of course, creating a new model and building a new coalition is no simple act of will. Our historic models were forged by specific presidents at distinct historic moments: Franklin Roosevelt in response to the Great Depression and Lyndon Johnson in response to the civil rights upheaval. But absent a moment beyond anyone's making, Democrats can embark on thematic projects that stake broad claims to the middle class, offer a distinctive understanding of the economy and expansive views of America's world position, and rebuild public confidence in the public sphere.

Democrats are positioned to take up the cause of domestic investment and American economic strength; they can address the declining or stagnant living standards of the majority and the forces menacing the modern family; they can acknowledge the values and burdens of the middle class and the excesses of the corporations in particular. Democrats can elevate these subjects into a revitalized statement about the party's purpose and identity.

Within this broadened discourse, intrinsic Democratic principles need no longer be submerged or appear disfigured. Principles such as equity and opportunity, a populist skepticism of private power, and a government able to respond to people in need and to lead the nation, take on new life and meaning and create distinctions that make voting worthwhile.

The Middle-Class Project

The Democrats need to reassert their claim to represent the majority of working Americans. The working middle class needs to figure at least as centrally in the party's identity as the traditional blue-collar imagery of the New Deal coalition because in our time the working middle class constitutes the broad majority.

To reach the middle class today, Democrats need to accommodate "middle-class consciousness," containing three primary and interconnected principles: work, reward for work, and restraint. Most Americans, including both those who formed the New Deal coalition and those who constitute the potentially expanded base, believe that work is a central value. Working people contribute to society, create the wealth, and carry the burden of taxes. They have learned and accepted the rules that govern social behavior, and they expect, in turn, to get a fair reward for their work. As the primaries were coming to a close in June 1988, voters thought Michael Dukakis's references to "good jobs at good wages" signalled a respect for work, and they inferred that he was "a middle-class kind of guy." That was all obscured by August; the lesson should help guide the future.

The middle class today perceives itself as "squeezed" between the rich and the poor, neither of whom play by the rules, but seek their reward through shortcuts or special claims—tax breaks, windfalls, and welfare. Middle-class consciousness deplores the lack of "values" today, which, in context, means the failure to honor work and recognize limits. To many, society seems to be spinning out of control and to be forgetting the people who carry the principal burdens. Middle-class voters believe that even though they carry disproportionate burdens (paying the taxes) and play by the rules (working hard), they get few of the benefits.

In real terms, middle-class and working families are indeed facing tougher economic odds, particularly those under 45 years of age. The bottom 40 percent of the population have lost income since 1979, and the middle 20 percent have stayed even only by the grace of working spouses. Home ownership has been increasingly frustrated (down 8 percent for young adults during the 1980s), and many face rising costs for day care for their children and long-term care for their parents. According to a CBS poll, while 55 percent of baby-boom voters believe the future will bring them better jobs and more money, they also believe that their children will have a "harder time." Children have become the central focus of discussion, perhaps the displaced object of all those unaddressed anxieties.

The middle class feels aggrieved and is experiencing economic difficulties, producing, in our polling research, gloomy assessments about the future: "the middle class is dying out"; "there will only be two classes, the poor and the rich." Many anticipate facing substantial costs in the next four years with long-term care (42 percent across all age groups), college tuition (36 percent), buying a house (21 percent), and child care (18 percent, rising to 38 percent for those under age thirty). Just a quarter of all voters expect any significant help or service from government, but a majority favor it nonetheless: 65 percent favor help with college costs, 74 percent with parental leave, 71 percent with long-term care, and 55 percent with child care (70 percent among those who expect to face the expense).

The liberal validation of middle-class values and concerns need not divide the middle class from the poor. After all, most poor people also work, or want to work, and identify strongly with middle-class aspirations of security and upward mobility. Thus Democratic conservatives make a grave mistake when they associate this set of "middle-class" issues with a simple move to the right, abandoning the poor, or rejecting affirmative government. Indeed, it is the link between the broad working middle class and affirmative government that allows Democrats to define a majority politics.

The National Investment Project

With rising apprehension, voters have watched the intellectual disarray about America's economic life. There is no new ascendant model, only the ghosts of past orthodoxies. As voters watch the looming budget and trade deficits, the rising foreign presence in the United States, and America's weakened position in the world, they know something important is amiss. Despite the short-run strength of the economic indicators, voters lack confidence in the economic recovery and the state of the country. Large numbers believe the good times are just a mirage and the future is endangered.

The impact of America's "economic decline" in the world context is already pronounced: only one in four persons believes the United States is now the leading economic power in the world, one in three has lost a job or knows somebody who has because of trade, and seven in ten believe that trade now hurts the economy. Two-thirds say growing foreign investment is a very serious problem. Americans are anxious to "put our own house in order"; they cannot understand why the nation's leaders have allowed the drift and decline.

That is why investment is such an important concept for Democrats. It expresses the widespread aspiration for national renewal and suggests a series of elements:

Economic strength. Investment represents a commitment to the primacy of economic strength in the definition of American security. Under this banner, Democrats can emerge as the party prepared to meet the challenges that rob us of our autonomy, sovereignty, and security.

Nationalism and internationalism. Investment represents a determination to give primacy to America— our people, technology, and ownership. Yet it is also internationalist, for investment provides America with the opportunity to play more effectively on the world stage.

Activism. Investment requires a more expansive role for government to encourage productivity growth, to foster technological innovation, to uplift the population, to revive American industry, and to open up markets.

Economic policy. In the realm of policy, investment contains a logic that favors taxing unproductive speculation and excessive luxury consumption, rewarding productive private investment, and emphasizing investment in decisions about public spending.

Social welfare. Under the rubric of investment, social programs take on a new meaning as a way of expanding "human capital." Everybody has an interest in literacy, health, productive work, and education. Voters are less tax sensitive and more receptive to social spending the more they are convinced that programs will offer broad benefits.

Values. Investment contains two positive values—reward for work and self-restraint—that remedy Democratic troubles in other contexts. Investment means encouraging savings and productive work and discouraging excesses of consumption and profit-taking.

Under the banner of investment, Democrats can become a voice for a new common sense. The political logic of investment represents a challenge to the present emphasis on defense spending. As the Soviets have become less threatening, voters have concluded that our security depends more on economic than on military power. Democrats need to redefine their domestic agenda as shift in favor of productive national investment designed to protect America where its security is now in greatest jeopardy.

The Populist Project: Corporate Accountability

The Democrats must remain the party that checks the excesses of private power. That is why voters turn instinctively to the Democrats on the environment, social insurance, and tax fairness. Yet in recent years, anxious not to look out of fashion, Democrats have toned down their rhetoric, even supporting new tax cuts for the rich. But that misses the public mood that still responds strongly to a populist message: four out of five voters, for example, support a tax increase for individuals earning over $240,000.

Voters are ready for an ambitious populist project, linked to the new emphasis on national renewal. The Reagan and Bush administrations introduced a new social compact that gave the wealthy lower taxes in exchange for more productive investment and that asked workers to give up higher wages and tolerate higher profits now for the promise of good jobs and economic growth. The wealthy did receive cuts in their effective tax rates, and workers gave up higher incomes. Between 1979 and 1986, real wages stagnated or slipped for the bottom 60 percent of the population. Meanwhile, incomes rose sharply for those in the top fifth.

But did corporations and the wealthy keep their bargain with the American people? Americans see corporations as more interested in mergers and acquisitions than in productive investment and the creation of jobs. They see defense contractors, up to their elbows in corruption, cost overruns, and failing weapons; they see a savings and loan industry, guilty of fraud and extravagance yet passing off its losses to the taxpayers. Americans see Japanese companies capturing advanced technology while American companies seem unwilling to join the battle; they see corporations more interested in outsourcing and foreign investment than in generating jobs in America.

Many Americans feel, therefore, that the corporate community has failed to keep its end of the bargain. The Democrats are in a position to demand an accounting. They can insist on more honest business practices, a higher corporate tax burden, a more active pursuit of new technology, and greater investment in American jobs. Democrats, in short, can offer a new compact with the American people to replace the unkept deal of Reaganomics.

Reconstituting a Democratic Vision

This is no easy road. The path is strewn with older liberal models that enjoy little support in the public and color the Democrats as partial, narrow, and out of the mainstream. Republicans will be quick to drag out Willie Horton and the pledge of allegiance. Conservative Democrats will ridicule the Dukakis tank and helmet. The whole project could collapse, as Democratic leaders try to build a new political bloc, based on common interest as well as common justice. Critics will interpret their economic nationalism as protectionism and their populism as "class warfare." Nonetheless, by evoking the themes of a squeezed middle class and working families, the need for national investment, and a new populist compact, the Democrats can respond to deep voter concerns and reorganize the disturbing "facts" of American life into a coherent story about the nation's problems and its path of recovery. Only with such a new model will Democrats be able, once again, to speak for both the people and the nation.

[12]

JEFF FAUX

The Myth of the New Democrat

Becoming a media buzzword is the public relations dream of every Washington policy cabal. It is the signal that the media is ready to collaborate. The great PR success story of the 1980s was the "supply-siders." The term, which suggests a conservative concern with investment and producer efficiency, is still applied to those who promoted the decidedly demand-side Reaganomics of economic stimulus through the deficit financing of military and private consumption.

So it is with the "New Democrats." The label creates the image of a collection of Democratic politicians and policy technocrats freeing the party from its bondage to a liberalism that is out of touch with mainstream America. Closer to reality, the term reflects a confused attempt to bring intellectual respectability to the moderate-conservative coalition that has ruled Washington for most of the past twenty-five years.

There is a great deal of overlap between New Democrats and those politicians who used to be known on Capitol Hill as Boll Weevils —southerners who rose to committee chairmanships as Democrats and voted like Republicans. New Democrats include Senators David Boren of Oklahoma, Sam Nunn of Georgia, and John Breaux of Louisiana, and Congressmen Charles Stenholm of Texas and Dave McCurdy of Oklahoma. Southern conservatives who favor big business and expensive military budgets while opposing social spending are hardly new. They have been a fixture in the party even longer than big-city northeastern liberals.

But all New Democrats are not southerners. And those who sell their political wares under the New Democrat label insist they are an entirely new political phenomenon. In a June 6, 1993, *Washington Post* op-ed, Al From, director of the Democratic Leadership Council (DLC), which holds the principal copyright on the New Democrat label, tells us their opinions add up to "a new public philosophy—a synthesis of progressive ideas and a nonbureaucratic approach to governing, grounded in mainstream values." He quotes Bill Clinton, when the latter was the chair of the DLC, saying that it "plainly rejects the old ideologies and the false choices they impose. Our agenda isn't liberal or conservative. It is both, and it is different."

The New Democrats score points with their criticism of the liberals, and some of their specific policy suggestions are reasonable if not terribly new. But their reach to establish a new ideology far exceeds their intellectual grasp. When faced with such central public problems as falling real incomes, impoverished cities, uncompetitive industries, and stubbornly high unemployment, their vision falters. Like their own caricature of the Left, the New Democrats are trapped in a "politics of evasion," obsessed with abstract debates over social values, while the nation stumbles into decline. If it turns out that Bill Clinton truly is a New Democrat, then he was elected on the basis of bait-and-switch advertising, and America's next four years will be much like the last four.

The promise of being beyond left and right has perennial appeal in American politics. As George Lodge of the Harvard Business School pointed out years ago, we are among the most ideological of peoples, yet the conventions of American political life hold that politicians must present themselves as nonideological problem solvers. This has advantages. Ideological rigidity is not helpful in a complex, changing world, and liberals and conservatives can learn from each other. Moreover, there is a case for a posture of pragmatism; in any election, 35 to 40 percent of the electorate is locked into one party or the other; the contest is for the middle. Not surprisingly, most candidates for president present themselves as more "centrist" than the mainstream of their party.

So there is a useful role for honest "plague on both your houses" politics in America. But those who carry the intellectual baggage for the Democratic Leadership Council do not curse the House of Liberalism and the House of Conservatism with equal fervor. For them, liberals are clearly the enemy.

The spine of the New Democrats' argument is this: for the last twenty years, the Democratic Party has been dominated by its extreme left wing, which is out of touch with middle-class America. New Democrats represent a set of new, bold ideas uniquely relevant to the nation's problems. These ideas will bring back "Bubba"—the stereotype of the Reagan Democrat who defected from the party in the 1980s.

William Galston and Elaine Kamarck laid out the political case against liberals in a 1989 booklet, *The Politics of Evasion*, which became the guiding political manifesto of the DLC. In it, the authors, both of whom now work in the White House, declared that since the late 1960s the Democratic Party had been beset by a rigid "liberal fundamentalism." As a result, the public has come to associate Democrats with politically bizarre attitudes like "tax and spending policies that contradict the interests of average families: with welfare policies that foster dependence rather than self-reliance." According to Galston and Kamarck, "Liberal fundamentalism has meant a coalition increasingly dominated by minority groups and white elites—a coalition viewed by the middle class as unsympathetic to its interests and its values." Echoing the twenty-year-old analysis of Kevin Phillips, Galston and Kamarck tell us the result is a political realignment working against the Democrats. Proof is that after 1988, the Democrats had won only one out of the preceding six contests for the White House.

The notion that the Democratic Party is a captive of left-wing extremists is a familiar one to readers of the American press. It has been a staple of conservative Republican doctrine since 1932. In itself, this does not make the point incorrect, although it suggests that it is a bit musty. Reminiscent of the analysis that has been nurtured for decades in places such as the *National Review*, New Democrats have a tendency to argue at a level of abstract generalization that permits them to leap over some facts that would otherwise puncture their case.

The first set of facts is historical. With the exception of McGovern in 1972, in five of the last six presidential campaigns, the Democratic candidates—Humphrey, Carter, Mondale, and Dukakis—ran as centrists. Humphrey was the establishment candidate against Robert Kennedy and Eugene McCarthy. Carter ran as a conservative southerner moderate on race. The centerpiece of Mondale's campaign (for which Galston served as chief issues adviser) was deficit reduction. And Dukakis ran as a technocrat who, until the last two weeks of his campaign, avoided attacking Ronald Reagan because he didn't want to sound too partisan. Even McGovern didn't run as a "tax and spend" Democrat; a central part of his platform was a proposal for a huge middle-class tax cut. Indeed, the Carter presidency—the failure of which still weighs heavily on the Democratic psyche—was the exemplar of the New Democrat spirit. The *New Republic* reports that when Al From talked with Carter about forming the DLC, the latter said: "Boy, could I have used a DLC to back me up."

Well, say New Democrats, it wasn't necessarily the candidate who was too liberal. It was the Democrats at the convention who were too liberal—that is, Ted Kennedy challenging Carter, Jesse Jackson challenging Mondale and Dukakis. In this version, the sin of the liberal fundamentalists is not that they have taken over the party but that they have taken over the *convention* every four years and forced the candidate to accept a far-out platform that has been an albatross around the candidate's neck.

For this theory to be credible, the New Democrats have to argue that the 1992 convention was different. Inasmuch as they claim credit for

Clinton's victory, they have to claim that 1992 was *their* convention. True to form, the press generally has obliged by favorably contrasting the 1992 convention with the "liberal" conventions of 1988 and 1984. According to accepted wisdom, these two previous conventions were dominated by demanding minorities, feminists, labor unions, environmentalists, gays, and people with bizarre "styles" of political behavior. But as media critic Jim Naureckas has pointed out, the press ran the same story of moderation during the previous conventions as well. According to Naureckas, "every convention since 1984 has been hailed by journalists as the one where the 'special interests' lost their influence." He quotes press report after press report praising Dukakis in 1988 for appealing to "the middle ground and the middle class" (*New York Times*). For using words like "family, community, honesty, patriotism, accountability, responsibility, opportunity" (*Chicago Tribune*). For abandoning "the expansive promises of Democratic Party platforms of earlier years—the crowded bazaar of special interests and special pleading" (*Washington Post*).

In 1984 the *New York Times* headlined: "Democrats' Platform Shows a Shift from Liberal Positions of 1976 and 1980." The press lauded Walter Mondale's acceptance speech for its break with the past. "Look at our platform," said Mondale, "There are no defense cuts that weaken our security, no business taxes that weaken our economy. No laundry lists that raid our Treasury." Mondale himself, according to columnist David Broder, "embodies all the traditional middle-class values of the rural Midwest." Joining the journalistic consensus of the 1988 convention was Elaine Kamarck, then columnist for *Newsday:* "Interest groups and their demands were barely visible."

Naureckas concludes that "when the 'pragmatists' lose badly with their centrist approach, they are repainted after the fact as radicals, so the strategy of tilting to the right can be tried again and again."

No reasonable reading of history since 1972 supports the premise that an extremist coalition of minorities and white liberals has dominated the Democratic Party. Nor can one make the case that those on the left of the party have been somehow destructive or disloyal. They ran their candidates and tried to influence the platform. When they failed, they rallied behind the centrist candidate. Certainly the liberals have supported recent centrist candidates, starting with Jimmy Carter, with more loyalty than the conservatives showed to the candidacy of George McGovern. The 1992 campaign is a case in point. The liberal coalition—labor, environmentalists, minorities, fundamentalists, gays—were the shock troops of Clinton's political army. They were the activists who knocked on doors, raised money, and organized precincts. In contrast, many New Democrats seemed to spend their time complaining that Bill Clinton was allowing these people too much say in the campaign.

Liberal loyalty to Clinton continued throughout the troubles of his first seven months in office. They stuck with his budget even after it had been gutted of the domestic spending that was at the heart of their agenda. Senate Democrats like Ted Kennedy and Paul Sarbanes battled for the president's budget, which disappointed their constituencies. At the same time, New Democrats like Boren and Breaux were willing to ruin Clinton's presidency in its first year in order to protect the oil and gas industry. The liberals' reaction to the creation of an economic inner circle of deficit hawks—Bentsen, Rubin, Panetta, and Rivlin—and the subsequent insulting appointment of David Gergen was silence. The New Democrats' reaction to the appointment of Lani Guinier was to throw a tantrum, forcing Clinton to withdraw his candidate in an embarrassing public defeat.

In their 1989 New Democrat manifesto, Galston and Kamarck set up and effortlessly demolished a series of straw men, the supposed "myths" through which liberal fundamentalists have succeeded in getting the Democratic Party to evade reality. One is the argument that greater mobilization of minorities will automatically return a Democrat to the White House. They belabor what people who understand simple addition know: there are not enough potential black and Hispanic voters to outweigh white, working-class Democrats who would be alienated by a campaign aimed at minorities. That is why they are known as *minorities*. The argument of Jesse Jackson—the primary target of Galston's and Kamarck's attack—was that Democrats should be appealing to the working class as a whole. One may object that Jackson is not the most effective person to make the appeal, but that is another question. Ironically, Galston and Kamarck divide the working class along racial lines in attacking this class mobilization thesis, and a few pages later they criticize the Left for believing that race is the main reason for the white, working-class departure from the party.

The most interesting of the purported "myths" is the supposed thesis that, as Galston and Kamarck phrase it, "it's all economics." Even discounting the extremist formulation (no serious Democrat believes it is "all" anything), Galston and Kamarck think this is "a very powerful tactic in the politics of evasion," because "it allows Democrats to avoid dealing with problems of vulnerability on national defense and social issues."

New Democrats insist that noneconomic appeals to the white middle class should take precedence. Writing in 1989, Galston and Kamarck tell us that the next Democratic candidate must be fully credible as commander in chief and "squarely reflect the moral sentiments of the average American." They grant that he needs to have a "progressive economic message, based on the values of upward mobility and individual effort." But they maintain that the white majority doesn't respond to progressive economic messages because people dismiss the Democrats on the basis of foreign policy and social issues. So next time around —1992—the Democrats need a candidate whose strengths lie in social and foreign policy. "Above all, the next Democratic nominee must convey a clear understanding of, and identification with, the social values and moral sentiments of average Americans."

They got the 1992 election dead wrong. Bill Clinton's strength was not as a credible commander in chief—whether in Vietnam or the Persian Gulf—and he spent the campaign avoiding George Bush's call for debates on morality. Had the unemployment rate in October 1992 been 5.5 percent instead of 7.5 percent, there is little doubt that George Bush would be president today. Clinton's campaign was so focused on "the economy, stupid" that the very phrase has become a political cliché.

Moreover, Clinton's message on the economy was unmistakably liberal. He constantly attacked the "trickle-down" economics of the Republicans. And after outbidding George Bush with the promise of middle-class tax cuts flopped in the early primaries, Clinton overruled his DLC advisers and shifted to an emphasis on more government investment spending both as a way to jump-start the economy and to create more good jobs over the long run. He even argued that closing the public investment deficit was every bit as important as reducing the fiscal deficit.

But as Naureckas pointed out, the press lets the party conservatives rewrite history every four years, whatever the outcome.

There is some legitimate criticism to be made of the Democratic Party's activist left wing, but the New Democrat critique misses the target. The central failing of the Left is that it has not come to grips with the question of economic growth and stability in the new global economy. To some degree, the Left still views the world in the framework of the 1960s, when a growing pie of income and wealth could be taken for granted and progressives could focus on how to slice it.

Like the "liberal fundamentalists" they criticize, however, the New Democrats have practiced their own "politics of evasion" in avoiding the issue. In his credo for the New Democrat, Al From denounces both the "borrow and spend" policies of the Republicans and the "tax and spend" policies of the Old Democrats that have failed to solve the country's economic problems. The failure, he says, "has produced two decades of anemic gains in personal income."

Again, the "plague on both your houses" stance is at odds with history. Jimmy Carter actually cut taxes in midterm, a precursor to Reaganomics. Lyndon Johnson was not a "tax and spend" Democrat. In fact, history blames Johnson for not raising taxes to pay for the Vietnam War. Kennedy cut taxes, as did Truman before he raised them to pay for the Korean War. Postwar presidents—Democratic and Republican until Reagan—did use an unindexed income tax structure that automatically generated accelerating revenues with economic growth, but one has to go back fifty years, to Roosevelt's financing of World War II, to find a Democratic president's economic policy that could be described as deliberately "tax and spend."

Once having set up the false dichotomy to place the New Democrats in that safe haven "beyond left and right," From runs out of gas. Faced with the question of how to reverse this two-decade slide of income and growth, he ducks: "No one has convincingly solved this riddle," he says. "But while economists search for answers, we need to reduce the deficit and long-term interest rates." One might wonder why, if we haven't solved the riddle of our economic problem, we should opt for the solution of deficit reduction. Macroeconomic policy aside, it is reflective of how "new" the philosophy of the New Democrat is. From is telling us what Michael Dukakis told us in 1988, Walter Mondale in 1984, and Jimmy Carter in 1980 and even George McGovern in 1972—that we must reduce the budget deficit. Indeed, if there is one plank in the economic platforms of both Democrats and Republicans that has not varied over the twenty years of anemic economic growth, it is the well-worn demand for deficit reduction.

In any case, New Democrats seem to prefer turning the conversation to social programs. In the summer of 1993, the DLC commissioned a poll of Perot voters which showed that three-quarters of them did not list the deficit as either the first or second problem facing the country. But the Perot voters did favor "radical change" in government more than did those who voted for Clinton or Bush. According to the *Washington Post*, when asked for an example of what radical change in government would appeal to Perot voters, Al From and pollster Stanley Greenberg "were initially stumped.... They then said welfare reform was the kind of change that would appeal to Perot voters."

But the welfare reform the New Democrats say they favor hardly breaks new ground. It is the traditional combination of a generalized denunciation of personal irresponsibility and support for specific programmatic changes liberals have advocated for years. New Democrats advocate ending welfare after two years. In fine print they want public sector jobs for all those who can't get work in the private sector, subsidized training, more earned income tax credits, and universal health care. And they want an initial $5 billion to finance it. One can argue over the details, but this is the kind of program that liberal welfare policy analysts have been talking about for years. Dukakis made welfare reform a central piece of his platform. The problem—as From says and everyone knows—is delivering on the commitment. What's new?

Indeed, when one actually reads the New Democrat social policy literature, it is hard to see what all the fuss is about. New Democrats move easily from a call to arms against the liberal fundamentalists to the level of cliché, that is, the belabored insistence that New Democrats are different because they are for Opportunity, Family Values, Individual Responsibility, Better Government, and so on. But when we get to programmatic details, the trumpet begins to squeak. New Democrats say they are for investment in education, for example, European-style worker training, and help to college students in return for community service. In terms of the specifics of social policy, New Democrats simply do not represent a radical departure from the things that the liberal wing of the party, its convention delegates, and its losing centrist candidates have been saying for years. It seems again that it is not liberalism they are quarreling with; it is the liberals.

New Democrats claim government reform is a new centrist idea. Yet Democrats, at least as far back as the Johnson administration's effort to promote "zero-based budgeting," have been much more interested in having government operate efficiently than have Republicans. Many of the specific proposals to free government agencies from the tyranny of annual budgets, to consolidate agencies, to promote public-sector flexibility, and to inject more competition into the delivery of services are reasonable and indeed are part of the evolving American debate on public administration. By focusing some presidential attention on these issues, New Democrats have helped move the discussion forward. But when these issues are elevated to the level of a new public philosophy and used to attack liberals, the thinking becomes muddled and superficial, and the politics become conservative—encouraging the cheap shots against the public sector that have so poisoned popular political discussion in America.

Thus New Democrats roll out the anecdotes about government inefficiency: how long it takes for government to purchase new computers, how conscientious bureaucrats are frustrated in their efforts to save the government money by cutting red tape, how agencies are balkanized. There is much truth to these complaints, but to lay blame at the feet of liberal fundamentalists is absurd. It is not the liberals who entangle government agencies with restrictions and contradictory rules. More often than not, bureaucracy is a response to the micromanagement of government agencies by legislators with economic interests to grind.

New Democrats claim they want to improve government to make it more credible. A worthy liberal sentiment. But the missiles of their reform are typically fueled by conservative obsessions with reducing labor costs and the size of government and are locked onto public sector labor unions as the ultimate targets. New Democrats also depart from liberals in showing little interest in the misallocation of resources represented by a bloated post–Cold War military budget. And although they promote competition and privatization of public services, their zeal for efficiency does not extend to the possibility of socializing activities where the public sector's record is superior—like the federal government's more efficient administration of Medicare as compared with the performance of private health insurers.

The New Democrat "reinventing government" balloon gets much of its lift from the hot air associated with the word "empowerment." Like Jack Kemp, they use it to oversell marginal and often counterproductive reforms such as tenant ownership of public housing, enterprise zones, and privatization. But Kemp's political agenda is to split minorities from the Democratic Party. He knows his history: the Great Society of the 1960s championed grass-roots empowerment as a substitute for big-time spending for the cities. It came to political grief when moderate and conservative Democratic officials decided that people were taking the promises too seriously. New Democrats may be playing with fire. Also like Jack Kemp, despite abstractions about empowerment, they are hostile to organizations that attempt to give any real power to the lower two-thirds of the income distribution. For example, they are hostile to labor unions, which are the major mechanisms in a market system for giving working people some measure of control in the workplace.

Tax reform is another area where the New Democrats' claim is more than their due. The Left has been making the case for reform for over twenty years. What liberal fundamentalist is not for taxing the rich, giving the middle class a break, and providing tax relief for the working poor?

Like many liberals, by focusing on tax issues, the New Democrats evade the deeper structural changes in the economy that are eroding middle-class incomes. In fact about 80 percent of the increase in income inequality in the 1980s occurred before taxes. Having no answer to this "riddle," they fall back to intellectual pillow fighting with liberals.

The shallowness of the New Democrats' intellectual claims was revealed in an extraordinary debate on the MacNeil-Lehrer News Hour between Senator Charles Robb and Jesse Jackson in November 1989. Before his career was derailed by his falling out with fellow DLC-er Governor Doug Wilder of Virginia, Robb was a leading New Democrat hopeful for the 1992 race. He had just delivered the keynote speech to the Democratic Leadership Conference in which he challenged Democrats to choose between "liberal fundamentalism" and "mainstream values."

Jackson said he didn't know what liberal fundamentalism was. He said he is for aid to education, a war on drugs and poverty, a requirement that S&Ls that got bailed out invest more in their local communities. He said he was for a strong national defense but that he thought that building 100 stealth bombers at a half-billion dollars apiece when we could use the money for health care was not a good idea.

Robb's reply was: "On the basis of what he's suggested, there's not that much difference. We can find common ground and have previously. The concern here is also with style." Robb did not define what he meant by style. The exchange reinforces the notion that there is a murkier agenda at foot here. The line drawn in the sand gets filled in quickly and another must be drawn. The ground shifts from substance to style. The problem turns out not to be the liberal program but the liberals.

The New Democrats' mantra about social values and moral sentiments works as a political platitude. It doesn't work as a strategy for the Democrats. The fact is that in modern times national Democrats have always been somewhat out of sync with the social values of the average, white, and middle-class American. It is, after all, the progressive party. Its historic function is in part to champion the upward mobility of those who are different—immigrants, blacks, Hispanics, women wanting equal opportunity, gays in the military.

This is part of the burden of being a Democrat. Lyndon Johnson was right; the Civil Rights Act lost the South for the Democratic Party. The problem did not start in the 1960s, or even the 1950s; Harry Truman desegregated the armed forces in 1948. In the 1930s, Franklin and Eleanor Roosevelt were excoriated in racist limericks and jokes in working-class taverns and church suppers for their sympathies for blacks. Since the end of World War II, Democrats have also been seen as less hawkish than Republicans on foreign policy. Whatever the reality, to most voters Democrats were soft on communism, less supportive of the military, more interested in diplomacy than the big stick.

Nonetheless, the working class voted Democratic because Roosevelt, Truman, Kennedy, and Johnson were seen as on their side on the central issues of jobs and economic security. The Democrats were for full employment, progressive taxes, and spending money to help the little guy. This identity was so powerful that Hubert Humphrey, dragging a party that had been splintered on race and shattered by the Vietnam War, almost won the 1968 election.

The identification faded under Carter, the first New Democrat. Carter ran against the government and governed as a middle-of-the-road conservative. Bewildered by the "riddle" of economic stagflation in the late 1970s, he reached for the old Wall Street bromide of deficit reduction and tight money. He cut domestic spending to balance the budget and hired Paul Volcker to strangle the economy with high interest rates. Voters in *New York Times* and CBS exit polls in November 1980 named unemployment as the number one reason for voting against Jimmy Carter. Strikingly, the subject rates exactly one citation in Carter's 600-page memoir of his presidency.

The New Democrats are a continuation of the politics of Carter, which in various forms has dominated the party ever since 1976. Their insistence that the nation cares more about social issues than economic ones reflects a fundamentally conservative view of the world, one in which the major economic forces shaping society are seen as beyond political control. This inevitably leaves economic policy decisions in the hands of those who purport to speak for the business community—primarily the high rollers in the financial sector for whom low interest rates and slow growth take much higher priority than full employment.

This has been the real politics of evasion that has characterized the Democratic party over the last two decades of anemic income growth. The party has abandoned the search for a strategy to create good, permanent, full-time jobs with rising wages and benefits for Bubba and the rest of the party's basic constituency—the bottom two-thirds of the working class. Bubba may not like minorities, and minorities may not care much for Bubba. But they like less the prospect of working for the rest of their lives in a series of short-time, service sector jobs at a buck over the minimum wage.

Despite their claims to be the intellectual vanguard of the party, New Democrats have remarkably little curiosity about the central policy question the party faces. Al From says we must wait for the "economists" to solve the riddle of slow growth. Thus the faction of the party that attacks the Left for being elitist tells us to hand over the decision on the country's economic future to some shadowy group of unnamed scholars—and while we are waiting, let's listen to our betters on Wall Street who tell us to keep the lid on job growth.

People who purport to speak for the party's future should be less patient. The economic riddle is not insolvable. We already know the essential pieces of a high-wage answer. Clinton himself was on to it in the campaign. For those who need the authority, Nobel Prize economists have endorsed an investment-led growth strategy to put people to work now doing things that will make the economy more productive in the future. This will require a civilian public sector that is stronger, not weaker—and probably larger, not smaller. It will require a government that plans ahead and does not hide from the questions of how to deploy America's technology and labor force into the industries of the future. This, in turn requires a political party that gives the interests of producers at least as much attention as the interests of bondholders. And this in turn requires an intellectual leadership willing to engage the public in a mature dialogue over economic policy, rather than one that at the first sight of trouble will abandon the public sector to the political lynch mobs led by the likes of Ross Perot, Newt Gingrich, and David Boren.

Talk like this makes New Democrats uncomfortable, primarily, it would seem, because it makes Old Republicans uncomfortable. But in the absence of an economic program that might speak to the party's constituency, there is little room for compromise between its right and its left. Reflecting the strains in the larger society, the Right and the Left are trapped in deadly political combat over unresolvable issues of "style," like two scorpions trapped in a bottle. Moreover, lacking the will to risk exploring an economic strategy that would undercut their Republican affectations, New Democrats release the very forces they claim to want to suppress. Among Democrats, social liberalism, or liberal fundamentalism, is the natural corollary of economic conservatism. For example, if you can't spend money to put disadvantaged minorities to work, you are driven to support their upward mobility through affirmative action —which is what really makes Bubba crazy.

So in the end, the New Democrats do not live up to their billing. Their program cannot hold together. It is a tired mixture of conservative intention watered down with liberal tinkering in the hope that it will fill in the crack in the center. But it cannot build a new future for the party because it does not address the new economic reality. Neither can their effort to read the left wing out of the party succeed. Minorities, labor, feminists, and environmentalists were indispensable in Clinton's victory. Not only do they ring the door bells, organize the precincts, and raise the money, but it is ultimately on the left where the passion resides for the very idea of the Democratic Party. Take that away and Republicans will rule America for as far into the future as you can see.

[13a]

WILL MARSHALL

Friend or Faux?

Jeff Faux's "The Myth of the New Democrats" (*TAP*, Fall 1993) is illuminating—but in unintentional ways. It highlights the unresolved tension in *The American Prospect*'s editorial persona: though dedicated to rethinking old liberal assumptions, the magazine often shies from conclusions that defy liberal orthodoxy. *TAP* thus oscillates between earnest stabs at policy innovation and purse-lipped attempts to suppress heresy and enforce liberal dogma. Faux's polemic falls in the latter category.

Still, a *TAP* cover story on the New Democrats and the Democratic Leadership Council (DLC) represents progress of a sort. The exercise forces Faux to grapple with New Democrat ideas on their merits rather than simply dismiss them as "conservative"—a favorite tactic in the Left's politics of evasion. Honest debate might even advance the cause New Democrats share with *TAP:* the reconstruction of contemporary liberalism as a progressive force for national purposes.

Faux accuses New Democrats of being abstractly philosophical, substantively thin, little more than crypto-Republicans and yet, in the end, not all that different from traditional liberals. Confused *TAP* readers can judge for themselves by reading the Progressive Policy Institute's (PPI) *Mandate for Change*. Oddly, Faux never mentions this key New Democrat manifesto, rummaging instead through old news clippings to make his case. That's a shame, for *Mandate* sets out, in ample detail, policy innovations that challenge what candidate Bill Clinton acidly called the "brain dead politics of both parties."

What Faux essentially asks is, Why do we need New Democrats? But he doesn't want to hear the answer: that the party's establishment has been too busy defending the status quo—old policies and old programs—to adapt liberalism to such new realities as the globalization of commerce, the shift from mass to flexible production, the spread of information technologies that undermine the authority of central bureaucracies, and the impact of suburbanization on American politics. These changes require a fundamental rethinking of the liberal enterprise.

Unfortunately, for many Democrats solidarity, not adaptation, remains the overriding imperative. But solidarity won't expand the party's shrinking base. On the contrary, the evidence shows that exactly the opposite takes place—that yielding to the demands of pressure groups undercuts Democrats' ability to set broader public goals, and in so doing has turned many middle-class voters against us.

DLC Democrats are trying to move liberals beyond this self-defeating, circle-the-wagons mentality. Their initiatives—public investment, voluntary national service, youth apprenticeship, community policing, entrepreneurial government, and social policies that reinforce work and family—are intended to unite the interests of the party's core with those of an increasingly suburban national electorate.

Liberals seem embarrassed by this effort by New Democrats to bring these once and future Democrats—largely white and middle class—back into the fold. The underlying assumption, which Faux makes explicit, is that such voters are inherently reactionary—never mind that the working middle class was the party's mainstay from Andrew Jackson through Lyndon Johnson. Faux derisively calls these folks "Bubbas," though of course Northern ethnic whites have also deserted the party in droves; witness the recent election results in New York and New Jersey. (Perhaps he has forgotten that white union members gave half their votes to Ronald Reagan.) The inevitable conclusion here is that fighting for votes in the heart of America's middle class would somehow sully the party's purity. Left liberals dream instead of a rainbow coalition that pointedly excludes white males. Such intolerance—at once undemocratic and politically obtuse—is what makes the New Democrats' base-expanding strategy so vital to the future of progressive politics.

That strategy begins with political realism. In *Politics of Evasion* (1989), PPI argued that the party's losing streak in presidential elections was not a series of flukes but instead reflected a deeper syndrome—the replacement of the New Deal's middle-class populism after 1968 by a new paradigm of special interest liberalism. According to authors William Galston and Elaine Kamarck:

> In the past two decades, liberalism has been transformed. The politics of innovation has been replaced by programmatic rigidity; the politics of inclusion has been superseded by ideological litmus tests. Worst of all, while insisting that they represent the popular will, contemporary liberals have lost touch with the American people. It is this transformed liberalism that we call "liberal fundamentalism," on which the electorate has rendered a series of negative judgments.

Notwithstanding Faux's revisionist account—which fancifully casts George McGovern, Walter Mondale, and Michael Dukakis not as liberals but as DLC-style centrists—the 1992 election results confirmed PPI's analysis. Clinton presented himself to the voters as a "Different Kind of Democrat," one who at last understood and sympathized with "the forgotten middle class." Clinton's was the most politically incorrect Democratic primary campaign since Robert Kennedy's in 1968. Like RFK— the prototypical New Democrat—Clinton refused to sentimentalize the poor or condescend to black Americans by treating them as a monolithic bloc with one set of opinions. He stressed economic opportunity and mobility rather than wealth transfers, took a tough-minded line on crime, welfare dependency, and international security issues, and called for a new ethic of personal responsibility to temper demands for entitlements. He avoided divisive litmus tests that have frustrated the party's quest to rebuild an alliance between working middle-class whites and blacks.

Inconveniently for Faux, the 1992 nomination contest offered Democrats a clear choice between unadulterated liberalism and Clinton's amalgam of traditional and New Democrat themes. Anointing himself the "real Democrat" in the race, Senator Tom Harkin ran as the unapologetic apostle of liberal fundamentalism. He followed the classic "unite the base" strategy, only to find that even liberal primary voters had lost faith in electoral appeal of the old redistributionist nostrums.

The problem is not just an ossified liberalism, however; the dominant ideas of both parties have outlived their time. Americans are loath to choose between Democrats' special interest liberalism and Republicans' "neocapitalism" (the term is Robert Bellah's). They despise the Washington political game, in which the two sides seek to sharpen partisan differences rather than bridge them so that the nation can solve its problems. As E.J. Dionne wrote in *Why Americans Hate Politics*, people believe that "liberalism and conservativism prevent the nation from settling the questions that most trouble it."

New Democrats look beyond the left-right debate to a new synthesis that combines the valid insights from both sides in a new agenda for progressive reform. Consider the following examples.

Enterprise Economics. Notwithstanding Faux's claim that New Democrats subordinate economic to social policy, the first four chapters of *Mandate for Change* elaborate an "enterprise economics" tailored to the new requirements of global competition. PPI's Robert Shapiro and Doug Ross (now an assistant secretary at the Labor Department) maintain that the globalization of capital markets and production undermines both supply-side efforts to increase investment by cutting taxes on investors' profits and traditional liberal policies to pump up demand or micromanage the distribution of resources among industries.

Enterprise economics replaces obsolete "tax and spend" policies with a new strategy of "cut and invest." To make U.S. firms and workers more productive, it calls for substantial new public investments in education and job training, research and development, transportation, communications, and other public infrastructure systems. But New Democrats would pay for these investments by cutting and rechanneling unproductive federal spending rather than by raising taxes on the middle class.

The hard truth for liberals is that deficit reduction is a prerequisite for expanded public investment. Large, permanent federal deficits disable progressive government. Only by showing the ability to discipline federal spending and distinguish between consumption and investment can liberals regain the public's trust. Moreover liberals should, on principle, stop defending tax-and-spend subsidies and trade and regulatory protections for particular industries or for wealthy people. They insulate firms from the competitive forces that drive flexibility and innovation, and so leave workers less equipped to succeed in a global economy.

Faux makes a fair point that New Democrats have not solved the deepest economic riddle facing the country: the slowdown in U.S. productivity growth since the early 1970s and the resulting stagnation of family incomes. We're working on it. One thing, however, is certain: Faux's prescription—huge new dollops of federal spending—won't do the job. The federal government has been running deficits of $250 billion and more for years; there is no evidence that higher federal spending and even larger deficits would strengthen the economy. On the contrary, greater deficit spending would bring higher long-term interest rates that would slow the economy and its stimulative effects would be diffused throughout globalized markets. The truth is, economic models that prescribe mindless budget cutting or heedless deficit expansion are equally antique.

Trade Expansion. Support for liberal trade is one of the Democratic Party's most venerable principles. It is also essential to reviving the U.S. economy: from 1986 to 1990, 25 percent of U.S. job growth came from expanded exports. Yet Faux and congressional liberals made common cause with Ross Perot, the hierarchy of organized labor, right-wing nativists, and others to demonize the North American Free Trade Agreement. In part, opposition to NAFTA stemmed from valid fears of the often harsh impact of globalization on traditional manufacturing. Let's be candid: it also reflected labor's determination to save specific jobs in specific industries, even at the expense of U.S. workers' general interest in expanding markets for their products.

This is old-fashioned protectionism, however much you dress it up with high-minded concern for the environment or for the wages and

working conditions of Mexicans. However, the conservative alternative
—global laissez faire without so much as a glance back at the people and
communities caught in the crosswinds of economic change—isn't any
better.

New Democrats aim for a new synthesis on trade that acknowledges
both the benefits of trade expansion as well as the jarring effects of global
competition on some U.S. workers, industries, and communities. This
approach envisions a new compact with American workers aimed at
providing new sources of job security to replace those now dissolving
under the pressure of international competition. It would include, for instance, school-based apprenticeship to help noncollege youth acquire career skills and a new "employment insurance system" to help vulnerable
workers get access to education and job training. Reinforced by reforms
of our education, health care, and welfare systems, such initiatives can
endow U.S. workers with the resources, flexibility, and security they
need to brave the challenges of global competition.

Reinventing Government. Faux misreads the New Democrats'
push for "reinventing government" as merely the latest call for stream-
lining federal bureaucracies. In fact, the goal is to revamp the organizational culture of the public sector. The premise of reinventing government is that top-down, centralized bureaucracies served useful purposes
during the industrial era but are lumbering anachronisms in the information age.

The notion of entrepreneurial government sets off alarms on both the
left and the right. Despite rising public spending, liberals view the failure
of bureaucratic systems, whether public schools or welfare or federal agencies, as a function of financing; if only we spent more, we'd get better results. Conservatives oppose on principle government's intrusion into the
domain of market competition and private preferences; just get government out of the way, and our problems will take care of themselves.

For New Democrats, the issue is not whether government should be
bigger or smaller, but whether it can be made a more responsive, effective, and democratic instrument of public purposes. Examples of a new,
nonbureaucratic model of public activism include the charter school
movement for public school choice; "green taxes" or charges that harness
market forces to make polluters pay to clean the environment; and actions by such Democratic mayors as Chicago's Rich Daley and Philadelphia's Ed Rendell to privatize some city services and inject competition
into others. Vice President Gore's National Performance Review likewise
proposes to hold federal managers accountable for results, make some
federal agencies compete with private vendors, and reform the civil service system so that managers can reward federal workers who excel and
weed out those who don't perform.

Americans believe government is broken and must be fixed. Liberals can try, against all evidence, to argue otherwise. The New Democrat alternative is to begin the painstaking work of reviving public confidence in progressive government by making government work.

Social Policy. Faux chides New Democrats for focusing too much on social issues. Evidently, he sees crime, welfare dependency, illegitimacy, family dissolution, intergenerational poverty, and their concatenation in our decaying cities as chiefly economic problems: get the economy booming again and the rising tide will cover our blighted social landscape. Such economic reductionism overlooks the complex interaction of economics and culture. It drains politics of moral sense. And it ignores an overwhelming consensus that our social systems cannot offer real opportunity if they fail to reward sound values: work, family, individual responsibility.

TAP readers curious about how social issues and racial polarization have dimmed liberal prospects should refer to *Chain Reaction* by Tom and Mary Edsall, analysts with impeccable liberal credentials. But consider one especially dramatic example: the meltdown of urban liberalism. From Los Angeles to New York, the failure of largely Democratic urban coalitions to arrest the dreary cycle of violence, economic stagnation, and middle-class flight has allowed Republicans to run as insurgents against feckless and corrupt city machines. In Los Angeles, Republican Richard Riordan won on a reform platform that resembled Bill Clinton's own "New Democrat" agenda. In overwhelmingly Democratic Jersey City Wall Street Republican Bret Schundler was reelected with 40 percent of the black vote and 60 percent of the Latino vote. In a close election that left the city sharply divided along racial lines, New York voters chose a Republican mayor for the first time since 1965. The evidence strongly suggests the decline, and perhaps the fall, of an urban politics characterized by high taxes, poor services, wealth transfers, and racial and ethnic entitlement—what Jim Sleeper has called "civic balkanization."

Faux seems oblivious to these maladies of modern, pressure group liberalism. New Democrats see them as emblematic of the poverty of a liberal materialism based on narrow interests and selfish demands for government entitlements. To succeed in the information age, Democrats must compete on the basis of broader ideas and principles that speak to the nation as a whole. The New Democrats' approach—which combines resolutely progressive ideas, nonbureaucratic ways of governing, and mainstream America values—moves the party in that direction.

[13b]

JEFF FAUX

The Evasion of Politics

Will Marshall makes my point. You wouldn't know it from his comments, but my article examined the contradictions in the New Democrats' claim that they represent a new progressive element in American politics. I concluded that the claim is false, and that its political appeal is in the intellectual and moral cover the claim provides for those who want to make the Democratic Party look more like the party of moderate Republicans.

Marshall does not engage the substance of my critique but instead offers a cliché-driven restatement of New Democrat ideology. Once again we have the familiar generalization about liberals. In the first three sentences, we have "liberal assumptions," "liberal orthodoxy," and "liberal dogma." And once again we have the hyped-up list of mainstream policies ("enterprise" economics, "entrepreneurial" government) that he claims represent new ideas but are, for the most part, watered-down versions of proposals liberals have been making for years.

Let's start with the phrase "the party's establishment," which Marshall uses to restate the core theory of New Democrat politics, that is, that the Democratic Party is run by "liberal fundamentalists" (elsewhere described as minority groups, labor unions, and white, elite, liberal purists) who are busy defending the "status quo—old programs and old policies." His authority for this are the sweeping generalizations of New Democrat writers William Galston and Elaine Kamarck, whose work I criticized in my article. This is like responding to the case against monarchy by citing the opinions of George III.

Marshall's idea of who is in the Democratic Party establishment is curious. In Marshall's view, its members are not power brokers like Robert Strauss, Clark Clifford, or Warren Christopher, or the big-time lobbyists like Tommy Boggs, Stu Eizenstat, or Ann Wexler. Lloyd Bentsen, Tom Foley, George Mitchell, and Sam Nunn are not to be seen. Nor is the establishment Washington glitterati who show up at the Democratic Leadership Conference's $1,500 a-plate black-tie galas. Poor Bob Strauss, spending all that time at White House dinners, having presidents and cabinet officers snap to attention when he calls on behalf of his clients. All this time he thought he and his friends were the Washington establishment. No, in the Orwellian world of Will Marshall, Strauss and gang are the "New Democrat outsiders." In this world, the party's strings are pulled by unnamed minority groups and purist liberals defending unspecified "old programs" and "old policies." Could have fooled me.

Washington is full of lobbyists for every cause. But to anyone who knows the town, the idea that, say, the Coalition for Human Rights wields as much power as any of a hundred business trade associations or any one of the Fortune 500 is absurd. Yet this nonsense continues to play well in the media; pundits learn early that it is in their career interest to avoid excessive attention to who greases the skids in Washington. Among those who run and manage newspapers, stories about big business influence quickly become tiresome "old politics." Much more interesting is the story of how politicians tremble before left-liberals dreaming of their rainbow coalition.

Marshall dismisses, without challenging the evidence I presented, my conclusion that most recent Democratic presidential candidates ran centrist campaigns. Then he blatantly misstates what I said. My exact words were, "With the exception of McGovern in 1972, in five of the last six presidential campaigns the Democratic candidates—Humphrey, Carter, Mondale, and Dukakis—ran as centrists." But it is even more revealing that Marshall leaves Carter off of the list. My point was that Jimmy Carter was the first New Democrat. If Marshall actually had thought through his position, one would think this would be an important issue to engage. He explicitly defines the problem of the Democratic Party as having arisen after 1968 and, presumably, ending with the election of New Democrat Clinton. George McGovern—the liberal—was blown away after 1972 and since then his influence on the party has been virtually nil (although conservatives periodically drag out his name and beat it up in public). Carter, on the other hand, was clearly the most influential force on the party during the years since 1968. But Carter is inconvenient; so he is expunged from the New Democrat history books. Indeed, Marshall's only rebuttal to the evidence I offered on the recent history of the party was to accuse me of rummaging through "old news clippings." That's a lot of what history is about, Will. It helps to smoke out people who are constantly "reinventing" themselves.

Fortunately for the New Democrats, the pundits don't much care about history, either. So there is no challenge when New Democrats like Marshall pluck dead Democratic heroes out of the past and put them to work at their ideological ax grinding. In one fell swoop, Marshall presses into such service every Democratic president from Andrew Jackson to Lyndon Johnson. (Again, where is Jimmy Carter?)

The notion that the Democratic Party is now composed of something called "special interest liberalism" as opposed to the romanticized past of a "New Deal middle-class populism" when people were united in the pursuit of the common good is, as I explained in my article, muddled. If ever there was a coalition of special interests, it was the New Deal: labor and farmers; minorities and racists; bureaucrats and small business. Coalitions are what achieving power in democratic politics is about.

Marshall's attempt to cast the memory of Robert Kennedy into this ideological puppet show is particularly inappropriate. It was Kennedy who challenged the centrist Johnson and the Washington military and political establishment over the war in Vietnam. He also challenged the centrists of the day with the community development program inspired by his experience in Bedford-Stuyvesant. As the person who designed and ran that program, I can attest that its spirit and perspective are not captured in the New Democrat view of the world.

By bowdlerizing history and defining only the Left as "special interests" and limiting their criticism of Republicans to the far Right, New Democrats indulge in the conceit that they alone reside somewhere in the cosmos beyond liberalism and conservativism where the "national" interest lies. This is humbug. The sanctimonious position that my interests are "national" and your interests are "special" stops common sense political discussion. But perhaps that is the point. Because interests, ideas, and ideals are different, the democratic process is inevitably confrontational.

It is Marshall's particular point that this confrontation between the Left and the Right has become worse in the last 20 years, thus spawning a yearning for New Democrat centrism. But there is little evidence that the 1990s are more confrontational than the 1960s. There is, instead, plenty of evidence that people today are angry and frustrated with the political process. My article takes the position that these attitudes are mostly driven by the decline in living standards and anxiety about the economic future, and restoring economic growth is the central problem a progressive politics must address.

My point is not that economics is the *only* problem. Who does not agree that society is plagued by violence, family breakup, and irresponsibility? But New Democrats—like many social issue activists on both the Right and Left—seem to prefer endless pontificating about the state of the human heart, over which they admit government has little influence, to getting on with the business of creating jobs, rebuilding cities, and educating children, about which government can do something. There is, after all, a pretty clear link between economic distress and social dysfunction. But stimulating development and jobs costs money. It also means making private economic institutions, as well as public bureaucracies, more accountable to the communities in which they produce and sell. New Democrats do not seem to have much stomach for the task. It's much easier to pretend that poverty can be eliminated by yet another reinvention of the welfare system.

Ironically, the one political personality over the last dozen years or so who has consistently and credibly offered a message of individual responsibility to combat the violence and hopelessness of the inner city has been Jesse Jackson, political enemy number one for the New Democrats. Their fierce hostility toward Jackson strengthens my suspicion that for New Democrats lecturing the poor on their social obligations is less about solving the problems of the disadvantaged than it is about assuring the advantaged that social justice can be had on the cheap.

In this context, Marshall's formulation of "solidarity" versus "adaptation" is revealing. In common usage, these two words are not opposites. Marshall puts them in opposition to set up a straw man: the Left as the obstacle to change. The obvious target here is the labor movement—for whom the term "solidarity" has a deep meaning.

No serious person argues against adapting to change. History and nature force adaptation. The question is, how? Here we come to a real issue. Like mainstream Republicans, New Democrats would have us face the unfettered global marketplace as individuals. The labor-liberal tradition in America, on the other hand, is one that stresses adapting to changes in the world as a community, as a nation. The theory is that through collective action, we can guide and master change, not simply respond to it. And if this means slowing down the rate of change to reduce the level of dislocation and human loss, then so be it. This is an old debate driven by differences of class and values. Like the Republican Right, New Democrats talk incessantly about "values." But as one probes for that word's operative meaning, it turns out that the highest priority is given to the measures of worth created by buying and selling in the international marketplace. On every major issue, New Democrats come down on the side of prices rather than values.

The debate over NAFTA illuminated this question as few recent issues have. In one sense, the debate was a test of Marshall's extraordinary claim that the New Democrats, with their conscious strategy of ingratiating themselves with big business, speak for America's "working middle class." Whatever one thinks about the general idea of freer trade with Mexico, anyone who actually reads the 2,000-page-plus package cannot help but be struck by the disparity between the way it provides detailed protections for those who invest and the way it leaves defenseless the interests of those who work. Indeed, that is its purpose. None of the governments involved need NAFTA just to lower trade barriers. They could have done that with a one-page letter of agreement.

Thus, the list of allies to the pro-NAFTA New Democrats contains few surprises: George Bush, Ronald Reagan, Jimmy Carter, Gerald Ford, Richard Nixon, Henry Kissinger, all living ex-treasury secretaries, the chief executive officers of virtually every major corporation, just about all of the national media, probably 90 percent of the nation's academic economists, and the massive resources of the U.S. and Mexican governments. In the world according to Marshall, NAFTA represents the spirit of working-class populism in revolt against the establishment. But polls taken just before the NAFTA vote showed that college graduates and those making over $50,000 were for NAFTA. Non-college graduates (75 percent of the labor force) and those making under $50,000 were overwhelmingly against it.

Perhaps this upside-down view of class divisions accounts for Marshall's odd comment that my use of the word Bubba was "derisive." The term was a political allusion that obviously went over Marshall's head. My specific inspiration was a puff piece for the New Democrats by conservative Fred Barnes in the New Republic in which Clinton is depicted as "crying out privately for more centrist input. On speech drafts and memos, he jots plaintive questions like, 'Where's Bubba?'" Get with the program, Will.

Of course, Marshall offers the obligatory sympathy for workers with "valid fears of the often harsh impact of globalization," and goes on to express New Democrats' pious hopes that the problems will be solved by retraining programs. Even if we strain our credulity by accepting this premise, the fact is that all we have is a promise that such programs will be available sometime in the indefinite future—if we ever find the money.

If New Democrats were serious about their own proposals for economic security, they would have insisted that we put these programs in place before NAFTA. Moreover, the demand of New Democrats that we give priority to deficit reduction over economic stimulation guarantees that the economy will be operating at high levels of unemployment for years to come, and that long-term erosion in the living standards of the average American worker will continue. The fact is that without maintaining a strong demand for labor—"full employment" as the New Deal middle-class populists used to call it—the structural shifts necessary for this nation to successfully adapt to economic change will be constantly undermined by working-class economic fears.

Marshall's regurgitation of the New Democrat policy agenda is not impressive. As I said in my article, there is much in it that any sensible liberal supports. The practical problem is that in the real world, New

Democrats don't seem to be willing to put their money where their mouth is and pay for the programs. The ideological problem lies in the bizarre logic that an agenda of compromise between Right and Left represents a new political philosophy beyond Right and Left, which in turn justifies drumming liberals out of the Democratic Party.

Like intellectual claim-jumpers, New Democrats seize policy innovations from anywhere and tout them as unique to themselves, even when they contradict each other. Marshall wants more spending and spending restraint. He wants new priorities and not a word about the still-bloated military budget. His listing of proposals is devoid of context, as if liberals haven't been fighting for years for public investment, job training, and welfare reform. Marshall announces that crime is a major problem in America as if no one else in the Democratic Party has ever noticed.

And what is the program? When writing for us policy wonks (look it up in *Mandate for Change*), it consists of a national police corps, community policing, the Brady Bill, and better funding for drug treatment and education efforts. Can anyone distinguish this list from the generic liberal strategy? I'll grant there is one difference: when it comes time to pander to middle-class anxieties, New Democrats celebrate the death penalty, coyly obscured for readers of *The American Prospect* as Bill Clinton's "tough-minded line on crime." This, we are told, is a new courageous and innovative progressive position.

For New Democrats, hardly a political sparrow falls from the sky that they do not claim is a portent for their cause. Marshall glories in Democratic defeats in Los Angeles and New York. Democrats lose in New Jersey and Virginia, and DLC president Al From tells the admiring *Wall Street Journal* that the election was "a great day for New Democrats." But isn't Virginia the home of the New Democrats? And if, as the New Democrats would have it, crime is the single most important issue, why did Governor Jim Florio lose, when his "tough-minded" position on crime was to the right of his Republican opponent? Polls showed that Florio won substantially among those who thought crime was New Jersey's biggest problem. Forgive me for suspecting that had Florio been reelected it would have been hailed as another vindication of the New Democrat strategy.

My response does not by any means exhaust the contradictions embodied in Marshall's letter. The interested reader will pick out more of them without much trouble—particularly those designed to convince us that the political cynicism of New Democrats really reflects their moral superiority over liberals.

There is, of course, always a case to be made for cynicism. So let New Democrats argue that it is smart politics for Democrats to attack liberal labor, and minority constituencies. Let them try to persuade us that

Bill Clinton can be reelected on George Bush's economic program. Let them make the case that Democrats should appeal to white males by stuffing more people into the electric chair.

But spare us the crocodile tears for the working class. And spare us the pretense that this represents a serious rethinking of liberalism.

[14]

WALTER DEAN BURNHAM

The Politics of Repudiation 1992: Edging toward Upheaval

For a generation the United States has experienced a complex and deepening crisis of its political and economic order. Three pivotal and highly abnormal elections have punctuated this crisis. In 1968, undermined by the Vietnam War and the civil rights revolution, the New Deal order collapsed. A new electoral regime emerged from the ruins, marked by three main features: normal Republican control of the presidency; divided government as the (unprecedented) norm; and a candidate-dominated "permanent campaign," in which a capital-intensive personalism crowded out labor-intensive political parties.

In the 1970s, severe economic crisis replaced Vietnam as a driving issue. Its effects (stagnation and price-inflation coupled with low real interest rates) were reinforced by signs of foreign policy weakness and the emergence of the socioreligious right. The stage was set for Ronald Reagan and right-wing "conviction politics" designed to stop the rot on all fronts. A massive policy realignment ensued as Reagan and his allies launched their brand of political, economic, and social revitalization, confident that their new regime was both viable and durable.

But the 1992 election repudiated that attempted synthesis and its rhetorical, coalitional, and public-policy regime. Its policy consequences will long outlive the political order—particularly public debt exceeding 50 percent of the 1992 gross domestic product. Even Republicans agree that the Reagan-Bush era in American political history is over, mainly because it failed economically. The promises and dreams of the 1980s were liquidated not only by persistent recession but by its association with a massive, structural downsizing of American capitalism. More than any of its postwar predecessors, this recession has raised acute anxiety within

187

the broad American middle class—anxiety not just for their own future but for their children's. Average real family income eroded under George Bush and growth was lower across this presidential term than in any during the past sixty years.

Considering that two entire political worldviews and regime orders associated with them had achieved bankruptcy within the space of a dozen years, we should hardly wonder that public demands for "change" were as loud as they were unclear or confused. Nor is it surprising that the general political atmosphere among the electorate in 1992 was so disturbed and filled with rage against politicians or that for a few weeks in early summer Ross Perot led both major-party candidates in the polls.

To a quite unusual extent, 1992 presents a broad panorama of analytic issues associated with American presidential elections. An incumbent president running for reelection was defeated, but this was no ordinary defeat. Both his conduct in office and his defeat at the polls identify for us just what kind of incumbent George Bush was. Ross Perot, capitalizing on an immense breadth of public discontent with the existing order and its leadership, won the third largest share of the total vote ever secured by a nonmajor-party candidate in American history. Our task here is to attempt to provide a reasonably integrated account of what happened and why in the pivotal election of 1992.

The Permanent Campaign and the Interregnum State

Out of the crisis of the 1960s, a genuine critical realignment crystallized, unlike any in previous history. Its main characteristic was not a shift in voting preferences but the partial dissolution of the traditional linkages between elite and public, mediated by the traditional party system. At the presidential level, the McGovern-Fraser commission reforms led to direct primaries at the center of the nominating process. This formed a major break with the past and seemingly energized grass-roots voting participation. But at almost the same moment, a series of other "reforms" stimulated political action committees and other forms of political entrepreneurship. These combined with the rapid growth of campaign technology—polling, focus groups, targeting, paid ads, and personalist campaigns—to shift the entire system away from voting participation and toward financial participation. In what Sidney Blumenthal was the first to call the "permanent campaign," congressional incumbents made sure that no reform was undertaken that could give their challengers an even break, and the money rolled in.

The decline of party in turn led to a decline in the competitiveness of congressional seats (one sees glimmerings as early as the 1966 congressional elections). Apart from temporary upticks in 1974 and 1982, this trend continued from the late 1960s through 1988, a year when incumbents in House races seeking reelection numbered more than 400 of the 435 members of the House, and their reelection rate hit 98.5 percent. More generally, as a comparison of presidential and senatorial election outcomes also clearly demonstrates, for the first time in American history discrete electoral coalitions—different ones for different offices—emerged. Thus in 1984 Ronald Reagan was the winner in 375 congressional districts, only 182 of which also elected Republican representatives. How did incumbents on the Democratic side do so well? It was easy: All they had to do was run *on average* 19 percentage points ahead of Walter Mondale in their districts.

This intersected with the chief, *governing* feature of this sixth electoral era,* which I call the "interregnum state": the *divided government* that has lately intrigued political scientists. (See Richard Valelly, "Divided They Govern," *TAP* Fall 1992.) The critical realignment of the late 1960s led to a normal Republican majority in presidential elections five out of six elections, twenty of twenty-four years since 1968–69. For six years during this period, a quarter of the time, Republicans also enjoyed a majority in the U.S. Senate, but never in the House. The Madisonian separation of powers and its policy-fragmenting implications were thus reinforced by changed behavior in the electorate; the opposite of what the traditional party system (at its best) was designed to produce. Instead, by 1989 George Bush entered office with fewer partisan supporters in Congress than any of his predecessors across two centuries of American politics.

The Republican House minority in 1981 was large enough, in conjunction with Republican control of the Senate, to enact the major features of Ronald Reagan's tax-and-budget "revolution." But these forces were not strong enough to permit a complete clinical experiment in squaring the policy circle: cutting taxes, raising defense spending, and cutting enough outlay elsewhere to keep the budget deficit from exploding. This was to have long-term political consequences, not least of which was the Perot candidacy of 1992. On an increasingly exaggerated scale,

---

* Readers interested in the previous five eras should consult the author's *Critical Elections and the Mainsprings of American Politics* (New York: Norton, 1970), which suggests that the political history of the United States can be divided roughly into chronological eras, "systems," or regime orders, each separated from the other by a "critical realignment" of voting preferences, sociopolitical cleavages, and issue coalitions. These eras are: the early Federal period (circa 1780–1824); the democratizing or Jacksonian era (1828–1860); the Civil War era or "system" (1854/60–1892); the industrial-capitalist era or "System of 1896" (1894/6–1932); the New Deal era (1932–1968).

divided government produced a bizarre mix of collusion, collision, and buck-passing in public policy—the very negation of accountability.

It is no wonder that the first omnibus budget resolution presented to the House in October 1990, after months of tortuous negotiations among top congressional and executive leaders, was voted down in a wave of resentment among ordinary members of Congress who had been cut out of the whole process. It is no wonder that a key factor in the collapse of public support for George Bush in 1992 was his repudiation of his 1988 pledge, "Read my lips: No new taxes." It is no wonder that by 1991, the Kettering Foundation should find extraordinary levels not of apathy but of anger, rage even, against politics and politicians, captured so well in E.J. Dionne's *Why Americans Hate Politics.* Ordinary Americans, like ordinary members of Congress, strongly resent being dealt out of a political system that affects their lives while being expected to pick up the tab or provide the votes. Nor, given all this, is it any wonder that the voters of all fourteen states that had term limits proposals on their ballots in November 1992 approved them. This may be (as I believe) a bad idea whose time is rapidly coming. But it represents an enduring truth of American politics that for every action that closes off the elite world within the Beltway from the voters outside, there is likely sooner or later to be an equal and opposite reaction arising from said voters.

Significantly, while surveys throughout the 1980s indicated popular support for divided government, polls in 1992 showed a swing in attitude: most Americans now preferred candidates of the same party win the presidency and control Congress too. In the foreseeable structure of electoral politics, this party can only be the Democratic Party. It remains to be seen whether its new team can govern effectively, but for the moment the electorate is giving it the chance. Thus there is an implicit "race" underway between the willingness of the voters to entrust government to the Democrats and the current passion for term limits. The latter is the latest upsurge of a basic idea-set going back to the Progressive era at the turn of the century: that mechanically imposed, immaculately conceived structural solutions can work to cure the ills of American democracy. The former places real contestation at the heart of politics through parties that are vital and coherent enough to address the problems of the country. We shall see, across Bill Clinton's term and later, how this race will be decided in our own time.

From 1961 through 1981, the country endured five aborted presidencies in a row, four of which were repudiations (Johnson, Nixon, Ford, Carter): a sequence also without historical precedent. Now it has repudiated yet another. There do appear to be rare occasions in American political history when a consensus develops that we simply cannot go on like this any longer, that the impasse in our collective affairs has become insupportable. Some such consensus crystallized between the extraordinarily revealing Pennsylvania Senate election of November 1991 and the spring of 1992, and it was to be fatal to George Bush's bid for reelection. Nor was this a narrow loss. Measured in sheer quantitative terms, George Bush's loss of 15.9 percent of the total vote between his first election and his second was exceeded only three times in *all* of American history: in 1932, when Herbert Hoover's share of the total vote declined 18.6 percent from 1928; in 1800, when John Adams experienced a decline of 20.4 percent from 1796; and in 1912, when (with Theodore Roosevelt stealing more than half of the Republican electorate) William Howard Taft suffered an erosion of 28.4 percent of the total vote from his 1908 level. Whatever else 1992 may have been, it was a classic case of a landslide vote of no confidence in an incumbent president and the regime he led. Of twenty-nine incumbents seeking reelection or election to a full term across two centuries of American history, in terms of this measure of interelection swing, George Bush in 1992 ranked twenty-sixth, no mean feat that.

Thus in less than a generation, two whole ways of doing our political business, interest-group liberalism and now Reaganite capitalism redux, have been swept into the discard. We should not wonder at the deep sense of rage, bafflement, and confusion that marked the electoral season of 1992 from New Hampshire in March to November's final outcome. Can a system experience personal and structural repudiations of this magnitude, and within very few years, before the system itself is placed at risk? Some such question lies at the heart of the remarkable election of 1992.

Bush: A Third-Term Understudy

If Jimmy Carter had many of the attributes of a historical accident (as I think he did), George Bush seems almost a historical inevitability. He is a near-classic exemplar of a category of presidents extending across political history—the failed understudy.

In twenty-four of the fifty-two presidential elections held since 1789, incumbents originally elected to a full term have run to succeed themselves. Of these, fifteen won, while nine lost their bids for another term. Five of these losers, along with a narrow winner (Madison in 1812), form a distinct subset. Each was chosen to carry on the policies of a recently successful and policy-innovative regime, under conditions where the previous leaders of this regime are unavailable for an additional term themselves. George Bush is the first of them in sixty years. These six "understudy" or "conservator" candidates are: John Adams (Federalist, 1797–1801), succeeding George Washington; James Madison (Demo-

cratic-Republican, 1809–1817), succeeding Thomas Jefferson; Martin Van
Buren (Democrat, 1837–1841), succeeding Andrew Jackson; William
Howard Taft (Republican, 1909–1913), succeeding Theodore Roosevelt;
Herbert Hoover (Republican, 1929–1933), succeeding Calvin Coolidge;
and George Bush succeeding Ronald Reagan.

What else do these men have in common? For one thing, all faced
crises that grew directly out of the policies of their predecessors and their
regimes, which buffeted the understudies' term of office. Second, each of
them (with perhaps the admitted exception of Hoover) succeeded presidents who were regarded as heroic, charismatic or successful in their
own time: acts that were indeed hard to follow, sorcerers whose appren-
tice successors would have had to be truly remarkable to fill the voids
left behind. But, third, each of them was selected precisely to give "four
more years" of the same, not to engage in even timely innovations on
any large scale. George Bush, for example, was selected (and elected)
precisely because he was expected to preserve the Reagan legacy in as
nearly pure and undefiled a form as possible. People chosen as understudies, one may assume, are chosen precisely because they are *not* inno-
vators, and the "vision thing" seems much less of a problem when the
point of the exercise is conservation of the political gains and commitments secured during the immediate past.

Fourth, each of them came to office replete with exceptional *resumes*.
Adams, Washington's vice president, had been a key intellectual and ac-
tor before the establishment of the constitutional order in 1787. Madison
had been Jefferson's secretary of state, as had Van Buren (in addition to
the latter's additional services as vice president). A superb insider politician who was a true innovator in building party organization to channel
the new mass electorate, Van Buren had extensive partisan experience as
well. Taft had been selected initially to be governor-general of the newly
acquired Philippines, a job he loved, and subsequently became Theodore
Roosevelt's secretary of war. His is the classic case of being hand-picked
by his predecessor to succeed him. Hoover, with impressive credentials
in organizing relief efforts in Belgium and Russia, served Harding and
Coolidge faithfully as secretary of commerce, an important job in the age
of corporatism. George Bush had perhaps the most glittering *resume* of
all: not only Ronald Reagan's vice president for eight years, but before
that Republican national chairman and (under Gerald Ford) director of
the CIA.

The *resumes* underscore the integral and basic relationship between
the understudy and the regime he comes to represent. These men were
anything but political outsiders. But they also tended to share a fifth
characteristic: As insiders they not only lacked the common touch but
were often perceived at the time—sometimes even by themselves (Madi-

son and Taft, for example)—as lacking elemental qualities needed for effective presidential leadership. Each in his own way was conspicuously vulnerable to attack as elitist, out of touch with the public, and indifferent to the plight of ordinary Americans—a charge that was reinforced in most cases by their rigidity and inadaptability.

The sixth and final attribute of these understudies follows: All but Madison lost their bids for reelection. (He was saved by the unique structural characteristics of the so-called "first party system" and the hegemonic position of the Jeffersonian Republican Party in it.) But, Van Buren apart, these were no ordinary losses. Their share of the total vote from their first to their second races collapsed by a mean 16.9 percent. This contrasts with a decline of 6.8 percent for the five other incumbents losing their seats, and an increase averaging just under 4 percent for the eighteen incumbents (excluding Madison) who were reelected. All five of the bottom-swing presidents (those with the largest losses from their first to their second election) were third-term understudies. The only other presidents who came close were Gerald Ford in 1976 (–12.7 percent from Nixon's total in 1972), who had never been elected nationwide even as vice president, and Jimmy Carter in 1980 (–9.1 percent, as compared with Bush's –15.9 percent in 1992).

The 1992 Republican campaign was true to context. Exceptionally clear warning had been given to Bush and his campaign staff by Harris Wofford's trouncing of Richard Thornburgh in the Pennsylvania Senate race one year earlier (as Adams and the Federalist elite had been put on clear notice by the same state's 1799 gubernatorial election). Nothing worthwhile was done in response, thought many Republicans who were keenly aware of what was going on. The party convention at Houston, with its dramatic and off-putting stress on family values and the agenda of the socioreligious right, put its worst foot forward just as did the 1964 Goldwater convention and the 1972 Democratic convention that nominated George McGovern. But these had been *out-party* assemblies; here, in 1992, an *in-party* was providing a symbolically similar, off-putting show, something the Republicans had previously avoided even in the pits of 1932.

Thereafter, anything-but-the-economy—chiefly stressing doubts about Bill Clinton's character and trustworthiness—became the overriding theme of George Bush's message to the voters. After all, something similar had worked in 1988, hadn't it? But in 1992, voters weren't buying, and remarkably, in the second presidential debate a small number of them in the room forced the thematics back onto substantive economic issues. It was in this debate, when Bush kept looking at his watch and stumbled when asked how he personally had been affected by the recession, that his defects as a candidate were brought home—literally—to tens of millions of viewers; he was "out of touch" and he "just didn't get it." In the end, he broke another kind of historic record. Receiving just 37.5 percent of the total 1992 vote, he ranked twenty-eighth of the twenty-nine incumbents running for a full term across two centuries. Only Taft in 1912, with less than half of his party still behind him, and a former President as the third party candidate, did worse (23.2 percent). Even Hoover in 1932 managed to hold on to 39.6 percent of those voting in that election.

Bill Clinton and the "New Democrats"

After the dazzling success of Operation Desert Storm, which pushed Bush's approval rating to 90 percent, the presumed heavy hitters on the Democratic side found one reason or another not to present themselves for consideration, and by very early 1992 a group of secondary candidates had emerged. One of these was the "obscure" governor of a small and backward state, Bill Clinton of Arkansas. Now is hardly the time for any kind of extensive review of the entire campaign, which in any case has already been covered remarkably well by the print media in the public domain. Through thick and thin, good times and bad, Clinton—like the Energizer bunny in the TV ads—just kept on going and going and going. Demolishing his opponents within the party, his successful tactical choice for the general-election campaign was to take the high road and focus on what his campaign manager, James Carville, had tacked up in the campaign office: "The economy, stupid." He had given abundant evidence that he was very smart, capable of absorbing vast amounts of information and making some sense of it, gifted (perhaps at times too gifted) with words, and perhaps one of the really great natural hands-on politicians of our day. All this was not enough to still persistent public doubts about him (hence one reason for the size of Ross Perot's vote), or to give the public a clear sense of who the "real" Bill Clinton was. But it was more than enough to win, especially in the context we have been describing.

Bill Clinton's rise does represent a real break with the Democratic Party's past, but the nuances of that break have yet to be defined. When Ross Perot bowed out of the race on July 16, citing as a reason a "revitalized Democratic party," he was pointing to a situation in which a candidate less liberal than the party as a whole (and, except perhaps for Jimmy Carter, than its previous nominees) had been selected as its standard-bearer. It was no coincidence that Clinton had been a leading figure in the Democratic Leadership Council (DLC), an intraparty group whose aim was to move the party and its choice of nominee toward the center of the American political spectrum. With old-style interest group liberalism dead beyond retrieval as a dominant part of any winning presidential coalition, and with its coffin double-sealed by debt, deficit, and basic economic-reproduction problems left behind as a prime legacy of the Reagan-Bush era, the specific 1992 conjuncture was especially favorable for producing a nominee who could win a presidential election, even though a Democrat. As usual in such cases, the man and the moment met: Clinton carried the suburbs, won pluralities in all family-income groups under $75,000 per year, won the support of far more than half of the Democrats who had voted for Ronald Reagan in 1984 (69 percent to 31 percent for Bush on a two-party basis), held Bush to a tie among white voters as a whole, and otherwise enjoyed an exceptionally broad plurality sweep over the incumbent everywhere except the South and isolated pockets elsewhere.

Yet the apparent rightward shift is more complex than that advertised by the DLC. For Clinton believes in activist government, is married to a feminist, and began his tenure as president-elect by reaffirming his support for gays serving in the military. Although he made the necessary inroads into the middle class, he did it without writing off blacks, gays, feminists, greens, or trade unionists—the dreaded "liberal fundamentalists" in the dismissive phrase of DLC demonologists William Galston and Elaine Ciulla Kamarck. Indeed, his support among traditional liberals was about normal, or even better.

The most enduring reality of modern American electoral politics at least where economic issues are concerned—is that the Democrats have been the pro-state party and the Republicans the anti-state party. Clinton and his coalition of supporters will have as a prime objective the reclamation of this heritage, while overcoming their image as the party of bureaucracy. Despite the Democratic Leadership Council's embrace of Clinton and its own resolute centrism, government once again is to be seen as capable of making positive, indeed essential, contributions to a twenty-first century American economy in a thoroughly competitive and interdependent world.

What such a vision has going for it, in truth, is not the clarity of its program (yet) but simply the force of circumstances, *la forza del destino*. To remain competitive in the longer run with our economic rivals and to revitalize the domestic economy and thereby the well-being of the country's inhabitants and their progeny, some such development of a new role for the state will be a major part of the price. It could just happen that, with success along these lines, the older Republican state-as-(necessary?)evil ideology will become as *passé* as the once-sacred doctrines of isolation became in the 1940s and 1950s. But to succeed, Clinton will have to take on sacred programmatic cows, which could make him enemies in Congress. If he doesn't redefine a convincing, affirmative role for

government, he will not be doing his job of building the harmonistic political economy that is central to this new effort to find a way out of crisis
and decline.

Clinton of course takes office as a minority president, elected by just
42.9 percent of those who went to the polls. Leaving aside the special
case of John Quincy Adams in the free-for-all of 1824, fifteen of our fifty-
two presidential elections have produced minority winners. Clinton's
support ranks third from the bottom in this category: only Woodrow
Wilson in 1912 (41.8 percent) and Abraham Lincoln in 1860 (39.8 percent)
were elected with a narrower base of support.

On the positive side, it is noteworthy that in terms of an elected minority president's percentage lead over the runner-up, Clinton finishes a
robust fourth out of these fifteen cases (5.5 percent); and if percentages of
the electoral vote are used as a criterion, Clinton (at 68.8 percent) comes
in a strong second only to Wilson in 1912 (81.9 percent). Moreover, Wilson (at least in his first term) and Lincoln, below him in the share of the
vote, had personal qualities and political contexts favorable to active and
highly successful presidencies. Even Nixon, just above him at 43.4 percent, was both a reasonably strong and reasonably successful president
until ruination set in with the disclosure of the Watergate affair early in
his second term.

However, Clinton, with a considerably smaller working majority in
Congress than they enjoyed, would seem to have far less room for maneuver than Wilson or Lincoln. The budget deficit will also hem in his
programmatic running room, as will his tightrope act between the old
and new Democrats. Clinton has a clear constitutional mandate. Any
more extensive mandate will have to be fought for and won.

Alienation, Television, and Perot

Whenever major third entrants appear in presidential elections, they reflect a breakdown of the system's legitimacy: the greater the share secured by such candidates, the greater the breakdown. This has happened
ten times in American political history, with twelve cases of significant
insurgency (1860 and 1912 produced two significant-insurgency candidacies). With 18.9 percent of the total vote, Ross Perot finished a strong
third among these twelve. Moreover, the other two cases involved major
fragments of organized major parties—Millard Fillmore and the Whig-
Americans of 1856 (21.5 percent) and Theodore Roosevelt and his Progressive wing of the Republican Party in 1912 (27.4 percent). Perot's
showing is by far the most impressive ever achieved by that other category of third movements, the pure outsider or "protest" surge.

The data in the *New York Times'* early postelection survey makes it clear that, with few exceptions, Perot's support cut remarkably evenly across the whole spectrum. Perot was strongest among partisan independents, young men, liberal Republicans (a chemical trace in a sample these days!), and a few other categories, and weakest among blacks, Jews, the elderly, and a number of white Democratic voting groups. Regionally there were important differentials. Perot was strongest in New England—his best state was Maine, where fully 30.1 percent voted for him and he edged out Bush for second place—and in the Plains states and Mountain West. He was weakest in the greater South, except for the burgeoning states of Texas and Florida. Yet the general impression is that his appeal cut broadly across most voter categories without (unlike George Wallace in 1968) being concentrated very heavily in any. At the very end, the *USA Today*/CNN Gallup poll reported that when Perot voters were asked how they would have voted if Perot were not in the race, the response was 38 percent for Clinton, 36 percent for Bush, and 6 percent for "others"; 15 percent would not have come to the polls and another 5 percent gave no response. So Perot did not change the outcome. Had he not run, the only notable effect would have been to reduce the turnout from about 56 percent to 54 percent. As there is a distinct historic pro-Republican cast to those groups and areas most penetrated by Perot, this may be one more bit of evidence for our general case that Bush suffered a vote of no-confidence in 1992—though in this hypothetical exercise no landslide would have been involved.

Perot represents something quite new in American politics: the *enragé* billionaire Lone Ranger who demonstrated a near-perfect appreciation and use of television to build his following and sell his message. This message concentrated concretely on that part of the poisonous legacy of the past dozen years that produced the deficit and a hugely swollen national debt. But in more general terms, his claim was that the political system as such was broken. In a real sense, he virtually acted out the script that E.J. Dionne and others had been writing for sometime: it was necessary to transcend the politics of deadlock and finger-pointing, it was necessary to find some immaculate way of producing correct policy without traditional politics getting in the way.

The extraordinary breadth of his support across the land reflects at least two facts of contemporary political life in the U.S. The first of these is the power of "infomercials" and last-minute TV blitzkrieg backed by unlimited reserves of money to reach and appeal to "common sense." The second is the uncanny fit between Perot's general political symbolism and the pervasive public sense that Washington insiders and powerful interest groups had stolen the political system from the people.

This candidacy is a warning. It reflects some sort of dialectical acceleration in the decay of traditional parties and channels of authentic mass political action, a decay that I and others have discussed with growing alarm for the past twenty years. Vast numbers of Americans are now poised on the brink of taking a great leap into the unknown as they seek a savior from endless crises and an equally endless squeeze on their living standards. More than nineteen million did so in 1992. We have noted that the Democratic-led version of interest group liberalism went bankrupt in 1968, and conclusively in 1980, and that Reaganism led by the Republicans has achieved bankruptcy in its turn. If the new state-centered redevelopment synthesis of the Clinton years should fail in its turn, what then? Virtually nothing readily imaginable would remain in the repertoire; we would have played out all our options. At that point, one more heave could do the job: The first completely self-financed candidate in American history, Ross Perot becomes president after winning the 1996 election. At that point (if it ever arrives), we will enter an entirely new phase of our political history. In the wake of 1992, we are measurably closer to it.

Demographics and the Vote

The 1992 election was a repudiation, but not a radical realignment. Elections are won as a rule by shifts at the margins. Bill Clinton's 53.4 percent of the two-party vote is impressive under the circumstances, but it was no popular-vote landslide. And there have been considerably larger two-party swings in our recent past than the 7 percent pro-Democratic swing that occurred nationally from 1988 to 1992. The basic long-term demographic patterns within which this election was decided go back a generation; the overhang from the past is impressively powerful. Notwithstanding the collapse of both Carter and Bush, more than three-quarters of the variance in the 1992 distribution of votes can be explained by the aggregate voter-group preferences in 1976; in terms of basic voting alignments, not much has changed in sixteen years. When we ask which groups line up which way, the short answer is that given by Captain Louis Renault in *Casablanca:* Round up the usual suspects. Groups (very often overlapping, of course) that gave Clinton more than 60 percent of the two-party vote include, in order, blacks (88 percent), Jews (87 percent), voters in the lowest family-income bracket, less than $15,000 per year (72 percent), Hispanics (71 percent), members of union households (70 percent), the unemployed (70 percent), voters in the lowest education level, less than completed high school (66 percent), first-time voters (62 percent), and unmarried voters (60 percent). At the other end of the distribution are those groups in which Bush prevailed over Clinton. These include, in order, white voters (49 percent Democratic), those with a completed college education (49 percent), voters in the medium-high family-income bracket, $50,000-$74,999 (49 percent), voters in the South (49 percent), white men (47 percent), voters in the top income bracket, $75,000 and over (43 percent), white Protestants (42 percent), and white born-again Christians (27 percent). There are very few surprises in either list. The survey also makes clear that partisanship coupled with ideology forms a far more powerful long-term continuity factor than demographics.

Even without regard for the moment to the Perot presence in the race, the differentials in the 1988–1992 swing across voter groups make it clear that Bill Clinton's strategy of focusing on the economy and targeting his main appeal to the white middle class was brilliantly successful. This election was above all a revolt of the moderates, a point which the relative strengths and weaknesses of Perot's candidacy in the electorate simply underscores. Demographic and political groups with a two-party Democratic swing of 10 percent or more include Jews (+22); first-term voters (+14); moderate partisan independents (+12); members of union households (+12); voters with complete college educations (+12); voters aged 18–29 (+11); voters with some college education (+11); white men (+11); partisan independents, as a whole (+10); and moderates, as a whole (+10). Groups showing the least Democratic swing include liberal Republicans (–2); blacks (0); Hispanics (+1); liberals (+1); liberal Democrats (+2); conservative Republicans (+2); conservatives as a whole (+3); Republicans as a whole (+3); voters with complete high-school educations (+5); and voters with second lowest family incomes, $15,000–$29,999 (+5). And, according to a *USA Today* survey, Clinton carried suburban voters over Bush. Among Democrats voting for Reagan in 1984, their 1992 choice was Clinton, 55 percent; Bush, 25 percent; and Perot, 20 percent—a two-party Democratic lead of 38 points. Careful readers examining the Democratic percentages in the most-Republican groups discussed earlier will probably be less impressed by the expected (their relative ranking) than by the fact that Bush's lead over Clinton was generally very thin indeed.

With Perot in the race, net voter support for both major-party candidates declined from the two-party 1988 contest, but Bush's decline was more than five times as large as was that on the Democratic side (–16 percent versus –3 percent). George Bush lost 29 percent of his 1988 voting base, one of the largest single-election declines of its sort ever seen. This relative collapse covers a very wide and remarkably heterogeneous list of voter groups, being notably limited only among blacks (–8 percent) and Hispanics (–17 percent). And as Perot represented one considerable part of the public's overall judgment that George Bush had been weighed in the balance and found wanting, so his last-minute mini-surge reflected another basic reality of 1992: Bill Clinton had not completely closed his sale of himself as the agent of change from the rejected *status quo* of 1992.

Nonetheless, the highest strategic marks should be given to Governor Clinton, his master tactician James Carville, and other key actors in his campaign. To win, Clinton had to develop an appeal to "middle America" that recent Democratic nominees have lacked. He was successful in this, and in distancing himself from tight relationships with core interest-group liberal constituencies, yet without disavowing them—a deft balancing act. Ross Perot helped by drawing from segments of the electorate that might otherwise have drifted back to George Bush. The strategy was deplored by some urban liberals, but it may have been the only way through the maze to success in 1992. Despite his huge 1988–1992 losses, George Bush might very well have won this election confronted by a less dynamic opponent pursuing a more traditional Democratic campaign strategy. The key to success lay in capitalizing effectively on the revolt of the moderates, the preponderant majority of whom had voted for Reagan and Bush over the past three elections. Even in 1992, this could not have been done by just any Democratic nominee.

The Robust Republicans

Before the actual returns came in, the question hovered in the air as to whether this election was another 1932. It wasn't, because the old partisan voting linkages just aren't there any more and new ones have not been cemented. Republicans gained nine seats in the House contests and broke even in the Senate races. By contrast, the Republicans lost eighty-two incumbent congressmen in 1932. In 1860–61, Lincoln's position as a national minority president was much improved when more than seventy Southern representatives and twenty-one senators left the union with their states. With FDR, Wilson, and Lincoln, overwhelming legislative majorities accompanied the new administration into office. This is not the case this year. If 1992 was a landslide rejection of an incumbent Republican president, his party was scarcely affected.

This can be read in a variety of ways, of course. Republicans were chagrined that a "golden," post-reapportionment, post-scandal opportunity had been lost to make far greater gains than this. There were more open seats in the House (91) than at any time since the First World War. Considering the levels of public rage against incumbents the polls had monitored all year, a real slaughter of sitting Democrats seemed perfectly possible. Turnovers of as many as 150 House seats were contemplated. The payoff on election day, however, was surprisingly modest. Thirteen Democratic incumbents were ousted, as were six Republicans, while another three Democrats and a Republican lost to their opponents where apportionment forced them to run against each other. As for the open seats, Democrats won them by a 57–34 margin and partisan switches in this category canceled each other out. The Republicans' great expectations were once again dashed; but they were hardly irrational.

Following the civil rights act of 1982, Republicans pursued a very often successful "aggregation" strategy of drawing districts designed to elect blacks or Latinos and thus draw off votes on which many white Democrats had relied for their election. Many of the competitive seats narrowly won by Democrats in 1992 probably represent "land mines" for the future. Thus the 176 Republicans in the next Congress represent a situation that, from Clinton's point of view, could have been worse, and may very well become so across the 1990s.

The congressional election was notable on a number of dimensions. The number of House seats where there was no major-party opposition plummeted to 29, the lowest number (and proportion) since 1900. The number and proportion of competitive contests rose to the highest level in incumbent-held seats in nearly thirty years. Perhaps most notable of all was the strong pro-Republican vote shift in the South. This produced a situation where, for the first time in American history, the Democratic share of the congressional two-party vote was lower in the South (51.9 percent) than it was outside it (52.9 percent). This region's secular realignment toward the Republicans, speeded up in 1984 and 1988, is still under way; it has now fully rejoined the Union, and then some.

Still, despite seeming change, the overall impression is one of remarkable continuity. This is the more remarkable when one considers the "everything-up-for-grabs" atmosphere that was reported in the polls and reflected in a good deal of pre-election analysis. And if I have not spent any great time discussing the Senate contests, it is because the continuity level is greater still. In the end, only four incumbents lost their seats (Fowler, D-Ga.; Kasten, R-Wis.; Sanford, D-N.C.; and Seymour, R-Calif., the latter an appointee). The candidate domination that is a central theme of the sixth electoral era's "permanent campaign" remains alive and in fine health in 1992. This is one very strong reason for believing that while this election ended the Reagan-Bush era, it made no more than an occasional dent on the relationship between candidates and voters that so mark this particular era in American history. To the extent that this is so, the electoral regime set up in and after the critical realignment of the late 1960s has not yet run its course or been replaced by something basically different.

Interest group liberalism, in the sense first used by the political scientist Theodore Lowi in 1969 as an alliance between constituent groups and a benevolent state, has faltered because the state no longer effectively serves the demands of the groups and the groups no longer provide consistently reliable electoral support for the (Democratic) governing coalition. Yet at the same time, as the electoral continuities demonstrate, most of the groups are still there (only organized labor is notably weaker); indeed, the old interest groups have been joined by several new fervently active groups—feminists, gays, Hispanics, greens, disabled people, among others. And most still look, however skeptically, to the Democrats.

However, the state today is far less able than before the year 1968 either to provide tangible benefits or to broker satisfactory compromises hence the frustration and the interregnum. Interest group liberalism as a viable regime order may be dead, but as the 1990 election data show, the Democratic Party still depends heavily on a coalition of liberal interest groups, traditional and new. Indeed, leaving aside the white South, the Clinton coalition of 1992 looks remarkably like the Roosevelt coalition of 1940. What remains to be seen is whether Clinton can cement their allegiance, while simultaneously defining a transcendent national interest, to create a seventh durable electoral era and governing consensus.

1992: A Summation

In this essay, I have sought to locate the broad picture of this election and its setting in "political time" across American history. This picture may suggest rather darker colors than the occasion warrants. After all, it had become clear to American voters early in 1992, as it was clear to me and many others, that nothing constructive could be expected to happen if George Bush were reelected. This might not matter at a point where drift could continue a while longer; it mattered vitally in 1992. Clinton's election, with all the constraints duly noted, means that something more constructive is a possibility—and none too soon. For it is now a close to universal belief among Americans that time is not on our side.

As Abraham Lincoln famously observed in 1862, "The occasion is piled high with difficulty. We must think anew and act anew. We must *disenthral* ourselves, and then we shall save our country." Economists, policy specialists, and countless others have been hard at work spelling out our own piled-high difficulties and how they might be constructively addressed. Clearly, a new start must center on disenthralling ourselves about government's place in the political economy. This implies a government that can "work" and especially one that is widely seen to "work," and this in turn will involve myriad, highly disagreeable, changes in the behavior of Washington's politicians. Ross Perot's candidacy and the size of his vote are a clear warning; so more generally was the extremely disturbed state of public opinion throughout 1992. An exceptional burden is thus added to the inventory of burdens that poured down on Bill Clinton on November 3. For Clinton may well be the system's last chance. One suspects that he has already considered this possibility. And he may just be skillful and lucky enough to succeed in the task of reconstruction that now begins, by involving—as he must—both Washington politicians and the public in developing their own personal stake in his success.

[15]

Marshall Ganz

Voters in the Cross Hairs: How Technology and the Market Are Destroying Politics

Organize the whole state, so that every Whig can be brought to the polls ... divide the county into small districts and appoint in each a sub-committee ... make a perfect list of voters and ascertain with certainty for whom they will vote ... and on election day see that every Whig is brought to the polls.

—Abraham Lincoln (*Illinois State Register*, February 21, 1840)

Campaigns and elections are the lifeblood of American democracy and the principal means by which citizens form and express political opinions. Any less than full and equal electoral participation puts democracy at risk. Today electoral participation is neither full nor equal, and it is getting worse. Paradoxically, new campaign technologies and practices bear significant responsibility for declining participation. While making it easier to communicate with voters and to create Lincoln's "perfect list," direct mail, databases of voters, polling, and targeted advertising also depress voter turnout and fragment the electorate. The source of this conflict lies in the combination of the technology, the new class of political consultants it has empowered, and the marketplace institutions to which the management of campaigns are increasingly relegated (like so many other public goods).

The paradox demonstrates a fundamental American dilemma: the conflict between equality and liberty and, more specifically, the conflict between a politics based on equality of voice and an economics based on inequality of resources. To the extent that voice depends on resources, an unregulated political market guarantees political inequality. The new technology has given those with more resources access to even greater voice. As a result, many elections have become for most citizens exercises in choosing between two power blocs representing similar if not identical resource-rich interests.

Not surprisingly, fewer Americans are taking part. Election scholar Walter Dean Burnham reports voter turnout in presidential elections outside the South declined from 73 percent in 1960 to 54 percent in 1988. Participation expert Sidney Verba found that turnout for local elections during a similar period declined from 47 percent to 35 percent.

Verba also found that the well-known bias that favors higher electoral turnout among wealthier voters is even greater for other forms of participation. Families with incomes below $35,000 comprise 54.6 percent of the eligible electorate but only 50.3 percent of voters. On the other hand, those earning more than $50,000 make up 24.6 percent of the electorate and 28.1 percent of voters. In campaign hours, the lower income group contributes 35.5 percent, while the upper income group contributes 50.1 percent. In campaign dollars, the lower income group gives only 16.5 percent, while the upper income group contributes 71 percent. Indeed, the top 10 percent contributes 50 percent of all the money that supports political campaigns.

Because politicians pay more attention to the people who put them in office, this pattern of participation means the interests of a major portion of the electorate, if not a majority, are consistently left out of the political calculus.

The mechanisms by which elections are conducted are a kind of electoral "means of production" for the polity. Electoral mechanics define who takes part, how they take part, what resources are needed to take part, and thus whose interests the outcome will reflect. The introduction of radical new communications technologies has dramatically altered the way in which elections are conducted. This revolution, in turn, has altered the political system itself.

Hunters and Gatherers

Since the 1830s, American political campaigns have pursued one of two basic strategies: vote "gathering" that maximizes turnout or vote "hunting" that minimizes it. During the nineteenth century, political parties "gathered" votes by using marches, rallies, patronage, and a partisan press to mobilize known supporters; in 1896 turnout outside the South reached a peak of 86 percent. Early in the twentieth century, however, an establishment fearful of populism and new immigrants used restrictive voting measures, such as voter registration, as well as a nonpartisan press and new advertising and broadcast technologies in a "hunt" for the "responsible" but undecided voter. By 1920, turnout outside the South had declined to a new low of 57 percent. With the political upheavals of the 1930s, vote gathering resumed as newly organized unions and a revitalized Democratic Party generated new political resources that were applied to renewed voter mobilization. Turnout increased, reaching 73 percent in 1940.

Modern campaigning, which began with polling and television in the 1960s, marked a return to vote hunting. Although polling developed from demographic studies by Gallup and Roper in the 1930s, it reached public acceptance only in the early 1960s when Lou Harris achieved fame as John F. Kennedy's pollster. Polling enabled politicians to learn voter opinions without attending to constituency leaders or the voters themselves. It became possible to "know" the electorate without having a relationship with it. Polling also created a role for the electoral expert whose "expertise" derived not from political or organizational experience but from mastery of the new technology.

Television transformed political campaigning along with much of American life beginning with the 1952 Eisenhower campaign. Television was also credited with Kennedy's presidential victory over Richard Nixon in 1960. Television transformed JFK's state primary victories into national events, creating a momentum Democrats could not ignore, and gave the photogenic Kennedy a critical edge over Nixon. By the 1970s, television advertising had become a key element in most major campaigns, as well as the principal factor driving up their cost. Television also introduced a second technological expert—the "media adviser" typified by long-time Democratic campaign consultants Tony Schwartz or Joe Napolitan.

Computers, which had been used to support polling, began to have a separate influence in the 1970s. Computer technology made it possible to develop direct mail fund-raising campaigns on a large scale but with precise targeting. About the same time, marketing companies learned to combine census data and polling information, enabling marketers to target consumers by zip code according to their lifestyle and preferences. As voter registration lists and other electoral data became computerized at the state, county, and city level, micro computer technology spread and there developed an industry of over 2,500 firms providing each campaign with targeted, custom-made lists. Consequently, voter contact strategies are targeted down to the level of the individual voter.

In 1984 Frank Tobe, a leading practitioner of computer targeting, described his mission:

Campaign managers ... need to be aware of the exciting, new delivery products for campaign messages afforded by today's computer technologies and decide which are most relevant and cost effective for the race they are working on ... computer-prepared laser letters, pre-filled-in absentee ballots, computer-generated slate cards, tasteful and stylish response devices, urgent looking (get out the vote) messages, polished and authentic looking endorsement letters, and hundreds of other computer prepared products all improved by some level of personalization far beyond simple inclusion of the recipients' name or city into the copy.

Meanwhile, modern campaigns have become even more expensive while voter turnout has fallen to a new low. Campaign expenditures climbed from $200 million, or $2.80 a vote, in 1964 to $2.7 billion, or $29.48 a vote, in 1988, but voter turnout outside the South fell from 73 percent to 54 percent.

The Professionals

Each technological innovation produced a new expert—or "consultant"—who provided access to the new tool for a fee. In the absence of strong parties or public regulation of campaign activities, candidates made deals directly with consultants. No longer was running for office an organizational activity; it was now an "entrepreneurial" endeavor. The premium was on the cash to buy expertise rather than the loyalty to command organization. The campaign manager or press agent of yore, often a party operative or associate of the candidate or his supporters, was replaced by a paid professional.

The arrival of television in the early 1950s provided professional campaign consulting with its real kick-off. In *The Rise Political Consultants*, Larry Sabato noted that by 1972, 168 out of 208 candidates for state office were reported as having hired professionals, as had 61 out of 67 U.S. Senate candidates, 38 out of 42 gubernatorial candidates, and 30 out of 37 candidates for attorney general. By 1986, after the introduction of computer targeting, consultant Frank Lutz reports that 85 percent of 138 senatorial or gubernatorial candidates hired professional pollsters, 94 percent had professional media consultants, and 4 percent had no consultants at all.

Ironically, the rise of the consultants was also spurred by the campaign finance reforms of the 1970s and the 1976 Supreme Court decision, *Buckley v. Valeo*, that declared spending limits unconstitutional. The legislative reforms attempted to regulate contributions rather than expenditures, thus trying to control supply rather than demand. The unabated demand for money, however, simply created a premium for fund-raisers with expertise in the new requirements. The contribution limits also placed a premium on the ability to raise large sums of money in small amounts from many donors. Direct mail fund-raising thus received a new boost, as did political action committees (PACs). The legacy of this legislation was to make campaigning still more expensive and the role of consultants still more critical.

The way in which consultants are compensated also drives up campaign costs. Consultants are usually paid a flat campaign fee plus a commission based on the cost of the services the campaign (the consultant) purchases. For example, a consultant paid a flat fee of $100,000 will also receive a commission of 15 percent to 20 percent of all the money spent on the television buy, direct mail, and even billboards. A typical television buy of $300,000 and direct mail expense of $250,000 will return the consultant an additional $120,000. Consultants also often own interests in their subcontractors (printers, mail houses, telemarketing firms, and so on), providing them with additional income. A consultant who produces a mailer for $.32 per piece will charge the client $.40 per piece. If a campaign sends, say, 27 mailings of 75,000 brochures each, the consultant nets an extra $162,000. Since top consultants handle from five to ten campaigns simultaneously, their earnings potential is impressive indeed.

The personal quality of consulting has inhibited the development of a competitive market. A winning reputation is so important that a candidate's capacity to raise money and discourage competition often depends on hiring the right consultant at the right time. Absent political parties with the resources to take advantage of the new campaign tools, and absent reforms to limit spending, consultants are able to sell their expertise for "all the market will bear."

The thrall in which many consultants hold candidates also gives these professionals greater control over the content of a campaign than candidates themselves. In a 1989 survey, 44 percent of political consultants interviewed reported that their candidates were uninvolved in setting the issue priorities in their own campaigns, and 66 percent reported candidates to be uninvolved in determining the tactics.

Consultants have thus come to play multiple roles: campaign manager, press agent, party, and even candidate. But for most political consultants, the motivation to get out the vote is private, not public, gain. For these professionals, politics is not a public domain in which each citizen is to have an equal voice. It is a business in which market principles apply and there is one criteria of success—winning. From the consultants' perspective, winning does not depend on who is right, who is the better candidate, or what is in the best interest of the community. As Stanley Foster Reed, founder of the trade journal *Campaigns and Elections*, put it in his 1980 premiere issue:

What makes the difference between winning and losing a political campaign? Is it the same thing that makes the difference between succeeding and failing in business? Yes! Management makes the difference. Management of resources: money, media, people.

Of course, candidates, parties, and constituency leaders also want to win, but this desire dovetails with the long-term interests of their political community. The consultant's calculus, on the other hand, considers only will it win and does it make money?

Although the consequences of this marketplace thinking for American democracy are serious and far-reaching, they are not the result of insidious forces or a malevolent cabal. They are the result of intelligent people making conscious and "utility maximizing" decisions under the current arrangements that govern American political campaigns.

Campaigns Old and New

The guiding principle of modern campaign management is "bang for the buck" —the allocation of each dollar to achieve maximum possible effect in the current election. Traditional campaigns took a more long-term, investment approach, building the party infrastructure through voter registration and precinct organization. The new campaign methods not only raise costs and empower consultants, they also require that money be spent in different ways. Today's campaign strategies have reached a new level of sophistication, where only those voters most likely to vote are wooed, messages change with demographics, issues are condensed into fleeting televised images, and campaign organizations are nearly as ephemeral.

Targeting I: Reducing the Universe. Traditional campaign strategy would expand the electorate and motivate voters to participate. A voter registration drive, for example, would increase potential support in the district by targeting pockets of unregistered supporters based on the density of partisan registration. Each campaign would then target its own partisans for mobilization and a portion of the other party's adherents for persuasion. Both campaigns would target unaffiliated voters for persuasion. This logic would lead to the targeting of 60 percent of registered voters for mobilization by one of the campaigns and 40 percent of registered voters for persuasion by both campaigns. An election day get-out-the-vote program would then focus on turning out all identified supporters to vote.

This was the strategy Senator Robert Kennedy's 1968 presidential campaign used in targeting California Latinos for pre-primary voter registration, especially in East Los Angeles. The extraordinary turnout from this community was a key factor in Kennedy's primary win. Today such a registration effort would never happen, on grounds that historically lower turnout among Latinos means that precious campaign dollars should be invested in persuading more-likely voters.

For the last couple decades, campaign consultants have been perfecting ways to restrict the electorate by "reducing the universe" of voters, long before Ed Rollins caused a furor by claiming he paid New Jersey ministers not to encourage their congregation members to vote in the gubernatorial race last September. The computerization of voter registration files and emergence of "list vendors" who purchase tapes of these files and convert them into customized, campaign-specific lists make possible this new approach to targeting. Matching voter files with tapes of phone directories, ethnic surname dictionaries, county assessor records, and voter turnout reports makes it possible to generate lists of voters individually profiled by their party affiliation, age, gender, marital status, homeowner status, ethnicity, and frequency of voting. Consultant Matt Reese explains how this information is used:

> Targeting is a process of excluding people who are not "profitable" to work, so that resources are adequate to reach prime voters with enough intensity to win them. Targeting provides an ultimate "lift" to the voter contact process, allowing maximum concentration of resources to a minimum universe.

Voter registration, for example, is rarely considered because newly registered voters are less likely to turn out than established voters. Also, it requires a "ground force" of volunteers or paid registrars. In the absence of an ongoing program, there are numerous problems of management, recruitment, and quality control in creating such a team for a single campaign.

The effects of this new campaign ethos can be seen in a hypothetical district, where 55 percent of the registered voters are Democrats, 35 percent are Republicans, and 10 percent are independent or "decline to state." The first step in applying the new strategy is to buy computer tapes that describe the district by party and by voter turnout. Of all registered voters, 24 percent have no record of voting, suggesting that they are gone, and 39 percent vote only occasionally, mainly in presidential elections. These voters are ignored because they are unlikely to turn out unless stimulated. The likely voters, a bedrock 37 percent of registered voters who vote in most elections, are the prime targets of the campaign. Among these, priority is assigned to the Democratic 10 percent, Republican 5 percent, and independent 2 percent judged to be "swing" voters based on their electoral or individual histories (a Republican living with a Democrat, for example). This 17 percent is targeted for persuasion and becomes the heart of the campaign, the real determiners of the issues the campaign will address. The remaining 20 percent of the electorate who are likely voters and are likely to be loyal to their parties are contacted mainly to inform them of the candidate's identity and affiliation. They are not mobilized because they are regular voters.

As of election day, 63 percent of registered voters will not have been contacted by anyone. If, as is typical, only 60 percent of the eligible electorate were registered, 78 percent of the eligible voters in the district would never be contacted. These uncontacted voters are far more likely to be of lower socioeconomic status than those who are contacted. They never hear from a campaign and thus will likely stay at home on election day or vote the way they always have. The assumption that past voting behavior is predictive of future behavior becomes a self-fulfilling prophecy. With both campaigns in last June's Los Angeles mayoral election using this kind of reasoning, it is not so surprising that, despite the city's troubles, less than 25 percent of the Los Angeles electorate turned out to vote.

Targeting II: The Segmented Electorate. After "reducing the universe" limits the campaign to just 37 percent of the registered voters, further targeting segments it for assault by direct mail. In a recent interview, Richie Ross, consultant to California Assembly Speaker Willie Brown, described the process:

> Once a consultant goes to work for a candidate, he or she will cross-reference the district's population over and over, until the desired geo-demographic groups have been isolated. These groups are always exceedingly narrow. The number of demographic groups targeted in a specific campaign ranges from 60 to 1,200 with the precise figure depending on the level of office being contested and the amount of money a candidate has to spend.... A typical congressional campaign might have around 300 groups targeted.

Information on each of these subgroups is matched with polling data, and the campaign messages are developed to deliver what Matt Reese calls "different—and compelling—truths" to those various segments.

Instead of a single campaign with a single theme that unifies a candidate's supporters, parallel campaigns emerge, each articulating themes narrow enough to appeal to the peculiar characteristics of each subconstituency. In a recent California Assembly campaign, for example, married Catholic homeowners learned that the candidate supported family values, while single Jewish women under age 40 found the candidate had been consistently pro-choice.

Although direct mail was originally developed for small-donor fund-raising, consultants adapted it to the delivery of the segmented message because it is far less expensive than television and can market politics to precisely the right voters.

Far from aggregating the interests of the electorate, the new campaign thus serves only to further disperse them.

The 30-Second Spot. As television has driven up campaign costs and given new currency to consultants, it has devalued the quality and content of political discussion. The quest for the six o'clock news sound bite and the reduction of political debate to visual-emotional images that can be conveyed in 30 seconds have been major factors in redefining American political discourse.

To the extent that voters depend on campaigns for political information, the "30 second rule" allows the medium to obstruct the message. Thus the emptiness Americans observe in their political dialogue may be mechanical as well as substantive in origin. Even worse, the 30 second bite has been a very effective tool for the negative campaigning that increasingly takes the place of issue differentiation between candidates who target the same voters.

Developments in targeting and direct mail, however, have made the economics of television advertising problematic for all but the largest campaigns and those in which district boundaries coincide with a particular media market. Television is so expensive because it is billed according to the size of the entire market a particular channel reaches. For example, if a candidate for the Los Angeles City Council in a district with 100,00 voters runs a television commercial, he or she pays for reaching all 10 million people in the Los Angeles basin.

A revival of televised political advertising may occur if it can become a visual version of direct mail. Newer wireless cable technologies and the proliferation of local and specialized carriers may both lower the cost and offer access to highly targeted audiences currently possible only through the mail.

Instant Organizations. When consultants determine a need for people-intensive tactics, they turn to "instant organization." For example, canvassing may be required to determine the identities of undecided swing voters who may then receive calls or mailings customized to their concerns. Or an election may be so close—and well funded—that occasional voters will be targeted for get-out-the-vote work. With atrophied party structures, weakened constituent organizations, and the increasingly lost art of building a campaign structure to recruit, train, and direct volunteers, consultants subcontract to purveyors of instant organization, or IO.

Providers of IO hire a paid staff to run field operations that dissolve at the end of the campaign, leaving candidate and consultant free of costly maintenance and accountability problems. IO generally entails paid door-to-door or telephone canvassers using prepared scripts to solicit voter support and who are paid on a per-head or bounty basis. The results of their contacts are then computerized and dovetailed with mailing or recontact strategies. That such efforts can be effective—for vote gathering as well as vote hunting—is demonstrated by the 1986 campaign of California Senator Alan Cranston. Six weeks before the election, after Cranston and his opponent, Ed Zschau, had spent $15 million each on television and direct mail, Cranston committed $300,000 to an IO get-out-the-vote effort. Computerized targeting identified "unlikely" voters who were supporters. The only work done by the precinct was turning them out to vote. The 160,000 unlikely voters who did turn out gave Cranston the 110,000 vote edge he needed to win.

In the absence of an institutional structure to connect with, however, almost all of these organizations have been abandoned by the candidate "the morning after" the election. Candidates' agendas shift to raising money to pay off campaign debt (and accumulate a new war chest), accommodating interest groups, and insulating themselves against opposition in the next election. This development, in turn, induces cynicism among organizers and volunteers who generally want to have a longer term role in policy as well as politics.

The "New" Campaign and American Democracy

These developments have eroded the quality of American democracy in four important ways.

Decline and Bias in Voter Turnout. New campaign methods undermine and bias voter turnout by failing to communicate with all but the most likely voters. This denies many people the resources and motivation they need in order to participate—particularly voters at the lower end of the socioeconomic spectrum.

Resources include political information and skills; motivation includes attitudes that encourage participation, a belief in one's political efficacy, and a clear political interest. Citizens of higher socioeconomic status generally have greater access to both resources and motivation. Sidney Verba found, however, that the motivational deficit can be compensated for when "group consciousness" makes a voter's interest in participation clearer or provides a heightened sense of efficacy. The resource deficit can be offset by organizational affiliation, which allows the activist to gain political skills and information. This explains the impact that unions had on American workers in the 1930s and that many Protestant churches have on African-American constituencies today.

Diminished voter contact also inhibits the formation of political opinion. In *The Reasoning Voter*, political scientist Sam Popkin reported that voters use the information they receive from campaigns, Popkin says, because they have limited information about government and are "open to influence by campaigners who offer them ... better explanations of the ways in which government activities affect them."

The voter's understanding of campaign issues is also directly related to the amount of debate to which he or she is exposed. Popkin found that "the more the candidates talked about an issue [in a campaign] and the greater their differences on it, the more accurately it was perceived." The logic of the "reduced universe" denies this information to the voters who most need it.

Finally, the "dehumanization" of voter contact techniques damages efforts to turn people out. Campaign activities that depend on popular participation for their effectiveness—such as voter registration and get-out-the-vote programs—have been widely dismissed as not cost-effective. Yet studies like those of political scientist Ray Wolfinger have verified that people are most likely to respond to other people. Wolfinger found that active precinct increased voter turnout in New Haven by as much as 10 percent.

Decline and Bias in Political Activism. Because the new campaign devalues all forms of political activism except for giving money, the role of the political volunteer has been all but eliminated. This dampens overall levels of participation and limits it to those with the financial resources to become contributors.

The decline of the volunteer has closed off an important source for recruitment of political leadership, and many people drawn to politics today must seek entry instead as employees or interns. The reduced demand for volunteer activity has also likely contributed to a decline in membership in political organizations, according to Verba, from 8 percent of the citizenry in 1967 to 4 percent in 1987.

The Weakening of Civic Society. The new campaign has undercut broad-based democratic organizations through which individual citizens have traditionally participated in public life. Traditional democratic organizations, which rely heavily on volunteers, once served as important "schools for democracy" where citizens acquired resources and motivation for active political participation. These organizations—parties, unions, political clubs, and civic groups—help formulate political choices and provide organizational mechanisms to encourage voting. The atrophy of these associations and the rise of Washington-based lobbies that do little more than seek members' money through direct mail both reflect and reinforce the rising influence of money and the declining importance of citizen participation.

Erosion of Common Interest. Segmented voter interests have undermined incentives for political leaders to articulate and act upon those interests citizens do share. Indeed, intensity of political voice seems to have become directly related to narrowness of vision, while breadth of vision is related to weakness of voice. Much of this "narrowness" can be directly traced to the new campaign and its approach to "political marketing."

The reduction of individual voters to demographic abstractions has even dampened the incentive of citizens to intelligently translate their own competing interests into coherent politics. A voter receives one piece of mail as a married Catholic, another as a 30-year-old professional, and still another as an "environmentally concerned" citizen. Each piece of propaganda asserts the overwhelming importance of its own priorities and course of action. The set of concerns that least enters the campaign are those of citizens of lower socioeconomic status. As a result, the marginal voters are rendered invisible, as their concerns go unrepresented, and silent, as their capacity to articulate those concerns remains undeveloped. Thus instead of providing an experience in "strong democratic talk" that helps to define and articulate common interests, the new campaign is a political cacophony in which one coalition of dissonant and powerful interests seeks to defeat another. This offers a grim prospect for the future of American democracy.

Restructuring Voice

The introduction of new political technologies has crippled the American attempt to combine equal voice in politics with unequal resources in economics. Technology, however, is only a set of tools. The critical factor is the "free market" approach to the management of politics and elections. Weak parties and an ineffective method of governing elections has allowed the new tools to enhance the power of those with the resources to buy access to them.

Establishing equality of political voice for all Americans will require major institutional change: a reconstruction of the political parties and the public allocation of campaign resources.

Despite their weakened condition, political parties remain one of the few institutions with which a significant number of Americans still identify. The rule of thumb in most campaigns is that 80 percent of voters will vote for the party with which they are registered. Political parties also have the framework of a democratic structure through which participation can take place. They are uniquely positioned to have a strategic interest in gaining more adherents and thus in expanding the electorate.

Partisan "reconstruction" would begin with measures enabling them to build their own financial base from resources unavailable to candidates running for office. These resources could be used as the political capital to invest in the following partisan infrastructure:

- party-owned computerized voter files available to all endorsed candidates;
- voter registration drives targeted on the non-participating voter with the intent of expanding support for the party;
- ongoing precinct organization available to support endorsed candidates but not dependent on them for finance;
- "generic" media campaigns targeted at the non-participating electorate encouraging them to join the party, etc.

Reconstructed parties could then become vehicles for currently disempowered interests to reenter the political process and serve as a means for rebuilding a politics of inclusion and common interest.

Second, the cost of campaigns must be reduced and equalized, attacking the demand side of the equation by allocating the availability of political resources in an equitable fashion. The mail, the radio waves, and the television airwaves belong to the public, and access to them by political campaign—as to any limited public space—should be allocated by the public in the public interest.

In other words, bona fide candidates should receive equitable but limited access to the mail, radio, and television. This would limit the need for funds, soft and hard, thereby reducing the incentive to raise them. Public finance could be provided to campaigns agreeing to operate within this framework and denied to others. This would avoid problems created by constitutional inhibitions to limitations on campaign spending per se and yet reduce the incentive for ceaseless, seemingly limitless, fund-raising. Limiting what could be purchased and the money available to purchase it could force candidates to turn back toward volunteers, parties, and other organizations able to provide the human power, which could then provide the "edge" in winning a campaign.

The paradoxical impact of the new technology is captured most clearly by the authors of *The Electronic Commonwealth*:

> Here we come to an essential irony about the impact of the computer age on our democracy. In theory, the computer is a vast force for equaliz-

ing access to information: no information is so remote or closely held as to be unobtainable by the average citizen. In practice, however, the computer tends to widen the information gap between economic classes.

The political challenge which we face is to gain control over the consequences of our own technology, finding ways to use it to bring the goal of a democracy of "equal voices" ever closer to reality. It is, however, only through a mastery of the politics of our time that we can hope to succeed.

[16]

Bruce Ackerman

Crediting the Voters: A New Beginning for Campaign Finance

When Americans register to vote, they should be issued a credit card by a special public company. Call it the Patriot card and color it red, white, and blue. This card will become the basis of campaign finance.

Suppose each voter's card were automatically credited with a $10 balance for the 1996 presidential election. To gain access to this red-white-and-blue money, candidates should be obliged to demonstrate significant popular support by gathering an appropriate number of voter signatures. In exchange for these signatures, the Patriot company would open an account that granted the candidate an initial balance of red-white-and-blue money—say, one million dollars for presidential aspirants. Candidates could then spend their initial stake on a series of advertisements to convince Patriot holders to transfer more red-white-and-blue money to them. Some candidates will, of course, soon see their initial Patriot balance shrink to zero; others will generate tens of millions as the campaign proceeds.

Under this system, only red-white-and-blue money may be used to finance political campaigns. The use of greenbacks would be treated as a form of corruption similar to the use of greenbacks to buy votes.

Reforming Reform?

A democratic market society must confront a basic tension between its ideal of equal citizenship and the reality of market inequality. It does so by drawing a line, marking a political sphere within which the power relationships of the market are kept under democratic control. Over the past 150 years, Americans have taken two large steps in this direction.

The first, completed during the age of Andrew Jackson, was the abolition of property requirements for voting. The second development, the secret ballot, came a half-century later. Before this reform, people could buy your vote and hold you to your bargain by watching you at the polling place. Even if you refused a bribe, you were subject to retaliation from your employer or other rich folk. Only with the use of the secret ballot, in the late nineteenth century, did Americans begin to build a political sphere that was insulated from the inequalities of the market.

Since then, we have been trying to take the next step. Just as the nineteenth century made it tough to buy votes, the twentieth has tried to make it hard to buy candidates, most recently in the 1974 amendments to the Federal Election Campaign Act. Yet these efforts have been painfully ineffective; they have even backfired.

This failure has had multiple causes: the power of vested interests, underlying uncertainties about the ideal relationship between liberty and equality, and between money and speech. But there is another cause as well—primitive regulatory thinking. For too long, debate has focused on two strategies: (1) limit the kinds and amounts of private money introduced into the system; (2) add government funds dispensed by a centralized bureaucratic agency.

But there is a third way, which deploys an increasingly familiar reform technique: the voucher. From welfare to education to health care, voucher proponents make the same basic point. The alternative to a market is not necessarily a slow-moving and potentially oppressive bureaucracy. If the root of the difficulty is extreme inequality, a voucher system permits the creation of a new currency, distributed on more egalitarian lines, that retains many other advantages of a market system.

The voucher isn't a panacea. Curiously, however, its potential has been largely ignored in an area where it shows itself off at maximal advantage: campaign finance.*

---

* Voucher proposals were more seriously entertained in the 1960s and 1970s than recently. For example, Senator Metcalf proposed a primitive voucher scheme in 1967, and there is a useful discussion by David Adamany and George Agree, *Political Monthly* 189–92, 196–201 (1975). More recent treatments seem to ignore the voucher alternative. See, for example, David Magleby and Candice Nelson, *The Money Chase 200* (list of proposed comprehensive reforms, 1990). Professor Philippe Schmitter of Stanford University has generously shared with me some unpublished work that uses the voucher technique as part of an ambitious effort to rehabilitate corporatism in democratic theory. Since I am unconvinced of Schmitter's larger goal, my voucher proposal diverges from his in basic aim as well as countless particulars.

The Core of the Problem

Consider how the two traditional reform strategies combine to create insuperable obstacles to effective action. By restricting the amount of green money sloshing through the system, we create two big problems. Most obviously, we have reduced the amount of political debate. While money isn't speech, it makes effective speech possible, especially in an age of mass media. This generates anxious doubts. Egalitarian reformers begin to seem grimly repressive. Do we really want equality at the cost of shutting down debate?

Restricting the flow of cash may also skew the balance of power between incumbents and their challengers. Incumbents go into each campaign with the accumulated reputation they have generated through years of great visibility. Challengers need lots of cash to offset this advantage. By placing an overall limit on funds, aren't we allowing old-timers to tighten their grip on office under the banner of "reform"?

These questions endure despite the second traditional strategy: government finance through a centralized bureaucracy, which typically gives established parties a privileged position at the federal trough. Worse, the present system of public financing has not stemmed the flow of private finance; it has only diverted it into new and more insidious channels of "soft money" and has left the large donor and the large fund-raiser more influential than ever. Moreover, present law allows well-heeled candidates like Ross Perot and John Connolly to buy their way to the White House so long as they turn down the subsidy.

These loopholes erode the moral foundations of reform. Despite public financing, presidential politics continues to be a rich person's game. The loopholes permit the resurgence of special interest influence. They generate corrosive skepticism among ordinary people. And yet it is too easy to condemn the loopholes outright. At least they provide an escape hatch against the worst possible abuses of centralized public finance: Do we really want politicians to be entirely dependent upon the good will of government bureaucrats for financial assistance in their hour of electoral need?

Adoption of Patriot permits a straightforward answer that encourages decisive steps against corrosive loopholes. The new system controls the undue influence of wealth without transferring power from the general citizenry to an imperial bureaucracy. Under the proposal, the Patriot company would distribute a sum of red-white-and-blue money to cardholders that, when summed, will be greater than the total spent in the last election held under the green money regime. For example, if $10 in red-white-and-blue money were distributed to each of America's 130 million registered voters, the $1.3 billion deposited in Patriot accounts would quadruple the total sum spent by all presidential candidates in 1992. Even if lots of people never used their Patriot cards, more money would still be running through the system than previously without the heavy hand of bureaucratic direction.

Patriot also generates a much more egalitarian distribution of financial power than anything promised by traditional spending limitations. Those ceilings may cut down on the influence of very rich people and interests. They do nothing to confront the fact that the overwhelming majority of citizens give nothing to political campaigns, and that the small percentage who contribute are overwhelmingly from the upper classes. Under green money, Americans decide whether they are willing to send a $10 check to the Republican or Democratic candidate at the expense of an extra shirt for their six-year-old. Compare Patriot. Rather than pitting an act of citizenship against an act of private consumption, the voucher system presents a different choice: Do citizens want their Patriot balances "to go to waste" or do they want to take the time to decide which candidate should get the money?

The voucher plan transforms campaign finance from an inegalitarian embarrassment into a new occasion for civic responsibility. Each Patriotic decision will serve as a preliminary vote, encouraging card-holders to focus on the campaign as it develops and support the candidates of their choice at the time of their choice. These tens of millions of decentralized decisions replace acts of centralized authority that bulk large in the traditional subsidy proposals. Rather than authorizing a bureaucracy to determine when, and whether, particular candidates can share in governmental largesse, the Patriot plan places this decision in the hands of the citizens of the United States, where it belongs.

Designing Patriot

One appealing strategy is to begin with a narrow target: the presidency. In contrast to congressional elections, which have no public financing, we already have in the presidency a large program that seeks to substitute public for private finance. Patriot would simply do the job much better than existing centralized arrangements. If a pilot program were in place for the 1996 election, it would demonstrate concretely to ordinary Americans that they can indeed act constructively to provide a solution to the present disgrace. This demonstration could, in turn, generate a decisive swing in support of a significant expansion of scope on both federal and state levels. Existing doubts about expanding public finance do not revolve around matters of budgetary cost. It would cost much less than a billion dollars a year, for example, to expand Patriot to finance all congressional campaigns. Opposition is based instead on the pervasive suspicion that federal funding will be perverted by incumbents to insulate themselves further from the popular will. The best way to confront these fears is by demonstrating Patriot's capacity to empower ordinary people rather than Washington bureaucrats.

Of course, present discontent with Congress is already so high that it might be preferable to include congressional elections from the outset. The Patriot's cleansing effect on congressional elections is more likely to improve the quality of public life than, say, term limitations forcing the retirement of popular and seasoned members of the House and Senate after a few terms in office. If the Patriot is extended to congressional elections, a second design issue becomes even more important: many voters will have trouble making intelligent funding decisions. If primaries are included within the program, challengers will have a hard time piercing the anonymity barrier. For the scheme to function effectively, cardholders should be allowed to give their red-white-and-blue money to political brokers to spend where they think it will do the most good.

Millions will refuse to take advantage of this option and will insist on making their own decisions on candidates. But those who wish to delegate their choices should be allowed a broad range of choice. Many will select a political party to serve as broker, but they should also be allowed to transfer funds to a broad range of interest groups—PACs, if you will, representing the full gamut of political opinion.

While PAC-baiting is a part of the conventional wisdom, we should rethink the source of our unease. So long as PACs depend on the supply of green money, it is easy to see how they reinforce those special interests that are relatively advantaged by the market. If, however, PACs are dependent upon red-white-and-blue funds, why not let a thousand flowers bloom, leaving it to the good sense of citizens to determine whether a political party or a PAC or a particular candidate best expresses their vision of the public good?

Some political scientists may find this expression of faith in ordinary people naive. Rather than leaving the role of parties to the political marketplace, they argue that the integrative functions performed by parties are crucial to the operation of a democracy. On this view, it would be healthier in the long run if we refused to allow "special interests" to compete directly for red-white-and-blue funds, requiring them instead to compete for influence by participating actively within the parties.

I am unpersuaded, but more important, so is the Supreme Court. As we shall see, there is no reason to think that the Court will react to Patriot with hostility so long as it remains broadly open to the shifting currents of political opinion. Using it to entrench the power of existing political parties, however, will likely generate a much more hostile response from the Court.

There are many more practical problems to be considered. I hope I have said enough, however, to make my sketch sufficiently credible that we can step back from these important, but ultimately secondary, details to consider Patriot's place in the larger system.

Drawing the Line

A first basic issue revolves around the relationship between the new red-white-and-blue currency and the ongoing use of familiar greenbacks: Can greenbackholders continue to buy political advertisements in newspapers to announce their "spontaneous and independent" support of a candidate? And what of the normal discussion of political questions in newspapers and other mass media? Presumably these standard media will continue to be financed through green dollars. Should their intervention in political campaigns, then, also be restricted?

Fundamental questions—but there is nothing special about the voucher plan that generates them. Any effort to insulate campaign finance from the unmediated rule of money requires us to cut the world into (at least) two spheres—the sphere of "campaign finance" in which the role of green money is constrained (either though traditional reform measures or as part of a voucher plan), and the world of ordinary commodities, where ability to pay is measured exclusively in terms of green dollars. Unless the market or democracy is allowed to dominate all spheres of life, we must be prepared to draw some lines—pointing out those activities, like voting or campaign finance, in which the democratic aspiration is taken with special seriousness, and those spheres where we are more willing to live with market-generated inequality. Since line-drawing is a feature of all reform programs, the difficulties it entails cannot be used as a reason for rejecting Patriot and continuing with old-style campaign reform.

Wherever we draw the line, we will be obliged to distinguish close cases. For example, Patriot might mimic existing law by allowing rich citizens and special interest groups to spend green money on political advertisements so long as they act "independently" of the candidate's direction. But there is nothing sacrosanct about this line. It is a result of Supreme Court decisions that, as we shall see, do not control a constitutional assessment of Patriot. Congress should therefore feel free to bar all purchases of political advertisements with green money, even if the purchaser claims to be acting "independently."

This decision, it bears emphasizing, does not mean an end to independent political action. As we have seen, PACs will remain free to compete with candidates and parties—for red-white-and-blue money. If

PACs choose to spend their Patriot funds on an independent campaign rather than on contributions to candidates' war chests, that is their choice. Patriot simply deprives PACs of power based on the wealth of their clients; it does not deprive them of their freedom to operate on a more level playing field. If the American Medical Association can convince the doctors of the United States, and perhaps some patients as well, to transfer their ten red-white-and-blue dollars to them, rather than the Sierra Club or the Republican Party, Patriot does not prevent them from continuing to play the game of electoral politics, albeit on a reduced scale.

Nor will Patriot eliminate the power of green money. General purpose media—ranging from the *New York Times* to the *National Enquirer* —would remain within the green-money sphere. While they could only accept political advertisements in exchange for money coming out of a Patriot account, they would otherwise be free to comment on political matters. Think tanks will continue to shape their messages to win the support of rich donors. By redefining the sphere of political equality, I have no desire to abolish the impact of market-generated inequality on our political life. I am searching for a healthier balance in which the sphere of political equality is not overly compromised by the pervasive impact of wealth.

Similar line-drawing exercises await when we turn to consider the problem of the political volunteer. Whenever a citizen works for free on a political campaign, he or she is forgoing time that might have been spent on money-making activities. Should we conclude, then, that volunteers are really spending the market value of their time and that their "imputed wages" should be charged against the campaign's red-white-and-blue budget?

Though this suggestion might appeal to some economists, liberal democrats should reject it. The point of a political campaign is to inspire lots of Americans to act as conscientious citizens, putting their money-making cares to one side for a time to consider the public interest. One candidate should not be penalized if he or she successfully engages this civic spirit more than others. Volunteers are not in it for the money, and their energies should not be charged against the campaign's budget.

If so much is accepted, we confront a final question: How should we treat a candidate like Ross Perot, who wants to invest vast sums of green money in his own campaign? Just like everybody else. On the one hand, the fat paycheck Perot could have been earning as a business executive should not be charged to his campaign's Patriot account as an "imputed" cost of operation. On the other hand, Perot should not be permitted to throw his green money around to buy the presidency or any other office. Like every other American, his purchasing power within the sphere of campaign finance should be measured in terms of red-white-and-blue, not green, dollars.

Corruption

But won't our careful line-drawing efforts be undermined by outright corruption? If a credit card has a balance of 10 red-white-and-blues, what is to prevent its holder from selling this balance in a corrupt exchange for a couple of greens? This is what happens with food stamps, why not with more patriotic forms of "nonnegotiable" currency?

The analogy to food stamps is too quick. The illegal buyer of food stamps can go into any store and exchange them for commodities. The corrupt buyer of a Patriotic balance will have greater difficulties. He must spend time and energy making sure that his promisee goes to a card machine and dials in the codes that will authorize the transfer to the "right" political party or candidate. This will be very costly, given the relatively small sum the corrupting party will gain from each transaction. It will also be hard to keep the media ignorant of a mass effort at corrupt purchases by a political "machine." A misstep here can be disastrous. Wrongdoers will face criminal sanctions equivalent to those involved in voting fraud, and the media carnival following the discovery of "dirty tricks" will seriously damage the tainted candidates.

But we have more to fear than this low level kind of corruption. What is to prevent high-level managers of the Patriot company from abusing their positions of trust? The possibilities are many: leaking lists of contributors, cheating on the accounts, and so forth. While there are institutional safeguards that may be employed to check against abuse, who will guard against abuse by the guardians? There can be no fully satisfactory answer. However, the present system of presidential public financing has been relatively corruption free, and other public bureaucracies have discharged even more sensitive functions without too much abuse. For example, the Internal Revenue Service has done a pretty good job insulating itself from pressure by political ins to oppress the political outs. Is there any reason to suppose that Patriot cannot be controlled as well?

But Is It Constitutional?

Despite this prospect of reinvigorated democracy, will Patriot nonetheless be held unconstitutional by the Supreme Court? *Buckley v. Valeo* upheld public financing but struck down some of Congress's attempts to restrict the role of private money in campaign finance. Worse yet, the case has chilled innovative thinking ever since.

This is especially unfortunate because the Court's decision should have pushed discussion in the direction of Patriot. To see why, divide the *Buckley* opinion into two large chunks. One part expressed deep skepticism about Congress's comprehensive effort to reduce the level of private expenditure by citizens and candidates. While the Court upheld some of these limitations, it struck down others that it feared cut too deeply into the resources required by candidates and citizens for energetic public debate. A second part of the opinion took a very different tack, abandoning skeptical critique for enthusiastic support. The Court shifted conceptual gears when it confronted Congress's creative use of subsidy programs to control campaign abuses. Rather than striking down such efforts, the Court went out of its way to uphold Congress's broad authority to embrace wide-ranging innovation. The constitutional case for Patriot builds on this strong affirmation.

The question that induced the Court's change of course involved the financing of presidential elections. While Congress was offering candidates big federal subsidies for their fall campaigns, it attached a very significant string: any candidate who accepted the federal subsidy could not accept a single penny from the private sector. Over the strong dissent of Chief Justice Burger, the *Buckley* Court upheld this innovative condition. In doing so, it took one large step toward Patriot. Like the program involved in *Buckley*, Patriot requires each candidate to decline all green money in exchange for participating in its subsidy scheme. On this core question, there can be no doubt about the plan's constitutionality.

But Patriot goes further. It prohibits people like Ross Perot from refusing Patriotic dollars and insisting on his right to buy his way to the presidency with green money. It also restricts ordinary citizens to their red-white-and-blue money if they choose to support "independent" campaigns on behalf of their favorite candidates. On these particular issues, *Buckley* looks both ways. As we have seen, the case strongly supports congressional creativity in the design of innovative subsidy programs. At the same time, the more skeptical portion of the Court's opinion did invalidate restrictions on candidates and citizens that bear a superficial resemblance to those at issue here. In particular, it invalidated Congress's restriction on candidates who wished to finance their campaigns with their own greenbacks; it also protected the right of citizens to use greenbacks to contribute to campaigns that were "independent" of the main effort controlled by the candidates themselves.

In the lawsuit of the future, the challenge will be to convince the Justices that this part of *Buckley* does not apply to the new reform. Defenders of Patriot must show convincingly that it was one thing for *Buckley* to protect the use of greenbacks when people were not provided with red-white-and-blue money; quite another thing to invalidate Patriot's restrictions on green money when each citizen is compensated in a new political currency.

This shouldn't be too hard—so long as the Court is prepared to think through the reasons why *Buckley* was so skeptical about expenditure limitations. As we have seen, traditional reforms of this type endanger two distinct interests. The first is a macro-interest: whenever the law tells people that they can't legally buy political advertisements, it reduces the overall quantity of speech-related investment. The second is a micro-interest: regardless of its overall impact, expenditure limitations frustrate each individual's freedom to spend money in the way that he or she thinks makes the most sense. Given this dual threat, Congress's comprehensive effort to restrict private expenditure understandably set off constitutional alarm bells for the Court. While the pursuit of equality is an admirable ideal, are we not running it into the ground when we use it to reduce the resources that would otherwise be devoted to political speech?

Within this context, the Court set about scrutinizing particular efforts at expenditure limitation—passing some and rejecting others, including the two that resemble our Patriot limitations. Though many have questioned these judgments, I agree with them. Without a compensating subsidy, severe limitations on greenbacks can greatly reduce the overall amount of resources devoted to political debate. Since the vitality of this debate lies at the very core of the First Amendment, the Court was right to look upon an encompassing set of restrictions with skepticism.

But as we have seen, *Buckley* itself recognized that the constitutional calculus can be radically transformed by the addition of a subsidy. Since Patriot distributes four red-white-and-blue dollars for every green dollar spent in the last election, it will lead to more, not less, political debate. Given this fact, the Court should ask itself a new question when confronting Patriot's limitations on the use of green money by candidates and private citizens. Unlike *Buckley*, the constitutional antics of Patriot will not be able to argue that both macro- and micro-interests support invalidation. To the contrary, Patriot's defenders will point to *Buckley's* support of innovative subsidy programs and will urge the Court to support Congress in designing a program that will generate a much more vibrant political debate than the free market had produced. Rather than threatening the macro interest in free speech, Patriot is reinvigorating it.

In response, the restricted greenbackholders will only be able to invoke a vague intuition in defense of their micro-interest: "After all, it's *my* money. Why can't I spend it on an advertisement for a candidate rather than spend it on some trivial act of private consumption say—an extra television set?" Call this the brute property intuition. The constitutional question, simply put, is whether the Supreme Court would find this a sufficient basis to invalidate the new limitations on green money imposed by Patriot.

The Spirit of Lochner

There was a time when the right answer could have been yes. During the early twentieth century, courts constructed an elaborate jurisprudence guaranteeing property owners a fundamental constitutional right to use their property as they thought best. The spirit of the time was expressed by the famous *Lochner* decision of 1905. New York had passed a statute restricting the workweek of bakers to sixty hours. The Court invalidated the statute on the ground that it violated the freedom of the owners and employees to use their property and labor as they thought fit.

If *Lochner* were still good law today, I would fear for Patriot. Since the constitutional revolution of the 1930s, cases like *Lochner* stand as the great anti-precedents in the American legal mind. For Justice Scalia, no less than for Justice Brennan, it functions as a powerful symbol of negation, not commendation. Whatever constitutional rights Americans may plausibly claim in the modern era, all sitting Justices recognize one that Americans can't claim—and that is the Lochnerian right to use one's property any way one wants. Given the transvaluation of *Lochner*, even the present conservative Court will find it difficult to celebrate the rights of property as a reason for invalidating Patriot's restrictions on green money.

Constitutional Supermoney?

But assume I am wrong in all this, and that the ascendant Republicans on the Supreme Court are willing to breathe new life into the Lochnerian premise. Even this change would not be radical enough to endanger the constitutionality of Patriot. The *Lochner* principle has an unproblematic application within a social order where one kind of currency—color it green—serves as legal tender for all legal purposes. But it is precisely this world that Patriot is trying to replace. This multi-currency aspiration, moreover, is shared by a host of other voucher proposals. In education, health care, welfare, environmental control, policy discussion is awash with designs for special-purpose currencies. If a fraction of these initiatives become social realities, the wallets of the future will have a different design: lots of pockets containing monies of different colors, tenderable in different transactional contexts.

Within this brave new world, the neo-Lochnerian principle becomes conceptually inadequate. It is no longer enough to say that we have a right to spend money as we please; the question is *which* money do we have a right to spend—green *or* red-white-and-blue?

Or perhaps the question is better stated in terms of supermoney: Does the Constitution affirmatively require the creation of a single *supermoney* that must *always* be recognized as legal tender so long as any other kind of money is tenderable?

Since constitutional lawyers have been living in a single-money world, such questions are unfamiliar. As an active Court watcher, I am confident that the Justices, after scurrying to read the applicable precedents, would grant exceptionally broad discretion to the political branches in this area. If Congress insists there be only one currency, that's fine; if it wants to create specialized currencies in addition to an all-purpose money, that's O.K.; but if it wants to create "separate-but-equal" monies—each legal tender only within its own sphere—that's fine too. Since this predictable position leads to straightforward support of Patriot, one could leave the constitutional analysis at this point.

However, there are fundamental principles lurking here. The freedom that old-fashioned green money gives us to shape the contours of our lives is not to be taken lightly. Whenever the state decrees that one kind of money cannot be transferred into another kind, it constrains the freedom of those who would have made a different tradeoff. The proliferation of separate-but-equal monies, each for use in a different sphere of life, could lead to very real constraints upon our traditional practice of liberty. I am unprepared to say that such proliferation should be permitted to proceed without any serious constitutional scrutiny.

It seems wiser, then, to move beyond the conventional answer—the near-plenary power of Congress over the currency— despite the fact that the Court will almost certainly invoke it to sustain Patriot against attack. Whatever may be said of separate-but-equal monies in other emerging contexts, Patriot merits more than rubber-stamp approval. It deserves judicial recognition as a decisive contribution to a problem that gnaws at the very core of modern constitutionalism.

This involves the constitutional status of the American quest for distributive justice. Since the New Deal revolution, the Justices—from the Stone Court through the Warren Court through the Rehnquist Court —have been trying to carry off a delicate balancing act. On the one hand, they have consistently denounced the notion that the Constitution enshrines the market-generated distribution of wealth and income. On the other hand, the Justices have refused to take the idea of social justice to heart and interpret the Constitution's demand for "equal protection" as requiring any particular level of redistribution from the rich to the poor. Instead, they have sought to remove themselves from the business of defining distributive justice by delegating the task to the president and

Congress. While this step has insulated the Justices from the endless distributive struggles of the welfare state, it has also left a question gnawing just below the doctrinal surface.

Call it the problem of circularity. It is one thing for the Court to insist that it is up to the politicians to determine the justice of the green-money distribution so long as the politicians are selected through a process in which the green-money distribution does not play an overwhelming role. If, however, the green-money distribution does dominate politics, there is a very vicious circle: the Court defers to politics, which defers to green money on the question whether the existing green-money distribution is politically legitimate. In consigning the question of distributive justice to the political process, surely the Court does not suppose it is inviting the American people to play a shell game?

This embarrassing question does not bulk large on the pages of the United States Reports. Perhaps the Justices' insistence, in the reapportionment cases, on the principle of one-person, one-vote is part of an effort to reassure themselves, and the rest of us, that the circularity problem isn't too vicious—that the impact of the existing division of wealth, while substantial, isn't entirely undermining the constitutional credibility of political judgments about distributive justice. Perhaps the Justices reconcile themselves to circularity with the thought that there is not much they can do effectively to change matters, and that they must wait for mobilized citizens to insist upon the greater autonomy of politics from wealth.

This is where Patriot enters, breaking the circularity at its most vulnerable point. Patriot allows the Court to stop papering over some uncomfortable circularities whenever it defers to the political branches, interpretation of the constitutional meaning of equality. By insisting that *only* red-white-and-blue be used to run campaigns, Patriot allows the modern constitutional system to work according to its professed principles requiring property to justify itself to democracy, rather than the other way around.

If, in contrast, the Court were to invalidate Patriot, it would be sabotaging the collective effort to break the circle created by its own pattern of decisions. While the Justices doubtless would continue to say that the question of distributive justice is open for political determination, they would have destroyed the very program that would have endowed this claim with political reality. While I disagree with the Rehnquist Court on other points, I do not believe that the majority would seriously consider such a counterproductive step. Patriot, then, presents an easy constitutional case. Congress and the rest of us should confront it on its merits, without undue anxiety over hostile judicial reaction.

Campaign finance is reemerging as a high priority of the Clinton administration. But the newspapers are already full of fears of more grid-lock within the existing framework of reform proposals. Isn't it a good time, then, to redefine the framework?

[17]

James S. Fishkin

Talk of the Tube: How to Get Teledemocracy Right

American politics is suffering from a near-fatal attraction to direct democracy. Symptoms of this attraction include the proliferation of referenda, particularly in the western states, and the credibility given to Ross Perot's proposal to introduce "electronic town halls" in which television viewers would call in votes on current policy issues.

We have also brought elements of direct democracy into presidential selection by creating a nominating system dominated by the direct primary. Since 1968, when Hubert Humphrey won the Democratic nomination without entering a single primary, the number of states holding primaries has grown from seventeen to thirty-nine; primaries are now the televised battleground where the nomination is effectively decided.

In addition, a near-daily supply of opinion polls, reporting the approval levels of candidates and the popularity of various positions, has given us a system that is far more plebiscitary in its use of direct democracy than textbook analyses of American institutions would suggest. Political scientists from the late V.O. Key, Jr., to Giovanni Sartori have compared the interaction of television and opinion polling to an "echo chamber" in which polls bounce back impressions presented in the mass media. Despite their volatile character, these polls set the terms of political competition and dominate the agenda for public debate.

What's more, the media reports poll results as if they were solid constructions able to support platforms and candidacies. The political landscape is altered beyond recognition when presidential approval ratings drop from 91 percent to 30 percent, as they did between spring 1991 and summer 1992 for President Bush. Or when an enigmatic billionaire is able to climb the popularity of various positions, has polls from nowhere to become, if only briefly, the leading candidate for the presidency without contesting a single election. When General Schwartzkopf was substituted for Ross Perot as a presidential challenger in one poll, he did almost as well, revealing the flimsiness of the public information base on which the Perot challenge rested.

Three central factors—television, polling, and the impulse to bring the people directly into the process—have given us a thin democracy of stylized impression management. Yet, as I will suggest, these same three factors could be turned to a constructive purpose to give greater substance to our democratic processes.

Couch Potato Democracy

This campaign season has initiated a number of new variations on these themes. Some changes have improved the system in minor ways, while others have only increased the superficiality of our increasingly plebiscitary televised democracy.

The hallmark of the season has been the proliferation of opportunities for citizens to respond to what they see on television. Citizens have been given opportunities to join in the dialogue, to call in for information, to call in questions to live broadcasts, and to participate in town meetings. Supplementing the shrinking soundbite democracy of conventional news coverage, many hours of "talk show democracy" have been broadcast on national television. The advantage has been an increase in the breadth and spontaneity of the televised political dialogue. The disadvantage has been the addition of new pseudo-voices for "we the people" to the campaign process.

Conventional news coverage continues to filter opportunities for the candidates to talk directly with the public. In well-known, parallel studies, Kiku Adato and Daniel C. Hallin showed that the average candidate "soundbite," the period in which a presidential candidate could speak uninterrupted on the evening news, shrank from about forty-two seconds in 1968 to about nine seconds in 1988. Recent studies by the Center for Media and Public Affairs show that during the 1992 primary season, this shrinkage continued. The average candidate soundbite has now diminished to 7.3 seconds.

The move back to a more extended discourse would depend on the interaction of network norms of coverage and candidate calculations. CBS announced that it would attempt to counteract this trend with a guaranteed minimum length for sound bites of thirty seconds, but the policy has produced controversy because in practice, it ends up omitting candidate statements. Meanwhile, the candidates have learned how to speak in nine-second bites to get on the news. So for now the effective political discourse reaching the mass public is mostly the shrinking soundbite, a medium that reduces political debate to messages worthy of bumper stickers or fortune cookies.

A major factor counteracting this trend, at least during the primary season, was the loosely coordinated effort to broadcast debates. From December 15, 1991, to March 15, 1992, eleven debates were televised nationally. While these debates offered a substantive contribution for those who listened, they did not transform the effective political discourse reaching the mass public.

By and large, the public learned about the candidates from the soundbites the evening news produced rather than from watching the debates themselves. Ratings of the major network broadcasts ranged from a low of 2.1 for the climactic CNN/League of Women Voters debate before the New Hampshire primary to a high of 5.5 for the ABC debate March 5 in its "Nightline" slot. (Each rating point is a percentage of the 92.1 million television households and represents 921,000 households.) These ratings put the debates squarely in the bottom ninth of network programming in their respective weeks. Unlike the final presidential debates of the general elections, primary debates, when candidate selection is a live issue, have not attracted large audiences. (In contrast, the 1988 presidential debates in the general election were estimated to have drawn more than 160 million viewers.)

Notably, when these debates were turned into soundbites and newspaper stories, they were reported mostly in terms of whatever conflict, controversy, or confrontation they generated. The first debate, on NBC, was most notable for the flap over Jerry Brown's advertising his 800 number on the air and for Harkin holding up a dollar bill to symbolize the value of the middle-class tax cut. The CNN debate in New Hampshire was reported mostly in terms of the fire Paul Tsongas drew for his support for nuclear power. The Denver debate is remembered for Tsongas's response to Clinton that while he might not be "perfect," at least he is "honest." The Dallas debate was notable for Clinton's rejoinder to Brown that he should "chill out," a phrase that Hillary later took credit for in the press.

The debates were only intermittently enlightening (with the possible exception of the MacNeil/Lehrer debate on PBS), even for the few citizens who watched them. But the greater damage may have been that to the extent the debates did reach the public, they came as sensational, recycled soundbites. The debates, then, while a noble effort, did not transform the effective political discourse reaching the public.

Another noble effort worth mentioning is the opportunity the Discovery Channel provided to all the major candidates to communicate for twenty minutes each directly to the public, without the filters of pundits or editors. Unfortunately, the broadcast achieved a rating of only about

1.5, reaching about 1.2 million of the nation's television households. Because the format produced neither drama nor conflict, it was not widely reported and produced very few soundbites.

Talk, Talk, Talk

A major departure this campaign season has been the use of talk shows. Perot announced his possible candidacy on "Larry King Live" on CNN. Both Clinton and Perot fielded questions from viewer call-ins on the "Today Show" and "CBS This Morning." Perot held a two-hour "Nightline" town meeting on ABC while Clinton held a ninety-minute town meeting on MTV. In one of the most ambitious talk show forays into politics, Clinton and Gore appeared for two hours on "CBS This Morning" with questions from a studio audience, live satellite connections to remote locations around the country, and questions collected from viewer letters. This format was successful in combining viewer input from around the country with follow-up questions from the talk show hosts so as to yield a more sustained dialogue.

President Bush tried his hand at the town meeting format by talking with handpicked visitors to the White House on "CBS This Morning." Bush argued that town meetings were nothing new. He had, after all, campaigned in 1980 and 1988 with broadcasts of voter forums entitled "Ask George Bush." However, those forums were scripted, a practice that got Bush in trouble more recently when he complained to a live mike last December that he had been asked the questions in the wrong order in an ostensibly spontaneous question-and-answer session in a teleconference to a California teacher's convention.

The main benefit of talk show discussions with ordinary citizens has been the injection of spontaneity into the political dialogue. Talk shows permit us to examine candidates for longer than a shrinking soundbite and they do so under conditions that may produce spontaneous exchange. Instead of press questions focusing on the horse race and political strategy, ordinary citizens have tended to raise more substantive questions about the economy, health care, and other issues that touch their lives directly.

Still, while citizen questions on the talk shows have been notable for their substance (if not for their follow-ups), host questions retain a whiff of the sensationalism that is part of the regular agenda of such shows. Talk shows tend to treat politicians as just another group of celebrities. Hence it was Phil Donahue who relentlessly pursued Clinton about Gennifer Flowers and draft issues before the New York primary, only to be upbraided by a member of his studio audience who wanted substantive questions. And when Stone Phillips interviewed President Bush on

"Dateline NBC," the president threatened to cut the interview short rather than face a question about alleged adultery, a question Phillips was told he should be "ashamed" to ask in the inner sanctum of the Oval Office. Conversely, talk show democracy blurs the distinction between politician and media figure by allowing such figures as Pat Buchanan, Jesse Jackson, John Sununu, and David Gergen to alternate between roles.

Of course, the talk show or town meeting ideals hold out the promise of even more radical departures from conventional political coverage. In addition to lengthier, more spontaneous dialogue, television viewers may also see their reactions tabulated, in some process that appears analogous to voting. This was, of course, the basic idea behind Perot's proposal for the "electronic town hall." As Perot described it, major issues, such as the budget deficit or health insurance, would be explained on the air "in depth, not in soundbites." Viewers would then call an 800 number "by Congressional district." This feedback, Perot promised, would be tallied and used to get the White House and Congress "dancing together like Fred Astaire and Ginger Rogers."

Something very close to Perot's proposal briefly saw the light of day last January, after the President's State of the Union address. In a pilot for a possible series called "America on the Line," CBS tabulated about 300,000 viewer responses to questions about the President's speech and the state of the union. However, the viewers who decided to phone in their responses to the CBS program presented a distorted picture of public opinion, at least when contrasted with poll results from a representative sample asked the same questions (and reported by CBS). For example, 53 percent of "America on the Line" respondents said they were "worse off" now than a year ago, while only 32 percent of the representative sample said so. Only 18 percent of "America on the Line" respondents reported they were in the "same" economic situation as a year ago, while 44 percent of the representative sample reported being "the same."

This kind of electronic town hall has two fundamental defects—it is neither representative nor deliberative. It is not representative because the sample is self-selected. Instead of being chosen through the methods of modern survey research, through a random statistical process, viewers at home select themselves by their decisions to call in.

Viewers calling in to an 800 number constitute what Norman Bradburn, Director of the National Opinion Research Center at the University of Chicago, has called a SLOP—a self-selected listener opinion poll. A SLOP played a role in distorting media coverage of the Carter/ Reagan Presidential debate in 1980, when ABC used viewer call-ins (in this case with charges for calling a 900 number) to declare Reagan an instant two-to-one winner, as compared with random samples that viewed the debate as a close contest. Like the *Literary Digest* fiasco of 1936, which predicted a landslide for Alf Landon over Franklin Roosevelt, self-selected samples draw disproportionately from those who feel strongly enough to call. Large numbers do not by themselves offer any indication that the self-selecting viewers represent public opinion. CBS has reported that over 24 million calls were attempted to "America on the Line," but far more accurate results could have been achieved from a carefully constructed random sample of several hundred.

Neither is the electronic town hall deliberative. Citizens are expected to phone in their reactions off-the-cuff, have little opportunity for debate or for consideration of alternative views, and often they have little background information. This points to one of the biggest quandaries of direct democracy in a large nation-state: the belief that there is little reason to bother learning about candidates and issues because it is so easy to calculate that one vote is unimportant and will have little effect on the outcome.

One of the more inventive departures this election season has been directed at this problem of underinformed voters. The Center for National Independence in Politics has launched "Project Vote Smart" providing an 800 number, advertised on CNN, which citizens can call to get nonpartisan information about candidate positions. The same device, advertising a number for citizen information on television, has been employed by the notorious Floyd Brown (of Willie Horton ad fame). In a new twist on negative campaigning, Brown offers callers the chance to hear tapes of conversations between Gennifer Flowers and Bill Clinton.

In either case, the problem of individual incentives for information remains. Primaries, referenda, and opinion polls have brought power directly to the people, but under conditions where the people have little motivation to think about the power they are supposed to exercise.

Is there some way of getting over this problem of effectively motivating ordinary citizens to acquire political information and deliberate about it? Some recent experiments, both in this country and in Britain, suggest a new way of combining television and survey research. In five different British elections, Granada television took a random sample of 500 citizens from a benchmark constituency in northern England. After discussing the issues for a couple of weeks, these 500 citizens were transported to London, where they appeared in a televised question-and-answer session with the three party leaders, to be broadcast a few days before the British general election.

Unlike American "town meetings," which have employed either haphazard collections of people in a studio audience or viewer call-ins, the Granada 500 group was a statistically representative sample that was also prepared on the issues. However, the Granada 500 took no votes, made no decisions. It simply offered a new kind of forum for questioning the candidates, forcing them to confront issues of direct relevance to ordinary citizens.

The Jefferson Institute in Minnesota has been experimenting with "citizens' juries" that question candidates and deliberate about their positions. In cooperation with the League of Women Voters, it has held such juries in Minnesota (in a Minneapolis mayoral election and on various policy issues), and it plans to hold a similar forum, in cooperation with local television stations in Pittsburgh and Philadelphia, in the Pennsylvania Senate race this fall. In contrast to the Granada 500, citizens' juries vote on the candidates. However, it is worth noting that with juries of eighteen people, they cannot be statistically representative of the entire population, as a full-scale random sample would be.

Both the citizens' jury and Granada 500 use randomly chosen citizens who are given the opportunity to deliberate about public policy and who are, in addition, offered the chance to question candidates on television. These elements are both included in my own proposal for a "deliberative opinion poll" at the start of the primary season on national television. Instead of a random sample of a benchmark constituency, as with the Granada 500, or a group the size of a jury, as with the Jefferson Institute, I have proposed that we take a full-scale national random sample of 600 people and transport them to a single site where they can question the presidential candidates in person on national television. Even if the viewing audience were limited to the comparatively small audience of primary debates, the results of such a deliberative poll at the start of the primary season would receive enough coverage to play a major role in launching candidacies and issues so as to reform the "invisible primary"—the initial period of the nomination struggle that has come to largely determine the nominee in an increasingly front-loaded presidential selection system. Hence the timing of such a televised deliberative poll could give it an influence far beyond the 600 delegates and far beyond its viewing audience.

A deliberative poll harnesses to a constructive purpose the same factors that have, thus far, only trivialized our mass democracy—television, polling, and the impulse to bring the people directly into the process. A deliberative poll brings the people into the process but in a statistically controlled way; it uses the techniques of polling but under conditions where the responses represent more than echoes of shrinking soundbites; it uses television to amplify deliberation rather than to disseminate canned material or advertising.

An ordinary poll models what the public thinks, however little the public knows or pays attention. A deliberative poll, by contrast, models what the public would think—if it had more opportunity to think about the questions, more information about the issues, and opportunity to question candidates extensively. Like the advent of talk show democracy, a deliberative poll would add depth and spontaneity to the dialogue. However, it would do so with a carefully constructed sample that would have every incentive to pay attention and take the process seriously. Members of the sample, unlike ordinary citizens viewing the campaign at home, would be motivated to pay attention because they would appear on national television with the candidates. The problem of incentives for information and deliberation is solved for members of the sample, and the results are then amplified by the television broadcast.

I offer this proposal not as a panacea but as a televised demonstration of an alternative democratic model. Recall that the direct primary is, itself, a relatively recent innovation fostered primarily by the Progressives early in this century and, in a second wave of reform, by the McGovern-Fraser Commission reacting to the fiasco of the 1968 Democratic nomination struggle. Experimentation with alternative models is clearly called for, even if there is no single proposal that can, by itself, guarantee a credible system.

Last year I joined with WETA, the Washington PBS station, to attempt to mount a televised deliberative opinion poll, the "National Issues Convention" to be broadcast for three days over PBS at the start of the primary season in January of 1992. While the event was canceled for 1992 because it ran into funding difficulties, WETA has since joined with all ten of the nation's presidential libraries to sponsor the event in 1996 at the LBJ Library at the University of Texas at Austin. With luck and proper funding, the next primary season will begin with a deliberative opinion poll on national television.

To be sure, a televised deliberative poll or kindred forms of policy jury are neither a new form of direct democracy nor a substitute for the more usual forms of representative democracy. A functioning polity requires high voter turnout, responsible parties, a well-informed electorate, and competent elected officials whose job is to deliberate day in and day out.

However, our elected legislators are truly representative only to the extent that the voters pay attention. Otherwise, they exist in an echo chamber of their own. In that sense, a deliberative poll can serve as a kind of role model. It can demonstrate the capacity of ordinary citizens to appreciate the complexity of pressing issues; it can give elected representatives a more authentic form of feedback; and it can shame pollsters into resisting the temptation to oversimplify. Perhaps it can even help restore public interest in public issues. We shouldn't expect new forms of public deliberation to replace the ordinary mechanisms of democracy. Rather, we should appreciate their potential to infuse representative democracy with new life.

[18]

KAREN PAGET

Citizen Organizing: Many Movements, No Majority

Unless you are an activist yourself, your personal contact with the world of citizen politics probably occurs when your doorbell rings. A canvasser, usually a young person with a clipboard and leaflets, tries to engage you in a discussion of a contemporary problem, perhaps toxic waste dumps, pesticides in the food chain, or rising utility rates. If you sign a petition or contribute a few dollars, you'll receive more material. Engage in a longer conversation and you may be recruited for active membership.

You're also likely to encounter citizen organizing by mail or telephone. There, too, you're asked for a financial contribution to help stop wars, prevent nuclear holocaust, slow ozone depletion, or protect abortion rights, free speech, gene pools, or animals. Occasionally, you may

WORKS DISCUSSED IN THIS ESSAY:

Saul Alinsky, *Rules for Radicals* (Vintage Books, 1972).

Carl Boggs, *Social Movements and Political Power* (Temple University Press, 1986).

Harry C. Boyte, *The Backyard Revolution* (Temple University Press, 1980).

Harry C. Boyte, *Commonwealth* (Temple University Press, 1989).

Harry C. Boyte, Heather Booth, and Steve Max, *Citizen Action and the New American Populism* (Temple University Press, 1986).

Nick and Mary Lynn Kotz, *A Passion for Justice: George Wiley and the Movement* (Norton, 1977).

Gary Delgado, *Organizing the Movement: The Roots and Growth of Acorn* (Temple University Press, 1986).

Sanford D. Horwitt, *Let Them Call Me Rebel* (Knopf, 1989).

Frances Fox Piven and Richard Cloward, *Poor People's Movements* (Vintage Books, 1979).

Frank Reissman, ed., *The New Populism* (Temple University Press, 1986).

see rallies or demonstrations sponsored by these groups on television, but you will probably remain unaware of who or what is behind "Citizens for ..." or "Citizens against ...".

Citizen organizing, by neighborhood and by issue, is now entering its fourth decade and becoming a well established feature of the American political landscape. Some activists and theorists see it as a big departure from conventional politics. They credit citizen organizations with reviving grassroots democracy, empowering previously marginalized groups, introducing issues to the public agenda excluded by more powerful interests, transforming passive citizens into active ones, inspiring a new populist revolt, restoring a progressive political coalition, and addressing social problems government has failed to solve.

Citizen organizations have undoubtedly increased participation, particularly at the local level. Yet any close observer of citizen organizations discerns a paradox. Their growth has occurred at a time when, by most measures, civic and political participation has deteriorated. Voting turnout rates have declined steadily even as these organizations have grown. Partisan affiliation has dwindled, as money has become the most important form of participation. Citizens consume political information mostly through one-way channels. The general public distrusts political institutions in general and politicians in particular. And while serving as a new medium of public activism, citizen organizations face some important constraints on their political role, in part because of requirements for successful fund-raising and for retaining tax-exempt status. As a result of both the larger political context and the limitation of community organizing itself, this movement has not done as much to empower the poor, revive democratic citizenship, or create new political majorities as its adherents have hoped. How to understand and remedy those limitations is the subject of a continuing debate.

Ambiguous Activism

Though there is no precise definition of a citizen organization, even a narrow conception would disclose phenomenal growth in the last two decades. An estimated two million such groups operate in the United States, engaging perhaps 15 million people. Organizations range from community-based groups trying to keep crack cocaine out of their neighborhoods to national networks such as Citizen Action and the Association of Community Organizations for Reform Now (ACORN), which each operate in more than 20 states.

Neighborhood-based groups can claim a lineage that extends back to nineteenth-century ethnic, immigrant, and neighborhood associations. At least three more recent historical antecedents are evident. Numerous organizations grew out of the consumer, environmental, civil rights, welfare rights, antiwar, and feminist movements of the 1960s and 1970s. Among them are such well-known national groups as the National Organization for Women (NOW), Common Cause, Friends of the Earth, or the Nader-inspired Public Interest Research Groups. Other groups, such as Communities Organized for Public Service (COPS) in San Antonio, United Neighborhoods Organization (UNO), in Los Angeles, or Oakland Citizens Organization (OCO) in Oakland, have their roots in earlier organizing efforts exemplified by Saul Alinsky's work in the 1930s and 1940s in Chicago. Some of these groups are affiliated with Alinsky's training school, the Industrial Areas Foundation (IAF). Still other community-based organizations, often helping to deliver local social services, can trace their origins to the Community Action Programs of the War on Poverty.

Though ideologically varied, most community and citizen organizing can be loosely described as liberal or "social-change oriented." The groups have diverse and even contradictory goals, from promoting a more egalitarian politics to creating voluntarist alternatives to government. Some organizers who originally worked only with the poor have concluded that structural sources of poverty are not eradicable through local organizing. As a result, they have moved away from purely local antipoverty organizing and targeted more middle-class and national constituencies, even as their ideology and rhetoric continue to celebrate local democratic participation.

Many writers on community organization seem torn between their faith in the virtue of "the people" and their acknowledgement of the barriers that prevent citizen activism from adding up to the broad social transformation they seek. For example, Harry Boyte, in his several books, locates citizen politics in the Tocquevillian tradition of voluntary association—yet also as a populist challenge to corporate and bureaucratic power. Boyte's tone and emphasis have gradually shifted. His *Backyard Revolution* (1980) emphasized the anti-corporate aspect, while his latest book, *Commonwealth* (1989), stresses the inherent value of creating local democratic "spaces" in which democratic principles can operate. These spaces can include the neighborhood, workplace, schools, or local political organizations. Boyte still insists, however, that restructuring from the bottom-up carries a system-transforming punch.

Further left, political scientist Carl Boggs finds U.S. citizen movements disappointingly conservative. He compares them to an international wave of post-Marxian social protest, which includes feminism, pacifism, and especially the Greens. Where Boyte celebrates local organizing, Boggs argues that the political potential of American populism is limited by its localism and its participation in the political mainstream.

One fairly militant group that has moved beyond localism, while retaining an identification with the poor, is ACORN. In *Organizing the
Movement*, sociologist and former ACORN organizer Gary Delgado
writes that while community-based organizations do not "sufficiently
address larger social justice concerns," they still "demystify the economic
system ... help people get a sense of the way the world works, open a
path for them to think about how it could be, and provide them with an
opportunity to change at least a small part of it." Yet, like other authors
who are movement veterans, Delgado is candid about the practical difficulties of sustaining low-income organizing: the racial and class tensions,
the predominance of professional organizers who are white and male,
the difficulty of cultivating indigenous leadership, and the fragility of
members' organizational loyalty. Constituencies that by any objective indicator are poor can divide over something as basic as an income support policy. Poor people who work may not identify with poor people
who are dependent. Individual mobility rather than class uplift remains
a potent American ideal.

As this literature suggests, egalitarian process—"letting the people
decide"—does not always produce egalitarian outcomes. Local participatory democracy can challenge bank redlining—or sponsor a tax revolt. It
can attack corporate pollution and disinvestment—or the busing of
schoolchildren. It can politicize a hidden issue—or depoliticize it by
turning it into a therapeutic self-help enterprise. Boyte, whose vision is
civic and communitarian, views the oft-repeated fear of "excessive localism" as simply the left's ambivalence about democratic process. But for
others concerned mainly with empowerment or economic uplift of the
poor, the creation of local, democratic institutions, though laudable, is
seldom a sufficient response to the inequities and economic dislocations
caused by markets. The sheer scale of economic problems often dwarfs
the transformational possibilities of local institutions envisioned by
Boyte.

More conservative theorists of community, such as Robert Nisbet,
Michael Novak, Robert Woodson, Peter Berger, and Richard John Neuhaus, view local citizen efforts as squarely within the context of traditional American pluralism. These writers see a cluster of community
institutions that have deteriorated, including family, neighborhood organizations, churches, and other voluntary associations. Neuhaus and
Berger argue, "We are convinced that mediating structures might be the
agencies for a new empowerment of people in America's renewed experiment in democratic pluralism."

Andy Mott, vice president of the liberal Center for Community
Change, has written that for progressives, community organizations
"provide a vehicle for mobilizing people to fight for their rights and

become empowered and politicized," while for conservatives, "they provide a practical alternative to government agencies: they build self-reliance and self-help rather than dependence and bureaucracy." In *The Vermont Papers*, libertarian John McClaughry, formerly of the Reagan White House and now a Vermont legislator, and political scientist Frank Bryan see a residual "civic" and "humanist" culture transcending left versus right, promoting a return of decision-making authority to the community level. The conservative Heritage Foundation proposes a new emphasis in domestic policy, which also uses the language of empowerment.

Despite similar rhetoric, however, left and right divide over the appropriate role of the state. Boyte argues, "Citizens can use government to train, empower, organize, and teach, so that people are employed, day care centers are created, parents involved, communities organized, people encouraged and allowed to solve problems for themselves with the assistance of responsive public agencies." Where conservatives tend to see community groups as substitutes for government, liberals and radicals see them working in symbiosis with government to restore the imbalance of political and hence economic resources.

Invoke the name of Tocqueville, or the language of self-help, and citizen efforts are seen as quintessentially American. Political scientists point to membership in voluntary associations as one of the main stabilizing forces in the American political system. Invoke the name of Saul Alinsky, however, and extend the same principles to poor people trying to change social services or private investment patterns, and the patriotic aura tends to disappear.

Alinsky's Legacy

No one has yet done for the history of organizing what Taylor Branch's *Parting the Waters* and Harry Hampton's *Eyes on the Prize* have done for the civil rights movement. We are aided, however, by Sanford Horwitt's fine recent biography of Saul Alinsky, widely regarded as the father of modern community organizing; Horwitt succeeds in restoring much of the Alinksy lore to its original context.

Horwitt frames the central question of community organizing: Can people acting together at the local level become powerful enough to redress social and economic grievances, or do larger forces doom these efforts to failure? Alinsky devoted himself to finding an answer, and his life embodies most of the key conflicts and issues involved in creating "people's organizations."

Alinsky viewed much of the trade unionism of the 1930s as conservative because it organized those who already had jobs. He shifted his focus in the late 1930s to communities of the unemployed and low-skilled. What made him controversial wasn't so much this shift from workplace to community but his views on power and his advocacy of particular organizing tactics. Alinsky believed the poor were not just poor in resources, such as money, jobs, or social services. Rather, they lacked the power to affect the distribution of these resources. Liberals, he argued, believed that justice could be brought about through the use of reason or logical persuasion. Radicals, by implication himself, understood that only power made interests give way and that the tactics needed to dislodge power were often offensive to those who exercised it. Redressing grievances and creating power required the involvement of the poor themselves. No one, and especially not the social workers from the settlement houses, was entitled to speak for the poor.

While the prevalent "progressive" belief in the 1930s was that poor communities were socially disorganized, Alinsky discovered numerous organizations in even the poorest of neighborhoods, such as Chicago's Back-of-the-Yards. His method was slowly and patiently to knit together union locals, churches, service clubs, and other local institutions. The critical step toward building effective community power was developing the psychological power of individuals through the discovery of common interests that could be turned into strategic political action. What the poor lacked in resources, they made up for in numbers. Whether an organizing goal was a traffic light or a neighborhood health clinic, a victory strengthened the sense of both individual and group potency and the importance of organization. These concepts, now loosely referred to as "empowerment strategies," have had immense influence on contemporary thought about community organizing. Lately, however, the concept of empowerment has become extracted from its original context. In many groups, it has come to mean psychological fulfillment rather than political clout.

Alinsky's vision of a national umbrella organization that would reinforce and connect local efforts was never achieved, in part because his approach was unacceptable to mainstream funding concerns. He did succeed in raising church-based money (described by one admirer as "Sherman's march through the churches"), but even sympathetic funders were able to influence the location of some projects. Horwitt is one of the first writers to chronicle the complex relationship between organizers and financial backers.

Alinsky's conclusions after some forty years of organizing are less well known than are tales of his famous direct action tactics. Not long before he died, Alinsky concluded that poor people, or poor people and minorities together, do not constitute a majority capable of translating their concerns into significant change. In 1971 he wrote that organizing in the decade ahead would center on America's white middle class because of its power. Only belatedly, he said, are we beginning to understand that "even if all the low-income parts of our population were organized—all the blacks, Mexican-Americans, Puerto Ricans, Appalachian poor whites—if through some genius of organization, they were all united in a coalition, it would not be powerful enough to get significant, basic, needed changes." Horwitt also documents that although it is gospel among organizers that Alinsky was opposed to electoral politics, it is not true.

The Sixties

The reconstruction of organizing experiences during the 1960s is a more difficult task. Our sources are largely scattered in memoirs and biographies of activists or accounts of organizations such as the Student Nonviolent Coordinating Committee (SNCC) and Students for a Democratic Society (SDS).* In the mid-sixties many SDS leaders moved from campuses to cities such as Chicago, Newark, Cleveland, and Hoboken to build "community unions" sponsored by the Education and Research Project (ERAP) of SDS. Community unions joining blacks and whites were supposed to raise issues of economic injustice and overcome racism with class alliance.

ERAP projects were animated by notions of participatory democracy that were profoundly hostile to organization, hierarchy, and even leadership. A SNCC adviser to ERAP declared that the role of an organizer was "by his simple presence [to be a] mystical medium for the spontaneous expression of the people." By the late 1960s, however, most ERAP projects were judged failures by their own organizers, who were disappointed that they had largely degenerated into "stop-sign organizing." Although mobilizing community residents produced modest victories over the local traffic department, these victories had little or no impact on the larger structural issues of poverty. Like some of Alinsky's community efforts that didn't survive white flight to the suburbs, community unions foundered on the shoals of racial tension. Urban riots during the summer of 1967 effectively ended many of the projects.

---

* See, for instance, Sara Evans, *Personal Politics* (New York: Knopf, 1979); Tom Hayden, *Reunion* (New York: Random House, 1988); Jim Miller, *Democracy Is in the Streets* (New York: Simon and Schuster, 1987); Todd Gitlin, *The Sixties: Years of Hope, Days of Rage* (New York: Bantam Books, 1987); Winnie Brienes, *Community and Organization in the New Left, 1962–1968* (New Brunswick: Rutgers University Press, 1989); Kirkpatrick Sale, *SDS* (New York: Vintage Books, 1973); Clayborne Carson, *In Struggle: SNCC and the Black Awakening of the 1960s* (Cambridge: Harvard University Press, 1981).

The entry of government into this arena, through the OEO's Community Action Program, created new resources—and new confusion. Alinsky warned that the principle of poor people's participation was being perverted through patronage and money; untrained personnel were getting their "snouts into the trough." Similarly, ERAP organizers saw CAP agencies as "coopting" poor people. At the same time, city officials were viewing them as a serious threat and moved to eviscerate their independence. Federal sponsorship of organizing in the 1960s, however, did stimulate considerable activism in urban areas—thousands of people gained experience in the political process for the first time and trained thousands of new community organizers, especially among blacks and Hispanics.

The National Welfare Rights Organization (NWRO), founded in 1967, drew heavily on civil rights, SDS, and antipoverty activists. George Wiley, NWRO's leader and former director of the Syracuse chapter of the Congress of Racial Equality (CORE), mobilized the latent power of poor people to disrupt the system through sit-ins at welfare offices and other protest tactics, often demanding benefits that recipients were not receiving even though they were legally entitled to them. This "break the bank" strategy was intended to generate pressure from the bottom up to restructure national welfare programs. For the movement's theoreticians, Frances Fox Piven and Richard Cloward, these tactics were a kind of poor people's analogue to labor's capacity to strike. Yet, shortly before his accidental death in 1973, Wiley had reached conclusions similar to Alinsky's. Recognizing that welfare rights could amount only to "a minority strategy," Wiley wrote, "Only a broad-based movement aimed at the economic interests of a majority of Americans will ever succeed in bringing about the changes we desire."

The National Welfare Rights Organization, like many other organizations of the 1960s, no longer exists. But these experiences have influenced successor groups, albeit in different ways. Local affiliates of Alinsky's Industrial Areas Foundation have remained primarily focused on local community organizing, continuing to rely where possible on institutional bases such as churches and labor unions. Each of their 23 community projects operates a little bit differently. One project of long duration, COPS of San Antonio, Texas, seems to substantiate the claims of organizing advocates. Its strengths include financial independence, an emphasis on citizenship education and democratic process, the sustained creation of indigenous leadership (mostly Mexican-American), a concomitant lack of reliance on organizing staff, and the steady development of clout in San Antonio politics, whose governing structure was previously dominated by Anglos. Yet COPS's secret seems to be a common ethnic identity and a willingness—uncharacteristic of most community organizations—to plunge into local electoral politics.

ACORN, founded in Arkansas to focus on welfare issues, has expanded into 27 states. Its base has been enlarged to include a wider
range of working and lower middle-class constituents, such as farmers,
low-skilled laborers, and residents of poor neighborhoods. ACORN has
retained an emphasis on both economic issues and direct action tactics,
such as squatting campaigns in abandoned houses to dramatize the need
for affordable housing policies, as well as lobbying.

Citizen Action has become a federation of 20 or so state-wide organizations, such as Illinois Public Action Council (IPAC), Ohio Public Interest Campaign (OPIC), or Virginia Action. Like IAF, it has its own training
institute, the Midwest Academy. State organizations vary widely but
generally operate as coalitions of labor, environmental, civil rights,
women's, and senior citizens' groups. Some, like Massachusetts Fair
Share (now Massachusetts Citizen Action), organize their members
through neighborhood chapters. They all rely heavily on door-to-door
fund-raising, known as canvassing. (Canvassers are essentially contract
employees who are paid for their door-to-door work, and generally have
to meet pre-set quotas).

Founding Citizen Action leaders Heather Booth and Steve Max, both
veterans of sixties organizing, have tried to coalesce constituencies that
are often at loggerheads (such as labor and environmentalists) and to develop issues aimed at gaining majority support, such as toxic hazards or
utility rates. They have chosen environmental issues that organized labor
can support, such as disclosure of toxic workplace substances. In the
early 1980s, Citizen Action leaders reconsidered their position on electoral participation. Since then, state affiliates have had former members
elected to city councils and state legislatures and have tied issue campaigns much closer to election cycles.

These groups—IAF, ACORN, and Citizen Action—remain committed to the idea of empowerment of low-income people and economic
redistribution. Lately, however, much organizing activity has been shifting to nationwide, single-issue, and often middle-class constituencies
around such issues as abortion rights, environmentalism, peace, or the
rights of and claims of seniors, women, blacks, native Americans, and
the disabled. Yet, for multiple reasons, this broadening does not add up
to a coherent electoral alliance, or a viable successor to the New Deal coalition. For one thing, most organizers involved with poor people remain
skeptical of electoral politics for fear of cooptation and manipulation by
politicians. Mike Miller, head of the San Francisco Organizing Project, an
IAF affiliate, cautions that even powerful organizations need to be "wary
of becoming the tail on a candidate's kite." To encourage political participation, without adequate organizational power, Miller argues, is "the
stuff of cruel illusion." Likewise, ACORN's founding director Wade

Rathke has warned that in coalitions of poor and middle-class people, the latter will tend to dominate the former.

In addition to these philosophical beliefs, many veteran activists have bitter memories of the role that party and government played during the civil rights movement. Civil rights activists of the 1960s faced not only hostile local power holders, but a Congress dominated by white Southern Democrats who exercised disproportionate power through the seniority system. The event that long remained a symbol of the treachery of entrenched power was the refusal of party delegates, including liberals with a good civil rights records, to seat the integrated Mississippi Freedom Democratic Party delegation at the 1964 Democratic National Convention.

For very different reasons, the founders of consumer and public interest groups, such as Common Cause and the Nader network, also argued that partisan disinterestedness was the key to their legitimacy: "The strength of the public interest constituency depends on not maneuvering for its own electoral power. Its credibility results from battling for issues and for change without any hidden [partisan] agendas," writes former Common Cause president David Cohen in *Citizen Participation*.

In a curious convergence, the "good government" strain of middle-class organizing combines with the class analysis of radical lower-income community organizing to form a pervasive antipathy toward elections and political parties. So while there has been tremendous growth among citizens' organizations, the mistrust of electoral politics persists. Combined with funding imperatives, notably a reliance on tax-exempt financing, these features greatly limit the political potential of citizen organizing.

Organizing and Funding

Citizen organizing cannot be understood without assessing the effects of fund-raising on both the strategies of individual groups and the potency of their cumulative effort. Ever since Alinsky, citizen organizations have had to raise serious money to hire professional organizers. In the United States, of course, money is far easier to raise if donations are tax-deductible. But to receive tax-exempt funds, organizations must meet educational and charitable objectives established by the Internal Revenue Service. Thus, organizations formed for the purpose of tackling politically charged social or economic objectives apply for the tax-exempt status known as "501(C)(3)," often as their first organizational act. *In return, they have to promise not to engage in any partisan politics and, with some exceptions, not to engage in any lobbying.*

Organizations must worry constantly about violating their tax-exempt status and thereby putting themselves and their funders in jeopardy. Since most reform efforts are aimed directly at political change, to pledge nonpartisanship at the start is tantamount to tying at least one arm, if not two, behind one's back.

Some organizations have opted for another IRS status, 501(c)(4), which permits greater latitude in lobbying, including communication on issues and candidates with the organization's membership base. Nonetheless, these organizations must maintain, at least in rhetoric, a fuzzy line between nonpartisan and partisan activities. The larger and more sophisticated groups frequently establish parallel organizations to receive different kinds of monies and carry on different kinds of activity. But since the leaders often are on boards of both, they must behave in ways that allow their nonpartisan stance to remain credible.

One alternative to raising tax-free money is soliciting membership dues or small-donor support though such methods as door-to-door canvassing or telephone banks. Direct mail appeals may solve the problem of financial dependency on tax-exempt foundations, but they may bring other imperatives to the organization. Lists must target the right segment of prospective donors, and the appeal generally needs to be as sharply ideological and urgent as possible. Like a thirty-second TV spot, successful direct mail tends to rely on attention-getting "hot-button" issues. Though the canvass allows for more personal contact with the citizens, organizations face constant pressure to develop issues that will yield good fund-raising results at the door.

A major consequence of the necessity to compete for an always scarce dollar is that a "market niche" mentality has come to dominate many organizations and funders alike. To succeed in raising money, the leaders of each organization are forced to argue that their constituency, geographical domain, issue, or approach to the issue warrants support because it differs from all other competing groups.

For any issue area, picture a giant matrix, an expanded frame of tic-tac-toe. In each frame, cross the issue with a constituency or an approach and fill in the blank. For instance, in the health arena, organizations may combine gender and geography, as does the National Women's Health Network, whose letterhead heralds the organization as "the only national public-interest organization devoted solely to women and health." Combine gender, race, and geography, and fill in the Black Women's Health Network, based in Atlanta. Space doesn't permit the completion of the grid, but it can be constructed for any issue or constituency. This depiction of the landscape is not to disparage any organization's special identity; it is to say that issue and constituency organizing, as distinct from community organizing, has resulted in a systemic gridlock. This is only compounded when so many diverse reform objectives must be squeezed through a non-partisan, tax-exempt framework. This need to define a niche to survive financially means that the world of citizen organizations has come to mirror the dominant tendency in America's political culture of fragmentation and specialization. Modern techniques of funding (direct mail, telephone solicitation, some canvasses) have an effect on the electorate similar to television by substituting a largely one-way communication with citizens for two-way communication. One-way communication leaves individuals and organizations free from the task of reconciling competing or clashing interests. Demands in one policy sphere do not have to be weighed against others, nor is there a need to take into account the fiscal implications of policy choices.

There are few incentives, short of additional money, for organizations to coalesce with each other or with other constituencies, to work together on issues other than their own, or to develop a broader (common) vision. And, even though many organizers believe the lessons from the past dictate a move away from single-issue or constituency politics toward more majoritarian strategies that could be made manifest electorally, they remain frustrated in their attempts to encourage such a development. If what Theodore Lowi once called "interest-group liberalism" blocks the aggregation of majorities, so does interest-group radicalism.

Political Empowerment

Nowhere does the line between nonpartisan citizen organizing and partisan politics become more complex than in efforts to register and mobilize voters. Voter registration provides a unique window on the relationship between nonpartisan and partisan organizing, though there are no studies that examine the relationship in depth or assess the influence of funding imperatives. Such an examination would reveal the forces that have driven minority and low-income voter registration and other political empowerment efforts largely into nonpartisan organizations.

On the surface, the Democratic Party might be expected to be the major beneficiary of registration efforts among low-income and minority populations. The party, however, has consistently failed to undertake serious voter registration among those constituencies, even though candidates and parties should be better able to mobilize voter turnout than organizations that forswear partisan association. Voter registration, of course, is not an innocuous civic activity; it has the potential to shake up the status quo. Incumbents are seldom eager to see large numbers of new voters, with uncertain sympathies, added to the election rolls.

Prior to the passage of the Voting Rights Act of 1965, the Kennedy

Justice Department, constrained by the administration's ties to Southern officials, enlisted several liberal foundations to conduct voter registration campaigns. This intervention created serious splits within SNCC over whether direct action organizing or voter registration was the appropriate strategy. The first nonpartisan registration organization, the Voter Education Project (VEP), was established in Atlanta in 1963 and was headed by civil rights leader John Lewis, now Congressman from Atlanta, who left SNCC as a result of those debates. It is emblematic of the ideological confusion over the act of voting that it is regarded as both radical and conservative. In the early 1960s, voter registration was regarded by SNCC as an establishment strategy to coopt the movement; it simultaneously was sufficiently threatening to white Southerners that organizers were murdered for the act of registering blacks.

The Voting Rights Act may have created the framework for the enfranchisement of previously excluded minorities, but for the most part neither government agencies nor political parties were in any hurry to translate these rights into voting strength. That activity was pretty much left to civil rights organizations and liberal philanthropists. In the late 1960s minority voter registration activities in San Antonio, Texas and Cleveland, Ohio threatened incumbent office holders, who retaliated with Congressional hearings. Their wrath was directed primarily at private foundations, especially the Ford Foundation, which had made grants to the Southwest Council of La Raza in San Antonio to increase Mexican-American participation, and to CORE in Cleveland to increase black participation. In the case of San Antonio, the threatened incumbent was himself a Mexican-American.

Subsequently, the House of Representatives tried to outlaw all nonpartisan organizations from conducting voter registration with tax-exempt money from private foundations. In a 1969 compromise, the tax code was amended to require organizations doing voter registration with private foundation money to obtain a special status called 4945 (f). Organizations must work in five or more states, conduct registration across more than one election period, and not receive more than 25 percent of their money from any one source. This was intended to prevent individual campaigns from establishing tax-exempt fronts. While underrepresented constituencies, such as minorities and poor people, may still be targeted for registration, grants from private foundations may not be earmarked for a particular geographical area, and there can be no coordination with any campaign. It took the IRS nearly a decade to grant this designation to the San Antonio-based Southwest Voter Registration and Education Project (SVREP), an organization that grew out of the disputed La Raza-related organizing projects of 1969. Like VEP, SVREP was devoted to empowering Mexican-American voters through both voter registration and educational efforts. The Congressional hearings effectively chilled foundation enthusiasm for funding voter registration, and for a decade there was relatively little money for voter registration activities.

In the early 1980s, the first organization to target low-income constituencies for voter registration, Project Vote, was established with financial backing from organized labor. In an atmosphere of general concern over declining voter turnout and Reagan-era budget cuts, other newly created organizations applied for the special 4945 (f) IRS status, including HumanSERVE and the Midwest Voter Registration and Education Project. Older organizing networks, such as Citizen Action, added voter registration to their existing activities. And various philanthropists and foundations began efforts to increase the amount of funding available for low-income and minority voter registration.

For a moment in late 1983, it appeared that the Democratic Party was also going to launch a massive voter registration campaign. However, shortly after the party announced plans for such a campaign, Jesse Jackson entered the primaries. Many campaign contributors who might have been tapped for voter registration efforts were supporting former Vice President Walter Mondale and declined to give funds to the party for fear they would end up increasing the Jackson vote. Liberal donors did raise some funds for partisan registration during the general election of 1984. With Jackson even more prominent in the 1988 primaries, the same obstacles appeared.

In the period between 1983 and 1989, there was a substantial increase in citizen groups conducting voter registration. In some instances, experimentation led to closer ties between particular candidates and registering organizations. Citizen Action is an example of both the advantages and constraints of 501(c)(4) organizing. When Citizen Action's leaders decided to add voter registration to their other organizing activities, they attracted the attention of progressive politicians. From a politician's point of view, the advantage of Citizen Action is that its canvassers constitute a ready-made "volunteer" army. Citizen Action affiliates define as members any householder who contributes money or signs a petition. Under the IRS guidelines for "c-4" organizations, communication with members about candidates' stands on issues is permissible. Hence, once the monetary transaction is complete, the canvassers can give political literature to the householder. The Republican National Committee has filed an FEC complaint against Citizen Action and its affiliates, charging them with violating their nonpartisan tax status.

California's Center for Participatory Democracy (CPD) targeted low-income and minority people on a financial scale ($3 million) that was unprecedented for a nonpartisan group. While the center could legitimately claim many successes (it registered over 350,000 voters from target populations, of whom 57 percent turned out to vote), its dependency on the fund-raising skills of a single politician, California Senator Alan Cranston, led it into a trap which would destroy its capacity to raise money. One of the Cranston-solicited donations came from Charles Keating, a key figure in the savings and loan scandal. The accusation of tainted money not only decimated CPD's future registration plans but caused the collapse of another organization, the Forum Institute, which had been a wholesaler of voter registration funds.

Once again, private foundations have become gun-shy of voter registration. As tax-exempt groups, the more successful targeted voter registration drives become, the more at risk they become since "success" is almost always judged by election outcomes which, by definition, are partisan. Even worse, the new nexus of particular candidates and voter registration organizations, such as Cranston and CPD, contribute to the erosion of a political party role. Like television and candidate direct-mail, the new pattern encourages a highly personalized relationship, unmediated by party philosophy or program.

The fragmentation and specialization of issue organizing, and its disconnection from party organization, sets back the potential for a left/liberal electoral coalition. The issue groups cede this partisan territory to incumbents, candidate machines, and political donors. A self-fulfilling prophesy is at work. Citizen groups judge parties to be corrupt and useless; they mobilize activists and voters outside the framework of party, leaving the party all the more captive of candidates, donors, or both. The mutual antipathy of the issue groups and the parties is confirmed, and the gulf widens. The Democratic Party is presumably in business to aggregate electoral majorities. But the existence of the nonpartisan voter registration groups allows party leaders to avoid facing up to difficult coalitional issues and resolving the tension between its donors and voting constituencies.

Movements Without a Majority

Antipathy to party, by both radicals and civic reformers, has a venerable history. It was a key tenet of early twentieth-century progressivism. In reaction to urban political machines, progressives introduced such reforms as the city manager form of government and nonpartisan local elections. Critics of progressivism saw this antipolitical stance as limiting its power to achieve basic change. The same problem afflicts contemporary citizen organizing. Political parties are the only mechanisms we have invented in a democracy for coalescing constituencies and issues, mobilizing voters, and creating electoral majorities. E.E. Schattschneider's famous imagery of the American two-party system, as a large auditorium with only two exits, remains apt today: if you want to govern, a majority of people must follow you out one of the two doors.

One cannot argue that political parties in general have become obsolete, since the Republican Party today functions quite effectively. As Thomas Edsall of the *Washington Post* observes, issue donors on the Democratic side give mainly to "causes" and candidates, but not to party. On the Republican side, there is a far better integration of issue activism and party activism.

If anything, we are likely to hear increased claims for the potential of citizen organizing in the future. Even conservatives such as Congressman Newt Gingrich are laying claim to their brand of citizen empowerment as a "new paradigm" to replace the bureaucratic welfare state. To be sure, community organizations can play a crucial role in fostering participation, strengthening a democratic ethos, and in making government work. But claims that suggest such organizations can replace the state or the polity are as misleading as the notion that they could eradicate poverty. Those who embrace a more progressive conception of empowerment need to understand how decisively the dominant political culture—the connections between money and politics, schisms of race and class, pressures toward interest group fragmentation, and the weakness of party—have constrained contemporary organizing. If citizen organizing is to achieve its promise of reviving civic life and advancing the claims of the poor, it must do so without sentimentality and with a full understanding of its own history.

[19]

John B. Judis

The Pressure Elite: Inside the Narrow World of Advocacy Group Politics

In the 1950s, in the midst of what C. Wright Mills called the "great American celebration," mainstream political scientists conceived of modern American democracy as a more or less equal contest among large-scale groups—the most important being farmers, workers, and business. (Chapters Two through Five of V.O. Key's classic *Politics, Parties and Pressure Groups* were aptly entitled "Agrarianism," "Workers," "Business," and "Other Interest Groups.") Each social group had its own organizations from the American Farm Bureau to AFL-CIO to the Chamber of Commerce and the National Association of Manufacturers (NAM) and each enjoyed special power within one of the major political parties. Since almost every adult American was either a farmer, worker, or businessman, or married to one, almost everyone was represented within this pluralistic system. It was not the direct democracy of Athens, but it was as close to a representative democracy as a large modern nation could come.

This pluralist vision vastly overstated the extent to which America's pressure groups represented the general public or were equal in power to each other. Noting the narrow slice of the population who were active in these organizations and the preponderance of power wielded by business over labor, the political scientist E.E. Schattschneider commented in *The Semi-Sovereign People*, "The flaw in the pluralist heaven is that the chorus sings with a strong upper-class accent. Probably about 90 percent of the people cannot get into the pressure system."

Nonetheless, the pluralist vision reflected at least a shadow of reality. In the 1950s, no more than a dozen very large pressure groups dominated Washington politics. The labor movement represented about a third of the non-agricultural workforce and enjoyed enormous power in

Congress and the Democratic Party just as the key business and farm groups enjoyed the same kind of power within the Republican Party.

What distinguishes Washington politics today is the sheer proliferation of citizen organizations, trade associations, think tanks, and policy research groups. In its Spring 1991 directory of the most prominent Washington organizations, the *National Journal* listed 328 interest groups, 98 think tanks, 288 trade and professional associations, and 682 corporate headquarters. Many of the new citizen organizations such as the National Organization for Women (NOW), Greenpeace, and Common Cause boast memberships in the hundreds of thousands. Dwarfing even the AFL-CIO, the American Association of Retired Persons (AARP) has 28 million members, a legislative staff of 125, and 20 registered lobbyists.

But while the new organizations together claim far more members than the old—and therefore appear to be more representative of society as a whole—they have a far more tenuous connection to those whom they claim to represent directly. Many of them are what sociologist John McCarthy has called "professional movement groups." They are run entirely by their staff and by a board of directors that is often dominated by the staff. In organizations like the National Abortion Rights Action League (NARAL) and the Conservative Caucus, membership is primarily a fund-raising device to ensure continuous giving. Even in organizations that have local chapters and hold membership conventions, such as the National Audubon Society, the national staff and the board of directors control who is nominated for board positions and what information the members receive about the candidates. Moreover, in their funding, the new organizations represent almost as narrow an economic base as the old organizations of the 1950s. Many of them are supported by corporate and foundation contributions. Those that are supported by direct mail claim to represent a far broader public, but their donor profile tends to be overwhelmingly white, wealthy, and at least middle-aged. The best one can say about the bulk of these organizations is that they sing with an upper-middle-class accent. The old array of pressure groups fed false hopes of a new pluralistic democracy; the new—perceived by Americans as occupying a world unto themselves—fuel cynicism about special interests and about politics "inside the beltway."

The new organizations also have a very different relationship to the political parties than the old organizations did. The old organizations strengthened party representation by functioning as honest brokers within party conclaves. The new organizations contribute to political fragmentation and to the decline of the political parties. This reflects the circumstances of their birth: these groups arose independently largely because the old organizations and political party structures ignored or spurned them.

The New Pressure Group

Beginning in late 1950s, new political movements emerged that did not fit into the structure of the old Washington pressure groups and political parties. They included on one side the civil rights movement, the antiwar movement, the women's movement, the environmental movement, the movements for gay rights, consumer rights, and abortion rights, and on the other side the new conservative movement, the movements against racial desegregation and later against busing and affirmative action, the anti-abortion movement, and the right-wing evangelical movements. All these movements were initially outside the organized mainstream. Under the late George Meany, the AFL-CIO and the official Democratic Party were initially as hostile to the civil rights and antiwar movements as the established business groups and the Republican party were to Barry Goldwater's apocalyptic anticommunism and to Southern fundamentalism and segregationism.

Facing hostility from the Washington political establishment, these new movements created myriad organizations outside of Washington's established pressure groups. This was the origin of such groups as NOW, Friends of the Earth, SANE, Ralph Nader's Public Citizen, NARAL, the American Conservative Union, the Conservative Caucus, the Heritage Foundation, and the Moral Majority. But why did they choose to focus their activities on Washington?

The growth of these movements over the past three decades coincided with a dramatic expansion in the social and economic role of national government. Earl Warren's Supreme Court took an active role in shaping social relations—outlawing segregation and school prayer, granting the right to contraception and then abortion, expanding the rights of criminal suspects. John Kennedy used fiscal policy more consciously than any previous president to control the business cycle. Lyndon Johnson expanded the welfare state and convinced Congress to pass two major civil rights acts that outlawed racial and sexual discrimination. Richard Nixon sometimes promoted and sometimes acceded to an expansion of federal business regulation not seen since Woodrow Wilson's presidency, establishing new agencies like the Environmental Protection Agency, the Occupational Safety and Health Administration, and the Consumer Product Safety Agency, expanding old ones like the Office of the Special Trade Representative, and passing landmark regulatory legislation. Jimmy Carter created a new Department of Energy and carved a Department of Education out of the old Department of Health, Education, and Welfare, resulting, in both cases, in increased federal intervention. At the same time, Congress created its own regulatory apparatus through the expansion of its committees and staff.

This dramatic enlargement of official Washington's authority meant that many issues that had been predominantly local or state concerns from smog to abortion—became national concerns whose final resolution depended upon what the Supreme Court, Congress, and the President decided. As a result, both the old and the new movements became particularly concerned with influencing what happened in Washington.

From 1961 to 1982, the number of corporate headquarters in Washington increased tenfold, and there was a massive growth in trade associations and in lobbying firms. The number of lawyers in Washington tripled between 1973 and 1983. In addition, corporations began to fund new kinds of organizations from think tanks such as the American Enterprise Institute (AEI) to congenial environmental organizations such as the Nature Conservancy. In the 1980s, as trade disputes with Japan intensified, money from Japanese corporations—as much as a billion dollars over the decade—fueled a further growth in think tanks and lobbies concerned with defending free trade.

At the same time, the new social and political movements that had been spawned in the 1960s and 1970s increasingly concentrated their efforts on swaying Washington. Older environmental groups such as the National Audubon Society and the National Wildlife Federation began monitoring federal legislation, while new groups such as the Environmental Defense Fund and Greenpeace and the Citizens Clearing House for Hazardous Wastes based themselves in Washington. Common Cause and the Nader organizations were founded to fight corporate and government misconduct. The abortion rights and anti-abortion organizations focused on pressuring the Supreme Court. In the 1980s, People for the American Way and the Moral Majority joined the battle over court nominees and congressional legislation on school prayer. The National Rifle Association and Handgun Control locked horns over the new federal gun laws. The civil rights organizations devoted themselves to fighting for the renewal of the Voting Rights Acts and the Civil Rights Act of 1991.

The focus on Washington shaped the kind of organizations that emerged over these decades. Many of the new organizations located their headquarters in Washington, and some of those that had not chosen Washington initially, for example Friends of the Earth and the Cato Institute, later moved to the capital. Most of the groups eventually adopted a professionalized structure so that they were dominated by their Washington staff. This was partly a result of the groups' focus on influencing Congress and the White House and of the ebbing of grassroots political activity after the 1960s. But it also stemmed from the new kinds of funding that these groups enjoyed. The old organizations—from the AFL-CIO to NAM to the veterans' organizations or the American Medical Association—were financed primarily by membership dues. The new organizations were financed by grants from foundations, corporations, and unions, and by direct mail and neighborhood canvassing. This new form of funding laid the basis for the professional advocacy organization.

The Role of Foundations

The major foundations such as Ford and Rockefeller, which are independent of direct corporate control and which claim to be nonpartisan in their grants, were instrumental in the formation of the new organizations. Foundation support was essential to the civil rights movement's voting drives and to the founding of such diverse organizations as the National Council of La Raza, Ralph Nader's Public Citizen, the Environmental Defense Fund, and the National Resources Defense Council. Foundations that have been more strictly identified with the left or right— from Rubin and Stewart Mott on the left to Scaife and Bradley on the right—played important roles later in funding such groups as the Institute for Policy Studies and the Heritage Foundation.

By their nature, grants from foundations make an organization's staff less dependent upon members or constituents for organizational decisions, but as sociologist J. Craig Jenkins has argued, foundations also have encouraged professionalization. In studying foundation grants of social movements from 1953 to 1980, Jenkins found that only 17 percent of these grants went to "grassroots" organizations involved in protests and demonstrations. The rest went to the professionalized groups. Jenkins attributes the foundations' preference to their vaunted caution:

> Grass-roots organizations often lack a clear track record and are more likely to become involved in protests or other activities that might stir criticism. They are also more informal and decentralized, lacking the fiscal and management devices that foundations expect from their recipients. Professionalized organizations are centrally managed by single executive or professional staff. Their hierarchical structure is more intelligible to foundation boards, who typically come from business and academia, and affords greater assurance that the money will be used prudently as specified in the grant proposal.

Since the 1969 Tax Reform Act, foundations have also been limited to funding organizations that are not primarily "political"—meaning that they do not directly engage in lobbying or supporting candidates. Only nonpolitical organizations can receive tax-deductible gifts. This restriction has led the foundations to shy away from activist membership organizations. In 1968 the Ford Foundation provided the initial funding for the Southwest Unity Council for Social Actions, an organization intended to become a Mexican-American NAACP. But after the tax reform act, the Ford Foundation discouraged the new organization from taking part in local protests. Prodded by the Ford Foundation, the group renamed itself the National Council of La Raza and shifted its headquarters to Washington, where it became, in Jenkins's words, "a professional organization with relatively weak ties to a constituency."

The limits on tax-deductible gifts have in turn influenced the way in which organizations have defined their mission. Before the 1970s, a considerable gulf existed between the quasi-academic think tank such as the Brookings Institution that sought to influence the long-range views of government officials but did not have a specific legislative agenda, and the lobby or activist group that pressured Congress or the White House to pass or block certain legislation. In the 1970s, however, new organizations arose that were intended to circumvent the law—to maintain eligibility for tax-deductible grants from individuals and foundations while still seeking to influence official Washington. Policy research organizations and think tanks such the Heritage Foundation, the Free Congress Foundation, the Institute for Policy Studies, and later the Economic Policy Institute were not simply scholarly groups concerned with public policy; they had specific agendas and took positions on legislation, but they neither lobbied nor backed candidates. Some of these groups, the Heritage Foundation, for example, offered their donors memberships, but all of them, by their very nature, were professionalized organizations controlled by their staffs and by a board of directors representing their largest donors.

Some groups have tried to elude restrictions on tax-deductible gifts by creating nonprofit research or educational groups alongside lobbying organizations and political action committees. The educational group then becomes responsible for the organization's research and pays many of its salaries. Organizations that have adopted this structure include the American Civil Liberties Union, NARAL, Public Citizen, Consumer Federation of America, Eagle Forum, Conservative Caucus, and the Sierra Club. By its very nature this kind of cumbersome structure—requiring interminable bookkeeping and attention to grant writing and fund-raising—reinforces centralized staff control of organizations.

By their grants, the large foundations have also affected the kind of issues organizations have pursued as well as the way they have pursued them. In 1962 Kennedy administration officials used the promise of foundation support to lure the Southern civil rights movement away from militant demonstrations toward voter registration. In the environmental movement, the large foundations have favored the legal strategies and policy research of the Environmental Defense Fund over the less tempered methods of Greenpeace. Foundations often prefer studies of action to action itself; and they prefer studies with uncontroversial conclusions that will not call into question their own impartiality. As Robert McIntyre, the director of Citizens for Tax Justice, puts it, "They usually don't like anything controversial. If we changed our name to Citizens for Tax Thinking, we'd get more money." Similarly, directors of organizations concerned with trade issues have also complained that the foundations were reluctant to fund proposals that were not endorsed by established free-trade economists.

But this does not mean that the large independent foundations have partisan agendas, only that they rigorously follow the path of respectable opinion. When the controversial becomes widely accepted, they fund it. Their major impact is structural rather than partisan or narrowly political. They encourage professionalization and discourage militant protest strategies. They project their own caution and timidity onto the organizations that they fund. And they contribute to the decline of politics and parties by stimulating the growth of a new realm of organizational activity—issue-oriented, but nonpartisan—that is cut off from the compromise and deliberation that are essential to building majority political parties.

The more ideologically oriented foundations have tended to have a symbiotic relationship with their recipients. The Youth Project, now called the Partnership for Democracy, was founded in 1970 to act as a middleman between foundations and liberal and left-wing social movements and groups. The project's board has been made up of representatives from many of the organizations that receive funds from it. Scaife, Bradley, Olin, and the other foundations that fund conservative organizations are advised by leading conservatives such as William Simon and Irving Kristol. (Kristol earned his nickname of "the Godfather" partly from his role in arranging funding for conservative groups and individuals.) Whom these foundations fund reflects the priorities of leading conservatives rather than the distinct concerns of the foundation executives.

Even the exceptions prove the rule. Last December, the *Washington Times* reported what appeared to be an attempt by the $200 million Scaife Foundation in Pittsburgh to influence the agenda of the Heritage Foundation, the most important conservative institution in Washington. According to the newspaper account, foundation president Richard Larry forced the organization to adopt a program concerned with cultural policy. Heritage concurred by hiring former Secretary of Education William Bennett as the head of a new cultural program, funded by Scaife. Bennett was also a member of the Scaife board of directors. It seemed like a coup for Scaife, but in fact represented Heritage's willing acquiescence in a long-standing trend in the conservative movement. Heritage already had a staff member assigned to cultural issues. By Scaife's funding of

Bennett, Heritage gained a high-profile celebrity who will now help it exert influence over Scaife rather than vice versa.

Corporate Funding and K Street

Corporations and their private foundations contributed even more to the rise of new Washington-based organizations in the 1970s. Under attack from labor and the new consumer and environmental movements, and seeing their profit margins threatened by foreign competitors, businesses took the offensive. They vastly increased their lobbying budget in Washington. From 1971 to 1982, the number of registered business lobbyists increased from 175 to 2,445.

Corporations also flocked to set up political action committees —their ranks grew from 139 corporate PACs in 1974 to 1,204 in 1980. They revived the moribund U.S. Chamber of Commerce and funded new, powerful business organizations that were able to employ the media and grassroots lobbying techniques developed by the consumer and environmental movements. The Business Roundtable, composed of 192 large corporations, was credited with the defeat in Congress of Nader's proposal for a Consumer Protection Agency and the AFL-CIO's push for labor law reform. The American Council for Capital Formation successfully led the fight for reduction of corporate income and capital gains taxes. Business also funded think tanks that promoted deregulation of business, contributing to the rise of both the American Enterprise Institute—which before the mid-1970s was an insignificant backwater—and the Heritage Foundation.

During the 1980s, as trade battles heated up, foreign companies and foundations, particularly from Japan, poured more money into funding lobbies, public relations firms, trade associations, and think tanks in Washington. From 1986 to 1990, the Japanese contributed $1,015,000 to the Institute for International Economics, $1,812,408 to the Center for Strategic and International Studies, $1,610,684 to the Brookings Institution, and $846,000 to the American Enterprise Institute. The Heritage Foundation enjoyed substantial contributions from South Korean and Taiwanese companies and trade groups. The foreign contributions to think tanks were intended to reinforce congenial positions on trade and investment.

By the decade's end, foreign influence buying, combined with a sagging American trade balance, led to a backlash. A group of American corporations led by Chrysler, TRW, Corning Glass, USX, and Milliken began funding policy groups that favored using trade laws to protect American industries. These included the Economic Strategy Institute, founded by former Commerce Department official Clyde Prestowitz.

Corporations also funded coalitions to oppose changes in the laws of the General Agreement on Tariffs and Trade (GATT) favored by foreign countries. By the end of the 1980s, some of the fiercest lobbying battles in Washington were taking place between one business-funded lobby or policy group and another.

The influx of corporate money over the past two decades has created a burgeoning complex of law firms, public relations houses, lobbying firms, and policy research groups named after Washington's K Street, where many of them are located. This complex increasingly dominates politics in the city. National Republican politics has largely been run by the lobbying firm Black, Manafort, Stone and Kelly from which Charles Black and the late Lee Atwater came, while Democratic politics has been controlled by the powerful K Street law firms that house former Democratic officials and that have contributed Democratic national chairs Robert Strauss, Charles Manatt, and Ron Brown. The Democratic Leadership Council, chaired by Arkansas Governor Bill Clinton, and its policy group, the Progressive Policy Institute, were largely funded by former Democratic congressional aides turned K Street lobbyists. And many of these same lawyers and lobbyists now serve as trustees or members of the board of directors of the main Washington policy groups, from AEI to Brookings.

American and foreign corporations have also contributed to many organizations spawned or sustained by new social movements. These include NOW's Legal Defense and Education Fund, the Children's Defense Fund, many of the largest environmental organizations, including the Audubon Society, the National Wildlife Federation, and the Environmental Law Institute, the NAACP, the Urban League, the National Council of La Raza, and the Center for Community Change. The corporations had widely different motives for funding these organizations.

Corporate contributions to civil rights organizations largely stem from social conscience and from a commitment to social harmony and an educated work force. Many of the same corporations that contribute to conservative policy research groups also give to civil rights organizations that have denounced the kinds of policies that these research groups have favored. For instance, half of the corporations that fund the black policy group, the Joint Center for Policy Studies, also fund the Institute for Research on the Economics of Taxation, an organization founded by supply-sider and former Reagan Treasury official Norman Ture.

Some corporate gifts are intended to improve companies' images. Exxon and Weyerhauser hoped to improve their reputations among environmentalists through their contributions to the World Wildlife Fund, the Nature Conservancy, and Resources for the Future. Other corporations, faced with the prospect of change, have tried to throw their weight behind organizations that advocate the more palatable alternatives. In 1989, corporations gave $703,840 to the milquetoast Nature Conservancy and $3,175 to the Sierra Club. According to the *Corporate Philanthropy Report*, insurance companies, facing the likelihood of health insurance reform, now back research and programs that will preserve the private insurance industry's role and "head off unpalatable proposals such as shifting to a Canadian-style government health program."

The mixture of motives is epitomized by Waste Management, Inc., the $19-billion garbage collection giant and notorious polluter. Waste Management has given large contributions to almost every environmental organization to the right of Greenpeace, including the World Wildlife Fund, the National Wildlife Federation (on whose board of directors Waste Management CEO Dean Buntrock sits), the National Audubon Society, the Environmental Law Institute, Ducks Unlimited, the Sierra Club, the Natural Resources Defense Council, the Izaak Walton League, and the World Resources Institute. Waste Management intended its good works to deflect critics concerned about the $50 million in fines that the corporation has already incurred for illegal waste practices and for price fixing. The company accompanied its contributions with an aggressive advertising campaign in environmental magazines. For instance, it ran a full-page advertisement in the Wilderness Society's magazine that, under a photo of a butterfly, declared, "We profit by protecting the environment."

Waste Management also wanted to buy influence in the battle over environmental legislation and enforcement. In 1989, a year after Buntrock was named to the National Wildlife Federation's board of directors, he succeeded in getting Wildlife Federation president Jay Hair to set up a meeting between him and EPA administrator William Reilly. After the meeting, Reilly announced that he would challenge Southern states' attempts to restrict hazardous waste disposal. When the Wildlife Federation later signed a letter protesting the decision, Reilly told a reporter that he was surprised because Hair had "hosted the breakfast at which I was lobbied to do the very thing we are doing."

Finally, Waste Management has had a vested interest in passing stringent and complicated hazardous waste regulations that smaller companies would find too expensive to follow. According to an Audubon Society official, Waste Management is now underwriting that organization's attempt to strengthen the Resource Conservation and Recovery Act. Like the larger meat packing companies that pressed for food and drug regulation at the beginning of the century, Waste Management wants to use regulation to drive its competitors out of business.

Sometimes, corporate funding has seemed to induce organizations to steer clear of certain issues that might offend their donors, but usually only when a corporate representative already has considerable power within the organization itself. In the late 1970s, the NAACP refused to oppose the decontrol of natural gas prices. Most of the organization's leadership opposed decontrol, but Margaret Bush Wilson, who chaired the NAACP's board and served on the board of Monsanto, did not. Monsanto was also a big contributor to the NAACP.

In 1980 the Heritage Foundation called for the abolition of the Synthetic Fuels Corporation. But Heritage began equivocating when President Reagan appointed as head of the corporation Edward Noble, who was active in Heritage and served as a trustee of the Noble Foundation, a major contributor to Heritage. In 1985, when Congress was on the verge of abolishing the agency, Heritage produced a briefing paper on "Salvaging the Synthetic Fuels Corporation." "We saw Noble's hand in it," said one Capitol Hill aide who had previously enjoyed Heritage's support in trying to abolish the agency.

Corporations have sought influence primarily by throwing their weight behind organizations and groups that espouse alternatives they either enthusiastically back or prefer in the face of something they deem to be much worse. Through their contributions, corporations have established a decided superiority over their rivals and critics in every area that is of vital concern to them.

When Congress takes up tax issues, business can call on the American Council for Capital Formation, the CATO Institute, the Heritage Foundation, selected scholars from Brookings, the American Enterprise Institute, Ture's Research Institute, NAM, and the Chamber of Commerce. Labor can call on Robert McIntyre's tiny Citizens for Tax Justice. In defining the party's economic agenda, business cannot only command the loyalty of conservative and Republican organizations, but also of Democratic groups such as the Democratic Leadership Council that have been funded by lobbyists and their corporations. By contrast, liberal and labor Democrats can look to Heather Booth's Coalition for Democratic Values, housed in the top floor of a warehouse off a side street in suburban Maryland.

Much of the environmental movement is funded through direct mail, but as the recession has dried up direct-mail contributions, those environmental organizations that can gain large-scale corporate funding have continued to prosper while the more radical groups such as Greenpeace have had to cut back drastically in their staff and activities. According to the *Chronicle of Philanthropy*, only organizations that "seek market-oriented solutions don't feel the pinch." This means that their voice is now more likely to be heard, and, in Washington, the power to get your opinion heard wins battles.

Taken together, the corporate PACs and lobbyists, corporate officials manning new Washington offices, the Chamber of Commerce and NAM, the new organizations like the Business Roundtable, and the corporate contributions to like-minded organizations such as AEI have completely tilted the balance of power in Washington. Business has gotten its way for the last fifteen years in every major legislative battle that directly threatens it, from labor law reform to tax reduction and deregulation.

Labor's Diminishing Returns

The AFL-CIO watched the initial explosion of social movements with a mixture of confusion and disdain. During Martin Luther King's 1963 march on Washington, AFL-CIO head George Meany closed the federation's headquarters for fear that the march would turn into a riot. During the 1972 election, Meany implicitly aligned the federation with Richard Nixon's attacks against the "acid, amnesty, and abortion" of the new left and the McGovern campaign. But the United Auto Workers, which left the AFL-CIO in 1968 and did not rejoin it until 1981, and the industrial and public employee unions within the federation backed the civil rights movement, helping to found the Leadership Conference on Civil Rights.

Over the next two decades, as corporate lobbying expanded, these same unions also funded several coalition efforts, including the Full Employment Action Council and the Progressive Alliance, intended to counter corporate influence. In the late 1970s, after Meany had been succeeded by Lane Kirkland and after labor had been repeatedly drubbed on Capitol Hill, the AFL-CIO itself began reluctantly and haltingly funding organizations that it did not directly control. But the bulk of union funding still comes from individual unions rather than the federation.

During the 1980s, unions helped bankroll feminist, environmental, consumer, foreign policy, and citizens organizations, becoming the mainstay of such efforts as the Citizen-Labor Energy Coalition, now part of Citizen Action. Unions have contributed the bulk of the funds for two policy research groups, the Citizens for Tax Justice and the Economic Policy Institute (EPI) and have joined business in backing Clyde Prestowitz's Economic Strategy Institute.

The unions' role in founding EPI bears out the plight of labor. The AFL-CIO's Industrial Union Department (IUD) had regularly been doing studies of the decline of manufacturing, but the mainstream press ignored its efforts because they were seen as colored by labor's special interest.

After lengthy and sometimes difficult discussions with the policy intellectuals that were putting EPI together, union officials decided they would be better off following the corporations' example and funding a group that was committed to the same principles and ideas but not tainted directly by their label. In 1986 labor unions provided the money to start EPI, and the IUD's star economist Larry Mishel transferred to EPI, doing virtually the same studies, but gaining some attention from the press corps. Yet EPI remained haunted by labor's role. The press refers to the organization as "labor-backed," while never describing AEI and other business-funded groups as "business-backed." To secure its independence, EPI has successfully won some support from foundations and business.

Both Citizens for Tax Justice and EPI are relatively low-budget operations compared to AEI or Heritage. And labor's overall contribution to organizations like these remains minuscule compared to the amount of money corporations spend on think tanks and policy groups—perhaps less than one half of one percent. Labor also spends relatively little on lobbying. Since 1960, the AFL-CIO has devoted about 2.5 percent of its budget to lobbying Capitol Hill. By comparison, the National Rifle Association, a particularly effective force on Capitol Hill, spends more than 15 percent of its budget on lobbying. At one point, the American Petroleum Institute employed more lobbyists in Washington than the entire labor movement.

What clout labor has comes from its political action committee contributions to candidates and from its power as a genuine national membership organization that can summon its troops to punish and reward public officials. But as labor's percentage of the non-agricultural work force has dropped to 16 percent, its ability to counter corporate power has diminished still further.

The Power of Direct Mail

Many of the organizations that grew out of the social movements of the last decade including NOW, NARAL, Common Cause, and the Conservative Caucus use direct mail to raise the bulk of their money. The advantage of direct mail is that it renders an advocacy organization independent of large donors, whether wealthy individuals, corporations, foundations, or unions. Some major issues—like Common Cause's campaign finance reform, NARAL's defense of abortion rights, and the Conservative Caucus's campaign against the Panama Canal Treaty, for example—could not have been financed otherwise. Most of the large vested interests opposed campaign reform, and most of the foundations and corporations have found abortion too controversial. There are myriad smaller single issues such as gun control or opposition to federal funding of the National Endowment for the Arts that can be financed through carefully targeted direct mail. "Direct mail allows organizations to raise money for things that you don't always read about in the newspapers and that foundations and big donors are not interested in," says Republican direct-mail specialist Ann Stone.

But direct mail also has had its disadvantages. It is extremely expensive to finance. Nader's Public Citizen required a foundation grant to begin direct mail. Greenpeace relied on a loan from its direct mailer. It cannot be used by smaller policy research groups such as EPI whose work cannot be capsulized in a gut-wrenching direct-mail letter. By encouraging political groups to define their own purposes narrowly and through single issues, reliance upon direct mail contributes to the fragmentation of American politics. And while its social universe is larger than that of corporations and very wealthy large donors, it is primarily upper- and upper-middle class and is therefore only appropriate for issues that appeal to that segment of America. While direct-mail solicitation allows groups to communicate part of what they are doing to the world outside Washington, it provides little real link between that world and Washington pressure groups.

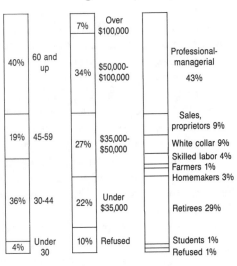

Figure 1.
Direct-Mail Donors to
Progressive Causes

Source: Peter D. Hart Research Associates, Inc., "A Survey of Attitudes among Donors to Progressive Causes," December 1990.

Direct mail was first used in 1964 by fund-raiser Marvin Liebman for Barry Goldwater's presidential campaign, which could not rely on traditional business sources. In 1970 Roger Craver, a former fund-raiser for George Washington University, used it to launch John Gardner's new good-government organization, Common Cause. Gardner, a former secretary of Health, Education and Welfare, had become frustrated trying to create a consensus among the labor unions, foundations, and corporations that funded the National Urban Coalition, and wanted a way of raising money that would free him from large funders with conflicting priorities.

In the early 1970s Richard Viguerie, who had been Liebman's assistant, began using it to finance new conservative organizations, including the Conservative Caucus and the National Conservative Political Action

Committee (NCPAC). In 1976 Viguerie associate Stephen Winchell branched out on his own and begin raising money for the Heritage Foundation, which depended on direct mail for much of its expenses in its early years and still raises about 40 percent of its funds that way. Meanwhile, Craver set up his own firm in 1976 and began raising money not only for candidates, but also eventually for NOW, NARAL, Planned Parenthood, Greenpeace, Handgun Control, and the whole array of liberal social-movement organizations.

Direct mailers boast that direct mail is a democratic means of raising money, but it is democratic only in comparison with fund-raising from corporations and the very wealthy. From 1970 through the mid-1980s, the direct-mail universe was very similar for both liberal and conservative organizations. It was predominately white, male, fifty-five years old and over, and with an income over $50,000. Craver refers to the liberal side of this constituency as the "toiling masses of Westchester and the peasants of Beverly Hills."

Conservative organizations like Heritage or Free the Eagle still rely on this older, male, well-to-do donor. Their funding base has not expanded and has probably shrunk slightly over the last two decades. But according to a survey that pollster Peter Hart did for Craver, Matthews, Smith & Co., the liberal social movements are now drawing almost a quarter of their funds from women donors age thirty-five to forty-five who have a mean income of $55,000. (See Figure 1) While the class base of Craver's mailing list has not changed, its age and sex have. This trend has already given liberal social-issue groups a decided advantage over their conservative counterparts.

Most organizations that raise money through the mail ask their donors to become members. A few groups such as Common Cause and NOW have tried to maintain real memberships through the mail, with local chapters and membership election of officers, but for most of the organizations, including NARAL, Planned Parenthood, Handgun Control, the Heritage Foundation, and Conservative Caucus, offering membership has served merely as a fund-raising technique that has allowed an organization to come back annually for contributions. It has sustained professionalized advocacy organizations.

Even in those organizations that have real members, the very size of the membership generated by direct mail has frayed the ties between the Washington headquarters and the organization's members. Typically, an organization such as Common Cause or NOW can be divided into four groups: the top staff and board of directors; an activist cadre of one to five percent who work in chapters and attend national conventions; the 25 percent of the membership that take the trouble to fill out membership ballots and opinion surveys; and the remaining passive members

—about 70 percent—whose primary contribution is to send an annual donation.

The passive members influence the organization largely by increasing or decreasing their contribution and their numbers. In the last year, for instance, environmental organizations have suffered a sharp falling off in their direct-mail receipts not only because of the recession but also because the average donor no longer believes that the environment is threatened, while women's organizations, buoyed by anger from the Anita Hill-Clarence Thomas hearings and the looming battle over *Roe v. Wade*, have experienced an upsurge in contributions. Similarly, many New Right organizations furiously expanded their contributions during the last Carter years, but then went broke after Reagan took office and removed the specter of a reigning liberalism.

In the direct-mail membership organization, the key group is the activist cadre, who, if they combine with a faction within the Washington staff, can effect real changes in the organization. In 1982, for instance, Common Cause's activists united with staff members to change the organization's focus from good-government issues to stopping the MX missile, even though the organization's polls showed that the group's membership was less concerned about the MX than about the organization's traditional issues. In 1989 NOW's activists forced the organization—against the better judgment of many of its leaders—to consider building a feminist third party.

However limited their representation, organizations such as NOW and Common Cause do represent an advance in democracy. But the majority of organizations are less like NOW and Common Cause and more like the Conservative Caucus, NARAL, Greenpeace, or People for the American Way. However noble their cause, they pursue it largely within a closed universe. They are accountable to a larger public only through the ultimate veto power that these donors hold. And these donors, far from being representative of the country at large, embody a small slice of upper-income America.

Organizations that are dependent on direct mail also are limited by the preoccupations of their own donor base. The donors to organizations like NARAL or the Sierra Club tend to fit the profile of the Baby Boomer—liberal on social and environmental issues and on foreign policy, but fiscally conservative, often suspicious of unions, indifferent to poverty except in the most melodramatic forms. None of the major organizations that rely on direct mail emphasize the redistribution of income, the rebuilding of cities, the rights of workers to join unions, the need for national health insurance, or the kind of environmental issues that plague working-class neighborhoods.

Canvassing the Middle Class

Some of those organizations that want to work on populist economic issues have discovered an alternative to direct mail and to contributions from business, labor, and foundations. In 1974 Chicago activist Marc Anderson, inspired by the example of door-to-door encyclopedia salesmen, began canvassing to raise money for Citizens for a Better Environment. Anderson introduced canvassing techniques to Ralph Nader's network of Public Interest Research Groups and to Citizen Action, a group of liberal state organizations that were emphasizing economic issues. Other national organizations, including Greenpeace, ACORN, Clean Water Action, and SANE-Freeze, now use canvassing to fund their operations.

Contributors to canvasses tend to be less well-to-do than direct-mail donors and more receptive to middle-class or even working class economic issues. Two years ago, Citizen Action did a profile of its donors (see Figure 2) and found that 58 percent have household incomes of less than $40,000.

Unlike the direct-mail donors, Citizen Action's donors identified jobs and unemployment as key issues. Yet Citizen Action's donor base was by no means working-class. One-third or more of those from thirty-five to fifty-four years old earned $50,000 and half of the donors identified themselves as either managers or professionals. Canvassing does widen the political universe in which groups operate—making it possible to raise money for economic issues—but it does not alter it dramatically.

Figure 2.
Donors to Citizens Action from Door-to-Door Canvassing, 1988

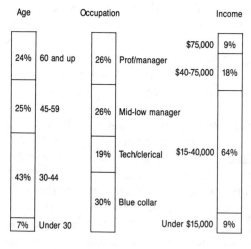

Source: Citizen Action.

When organizations began using canvasses for raising money, they also saw it as a way of educating citizens and gaining active members. Most canvassing groups continue to call their donors "members," and canvassers ask people not simply for donations, but to buy a membership. But over the last decade, canvassing has degenerated into a fund-raising technique for professional organizations that are run by their staff. Jo Patten, an official of a Chicago citizens group who has been active in several canvassing organizations, says, "Technically, it is membership, but membership means nothing. You can have no impact on the organization. Internally, it is viewed as first and foremost a fund-raising method."

Adoption of a canvass has even led some organizations to abandon the group's grassroots tradition. In the early 1980s, the peace organization SANE adopted a canvass to raise money. When it proved highly successful, SANE's director changed the organization from a chapter-based, activist group into a professionalized, staff-driven Washington organization with paper members recruited by the canvass. By 1988, when it merged with the nuclear freeze movement, SANE had become a Washington-based fund-raising shell.

Harry Boyte, the author of *Community is Possible* and an early proponent of canvassing as a means of building democratic organizations, is now disillusioned with its results. "Organizations that are heavily canvass-based not only pose issues in black and white, but lose any possibility for a strong membership base, because the money doesn't come from the members," Boyte observes. "The members don't have a sense of ownership or the challenge of raising money. [Saul] Alinksy is right that people don't have any strong stake in an organization unless they own it."

Yet for national organizations that deal with gas prices, health care, toxic waste, and other working-class economic issues, canvassing remains far more viable than direct mail or soliciting financial help from foundations, corporations, and unions. Direct mail does not work with people worried about their jobs; foundations and corporations appear interested only when discrimination occurs or when the poor huddle in front of Park Avenue apartments; and unions have their own diminishing membership to worry about.

Sociologist Pamela Oliver believes that the degeneration of organizations using the canvass into professional advocacy groups is the result of the decline of public political activity over the last decade rather than an outgrowth of the canvass itself. "Canvassing is a poor way of raising money," says Oliver, "but what is the alternative?"

Oliver is probably right, but the point remains: Canvassing by itself does not currently contribute to genuine mass membership organizations any more than direct mail does. And in the absence of a popular upsurge outside Washington, the existence of several national organizations that rely on canvassing has done little to mitigate the overwhelming tie of most Washington organizations to upper- and upper-middle-class wealth and concerns.

The New Power Centers

Political democracy has been breaking down in Washington. The break-down began with the decline of the political parties. The parties have lost much of their power and coherence, the victims of misguided reform and the replacement of the precinct captain and street corner rally by the political consultant and television advertisement. Popular institutions that supported a civic political culture, the labor union, the neighbor-hood bar, and the ward organization—have withered or disappeared.

The new lobbies, research groups, and think tanks that have arisen over the last three decades have not provided an alternative link be-tween citizens and their government. Instead, they have become central-ized bureaucracies as remote from the average citizen as the government itself. Moreover, these new organizations—through their focus on single issues or through studied avoidance of partisanship—have contributed further to the decline of parties and of politics as a process of public de-liberation and compromise toward common ends.

In the 1950s, pluralist theorists vastly overrated the power of the la-bor movement to act as a countervailing force to business, but labor in that era was a hulking Behemoth compared to what it has become. While labor's role in politics and pressure groups has steadily diminished, the power of business has vastly increased. Business and its organizations and lobbyists dominate the higher reaches of both political parties in Washington and set the agenda in the debate over the economic issues that directly concern it. About 8,500 of the 12,500 lobbyists, consultants, and lawyers listed in the current *Washington Representatives* work for American and foreign corporations.

As labor's role has diminished, business's lobbying has become nar-rower and more self-interested. It has had to concern itself less with chal-lenging labor's right to speak for the entire society and more with secur-ing its prerogatives and profit margins.

If there is another power center in Washington, it is the organs of so-cial liberalism and environmentalism—groups like NOW, NARAL, Com-mon Cause, Handgun Control, the Children's Defense Fund, the World Wildlife Fund, and the ACLU. Together, they employ about 2,500 Wash-ington lawyers, lobbyists, and public relations experts on their behalf. The power of these organizations now dwarfs that of the conservative social-issue organizations, lending credence to the charge that liberals rule Washington. But these organizations represent overlapping constitu-encies with many of the business groups. They do not reflect a compet-ing, but often a complementary vision of society: one that combines fiscal conservatism with a firm opposition to environmental pollution and ra-cial and sexual inequality. The liberalism of these organizations bears little resemblance to the economic liberalism of the New Deal and the labor movement. They represent the triumph of Hollywood, Cambridge, and New York's Upper West Side.

These two forces—business/economic conservatism and well-to-do social liberalism—have ruled American politics over the last fifteen years. During this time, Washington's politicians have fought off attempts to weaken environmental and social legislation even passing a strengthened Clean Air Act and a new Civil Rights Bill. But they have also acceded to a massive redistribution of wealth from the poor and lower-middle class to the upper-middle class and the wealthy, while acquiescing in the deregulation of corporations and banks. National Democrats have been particularly victimized by the erosion of parties and the growth of these new centers of power. Last spring, as the recession deepened, Robert Andrews, a freshman congressman from Bellmawr, New Jersey, recounted to me his utter bewilderment at how Washington works. While Andrews's constituents in his working-class Camden County district were becoming increasingly nervous about their jobs, Congress was preoccupied with the Brady gun control bill and a new version of the civil rights bill—measures, however meritorious, that were of no interest in his district. Echoing Ronald Reagan, Andrews described an "iron triangle" of interest groups that were dominating the Democratic Party and preventing it from attending to its traditional working-class and middle-class base. As a newcomer, Andrews saw clearly what many veteran Washington Democrats have accepted with resignation.

The Democrats' traditional middle class constituency, "Roosevelt's forgotten men and women," have also been losers in this transformation of Washington politics. Many of them know that they are better off because unions exist; they are far more concerned about jobs, taxes, and health insurance than about abortion, gun control, or exotic wildlife. As the pressure groups in Washington have proliferated, as billions of dollars have poured into the city to fund lobbies, PACs, and so-called public interest groups, these Americans have found themselves on the outside, watching with growing dismay as their own fate is decided by men and women they never elected, funded, or supported.

Part Three
Institutions

[20]

Richard M. Valelly

Divided They Govern

Since 1981 American voters have kept the national government divided between the two parties. We have had a Republican White House and a Democratic Congress, except in 1981–87, when Republicans narrowly controlled the Senate. This pattern, of course, could change if the Democrats retake the White House in 1992.

Polls suggest that voters increasingly approve of divided government. In 1981, 47 percent of the electorate preferred unified government,

---

WORKS DISCUSSED IN THIS ESSAY:

Alberto Alesina and Geoffrey Carliner, eds., *Politics and Economics in the Eighties* (University of Chicago Press, 1992).

Joshua Cohen and Joel Rogers, "Democracy and Associations," *Social Philosophy and Policy* 10, no. 2 (Summer, 1993): 282–312.

Gary Cox and Samuel Kernell, eds., *The Politics of Divided Government* (Westview Press, 1991).

Alan Ehrenhalt, *The United States of Ambition: Politicians, Power, and the Pursuit of Office* (Times Books, 1991).

Morris Fiorina, *Divided Government* (Macmillan, 1992).

Benjamin Ginsberg and Martin Shefter, *Politics by Other Means: The Declining Importance of Elections in America* (Basic Books, 1990).

William Greider, *Who Will Tell the People: The Betrayal of American Democracy* (Simon and Schuster, 1992).

Gary Jacobson, *The Electoral Origins of Divided Government: Competition in U.S. House Elections 1946–1990* (Westview Press, 1990).

David R. Mayhew, *Divided We Govern: Party Control, Lawmaking, and Investigations 1946–1990* (Yale University Press, 1991).

James A. Morone, *The Democratic Wish: Popular Participation and the Limits of American Government* (Basic Books, 1990).

David W. Rohde, *Parties and Leaders in the Postreform House* (University of Chicago Press, 1991).

Jack L. Walker, Jr., *Mobilizing Interest Groups in America: Patrons, Professions and Social Movements* (University of Michigan Press, 1991).

while 34 percent preferred divided government (the rest taking an ag-
nostic view). By 1989 these preferences had reversed: Now 45 percent
approved of divided government and only 35 percent backed unified
government, though very recent polls suggest some second thoughts.
Paradoxically, voters evidently dislike what they have wrought. As divided government has persisted, voter frustration has increased. Indeed,
divided government can be seen as both a symptom of voter disaffection,
and a cause.

Divided government appears to increase public cynicism about politics in two ways. First, when divided partisan government intensifies the
separation of powers of the American constitutional system, government
becomes stymied. Citizens, like the Founders, may think they are divid-
ing government to keep the rascals from doing damage. Yet the resultant
policy inaction sows deeper cynicism about politics and government.
Second, divided government creates a climate of scandalmongering, in
which each branch of government expends political resources embarrassing the other (Watergate, Iran-*contra*, the S&L scandals, Iraqgate) rather
than jointly tending to the national business. Over time, this discredits
both parties, blurs responsibility, and generates still more voter contempt
for government and politics generally.

This analysis is seductive, and at least partly true. However, several
recent books suggest it is overstated. Though we think of it as a characteristic of the 1980s, divided government has recurred regularly since the
1940s. In only eighteen out of the past forty-six years has the same party
controlled the White House and both houses of Congress. The Nixon
presidency, a period of legislative activism, coexisted with Democratic
control of the House and the Senate. Divided government was also common during the nineteenth century.

What's New, and What's Not

In a deeper sense, we have lived with divided government since the
Founding. Reacting to the Articles of Confederation, the Founders believed that the Constitution favored strong, if restrained, government.
But much of American political thought since then—from Theodore Roosevelt and Woodrow Wilson to Richard Neustadt and Walter Dean
Burnham—can be read as a recurring judgment that the Founders constrained government far more than they empowered it. It takes strong
politics and a mobilized electorate to overcome the constitutional bias
against government activism.

In the sweep of American history, bouts of effective governmental
activism have been rare: the Civil War and Reconstruction Congresses,

Woodrow Wilson's cooperation with party leaders in the Congress, Franklin D. Roosevelt's two strong working majorities in 1933–34 and 1937–38, LBJ's partnership with the 89th Congress in 1965–66. The ticket-splitting of the 1980s is more the rule than the exception—a case of the constitutional chickens coming home to roost. Still, the current era has generated more than a normal amount of squawking about accumulated problems that government seems unable to solve. The federal deficit has deprived government of resources to address national concerns, and the magnitude of the deficit itself stands as a monument to government's failure to act. So the electorate has evidently locked itself into a vicious circle of ticket-splitting, policy inaction, discontent, disaffiliation—and more ticket-splitting and more paralysis. Even if Bill Clinton should win the White House in November and enjoy a working majority in Congress, the process of political repair will have only begun.

According to several new studies by political scientists, however, we should not exaggerate the perils of divided government nor, by implication, the virtues of unified government—let alone more radical reform proposals imagining a move toward parliamentary government. These new studies add badly needed complexity to the conventional views that blame divided government, willy-nilly, for a multitude of sins.

Where most of the new studies fall somewhat short, however, is their failure to explore adequately the connection between divided government and perceived or real paralysis—and the resulting damage to public confidence in government itself and to key democratic norms. For one thing, divided government yields less accountable government. If both parties are the in-party, then policy failures are everybody's fault —and nobody's. Unified government may not be sufficient to revive strong politics, but it is probably necessary, at least in the current climate.

Divided government can also be a political red herring. For example, Republicans have long insisted that their failure to consummate a domestic program is the fault of Democratic control of Congress—control that is itself illegitimate, reflecting gerrymandering and the power of incumbency. The GOP 1992 platform states: "After more than half a century of distortion by power-hungry Democrats, the political system is increasingly rigged." The platform blames the chronic deficit on Democratic control of the Congress, and adds, "The only solution is to end divided government."

It is necessary to sort out the dynamics of divided government —where it came from, how it works, what can be fairly blamed on it, what unified government might portend—and what reforms are needed to reclaim politics, irrespective of divided government. One can begin by differentiating the causes of divided government from its consequences.

Causes of Divided Government

Political scientists generally make two kinds of argument about the causes of recent divided government. The first argument emphasizes the behavior of *politicians*, contending that factors such as congressional incumbency, or candidate-recruitment, tends to advantage one party over the other. Some of this literature views the past decade as an aborted realignment. Voters gradually shifted their presidential allegiance toward Republicans, but for a variety of structural or tactical reasons Democrats were able to cling to their control of Congress. The second view emphasizes the behavior of *voters*, and concludes that the voters' choice of divided government was rational, deliberate, and purposive.

A Rigged System? Drawing on three extensive academic literatures (on the electoral effects of congressional incumbency, reapportionment politics, and realignment), Newt Gingrich and other key Republicans view divided government as the product of Democratic success at riding out, through devious means, the electoral "right turn" that began in 1980. The case has superficial plausibility, since professional politicians do rationally protect their careers and incumbents have indeed gotten reelected more reliably than in the 1940s and 1950s.

Already advantaged by comfortable vote margins for all congressional incumbents, House Democrats supposedly used their committee positions to build up large war chests. Congressional Democrats also blanketed their districts with newsletters, shoring up the name recognition that helps reelection. Another part of the same "rigged system" were state legislatures—most of which are controlled by Democrats. These legislatures supposedly gerrymandered congressional districts to insulate House Democrats from an increasingly suburban electorate that gave Ronald Reagan a landslide in 1984 and George Bush a strong victory in 1988.

But though incumbents do exploit office, the "rigged system" thesis largely fails to explain divided government. Its fallacies are ably explored by Gary Jacobson and Morris Fiorina. If the system were rigged, why have Democrats done better in open House races? Why did they lose the Senate in 1980 and win it back in 1986?

While gerrymandering does occur, it doesn't explain lingering Democratic control of the House. Since 1952 Republican presidential candidates have received a significantly higher fraction of the vote than have Republican House candidates. Reagan got 57 percent of the national vote in 1984, but House Republicans got only 47 percent. For the most part, Republicans fail to capture the legislative branch because they attract fewer voters.

Incumbents appear strong, but their longevity can be exaggerated. Only 10 percent of those in the House in 1990 were there in 1968, even though incumbent vote margins have grown since then. As for campaign finance and incumbency, a big war chest can certainly scare away a strong challenger, leaving a seat effectively uncontested. But during the 1980s Republican challengers were much better endowed than Democratic challengers.

Do Democrats Have Better Candidates? A much more convincing argument holds that Democrats cling to legislative office, at all levels of government, because they field more attractive candidates. As both Alan Ehrenhalt and Gary Jacobson suggest, the Republicans have had a serious problem in candidate recruitment—one of the reasons why they have put effort into converting conservative Southern Democrat office holders to the GOP.

Democrats obviously have a more visceral commitment to politics and government than government-bashing Republicans. With the exception of able patricians like William Weld and James Baker, or such serious, supply-side intellectuals as Phil Gramm and Jack Kemp, talented conservatives tend to act on their creed and stay in the private sector. But talented Democrats, because they actually like government, will put up with the stress, long hours, constituent abuse, and the relatively low pay of local and state office, which in turn serves as a recruitment pool for congressional candidates. So Democrats often do have better candidates, a reality that grows out of their ideology.

Are the Voters Fools? A very different brand of explanation for divided government centers not on politicians but on voters. In this view, the voters are getting roughly what they want. Republican challengers were unlucky enough to pursue clear partisan realignment just when partisan loyalties, steadily weaker since the 1950s, were becoming too thin to support such ambitions. Most electorally active people have some kind of partisan loyalty, but increasing numbers no longer buy the party's entire program. Thus Republicans are split on cultural social, and economic fault lines and many Republican presidential voters hedge their bets by backing Democrats for Congress.

Voter ambivalence may be all too genuine. The electorate believes, for instance, that deficits ought to be reduced but also agrees, when asked by pollsters, that budgets for particular worthy purposes, such as the environment and education, ought to go up.

Fiorina, Jacobson, and others suggest that increasingly the voters active in both presidential and congressional elections, who happen to be better informed voters in general, are adopting some basic rules of thumb. There are quibbles among these analysts about the degree of sophistication, but all agree, first, that voters see the parties as offering different policy benefits, and, second, that voters associate their own preferences with a Republican presidency and a Democratic Congress.

Congress cannot face up to expansionist dictators and "evil em-
pires" nor can it broadly steer the economy, but the president can hardly
be an ombudsman for a constituent with a Social Security problem. When
weakened party loyalties and increasing distrust of government are fac-
tored in, the result is enough ticket-splitting to get divided government.

Fiorina is convincing when he notes the historic, system-wide perva-
siveness of divided government. Since 1946 divided government has also
spread rapidly to state politics, often pitting Republican executives
against Democratic legislatures. For Fiorina, this suggests that more and
more voters intend divided government and have become sophisticated
ticket-splitters. Unified government may well become the exception, not
the rule.

While Jacobson and Fiorina offer quite believable arguments—in
Fiorina's case, enhanced by simple but ingenious modeling—the direct
evidence for sophisticated voting is still only inferred from survey evidence. The great virtue of the thesis, however, is that it treats voters as
purposive: Voters are far more wary of government and politicians than
they used to be, and a near plurality seems to like divided government
even now, despite its chaotic results. Fiorina rightly calls for more research into ticket-splitting so that we can know just how much sophisticated voting is going on, and, in the meantime, urges skepticism about
the view that divided government is an evil.

In short, political science research does not find much support for
the contention that divided government is the result of illegitimate tactics by careerist Democrats. The Democrats include effective career politicians, of course—that's one of their strengths as a party. But true electoral realignments sweep aside yesteryear's "in party." We didn't have
nor could we have had such a realignment in the dealigned 1980s. The
real story is that Democrats went into the 1980s with advantages in legislative electoral arenas that the Republicans lacked, mirrored by disadvantages on "presidential" issues and presidential candidates that Republicans exploited.

If this approach explains the rational causes of divided government,
what about the consequences? The ticket-splitters in the electorate, after
all, do not make up a majority. What if they unintentionally (and, for
some, deliberately) stuck the rest of us with governmental deadlock and
political decomposition? Does the cool, rational logic assumed in the new
analyses of divided government's electoral origins also explain its consequences?

Consequences of Divided Government

Divided government seems to hobble governmental effectiveness in a variety of ways. However, these concerns are tempered when one takes a longer historical view, as do political scientists David Mayhew, David Rohde, and others. In the literature, three broad problems are attributed to divided government: policy inaction or incoherence, an obsession with political scandal, and an erosion of the political efficacy of the parties.

Policy Inaction, Flawed Legislation. The culpability of divided government is strongest on government's deferral of pressing problems, notably in economic and fiscal policy. Ginsberg and Shefter provocatively connect the national-level divided government of the 1980s to economic decline, fiscal irresponsibility, policy inaction, a failure to plan for economic competitiveness, and a subordination of national economic goals to a national security alliance with Japan. Each party is more devoted to retaining institutional strongholds than to fashioning as coherent national strategy.

Just how convincing are such charges? To test the hypothesis, David Mayhew did much tedious work, compiling a list of "important" legislation for the 1946–1990 period (during which the national government was often divided), 267 statutes in all. Mayhew's list was derived from the conclusions of leading reporters, policy analysts, and historians. He found that the rate of important policy making did not vary systematically across periods of unified or divided government.

Mayhew notes that most important legislation in the postwar period, 186 laws, passed with either two-thirds support or bipartisan majorities. He observes that Congress, contrary to its reputation, is more of a problem-solving institution than we often think simply because most of its members are committed to the ideal of making good public policy, as well as to the goals of getting reelected and achieving influence within Congress. Also, legislation doesn't come easily. To sustain a bill through all the veto points in the process requires legislative leaders to fashion majorities much larger than 51 percent.

Presidential skill, furthermore, doesn't neatly coincide with unified government; it can be found during divided government, as Reagan, Nixon, and Eisenhower showed. External events that demand problem-solving do not coincide systematically with unified or divided government. Finally, in a serious discussion of a phenomenon often dismissed by political scientists as being too soft for analysis, Mayhew shows that public moods demanding strong government span periods of both divided and unified government. There are constant policy-making pressures in Washington, surges of activism, often that last many years. Over the long run, both factors favor a rather high level of activism and policy making, divided government or not.

Is this view of the matter dispositive? Not wholly. Consider budget legislation in the 1980s. For many, the failure of government to match

revenues with expenditures is the signal failure of divided government—Democrats successfully defending outlays and Republicans successfully cutting taxes. However, while divided government in the 1980s
made this straddle possible, no such fiscal default occurred during the
sixteen years of cumulative divided government under Truman, Eisenhower, Nixon, or Ford. The new element that associated divided government with fiscal excess in the 1980s was the fierce Republican embrace of
what George Bush once aptly called "voodoo economics." None of Reagan's Republican predecessors believed that you could cut taxes and
increase revenues.

On the spending side, Mathew McCubbins's article in the Cox and
Kernell volume (written in the spirit of the volume's persistent focus on
parties) focuses on party conflict in a "bi-lateral veto game" and its resolution. He conceptually strips spending politics down to a stylized conflict over two types of programs, domestic spending and defense spending. Democrats preferred increases in one and reductions in the other,
and vice versa for Republicans. The outcome is basic game theory: since
neither side could get its first preference (more for its side, less for the
other side), they both agreed on the second preference (more for both
sides). The result, of course, was persistent, upward pressure on the deficit. Historically, Mayhew finds no such clear relationships between divided government and fiscal imbalance. But McCubbins's emphasis on
defensive partisan behavior in a fragmented system nicely captures the
dynamic of fiscal blockage, at least in the supply-side era.

On the tax side, a key piece of legislation, the Economic Recovery
Tax Act (ERTA) of 1981, played a very important role. Startled by the results of the 1980 elections, Democrats sought to shore up business support for the next election. Both parties competed to take credit for a supply-side bill that would spark economic recovery, setting off an infamous
"bidding war" that would have been improbable in a unified government. In a concise article in the volume edited by Alberto Alesina and
Geoffrey Carliner, Charles Stewart analyzes ERTA and other tax legislation in the 1980s. He estimates that about 90 percent of lost revenue over
the 1980s due to tax cuts is attributable to ERTA. Given Reagan's reso-
luteness in blocking major tax increases, divided government made it
impossible to recover lost revenue. Modest income and corporate tax increases as well as a large increase in Social Security taxes occurred, but
tax legislation after 1981 tended toward "revenue neutrality."

Divided government from 1981 to 1992 invited, in other words, complicated patterns of "gaming" between the two parties on spending and
taxing that, in turn, created a chronic deficit problem. Its real economic
consequences are still being debated—periodic fiscal imbalance has been
common in U.S. history since the Civil War, as Charles Stewart astutely

points out in the Cox and Kernell volume. But in the current era of government-bashing and festering economic and social problems, fiscal imbalance has symbolized government failure.

Increased public cynicism has probably been reinforced by the savings-and-loan scandal, a colossal case of bipartisan failure. In a lucid, sobering treatment of the "thrift debacle" in the Alesina and Carliner volume, Barry Weingast and Thomas Romer show convincingly the bipartisan, political origins of the crisis, emphasizing incentives and informational biases. The public was ill-equipped to assess the issue and was not cohesively organized as the thrift industry was. Since every member of Congress had many thrifts in his or her district or state, Congress tended to accept the available arguments. These favored, first, deregulation and, later, forbearance—letting the industry take time to work its way out of its difficulties.

Explicit treatment of divided government plays little role in the Weingast-Romer analysis. But their own account hints that Congress and the administration jointly delayed remedial action because they feared raising taxes or worsening the budget deficit—itself partly the product of divided government. In addition, the S&L scandal, like the deficit itself, suggests how divided government permits blame-sharing as well as credit-sharing. Both public deliberation and accountability suffered as a result of a blame-avoidance game. On balance, the contribution of divided government to policy inaction and flawed legislation from 1946 to 1990 across many policy domains is hard to prove, just as Mayhew says. But from 1981 on its contribution to economic mismanagement gets stronger, a point broadly consistent with more pessimistic analyses, such as Ginsberg and Shefter's *Politics By Other Means*.

Divided government has also been blamed for foreign policy incoherence. During the Iran-*contra* hearings, former National Security Adviser Robert McFarlane cited the Boland Amendment (prohibiting aid to the *contras*) as destructive foreign policy meddling. First Congress drew the line here, then it drew the line there. Circumventing Congress came easily—for who knew what Congress wanted?—but the process of circumvention damaged policy. Yet the problem with the general argument of foreign policy incoherence, as Mayhew points out, is that the country is never unified for long on foreign policy, even under unified government. Divided government may well add healthy checks and balances —as both the contras and the Sandinista party know.

In fact, divided government has often been associated with initiatives now recognized as statesmanlike, the most famous case being the Marshall Plan, launched during the "do-nothing" (read Republican-controlled) 80th Congress. There is simply no way, using any imaginable set of criteria, to judge foreign policies produced since 1946 under unified control as being consistently superior to those fashioned under divided control.

Scandalmongering. Ginsberg and Shefter argue that divided government in the 1980s encouraged "politics by other means." If Democrats couldn't win the presidency, they investigated and harassed the president's subordinates, while Republicans anxious to control the House used the ethics machinery to discredit the House leadership. If interest groups couldn't rally voters, they could buy elected officials. In time, the public reasonably drew unflattering inferences about people inside the Beltway: a plague on both their houses.

For some observers of American politics, a continuing round of ethics scandals feeds the kind of paranoia about government that Oliver Stone exploited with "JFK," a plausible point about the political origins of public cynicism. Equally serious, a certain administrative incoherence and timidity can set in. Administrators, wary of scandal, became excessively cautious. Appointments go unfilled, and talented people take a pass on a job offer because of some youthful indiscretion that could invite smears long afterwards.

There are, then, three related claims about scandalmongering. Divided government increases the rate of political scandal; that in turn increases public cynicism and hobbles government's ability to implement policy. But the rate of scandal-making does not vary systematically across periods of unified and divided government. Mayhew counted for the period 1946–1990 the number of days that the congressional committee investigations of the presidency, or executive response, were featured on the front page of the *New York Times*. There is no systematic relationship between periods of unified or divided government—none at all.

Capitol Hill launches investigations for at least two other reasons, factional and constitutional. Indeed, as Mayhew points out, a period of unified government can be associated with investigations that set the stage for tensions in a particular administrative or policy domain that will last for decades. If so, the case for a relationship between divided government and public cynicism and administrative incoherence is weak.

Scandals during both divided and unified government often reflect constitutionally mandated tensions. The Watergate and Iran-*contra* affairs, both associated with divided government, of course had political dimensions. But they also dealt with quite serious constitutional issues. Moreover, to dismiss recent crises of government as mere "scandals" is to trivialize the stakes. In Watergate and Iran-*contra*, or in lesser imbroglios, crimes and misdemeanors against democratic government all demanded scrutiny and response. The rate of congressional investigation in the post-World War II period (and probably the pre–World War II period) is at best only weakly correlated with partisan divided government. Party factions will go after one another as easily as different parties. And concerned congressional leaders will walk away from party loyalty toward the Constitution.

Death of Responsible Party Politics. An article of faith among most political scientists is the unimportance of parties within the Congress. As subcommittees and staff proliferated, abetted by the collapse of deference to leadership or any commitment to apprenticeship, such irrelevance grew. Congress is therefore unruly, hence the recurrent magazine covers picturing Congress as a baby in diapers. Mayhew summed it up best in an earlier, well-known book, *Congress: The Electoral Connection:* "No theoretical treatment of the United States Congress that posits parties as analytic units will go very far ... we are left with ... 535 men and women rather than two parties." All of this is supposedly compounded by divided government.

President Bush has set a modern record of thirty-one vetoes in fewer than four years. This has only sharpened the sense that running Congress is not an advantage for the Democrats as a party, and that minority status in the House has transformed Republicans into a kind of Weather Underground in suits. Committee barons freelance, Speaker Foley lacks fire in the belly, and everyone hustles money, subverting the party's historic social commitments. Meanwhile Newt Gingrich plots the fall of the Republic, or at least of the Congress.

There are two claims here: divided government thwarts partisan cohesion, organizationally and programmatically, and it intensifies illegitimate free-lancing, legislatively and in congressional campaign finance —or in a poisonous blend of the two. But this picture is also overstated, or just plain wrong. Rohde's finely counterintuitive analysis shows that party government is alive and well in the House of Representatives since the reforms of the late 1960s and early 1970s. His work is part of a renewed interest in congressional parties that can also be found in the Cox and Kernell and Alesina and Carliner volumes.

Rohde demonstrates a marked increase in party government in the House and Senate. To be sure, notwithstanding structural changes in legislative party cohesion, a Speaker's style can matter enormously. (Speaker Wright was a strong partisan and Foley a relatively weak one.) But, on the whole, far from weakening the Democrats and Republicans as coherent legislative parties, divided government has been associated with a strengthening. Rohde convincingly constructs a party cohesion index—that is, the proportion of votes on which a House or Senate Democrat supports the party position. The low for the House was reached in 1970, 27 percent, but by 1987 it had shot up to 64 percent; in the Senate it ranged from 35 percent to 52 percent in the same period. From the 92nd to the 94th Congresses, about 8 percent of the House was involved in the Democratic whip organization, but the percentage increased steadily to 40 percent by the 101st Congress.

During this period the Speakership was strengthened, becoming the apex of a system composed of regular whip planning meetings, policy-planning task forces, a Steering and Policy Committee, the Democratic Caucus, and the Democratic Study Group. The Rules Committee changed from being an obstructionist body to an operation that facilitated the Democratic Party agenda through increasingly sophisticated —and for Republicans oppressive—use of rules. Greatly aiding these changes was a sharp decrease in sectional tensions within the congressional Democratic Party, the result of the Voting Rights Act's impact on Southern politics.

Speaker Wright used this new system during his brief tenure to enact a party agenda, echoing earlier, now forgotten efforts and successes by Carl Albert and Tip O'Neill, both of whom forced strong, anti-recession measures on reluctant Republican presidents, in 1975 and 1983. Both the Clean Water Act and the Highway Reauthorization were enacted over Reagan's vetoes. Also passed were important savings and loan, welfare, farm credit, catastrophic health insurance, trade, and homeless bills. Indeed, Rohde's evidence suggests that policy planning and programmatic cohesion grew during the 1980s within the congressional Democratic Party. Forthcoming work by James Shoch of Dartmouth College, on trade policy, and Chris Howard of MIT, on social policy, will strengthen this implication of Rohde's research.

Nor is it clear that divided government promotes corrupt campaign finance. What does seem clear is that divided government in the 1970s helped stimulate the monitoring systems which generate the data that public watchdog groups use to call public attention to finance issues. On balance, public awareness of money's role in politics seems to have been helped by divided government. This isn't to dismiss the issue, which is too often ignored and misunderstood. Greider's controlled outrage in *Who Will Tell the People* wakes one up to it. Yet it is not analytically clear whether, or how much, divided government reinforces the power of organized money and social class in politics.

The overall case that divided government destroys parties is at best mixed. As Rohde suggests, party cohesion and ideological coherence, as well as coordinated policy planning, may actually grow under divided government. At the same time, party cohesion does not assure party accountability; and parties that do not seem accountable are parties that engender voter distrust.

Moreover, a party that shares governance may have difficulty functioning as a clear opposition. Divided government can increase collusion between the parties to avoid blame for policy inaction or failure, which in turn intensifies public cynicism against the whole system. In sum, divided government cannot have been the sole foundation of the recent crisis of governance. Its critics are putting too much explanatory weight on a pattern of electoral outcomes that has recurred since World War II, and that was common from the end of Reconstruction to the rise of McKinley. In the form it took from 1981 to 1992, divided government did, however, make it easier for government to become associated with major symbols of political failure, such as the chronic deficit and the S&L debacle. But restoration of public confidence will require more than control of both branches by the same party.

Political Renewal

Given America's constitutional institutions, political culture, and recent history, how shall we go about renewing politics? As James Morone's exceptionally interesting book shows in rich, historical detail, American political culture is deeply anti-political. American history is punctuated by political surges full of democratic yearning that well up from below. In many of them, people seek to abolish the messiness of politics in the name of "the people" and install a government founded in transcendental values of American community. The popular base of the Perot movement was a typical example.

Such democratic surges often ossify into the creation of new interest groups, and new allied federal agencies, such as the National Labor Relations Board in the 1930s, or the new environmental agencies of the 1970s. Yet the proliferation of constituencies and agencies only adds to the system's ungovernability. Thus, the stage is regularly set for broad disillusionment with politics, reinforcing the antigovernmental thrust of American political culture.

In ground-breaking work, the late Jack Walker constructed the first, reliable "census" across time of interest groups. He found that the older view of "stable unrepresentation" in the group system (to use a term coined by William Gamson of Boston College) no longer captures interest-group politics. Gaps in group representation have closed steadily since the 1930s due to constant intervention into the associational system by government and private "patrons," such as foundations, philanthropies and the media. For example, when the Kennedy administration established state-level commissions on the Status of Women, it laid the basis for the formation of the National Organization of Women, just as liberal foundations helped to finance the voter registration drive of the early 1960s.

Indeed, since the 1960s, the political system has been characterized by burgeoning interest groups—and declining electoral participation. Voter turnout and partisan affiliation have both decreased. As Ginsberg and Shefter observe, electoral politicians no longer have to engage in mobilizing the electorate. Today's politicians are all too comfortable with the "low voter turnout" environment in which they compete. It is a predictable milieu, and changing it is against their career interests. Thus, as the interest group system has become more pervasive and inclusive, the broader citizenry, paradoxically, has become more frustrated.

Perhaps, contrary to William Greider's title, The People don't need to be told—they have already grasped the intractability of representative government and have channeled their political impulses into avenues outside those mediated by party and election. Paradoxically, the number of political activists has increased just when millions have become electorally inactive. Reintegrating group activism with representative government and effective parties will be very tricky, for interest groups often seem to operate at the expense of parties, treating them as flags of convenience. (See Karen Paget, "Citizen Organizing: Many Movements, No Majority," TAP no. 2, Summer 1990, and John B. Judis, "The Pressure Elite," TAP no. 9, Spring 1992.)

Moreover, as William Greider suggests, because of the fragmentation and particularism of interest-group politics, the gain to inclusion is no match for the power of money. Also, the crisis of the labor movement—the most embracing and aggregating group of ordinary voters—has reopened gaps in representation. Hence the paradox of the contemporary system of representation: More Americans are highly active in politics, via interest groups. Yet in an age of partisan disaffiliation and group fragmentation, Americans are more disconnected than ever before. What gets lost, finally, is appreciation of democratic politics and government as aggregative and collectively valuable activities.

This, unfortunately, is the larger context for political renewal. For some analysts, such as those who formed the Committee on Constitutional Structure, the fate of the Carter Administration and the legislative and fiscal stalemate of the Reagan-Bush era suggest institutional and procedural reforms to create genuine unified government. In this view strong parties, a strong presidency, unified government, and responsible government all go together. Hence key figures associated with the committees, such as Lloyd Cutler and the Brookings scholar James Sundquist, call for constitutional reforms that would make our system more like parliamentary government. These include such ideas as "team tickets" (that is, voting for presidential, House, and Senate slates together), and changing congressional terms to give presidents time to see a program through. But these reforms, though appealing, are improbable, and they beg the question of how to redeem democratic citizenship under our present constitution.

One obvious inference is the need for stronger parties, to enlist citizens in the business of politics and to bridge the constitutional separation. Without strong parties, even "unified" government can itself become a kind of divided government, as the Democratic Party has often been throughout its history. Without a strengthened Democratic Party, a Clinton administration could go the way of the Carter administration, succumbing to the still potent factionalism in the three party groupings—the Democratic Leadership Council, Jesse Jackson and his various constituencies, and the AFL-CIO/Kennedy alignment. A Clinton administration, like Reagan—and unlike Carter—would have to take advantage of the party-building opportunities of White House incumbency.

Deepening voter alienation also reflects the widespread perception that the political deck is stacked—that only insiders have influence, that money talks louder than votes, and that both parties are corrupted. Greider's muckraking uncovers damning details about how money talks and constricts national debate about what's feasible. Here again, ordinary people are denied political influence for reasons deeper than the fact of divided partisan government. Fundamental campaign finance reform is only the beginning of a cure.

Political efficacy, citizen participation, strong parties, and government competence are mutually reinforcing. In the heyday of the New Deal coalition, notwithstanding its exclusions, each factor operated in tandem with the other to make for a strong polity, and invited further inclusion. Since the late 1960s, that cycle of reinforcement has ended. Divided government has compounded this political reversal.

But unified government—under the Democrats, at least—would have to work mightily to repair the damage. Political renewal can perhaps be built on the upsurge of citizen activism, but it will have to take care that such activism does not come at the expense of parties, or of voter confidence in the polity as a whole. Certain measures, like the "motor voter bill" recently vetoed by President Bush, or fundamental campaign finance reforms, point in the right direction. But they only whet one's appetite for a whole new genre of strategies to reclaim politics.

When all is said and done, it is hard to imagine political renewal occurring in the absence of a strong president who has a working majority in Congress and a healthy partisanship. In that sense, those who associate democratic decay with divided government are partly right after all.

[21]

Robert Kuttner

Congress without Cohabitation: The Democrats' Morning-After

On September 30, 1990, after being closeted for weeks at Andrews Air Force Base with White House representatives Richard Darman and John Sununu, Democratic congressional leaders brought back an agreement on the federal budget that the press initially treated as a historic compromise. It was actually an astonishingly Republican document—and a symbol of how deeply compromised the Democrats had become sharing power with a Republican administration. To slay the deficit, the agreement cut Medicare by $60 billion, limited any peace dividend, blocked new domestic spending, and relied on regressive taxes that would have increased the tax burden of the poorest Americans by 11 percent, the middle class by 3.3 percent, and the richest one percent of Americans by just 1.7 percent.

After ten years of deficits and failed supply-side dogma, why had the Democrats continued to accept the hand the Republican White House dealt them? "[Speaker] Tom Foley started off with the premise that if no budget were passed, we would be blamed," says a prominent liberal California congressman. "Once you accept that premise, the White House has most of the bargaining power."

Until one last, fatal miscalculation, the White House strategists had deftly exploited the Democrats' sense of their own weakness. The Democratic leaders felt lucky to have avoided a cut in capital gains taxes—and gamely backed the deal. The almost unanimous counsel of economists, editorial writers, and the Democrats' own leaders was to pass the budget, no matter what the cost to equity or party principle. "Deficit reduction is the only proven tool for assuring long-term growth," Leon Panetta, the budget committee chairman, declared, in a final speech beseeching skeptical Democrats to support the package. "Rise above your regional interests. Rise above ideology and partisanship, and cast a vote for the greater good of the country."

But late on the night of October 4, 1990, by a vote of 254 to 179, the House of Representatives rejected the agreement, when a defection of Republican back-benchers angry at the new taxes emboldened enough rank-and-file House Democrats to vote against the deal too. Then, in an unexpected turnabout, the Democrats abruptly recovered their souls or at least their wits. With Congressman Dan Rostenkowski's "Soak-the-Rich" alternative, they were back on the popular side of a powerful pocketbook issue, almost in spite of themselves. "Rosty," with his full-back's shoulders and working-class district, was symbolically perfect. "Finally," observed Democratic strategist Ralph Whitehead, "the Republicans have the briefcase and the Democrats have the lunch pail. Isn't that the way it's supposed to be?" By the end of the congressional session, the budget debate was usefully polarized—and the Democratic pole turned out to be the one that echoed voter sentiments as well as liberal ideology.

The effect was exhilarating to Democratic morale. The Democrats went on to make gains in the mid-term elections, and then to function as a surprisingly coherent opposition to an early shooting war in the Persian Gulf. So it is worth asking whether the 1990s will at last usher in an era of robust partisanship, in welcome contrast to the Democrats' prolonged, intermittent coma. To answer that question, one must first take a backward look at the sources of Democratic paralysis in the 1980s.

Cohabitation, American-Style

For more than a decade, despite profound differences between the two parties, congressional Democrats have often dwelt in cohabitation with the White House rather than defining a coherent opposition program. Frequently, they have seemed like the junior partners in a coalition.

The term "cohabitation" was first used to describe the peculiar coalition of the French Socialist President, François Mitterrand, with a conservative prime minister, Jacques Chirac, during the 1986–88 period when the Socialists had lost their working majority in the National Assembly. As it turned out, cohabitation better served the executive, who had far more residual power. When the brief experiment ended, Mitterrand grabbed most of the bedclothes and kicked Chirac out of bed, not vice versa.

Americans have more historical experience with cohabitation than have the French, but we have never previously had so long a period when one party controlled Congress and the other the executive branch. The House has been in Democratic hands for 36 years straight, and the

Senate for all but 8 of those 36 years, while the Republicans have held the White House for 18 out of the past 22. Thus, for an entire generation, divided government has been the norm. Robert Michel, the Republican leader of the House, has set a new record, serving in the minority for his entire 34-year career in Congress. It has become a cliche that the voters seem to like divided government. "They vote for Democratic congressmen to sponsor popular programs, and Republican presidents so they won't have to pay for them." Or divided government is said to reflect the voters' skepticism about government itself. A further explanation is that the Democrats still enjoy broad public support on bread-and-butter issues, while Republicans capture allegiance on the symbolic issues of patriotism, personal security, and mainstream cultural values.

Responsibility Without Power

At first blush, this lock on the legislative branch should have the effect of consolidating and energizing the congressional Democrats as a partisan opposition. But, in practice, the effect has been the reverse. As the long-term majority party, especially in the House, Democrats have come to see themselves as a party of government, with responsibility to Make the System Work.

Indeed, the more extreme the policies of Reaganism, the more Democrats were constrained by that conception of their role. In his first term, President Reagan was able to paint the Democrats as trying to add taxes and subtract program benefits—simply because he used preposterous economic assumptions and they used more realistic ones. "We tried to take the high road of responsibility, and we paid dearly for it," recalls Congressman Dave Obey of Wisconsin. "We ended up trying to compete with them over technical assumptions." Because it deferred difficult choices, Reagan's rosy scenario was so popular among the electorate that enough "Boll Weevil" Democrats in the House bolted to give Reagan a working fiscal majority.

Moreover, congressional Democrats have been whipsawed by the low repute of Congress as an institution—an ill repute that Republicans have adroitly marketed. Seemingly, the more they played a purely partisan role, the more they risked contributing to the public antipathy to the institution and, by extension, to themselves. But by failing to take a partisan stance, they obscured differences between the two parties, and ended up sharing responsibility for bad policies that most congressional Democrats actually detested.

The obstacles to effective opposition are also systemic. In a parliamentary system, the prime minister is leader of a legislative majority; parliamentary parties, therefore, tend to be relatively disciplined. But in our system, Congress is a co-equal branch of government, and legislative parties tend to be neither disciplined nor ideologically coherent, only a loose agglomeration of members elected in individual districts. This structure creates several independent constraints on the Democrats' ability to define a clear ideological opposition. In our system, an individual congressman is many things: an advocate and benefactor for his district; a subcommittee or committee chairman; an incumbent seeking to survive. Probably the weakest among his several identities is member of an opposition caucus. As the majority party in the House throughout the 1980s and the Senate since 1986, the Democrats controlled legislative committees. Absent a supermajority to override presidential vetoes, however, Democratic committee chairmen needed Republican votes and administration acquiescence to salvage even a shred of the programs to which they had dedicated their legislative careers. This also contributed to an absence of salutary polarization.

Moreover, the post-Watergate reforms of 1975 had a double-edged effect on party coherence. They usefully undercut the old seniority system, overthrew many entrenched conservatives, and elevated the party caucus. But the reforms also reflected a "good-government" procedural reformism rather than a substantive liberal agenda, and they cut loose each congressman to operate as more of a freelance. Many of the class of 1974 thought of partisanship as antithetical to good government.

One can think of other good structural, historical, or constitutional reasons why the Democrats' opposition to the Republican executive was blunted during the 1980s. But I will argue that virtually all of them let the Democrats off the hook too gently.

The Reagan Effect

Through most of the 1980s, Democratic congressmen and senators were dazzled by the apparent popularity of Ronald Reagan's ideas. Almost as shocking as the defeat of Jimmy Carter was the stunning ouster in 1980 of a generation of the most distinguished and effective Democratic Senators—Frank Church, George McGovern, Birch Bayh, Gaylord Nelson, and several more. It seemed entirely possible that the House might go Republican in 1982. As a consequence, especially in the first Reagan term, Democrats sought to associate themselves with Republican ideas. Many wished frankly to appear less Democratic and to win reelection as nonideological, loyal servants to their districts. Under Representative Tony Coelho, the Democratic Congressional Campaign Committee tried to recruit moderate-sounding congressional candidates who would be more acceptable to business. Under their new Ways and Means Chairman, Dan Rostenkowski, a man waltzed by the White House more than once during the 1980s, the Democrats put their own spin on the 1981 tax cut, sharing the credit and the blame and failing to define an axis of opposition. They had their own versions of other Republican themes, from deregulation and arms buildup to budgetary balance. In a reversal of the politics of the 1960s, Republicans defined the agenda and Democrats offered a pale, me-too imitation.

In hindsight, the loss of twelve Democratic Senate seats in 1980 was a fluke, not the beginning of a trend. Despite a far superior Republican national machine, surprisingly little of Reagan's popularity rubbed off on GOP congressional candidates. In 1982, as they regained some partisan fervor, the Democrats picked up 26 House seats. In 1984, despite the trouncing of Walter Mondale, the voters split their ballots in no fewer than 189 congressional districts that went for Reagan while returning a Democrat to Congress. By 1986 Democrats were able to take back the Senate. And notwithstanding an already anomalously large House majority, the Democrats have now picked up seats in three straight House elections. Yet throughout the 1980s, thanks in part to the mystique of Reagan's persona and to the politics of fiscal gridlock that virtually precluded an opposition program requiring affirmative use of government, Democratic legislators time and again played on Republican territory. Only episodically, when they championed the traditional Democratic issues, did they regain strength.

The Reality of Sisyphus

Why didn't the lesson sink in? In part, the congressional Democrats' chronic fatigue syndrome kept being reinfected by the dismal showing of their presidential standard-bearers. Each presidential loss—five out of six since 1968—began a new cycle of demoralization. The current mood of restored Democratic self-confidence is the third since 1980. Each time, the Democrats make one more Sisyphean effort to roll the rock back up Capitol Hill. And, of course, the latest would be shattered by a fourth GOP presidential landslide in 1992.

After Reagan's election, the Democrats were traumatized for an entire year. Belatedly, as the recession of 1982–83 deepened and Republican fiscal credibility sank, the Democrats mounted a successful, soul-restoring defense of Social Security—and the congressional party regained some gumption. But no sooner had they recovered partisan spunk when the Mondale blowout reinforced the feeling that whatever the Democrats were selling, the public wasn't buying. Mondale's defeat convinced House Speaker Tip O'Neill that Democrats should never again be the first to propose a tax hike. The 1986–88 cycle was more of the same: a restoration of partisan vigor in the 1986 mid-term election, real party energy around the Iran-*contra* scandal, a drawing of the line against further military buildup, high hopes for 1988—all dashed by the Dukakis debacle.

However secure their lock on Congress, Democrats are hardly immune to the impact of presidential elections. David Dreyer, formerly an assistant to Senator Gary Hart and to Representative Tony Coelho, now a senior staff aide to House Majority Leader Richard Gephardt, explains the psychology in morbid terms almost worthy of thanatologist Elisabeth Kubler-Ross. "There is always a grieving, a healing, and a hanging back after you have a defeat in a presidential election; it is natural for the party to turn inward and go through a period of self-criticism, if not self-immolation, as you reconstruct how it could have been done better, why we lost, and who was to blame."

Congress also generally gives a new president the benefit of the doubt. In Reagan's case, the attempted assassination a few months after he assumed office made him that much less vulnerable to partisan attack. "In 1981, everyone wanted Ronald Reagan to succeed," recalls former Speaker Jim Wright. "The country didn't want another failed presidency, so everyone bent over backwards to cooperate. Then after the assassination attempt, he came back with a real mantle of heroism. Here was a man back from the dead, a national treasure. We were at a terrible disadvantage, fighting a rearguard action." At the outset of the Bush administration, Bush made the Democrats' job harder by seizing the political center on issues like education and the environment. "To actually legislate, you had to compromise, which submerges partisan differences," says a liberal senator.

Unfortunately, despite the fact that Carter, Mondale, and Dukakis did not run as liberals, their defeat by more conservative Republicans lent credence to the claim by conservatives within the congressional Democratic Party that the logical lesson was to move right. If anything, Mondale suffered a blowout because he ran as the austerity candidate. Yet his defeat was seized by the opponents of "interest-group liberalism" and led to the formation of the center-right Democratic Leadership Council, preaching a message of guarded centrism. "One big impediment to our success was a whole group of our own people insisting that any talk of equity was political death," says Dave Obey. Dukakis, likewise, ran as a technocrat, the consensus candidate of the party establishment. He claimed that the election was not about ideology but competence; for this the voters adjudged him ideologically incompetent. Yet his defeat was also taken in some quarters as a repudiation of liberalism. Late in 1990, the congressional party at last reclaimed a winning liberal theme in tax fairness. Yet, as we shall see, there remain several obstacles to turning this win into a more generalized winning "story."

Congressional Leadership — an Oxymoron?

Despite the spillover effect of presidential defeats, and the constitutional fact that the Democrats are not a parliamentary bloc, a good deal of the blame rests with Congress's own Democratic leadership. A comparison of the three House speakers of the 1980s—Tip O'Neill, Jim Wright, and now Tom Foley—is highly instructive.

O'Neill, who became speaker in 1977, defined his role in rather traditional terms more as leader of the House than as leader of his party. He was treated rudely by the novices around Jimmy Carter, and in many respects he enjoyed a more comfortable relationship with Ronald Reagan. A fellow Hibernian and teller of tales, Tip shared many a post-session drink with Reagan. Whatever their political differences, the politics never got personal. A frequent O'Neill golfing partner was House Republican leader Bob Michel. O'Neill also gave a wide berth to the independent barons of the House leadership, the committee chairmen, which won him affection but at the cost of party cohesion.

There was bitter criticism of Tip early in 1981 by both House liberal and moderate back-benchers, for ceding practical control to the Republican-Boll Weevil coalition. "Tip's view was that it wasn't our job to offer initiatives," recalls a member of his leadership team. "We were to wait until the President offered an initiative, and then counterpunch." Gradually, O'Neill assumed a more partisan role, most emphatically in the Social Security rescue, but when he retired in 1986, he was still insisting that Democrats had to shed the tax-and-spend label and wait for the White House to move first on taxes.

Jim Wright, who became speaker in January 1987, was a whole other story. A populist Texan, he attempted to define the speaker primarily as a party leader, in this case an opposition party leader, more strongly than any speaker since the dictatorial Joe Cannon, who was dethroned in 1910. No sooner did Wright assume office, than he succeeded in forcing through an expensive clean water bill over Reagan's veto, followed by a highway bill and a trade bill passed the same way. He also succeeded in making sure that the budgets passed by the House were party-line, Democratic-sponsored budgets, rather than coalition affairs of House Republicans and Boll Weevil Democrats. In graphic contrast to O'Neill, he turned the House Democratic organization into the speaker's own machine. He wielded a heavy gavel, manipulating procedure in a way that violated many traditional House courtesies, infuriating Republicans and not a few Democrats.

Under the House rules, a "rule" governing the terms of floor debate for a bill may be approved by a simple majority. A rule, for example, can permit amendments or require a simple up-or-down vote. In the Senate, because of the unanimous consent tradition and the filibuster, a working majority is sixty votes and sometimes nothing less than unanimity. But a House leader who chooses to play hardball can turn his ample leverage to reward friends and punish enemies into a working majority, and thereby can make the House function almost in parliamentary fashion.

Wright did. In 1987, for the first time in forty years, the budget was passed on time, and every single appropriation bill was on the President's desk ahead of schedule. And for the first time in the Reagan presidency, the congressional Democrats in 1987 largely defined the shape of the budget. There would be $36 billion of deficit reduction— $18 billion in tax hikes, $18 billion in spending cuts, with half of that taken from the military and half from domestic spending. Wright even waded deep into foreign policy, conducting his own diplomacy with the Central American presidents, to make sure that the Arias peace formula was supported by Congress and not undercut by hawks in the Reagan White House.

Wright's downfall in 1989 in a hail of relatively petty corruption left the congressional Democrats with contradictory lessons. On the one hand, Wright's stance paid dividends for both the party and the Congress as an institution. Just before the beginning of his downfall, Republican House Whip Newt Gingrich, Wright's nemesis, told John Barry, author of an investigative biography of Wright, "If Wright survives this ethics thing, he may become the greatest Speaker since Henry Clay." The actual corruption—profiting from inflated book royalties on vanity books that had been peddled wholesale to interest groups; having his wife take a salary from a Texas developer who arguably benefited from his access to the Speaker; going to bat for a few Texas savings and loan executives—was relatively minor league. But his transgressions did give the opposition just enough dirt to destroy him. On the other hand, had Wright not been so fiercely partisan, so procedurally Machiavellian, the Republicans—Newt Gingrich in particular—would not have gone after him with such animus. Had he not been such a tyrant within the Democratic caucus, usurping power from the committee chairmen, more Democrats might have fought harder to save him.

Wright's downfall meant a reversion of power to the committee barons and less ideological coherence. The House Ways and Means Chairman, Dan Rostenkowski, a longtime rival of Wright who had wanted the speakership himself, was intermittently playing footsie with the administration. Rostenkowski was the leading House sponsor of the 1986 tax reform, an ideologically ambiguous measure that succeeded in closing loopholes and raising taxes on business at the terrible price of sacrificing the principle of tax progressivity. In between his two heroic performances, as 1986 champion of tax simplification and 1990 sponsor of raising taxes on the rich, Rostenkowski on more than one occasion let himself be the vehicle to break the Democrats' fragile solidarity in opposition to capital gains tax cuts. Were it not for Rosty's periodic equivocation, it is hard to imagine that Bush and Darman would have seriously expected to ram a capital gains cut through Congress. "Rosty is a true schizophrenic," says one close observer. "He has good Democratic roots and instincts, but he spends a lot of time on the golf course with millionaires. Both aspects play a role."

Rostenkowski's Senate counterpart, Finance Committee Chairman Lloyd Bentsen of Texas, was another intermittent Trojan Horse. Though seemingly born again as a relatively progressive "national Democrat" as Michael Dukakis's 1988 running mate, Bentsen remained fairly conservative on money issues, eager to cut deals that included a capital gains cut or special tax breaks for Texas oilmen. In this respect, both the parochialism and ideological diversity of key congressional Democrats have compounded the task of functioning as a coherent opposition.

Varieties of Degradation

In distinguishing the several sources of Democratic weakness, one needs to disentangle the different forms of corruption—the personal, the ideological, and the conjugal. Jim Wright's corruption was mostly personal —using his office for minor financial gain. For the most part, it was not ideological. Peddling collections of speeches did not make him any less progressive a Democrat. More insidious was the profound ideological corruption that resulted from the imperatives of campaign finance. The more Democrats relied on the largesse of business PACs, the more they tended to shade their progressive politics. The savings-and-loan scandal was only the most extreme case. Republicans, at least, believed in deregulation as a matter of ideological conviction. Too many Democrats supported it only because the S&L lobby helped to finance their campaigns. Moreover, if you spent enough time with high rollers rather than voters, they became the reference group that informed your view of the world.

Tony Coelho, the man who raised to a high art the bartering of access to liberal incumbents in exchange for conservative PAC contributions, combined both forms of corruption. Coelho's brand of corruption was the more ideologically corrosive. As Wright's floor leader, Coelho functioned as a tactically tough partisan Democrat, rounding up votes for the leadership, convinced that his fund-raising deals had not compromised his own basic values. But Coelho, too, resigned ignominiously, a step ahead of an ethics investigation, over—what else?—a savings-and-loan deal.

An even more subtle form of degradation is simply the ongoing corruption of shared government. If absolute power corrupts absolutely, shared power corrupts in a way that is barely perceived. "For a lot of these guys," says a longtime aide to a liberal senator, "life really isn't so bad. They get to govern, kind of. They don't get to set an ideological agenda, but within mainstream assumptions, they have a lot of authority. They can put their stamp, in part, on clean air, child care, and other good things. One of the consequences is that it blunts your ability to engage in combat; all the legislative incentives are to compromise, and to blur basic differences of principle." Thus, chronic incumbency undermines political democracy in two distinct respects. Inside Congress, it makes the ostensible opposition party a long-term partner of the governing party. Outside, it denies voters a sense of meaningful choice—my congressman will be reelected anyway, so why vote?—and discourages participation.

On balance Wright's partisanship was good for the Democrats. But in 1989, as he fell from power, his personal corruption, heavy gavel, and partisan scheming seemed all of a piece—a wheeler-dealer style that was bad for the reputation of the Congress and bad for the image of the party. His Senate counterpart, Majority Leader Robert Byrd of West Virginia, was not criticized as a wheeler-dealer, merely as a relatively ineffective anachronism.

To many Democrats, the team of Tom Foley of Washington State, who succeeded Wright, and George Mitchell of Maine, who succeeded Byrd, was the perfect antidote. According to Dave Obey, a leader of House liberals, who opposed the current leadership on the budget compromise, "Having someone of Foley's temperament was very important to the institution. People don't realize how close this place was to blowing apart." Courtly, far less of a populist, courteous almost to a fault, Foley reverted to the traditional role of a speaker almost above party. "He attributes to others his own decency," says a member who has worked closely with him, putting a criticism kindly. "Tom comes by his parliamentary caution honestly," says another member. "His own politics tend to be quite moderate." He won election in a traditionally Republican farm seat in eastern Washington State, which he held with barely 51 percent of the vote in the 1980 Reagan landslide.

"Foley and Panetta try to deal with the Congress the way they deal with their own districts," says a liberal aide not associated with the leadership. "From the beginning of their careers, their survival has depended on attracting local Republican votes by minimizing their Democratic party affiliation. But in the present national environment, that's the worst thing you can do. You have to have a banner. You can't win by persuading voters that you are personally brighter or more decent. You can only win by convincing voters that you are part of a party that has values and priorities different from the other party's. These guys have never practiced that kind of politics; they're uncomfortable with it. But it's more important than ever. Our party system, without a lot of people appreciating it, has evolved into a national system."

Mitchell also seemed perfect. Where Byrd seemed an old-fashioned inside player evocative of another era, Mitchell, although reliably liberal, was modern, articulate, and telegenic. A former federal judge and a genuinely nice man, he seemed anything but a wheeler-dealer. Mitchell also had a substantive interest in policy, having offered a full programmatic blueprint in 1988 that was largely ignored by the press.

War of the Newt

Yet the new leadership team did abysmally throughout the 1990 budget wars, until rescued by the clumsy miscalculations of Messrs. Sununu, Darman, and Gingrich. All the contradictions of the Democratic opposition party role were epitomized in the 1990 budget episode. As long as George Bush could insist on "no new taxes," the Democrats seemed stymied. Though tax-the-rich ultimately proved superior politics to soak-the-middle class, don't-tax-anybody clearly trumped both positions. As the economy softened and foreign lending to finance the deficit dried up in early 1990, Bush at last relented. Yet the Democrats remained boxed in, continuing to resist a genuinely populist program.

The summit conference at Andrews Air Force Base was an epic case of divide-and-rule. As the budget package took shape, the administration demanded that nearly all the concessions come from the Democratic side: no increases in income tax rates, regressive excise taxes, paralyzing cuts in Medicare, trivial military reductions, and, to add insult to injury, a capital gains tax cut. At several points, Darman and Sununu called negotiations to a halt over the capital gains impasse. At times, the relative accommodationists in the Democratic leadership—Bentsen, Foley, Panetta, Rostenkowski—sided with the administration. "It was really the administration and the House leadership against the liberals," recalls one liberal back-bencher. Remarkably enough, the most steadfast partisan Democrat throughout was Bobby Byrd, a moderate senator, yet old enough to remember a time when Democrats behaved like Democrats. On behalf of the Democratic Leadership Council, Executive Director Alvin From, on the eve of the historic vote, contributed a *New York Times* op-ed piece urging passage for the responsible good of the nation. Mercifully, Sununu, Darman, and Gingrich snatched defeat out of the jaws of victory—Sununu by refusing to budge on capital gains, Gingrich by leading a Republican defection over tax hikes. "If they hadn't overreached," says George Mitchell, "we would have passed a far more Republican bill."

Only when the first budget went down did Rostenkowski see his opening and come forward with a new bill, raising top rates. And even that was watered down somewhat by the Senate before finally passing both houses on October 28. It remains to be seen whether the congressional party can build on this windfall victory, which was less the result of their own cohesion than of Republican disarray. "There was real bitterness at Foley," says one senior legislator, even the beginning of talk that someone else should run for speaker.

House in Order?

What does the future portend? The budget win reminded congressional Democrats that economic populism is popular. The discouraging fact is that they backed into this realization. Foley continues to view himself as speaker of all the House, not as a Wright-style partisan. And Mitchell, though more partisan, is constrained by the fact that his job is to find sixty votes, not to define a clean Democratic position.

The budget win, however, did have the salutary effect of laying to rest, hopefully once and for all, the worry that by playing partisan hardball in defense of party principle, Democrats would make the institution look bad. Congress-bashing, so fashionable of late, has always been partly a canard, and a highly calculated one at that. After all, the one institution Republicans have been unable to capture during the 1980s was the Democratic House—"The People's House"—the branch of government closest to the voters. Not surprisingly, the ideological high strategists of Reaganism—the think tanks, *The Wall Street Journal* editorial page, Gingrich's Conservative Opportunity Society—have kept up a relentless drumbeat of attacks on the institution. (If you can't wash the dishes, break the dishes.) Congress, in this story, was a tyranny of incumbency, a swamp of special interest politics and personal scandal, a tax-and-spend machine unable to keep to a schedule or to set priorities. These charges drew some blood; they did make the congressional Democrats hypersensitive to the concern that failure to strike a budget deal would bring discredit on them. It also primed the press to treat voter anti-incumbent outrage as the big story of the mid-term election.

To understand the dynamics of Democratic paralysis, it is essential to distinguish the real institutional flaws in the Congress from the ones purely trumped up by Gingrich and the right-wing brain trust. In its Summer 1990 issue, *The Public Interest* published a virtual compendium of the conservative indictment of the Congress. Political scientist James L. Payne depicted Congress as "brainwashing" interest groups to demand more spending. Journalist Fred Barnes drew a lurid portrait of "Congressional Despots, Then and Now." Gary McDowell, a law professor, took Congress to task for fomenting judicial activism. The *Wall Street*

Journal's prolific Gordon Crovitz railed against Congress for micro-managing foreign policy. Others indicted it for its oversight of regulatory agencies and the Pentagon. In this medley of criticism, *The Public Interest* graciously included one token moderate, Norman Ornstein, and a token liberal, Nelson Polsby, both political scientists. And, to this reader at least, the Polsby and Ornstein pieces blew the rest away.

Ornstein accused conservative Congress-bashers of "situational Constitutionalism." After all, what were good conservatives doing attacking the most representative branch of government? Ornstein also demolished statistically the permanent incumbency claim. If Democrats were really hiding behind the shield of incumbency, the voters would stampede to Republicans when seats opened up. But in the past decade Democrats have won more open seats than have Republicans. Ornstein also obliterated the claim that Democrats have more seats by dint of gerrymandering.

Polsby, in a delightful essay titled "Congress-bashing for Beginners," recalled the liberal critique of Congress in the 1940s and again in the 1960s as deadlocking democracy. He wrote acidly, "What liberal critics of Congress needed was not constitutional reform. What they needed was the 89th Congress [1965–67].... What Bush needs isn't a weakened Congress so much as a Republican Congress." Polsby also challenged the currently popular ideas of a line-item veto and a limit on terms as radical attacks on the separation of powers. As Polsby and other critics of term limitation have observed, limiting tenure of service would give more power to unelected permanent staffs and to unelected lobbyists. It would encourage congressmen to incur IOUs while in office to be cashed in that much sooner. Even so, term limitation would not necessarily weaken the Democratic hold on the House, since Democrats keep winning most of the open seats.

Still, the phenomenon of the "vanishing marginal seat" is a genuine problem, for it denies more and more voters a meaningful electoral choice. But if we truly want more competitive races (rather than merely more Republican members), public financing of elections—leveling the playing field—is a far better way to engender true partisan competition than such artificial gimmicks as term limitation. Getting private money out of politics would finally break the back of both kinds of corruption—the venal and the ideological. Campaign finance reform would be far better for the democracy, and for the Democrats.

Republicans, however, are continuing to escalate their attack on the institution itself. The 1990 election was widely advertised as a coming repudiation of incumbents, presumably Democratic ones. The belated emergence of a real axis of economic cleavage—Republicans as protectors of the rich, Democrats as guardians of the middle class—saved the party from that fate. In the event, Republican incumbents suffered a great deal more at the hands of the voters than their Democratic colleagues. According to *Congressional Quarterly*, the average reelected Democratic incumbent received 3 percentage points less than his 1988 vote; the average reelected Republican incumbent lost 8 percentage points. Of formerly Democratic open seats, Democrats held ten of ten; of open seats previously held by Republicans, the GOP lost six of seventeen.

Arise, Ye Prisoners of Cohabitation

Even with more cohesion and bolder ideological aspirations, the Democrats will be constrained for at least three years by the deficit and the deficit-reduction agreement. The deficit has proved to be Ronald Reagan's time-release poison pill, his most lethal legacy. And although in 1990 the Democrats won the battle for greater tax fairness, Darman may have bested them on the fine print of spending limitation. Under the deal defense and domestic spending are capped, separately, until 1994. No money cut from defense can be redirected to discretionary domestic spending. Darman thereby managed to lock away any peace dividend for three years. However, one big loophole remains. Congress can expand entitlement programs, though only on a pay-as-you-go basis. Without violating the plan, for example, Congress could slap a surtax on millionaires and target the revenue for child care. This is an invitation for Democrats to think big, or not at all.

Will they? Admittedly, for good constitutional reasons, Congress is a less than ideal bastion from which to mount an opposition program. "It's an interesting commentary that we are thought of as the opposition party," says George Mitchell. "After all, there are more Democratic congressmen, senators, governors, state legislators, mayors, local elected officials, but we're considered the opposition solely because we don't control the White House. In a television age, the presidency has become the government."

Yet the other Democratic bastions are similarly compromised. Most Democratic governors are tangled in state-level fiscal knots. The Democratic National Committee (DNC), under Ron Brown, has been doing a far better than average job of offering a coherent Democratic program. Brown has also met regularly with the House Democratic Caucus, and on more than one occasion helped restrain a stampede to support a capital gains cut. Still, the DNC, compared to its Republican counterpart, remains chronically strapped for funds and is thus less of an institutional player.

Normally, an opposition philosophy is also defined by its elder statesmen. On this front, the Democrats are more bereft than usual. Most of the New Dealers are now deceased; the last survivors are in their seventies or older. Veterans of the Carter administration include many Democrats of the scuttle-to-the-center school, such as Stuart Eizenstat, Charles Schultze, and Robert Strauss, who think budget discipline is paramount, big spending got the Democrats in trouble, and equity has to be sacrificed to growth. These are voices of neoliberalism, if not conservatism.

Another reservoir of statesmen is former presidents and presidential candidates. These, unfortunately, are now famous mainly for calamitous defeats. And, although party philosophy may be defined in new presidential candidacies, the candidates first have an understandable need for product differentiation. Once nominated, they appeal for unity but along the way they are typically a force for division rather than cohesion.

For better or for worse, the congressional party must define what Democrats are all about. Paradoxically, by being clearer about what the party stands for, congressional Democrats make the Congress look better, not worse, as they did when Congress rescued the budget and Social Security, and began salutary debates on Vietnam, Watergate, the Persian Gulf, and such popular domestic issues as universal health insurance and child care.

The Democrats are not virgins, but for the moment they have climbed out of the presidential bed. They should stay out. It is, of course, far better to dwell in connubial bliss with a president of the same persuasion, and far easier to define a coherent ideology from the White House. But, first, a Democrat has to get there. That journey is still arduous, yet more likely to be successful if the party knows where it is going.

[22]

Nelson W. Polsby

Constitutional Mischief: What's Wrong with Term Limitations

On November 6, 1990, California voters by a modest margin amended their state constitution with an initiative that promises to produce far-reaching consequences. This initiative, numbered 140, one of 26 state-wide measures offered on the ballot, contained four main provisions:

(1) A lifetime ban on the holding of each major state constitutional office applied to persons who have served two terms, covering the offices of governor, lieutenant governor, attorney general, secretary of state, treasurer, and superintendent of public instruction.
(2) A lifetime ban on service in the state Senate after two terms, or eight years, and the state Assembly after three terms, or six years.
(3) A ban on the provision of a pension or retirement benefit for service in the legislature, other than federal Social Security.
(4) A sharp permanent reduction in the expenditures allowed for legislative salaries and staff, amounting roughly to an immediate 40 percent reduction in legislative staff.

I shall not deal further with the first of these provisions, because limitations on the terms of executives having control of large and experienced professional staffs poses somewhat different problems for government—though not necessarily for democratic theory—than the set of provisions applying to the legislature.

While term limitations in some respects weaken all public officials in their incentives and capacities to attend to and effectively perform their duties, ballot measure 140 did special damage to the state legislature. Term limitation proposals meant to apply to legislatures elsewhere, such as the U.S. Congress, are designed likewise especially to cripple legislatures.

It can, of course, be argued that legislators have no need of pensions, staff, or longevity to perform their functions adequately. Did not Cincinnatus, after all, leave his plow only temporarily? Would we not be better off if the makers of our laws arose directly from the people, represented them faithfully, and then returned directly to the people before they can be sullied by the poisons lurking in the superheated political atmosphere of the capital?

There are at least two difficulties with this Grandma Moses depiction of modern American political life. The first has to do with the size and complexity of the districts being represented by individual legislators. The second has to do with the size and complexity of the legislators' tasks as authors of legislation and monitors of the executive branch of government.

One may doubt whether there is a legislative district anywhere that is small enough, or homogeneous enough, to be capable of producing a series of representatives to a legislature so perfectly attuned to the constituency's needs as to require no effort on the part of the member to ascertain what those needs are. Whether or not such a constituency exists in principle, we can be reasonably certain that large constituencies, containing half a million or more people, as congressional districts do, or 300,000-plus people, as California state assembly districts do, require effort by representatives before these representatives can be expected to be adequate to the tasks of representation.

The belief in the spontaneous competence of good representatives belongs to an age and place where a relatively stable and well-accepted status system did much of the work of government. Amateur representation is historically the product of a status-ridden society, where people knew their place. People who inhabit more fluid and diverse societies, where people contend, negotiate, sue, migrate, or otherwise engage in mutually adaptive activities, require far more in the way of explicit attention from their representatives than Cincinnatus and his amateur colleagues are competent to give.

Translated into modern terms, the plea for an amateur legislature is a plea for legislators capable of representing only the most conspicuous elements of their constituencies. Perhaps this is all many modern legislators choose to do. But term limitations make legislators much less capable of choosing otherwise.

Equally serious are the consequences for the legislature as a body. Suppose we accept the notion, central to the term limiter's case, that state government, or national government, is somehow itself the problem. Would it not follow that it is in the interests of the people to equip their chosen representatives with the capacity to deal with the problem in all its complexity and difficulty?

The essential tool of a legislative body in dealing with any set of complex problems—including those posed by the rest of government—is its own capacity to form judgments about the merits of alternative proposals and diagnoses independently from whatever is advocated by the executive branch, the governor, lobbyists, fixers, hangers-on, and interest groups. The legislature's capacity to form an independent judgment arises from three things: a division of labor, in which individual members are assigned to specialize in a limited range of topics; longevity, in which they continue in their specialization long enough to familiarize themselves with the players, their interests, and the strengths and weaknesses of various arguments and proposals; and finally, their ability to purchase technical assistance responsive to their needs for analysis and understanding, in short, staff.

It follows that a constitutional amendment prescribing limits on the longevity of members of a legislature and limits on the amount of staff they may have to help them is an attempt to prevent the legislature from forming its own well-considered and independent judgment on matters its members must understand.

By no means, however, can we say that this exhausts the mischief enacted by California measure 140. We can say with some confidence that the capacity of the individual legislator to represent well has been deprofessionalized, and that the capacity of the legislature to act independently and competently has been severely maimed. But there is more.

Consider the social composition of a legislature that has been transformed into a body of temporary place-holders. To whom might membership be attractive? At least three sets of people: (1) the old (2) the rich (3) the bought.

A lifetime ban after six years of service and no pension can scarcely be a deterrent to a candidate who already has a pension, not to mention a short life expectancy. So we could expect that hale and hearty senior citizens might well enjoy the stimulus and the opportunity to serve that the people of California have devised for them. To be sure, there are obvious possible disadvantages to rule by the old. Elderly members of a legislature may be unable to work very hard. They may prove to be unusually stubborn, inflexible, or resistant to new ideas or new experiences. They may be out of touch with the vast bulk of the population they are supposed to be serving. Their health, or their hearing, or their physical robustness, may deteriorate on the job, making them unusually dependent rather than independent as policy makers.

These are merely possibilities. Older legislators may also be wise, disinterested, experienced, and public-spirited. With respect to most of the human qualities we would want to see in a legislator, the old might constitute a population only somewhat more risky than the population at large. Of course, they could not be expected to be entirely free of concern for the special interests of the old.

It seems unreasonable to expect utter selflessness from any group in the population. Even so, I suppose more than a few might advocate generous provision for the school-age population, even if it meant means-testing benefits to the elderly. Considerations of this kind would fortify arguments favoring a mix of demographic characteristics in a legislative body that seeks to represent a diverse population rather than an absolute bar to membership by elderly members.

But consider the next category, the rich, to whom pensions and occupational careers, legislative or otherwise, would mean little or nothing. Why would they seek to serve at all, except to further their own interests? Some, no doubt, do serve for reasons other than purely to defend their economic advantages. In Colorado, for example, where legislators are grossly underpaid, an unusually large number of well-to-do women, who do not need the money, can afford to serve, and many are reported to do so with distinction.

Nevertheless, it is very hard to justify a constitutional arrangement that systematically favors legislative service for a group so well able to take care of itself, if need be, in the private sector. And yet there can be no serious doubt that this is more or less the constitutional arrangement that Californians have voted for. The main sponsors of this plan in California were conservative Republicans and land developers, in short, friends of the rich. The main advocates of term limitations for members of Congress are Republican political operatives at the national level and trickle-down conservatives.

Finally, there are the overly dependent whom I have unkindly called the bought. We must recognize that term limitations greatly increase the dependence of those legislators who do wish to have careers, or have no extraordinary independent sources of income, on the money that interest groups can provide. Interest groups, many of which are currently allied with legislators, gain power over their legislative allies under term limitation conditions at three points.

First, interest group money is necessary to advertise new candidates for legislative seats in order to get them elected in the first place. Veteran legislators can depend on name recognition, habit, or constituent case work to reduce their dependency on contributions of cash. Indeed, well-entrenched incumbents can raise money more easily precisely because they can do more for interest groups than interest groups can do for them. Not so for novices.

Second, inexperienced legislators after they are elected need interest groups in order to help them understand political issues that come before the legislature. This is especially the case in the absence of legislative staff. Lobbyists have information. They are available to impart it. They offer alliances. They are indispensable to any legislative body with serious work to do.

But legislators must also have the capacity to keep interest groups at arm's length, so that those legislators who have the desire to carve out an independent path may do so. A reasonably safe seat, expectations of an honorable legislative career, a decent salary and pension, adequate staff, all play a part in providing that capacity. Without any or all of these things, interest groups gain influence.

What of the future? A legislator who knows that he has not much of a personal future in the legislature must consider in what arena his future lies. Will the member try for some other public office? Will the member become a lobbyist, or a lawyer in private or semi-public practice? The prospect of no future in the legislature does not mean no future at all. The California constitution does not now require that members completing their terms be taken out and shot. So here again the potentiality for undue dependence on interest-group alliances raises its head. And this may do great harm to the quality of the public service that legislators are meanwhile able to render.

It may nevertheless be too severe to characterize legislators under a term limitation scheme as "bought" because the dependence of so many of them on interest-group alliances and interest-group money will inevitably increase. There will always be at least a few people of high character in most human institutions. In designing institutions, however, as we do when we write or rewrite constitutions, it is only prudent to organize incentives so that it is unnecessary continually to rely on individual resources of character and self-restraint to prompt good behavior. Rather, we should want our representative institutions to be positively hospitable to a great range of our fellow citizens, especially those leading normal lives, with everyday concerns, families to feed, ambitions and thoughts for the future, in short, those with as full a complement of human attributes and qualities and potentialities as we can attract to the messy and inspiring business of self-government.

Term limitations short-circuit this process by making it too hard for too many sorts of people to participate. This debases the representative capacities of the legislature as well as the capacity of the legislature to play a constructive independent role in governance.

White House Chief of Staff John Sununu, presumably speaking for the President, has recently endorsed the idea of a constitutional amendment limiting the terms of members of Congress. The absence of something like the self-destructive California initiative process at the national level means that it probably won't happen. James Madison and his colleagues knew very well what they were doing when they made the U.S. Constitution difficult to amend.

Observers meanwhile should reflect upon the spectacle of self-proclaimed conservatives trumpeting their support for a constitutional amendment to rid themselves of Democratic members of Congress whom they don't seem to be able to defeat the old-fashioned way. If alleged conservatives will launch a fundamental attack on basic American political institutions on so trivial a pretext as their annoyance at having to make bipartisan compromises with a coequal branch of government, what are we to expect of nonconservatives?

Those who remember Robert A. Taft's encouragement of Joseph McCarthy or George Bush's more recent attempt to rewrite the First Amendment to prevent flag burning may not be surprised when conservatives exhibit an appalling shallowness of commitment to basic American institutions. It may be argued that constitutional arrangements are so well settled in America that they can withstand any amount of self-serving, opportunistic rubbishing. This, however, is not the contribution American conservatives ought to be making to political discourse.

[23]

Richard E. Neustadt

A Memo on Presidential Transition

1 . The Problem of Another "Hundred Days"

One hears all over town about "another Hundred Days" once Kennedy is in the White House. If this means an impression to be made on Congressmen, bureaucrats, press, public, foreign governments, the analogy is apt. Nothing would help the new Administration more than such a first impression of energy, direction, action, and accomplishment. Creating that impression and sustaining it become a prime objective for the months after Inauguration Day. Since an impression of the Roosevelt sort feeds on reality, and could not be sustained by mere "public relations," establishing conditions that will foster real accomplishment becomes a prime objective for the brief transition period before Inauguration Day.

But the "Hundred Days" analogy can also be taken—and is being taken—as an expectation of fulfillment for every sort of legislative promise in the Platform and the campaign. Everybody tends to think of his pet pledge as the priority accomplishment for Kennedy's first three months. Yet that timing only brings us to the Easter Recess of the First Session of a modern Congress!

EDITORS' NOTE: On September 15, 1960, Richard Neustadt, then a professor of government at Columbia, wrote a bold memo to candidate John F. Kennedy on issues for the anticipated transition. His memo, the first of a series, was subtitled "A Tentative Check-List for the Weeks Between Election and Inaugural." Professor Neustadt drew on his own insights from his influential book, *Presidential Power*, which had been published the previous April. Today, Neustadt continues to teach, at Harvard's Kennedy School. The memo, never before published, remains a classic. Depending on events in November [1992], it may take on new relevance.

These legislative wants are hard to square with a convincing demonstration of energy and accomplishment. "Another Hundred Days" as an impression of effectiveness is threatened by the promissory notes read into that analogy.

In terms of legislative action, the analogy to 1933 is not apt. Roosevelt then did not take office until March. He had four months to organize the take-over. Congress was adjourned when he entered the White House and was not due to assemble until December. It met in special session after his inauguration, on his call. It met, moreover, to deal with a devastating domestic crisis that was seen and felt by citizens, in their own lives, all across the country. Foreign relations, meanwhile, raised virtually no issues that could not be ignored or postponed. And Roosevelt had the patronage (old style) to dole out at a time when jobs of any sort were highly valued. What is the analogy with 1961?

In 1948, when Truman was reelected, there also was much talk of "another Hundred Days." But when he was sworn in a second time, Congress had been in session for three weeks, organized, bills introduced, committees working. No sharply felt, widely perceived crisis faced the country. Instead, in all the realms of Cold War and of welfare undertakings—most of them unknown in 1933—government agencies and private groups pressed diverse legislative claims, citing campaign promises as their authority and jostling each other in the rush to take advantage of Truman's "honeymoon." Weeks before inaugural, the groups concerned had gained commitments from Congressional leaders (whether they committed Truman, or he, them, is in dispute) for early floor fights on FEPC and on repeal of Taft-Hartley. By the time those fights had failed, the "honeymoon" was over and the Session far advanced with little else done. In legislative terms, it is 1949, not 1933, that offers an analogy—and warnings—for 1961.

Unlike Truman, Kennedy *may* come into office in the midst of some sharp, overt international emergency, or in the train of a sharp economic slump. It is at least possible, however, that January 1961 will be a time of many incipient crises but no "crisis." So was 1949.

It follows that, for the transition period between election and inaugural the guidelines ought to be: *Postpone whatever is postponable* in the mechanics of administration-building. Put off the novelties that have not been thought through. *Concentrate upon the things that are immediately relevant to showing real effectiveness* on and after January 20. And in the doing of those things, keep this objective uppermost. It is the key objective for the weeks after November 8.

The things that cannot be postponed are enumerated below. They are *roughly* in the order in which it seems desirable to deal with them, starting November 9.

2. Organizing for a First Message to Congress

The most important task in the transition *is the working out of strategy and tactics for an exploitation of the "honeymoon" ahead.* This means decisions on the substance, timing, publicity, *and priority* of legislative proposals to Congress. It means decisions of the same sort on discretionary executive actions. It means decisions on relationships between projected proposals and actions. It means weighing short-range gains against long-range troubles, political and other. It means judging what should be done in the President's name, and what should not, and how to enforce the distinction. It also means evaluating fiscal implications of proposals and of actions, both, and making some immediate decisions on taxation and the budget.

Not all of these decisions can be taken before January 20, but preparatory work needs to be far advanced by then: The issues should have been identified, the arguments defined, preliminary judgments entered well before Inauguration Day …

The *first* thing to do is to make a plan, *deciding tentatively on the timing and the scope of such a message.* This provides a target for everybody who has ideas, views, concerns about the program objectives of the new regime.

The second thing to do is to *establish "working groups" and get them moving* with the message as their target—both on things that should be asked of Congress and on things that could be pronounced done or underway administratively …

The *third* thing to do is to get a "bird dog" on the scene, *putting somebody in charge of staff work on the message.* This should be someone close to Kennedy, very much in his confidence and very much a "staff man" (but a tough-minded one). His job should be to see that all the working groups are working, the competitors competing, gaps filled, issues raised, arguments brought to focus, and the President-elect informed on who is doing what, with what, to whom. *This is a full-time job,* for the whole transition period and after. Its holder has to be much more than a draftsman; drafting is merely his hunting license; his hunting ground is foreign *and* domestic program, legislative *and* administrative. This is somewhat like Rosenman's work at message season in the Roosevelt White House, or like Clifford's and Murphy's in the Truman White House. But in many ways it is a broader and rougher job than theirs; they worked in an established context; this man will not …

3. Designating White House Aides

After Election Day the President-elect will need a *small personal staff* to operate through the transition period and to take office with him. A few staff aides are immediately necessary; their names and jobs should be announced at once, so that importunate office-seekers, idea-peddlers, pressmen, legislators, diplomats, and cabinet-designers know who and what they are. These necessary jobs include:

(1) **A Press Secretary,** whose work after the inaugural will be so much like his work before that he should have the title at the outset. On November 9, Kennedy will be transformed in the eyes of Americans *and foreign governments.* He will no longer have the leeway of a "campaigner." His statements will be taken with the utmost seriousness. *Everything* said and done in public need be weighed as though he were already President.

(2) **An appointments aide,** to guard the door and manage the daily schedule. Whether this person should be designated "Appointments Secretary" depends on whether he is meant to have autonomy, after inaugural, or to work as a subordinate of some other aide. If subordination is intended, hold off on the "Secretary" part of that title.

(3) **A "Number-one Boy,"** serving as a sort of first assistant on general operations, day by day. He could be called "Executive Assistant to the President-elect" and he could carry that title into the White House in lieu of Sherman Adams's title, "*The* Assistant to the President." It would be well to avoid reminders of Adams, not only for public relations but because, once in the White House, Kennedy may find that he needs several "number-one boys" for different aspects of the work; other things aside, Adams was a terrible bottleneck.

(4) **The message-and-program aide** indicated above. If the man is a lawyer, and if Kennedy wants him around for comparable work in later months, he might be designated "Special Counsel" (FDR's invention for Rosenman). But he could just as well be called "Special Consultant" and his long-run status left in abeyance for the time being. What counts in the short run is his standing with the President-elect, not his title.

(5) **A personnel consultant** (discussed below). Here again, it would be well to treat the job as ad hoc and avoid traditional White House titles for the time being.

(6) **A personal secretary** who might remain just that after January 20, or who might carry higher status and more general duties afterwards, depending on the President's convenience and her capabilities. Meanwhile, it would be well not to dispose of any traditional titles one might ultimately want for her.

These six should suffice as a nucleus to move into the White House, January 20, where they will find the Executive Clerk and his career assistants on the job for routine paper processing. Additional aides will certainly be needed for ad hoc troubleshooting before inaugural; still more so afterwards. But until the needs are felt to be both clear and continuing, and until the men have been tried on the job, there is no reason to announce their designation as permanent members of the White House staff. Nor is there reason to give them traditional White House titles ...

In designating personal staff, two rules of thumb are indicated:

First, appoint men only to jobs for which the President-elect, himself, feels an immediate and continuing need, a need he has defined in his own mind, and can at once define for them. If the need is immediate but not continuing, offer a "consultantship," or put the man in a department and borrow him back.

Second, give appointees titles that square with the jobs to be done and choose no titles without thinking of their bureaucratic connotations in the outgoing regime. A title may attract a lot of "customary" business that the President-elect wants handled somewhere else, or not at all, or on which he prefers experimentation. A title also may connote a ranking in the staff that he does not intend.

If these rules of thumb are followed, most of Eisenhower's current staff positions will fall into abeyance on January 20. There is nothing wrong with that.

4. Designating Science and Security Aides

Two of the positions in Eisenhower's White House present special problems:

(1) **The Science Adviser.** This post, created after Sputnik, is highly valued in the scientific community which would be disturbed if it were not filled by early December ...

(2) **The Special Assistant for National Security Affairs.** There will be no outside pressure for filling this post and NSC can operate without it, for a time at least ... But if, for reasons of his own, the President-elect wants to make an appointment, both the title and the duties should be considered, in advance, with particular regard for the intended role of the Secretary of State, *vis-à-vis* NSC.

5. Designating Executive Office Aides

Soon after November 8, the President-elect will have use for *a principal assistant, at one remove from personal aides, who can backstop the White House* in coping with programming and administrative problems from Inauguration Day on. If he is to be of maximum assistance from the start, *the job to give him is the Budget Directorship* ... This Budget Director-designate should be conceived as someone capable of broad-gauged, general-purpose service to the President, *picking up the staff work that personal aides cannot give time to on a continuing basis* ...

Besides the Budget Director, there are three top appointive officials in the Executive Office: the Chairman of the Council of Economic Advisers, the Director of the Office of Civilian Defense Mobilization, and the Executive Secretary of NSC ...

6. Designating Cabinet Officers

There is no operating reason why Cabinet officers and heads of major agencies need to be designated immediately after election. With "working groups" established and key staff aides appointed ... one does not need Cabinet officers in order to get moving toward a fast start after January 20. Indeed, there is advantage in holding off on most Cabinet appointments until staff and working groups are launched; Cabinet members then would have a framework to fit into and could not wander off on their own. As a rule of thumb: *defer Cabinet and major agency designations until early December.*

A possible exception is the Secretaryship of State. The Jackson Subcommittee favors using the Secretary not just as a department head but as a principal assistant *in the whole sphere of national security policy* ...

A second possible exception is the Cabinet post, if any, where the present incumbent would be retained as a gesture of bi-partisanship. Nothing of the sort may be contemplated. But if it is, then obviously the sooner it were done the better ...

In choosing Cabinet officers (and heads of major agencies), the President-elect will naturally consider the usual criteria of geographic, party, and interest-group "representativeness." *Three additional criteria are worth bearing in mind:*

First is competitive balance among major differences in policy outlook, on which Kennedy does not choose to make up his mind for all time. This is a very tricky and important problem in"representativeness." If the President-elect wants both "conservative" and "liberal" advice on economic management, for example, and wants the competition to come out where he can see it and judge it, he needs to choose strong-minded competitors *and he needs to put them in positions of roughly equal institutional power,* so that neither wins the contest at a bureaucratic level too far down for the President to judge it. For example, if the Treasury (a powerful post) were given to a "conservative," it would not suffice to put his competition on the Presidential staff; at least two Cabinet competitors would be needed in addition.

Second is the chance for useful reorientation of a department's role with a change in its Secretary's traditional orientation. The Eisenhower Administration, for example, has had an industrial relations specialist as Secretary of Labor, instead of the traditional union president or politician avowedly representing "labor's voice in the Cabinet." As a result, Mitchell has been able to act for the Administration in labor disputes and to keep a supervisory eye on "independent" labor relations agencies to a far greater degree than his predecessors. For the unions—to say nothing of management—were never content with "labor's voice" when they wanted to deal seriously with the Administration. An Arthur Goldberg is the only sort of "unionist" who could sustain and broaden this reorientation; otherwise, reversion to traditional selection risks the new usefulness of this department. Other examples could be offered: Treasury, for one, has often been a drag on State and Defense, in part because of the traditional orientation of its Secretary. A Lovett, or a Harriman (or a David Rockefeller!), who both meets the tradition and transcends it, could make a substantial difference in the future.

Third is the effect on long-run organizational objectives—and options—inherent in the personalities and interests of particular appointees. The case of CEA has already been mentioned; so have the cases of State, the Security Assistant, and the Science Advisor. Another example is the Budget Bureau. One more cost-accountant in the place would finish it off as a useful source of staff work for the President. Especially in the sphere of national security, the personalities and interests of initial appointees at State, Defense, Budget, and Treasury *will go far to decide* what can and cannot be done thereafter by way of improving "national policy machinery."

7. *Organizing for Appointments below Cabinet Rank*

This is an area in which the President-elect and his whole staff could easily get bogged down at no profit to themselves ... word should be passed to incoming department and agency heads that they will make nothing but trouble for themselves and the Administration by unselective replacements or massive importations of persons at Assistant Secretary level and below. Changes should be made selectively and at leisure, using the guide line, "Know who your replacement is before you make a change."

It is no accident that in 1953 the two most effective officers in the first weeks after Inauguration Day were Dodge at Budget and Humphrey at Treasury. These were the two agencies where there was no "purging" and where inherited staffs were told they would be treated as reliable until they turned out otherwise. Humphrey and Dodge were immediately effective because they immediately had staffs at work behind them. For a Kennedy Administration with the "Hundred Days" problem to lick, the lesson is obvious.

8. Reassuring the Bureaucracy

If one means to take the steps suggested ... above, one ought to get a maximum of credit for them from the bureaucracy. *This calls for an early public statement to the effect that government careerists are a national resource and will be treated as such* by the new regime. The reality of that intention will be demonstrated as those steps are taken. It will be demonstrated further if the working groups suggested ... above begin, informally, to draw upon the expertise of selected bureaucrats long before Inauguration Day.

The more career officials can look forward to January 20 with hopeful, interested, even excited anticipation, *the better the new administration will be served in the weeks after.* To instill negative anticipation is to cut off one's own nose to spite one's face. That was the effect in 1953.

9. Consulting with the Legislative Leadership

From Election Day on, several things should be kept in mind:

(1) The Vice President-elect will be looking for work.

(2) In 1949, the new Senate leader was chosen by the Democrats just before Congress met, with the proviso that Barkley keep the post until January 20. Is this precedent to be followed in 1961?

(3) Congress meets two weeks before inaugural; the Committee Chairmen—*the same faces as before*—will be looking for the "customary" laundry-list of Presidential proposals in every sphere; *in 1949, that custom helped to dissipate Truman's honeymoon.* They also will be thinking about going into business for themselves; some of them will be doing it. Finally, they will be touchily awaiting signs of recognition from the President-elect.

(4) When Congress meets, the Senate liberals apparently intend another rules fight.

(5) Congressional leaders will have to be consulted on, or at least informed of, the President-elect's immediate legislative plans. Their help will be needed in considering—and above all in sustaining—priorities. But consultation *with whom, how* above all, *when?* These questions will not necessarily look the same from the Executive side as from the Senate.

(6) The first *formal* meeting with the legislative leaders, whether before or after Inauguration Day, will tend to set the form, tone, member-

ship, and timing of future meetings. What purposes are these meetings to serve? Are they to be intimate sessions, *a la* FDR, or ambassadorial encounter, *a la* Eisenhower, with staffs present and minutes taken?

10. Giving Congress Agenda before the First Message

Hopefully, some non-controversial, simple, quick-action items could be introduced *before* Inauguration Day "on the President-elect's behalf," to "facilitate the work of the new Administration." Within reason, the more of these the better, and the wider their spread across committees the better ...

11. Establishing Liaison with the Eisenhower Administration

There seems to be no need for "general" liaison and no point in assigning anyone to do that meaningless job. Presumably, Eisenhower will suggest a courtesy meeting and briefing, as Truman did in 1952, and will offer assistance toward a smooth transition. If he does not offer, he could be asked. Once the offer is made (or extorted) it should be used to establish several *specific* liaison arrangements. These include:

(1) Access for the President-elect to all government intelligence sources and for the prospective Secretary of State to all the cable traffic he may want to see.

(2) Arrangements with the FBI for prompt security clearance of appointees.

(3) Access for a reliable associate of the prospective Budget Director to all aspects of the Budget Bureau's work in preparing the 1962 budget and in clearing legislation before January 20. This should be for the purpose of obtaining information, not participating in decisions.

(4) Arrangements for use of Civil Service Commission staff and facilities, and for information on expiring appointments in the hands of the White House Executive Clerk.

(5) Arrangements for consultation by incoming officials with their outgoing opposite numbers and with departmental staffs. No limitations should be accepted on the freedom to inquire and consult.

(6) Arrangements for taking over White House offices and budget.

It may turn out that the international or economic situation requires more than a courtesy consultation between Eisenhower and Kennedy; if so, the situation should be met as it deserves, with the proviso that Kennedy need make none of Eisenhower's decisions or accept commitments carrying past January 20. *This proviso cannot be a prohibition; the situation may be unprecedented.*

The President-elect must be prepared for a variety of international complications before inaugural. What they might be and how to meet them could be studied *now* by the Nitze group.

12. Organizing for Reorganizing

Not long after Election Day, it would be well to designate the members of the President's Advisory Committee on Government Organization ...

13. Setting Ground Rules for Press Conferences

The big "Press-Radio-TV," televised press conference is a recent innovation; it serves some purposes well; others badly. It does not accomplish some of the objectives served by the quite different institutions of Roosevelt's time. Whether any changes should, or could be made is open to question. It is a question worth pursuing with responsible journalists like Reston. *If changes are intended, they should be instituted at the outset;* the first press conference after inaugural will set a pattern hard to break.

14. Installing the "Shadow Government" in Washington

Very soon after Election Day, the President-elect will want to decide how fast and how formally—and in what facilities at whose expense—he wants his staff and Cabinet designees, and *ad hoc* working groups in Washington.

This automatically involves decision also on the timing of vacations *and of reconnaissance trips abroad* by Presidential designees, or by the President-elect. Shall they (or he) survey the free world? And when must they be back?

15. Preparing the Inaugural Address

It would be well *not* to begin this too early, but instead to wait until the main lines of a first message—that is to say of an initial program—had emerged. The Inaugural Address has to be a tone-setter. It will help to have a notion of what is to follow, before spending much time on this introduction. It will also help to wait until one knows what international and economic conditions to expect by January 20.

16. Arranging the Physical Take-Over

A number of troublesome details will have to be attended to. Some of them are unlikely to be settled without reference to the President-elect.

These include:
(1) Arranging White House office space and Executive Office Building space ...

17. Arranging Initial Cabinet and NSC meetings

Eisenhower surrounded these meetings with elaborate paper-work and preparatory consultations. Staffs have been created in each department to assist with preparations and follow-up. Also, Cabinet meetings now include more Presidential aides than department heads. Somewhat the same thing occurs in NSC meetings.

It is important that none of these procedures and arrangements continues, except as Kennedy specifically desires, after a chance to get his own feel for the uses of Cabinet and NSC. Yet the first meetings of these bodies could automatically perpetuate all sorts of Eisenhower practices. Past procedures will be carried on by career staffs unless they are deliberately interrupted.

It would be well, therefore, to confine early Cabinet meetings to department heads of Cabinet rank, along with the President's Executive Assistant, and to have only such agenda as the President may choose in consultation with his personal staff. As for initial NSC meetings, it would be well to confine them to statutory members, perhaps adding the Budget Director and the Executive Assistant, while the NSC Secretary stuck to "secretarial" service, with agendas chosen by the President ...

18. Program Development after Inauguration

Presumably the first message will not have been completed, or all fights on it finished, by January 20. This will remain to be put into final form. As that is done, attention would shift to amending Eisenhower's budget, the next great action with a deadline attached around which to organize Administration planning and decisions. At the same time, it will be desirable to get study groups working, in or out of government, on the desirable projects and programs, administrative and legislative, which are not to be, or cannot be, acted upon immediately.

These three steps—completing the first message, amending the budget, getting long-range studies started—will be major items of concern for the President's first weeks in office. They represent, really, a late stage in "transition."

Like everything before, this stage should be set in awareness of possible complications from abroad.

[24]

PAUL STARR

Can Government Work?

Americans may love their country; they may resent anyone showing the least disrespect for the flag. They may judge other countries to be better or worse depending on how closely those nations approximate the American political system. All the same, they regard their own politicians and government with a mixture of skepticism and scorn. In the United States, especially since Reagan, distrust of the government has virtually become a mark of the authentic patriot. To show some confidence in government may not yet be subversive, but it does raise suspicions.

Of course, skepticism about government is not an unreasonable impulse: a number of our recent leaders have seemed entirely worthy of it. A free people, moreover, ought not to be so taken with their government as to be taken in by it. But in a democracy, the government is their instrument for confronting problems that affect them collectively. When the citizens of a nation give up on the integrity and efficacy of their government—when they no longer believe that elections matter or that public institutions can perform reliably—they lose a power of their own.

For more than a decade now, the idea of public remedy has been in public disrepute. Many Americans have become convinced that there simply are no public solutions to our national problems. Or if there are, that Congress could not possibly enact them in a rational and coherent form. Or if it could, that we cannot afford the cost, not now, perhaps never. With suspicious modesty, we have managed to persuade ourselves that despite the genius of our democracy and the superiority of our economy, we are either too inept at government or too impoverished to remedy what ails us—or at least, what ails some of us.

The distrust of government is hardly confined to conservatives. Even many people with progressive inclinations are cynical about the integrity of political leaders, the intelligence of policy making, and the competence and efficiency of public services. They worry that liberalism, even their own liberalism, relies too much on government, though they are uncertain what other instrument could serve where government cannot.

Probably no bigger obstacle stands in the way of a revival of liberal politics than this: the many who think government doesn't work also think that liberalism means more of it. Even those who grant that some things are deeply wrong see no way through politics to put them right; and because they see no point to politics, to call upon their sense of compassion is almost no use. Besides, it is not chiefly compassion that we need to evoke, since compassion is for someone else. The distrust of government now blocks us from acting even on prudent, national interests that affect us all. But it is exactly for those purposes that a recovery of public remedy is most necessary. After years of deficits and deadlock, America is paying a great and growing price for politically incapacitating itself.

The Costs of the Conservative Default

The political capacity of a society springs from a variety of sources: the cooperation and confidence a government enjoys from its citizens and international allies; the coherence and ability of its leadership; the financial and organizational resources that it can marshal to carry out its policies. Andrew Carnegie once spoke of the "stewardship of wealth" as a responsibility of the rich. A nation's leaders have a corresponding democratic responsibility: the stewardship of political capacities and public wealth.

When conservatives came to power a decade ago, they promised to reduce the scale of government and its influence on society. Whether their policies have achieved that goal is open to question. But in one sense, they achieved a more drastic result. The reductions in income tax rates and military buildup of the early Reagan years—followed now by the burgeoning costs of the savings and loan bailout—have created a fiscal blockade against all new initiatives. To be sure, that blockade has had the happy result, from the conservatives' standpoint, of precluding or at least forestalling social programs that require new spending. But the deficit has also depleted America's political capacity to meet *any* new challenge.

The federal budget has by no means shrunk, but interest payments, the armed services, and Social Security now account for so large a share of expenditures that discretionary funds have been severely limited. In the face of unforeseen problems, such as AIDS, the S&L crisis, or the deterioration of nuclear weapons plants, the first responses have been avoidance, postponement, and budgetary chicanery. And in the face of unforeseen international opportunities, notably the upheaval in Eastern

Europe, we have not "stood tall." Rather, we have stood back, convinced that we could not afford to extend ourselves with financial assistance.

Conservatives have told us that fiscal pressure is a healthy political condition. Ronald Reagan often warned against any tax increase on the grounds that Congress would spend whatever additional tax revenue it had; supposedly, the money would just vanish into a black hole in the federal budget. But a perpetual fiscal squeeze has dangers of its own, now much in evidence. Not only has the squeeze constricted the political imagination and blocked quick responses to new problems; it has deformed public policy. The refusal at first to acknowledge new problems, and then to respond adequately to them, has turned out repeatedly to add to long-run costs. The inability to shut down savings and loans that month by month were effectively spending billions of dollars of the taxpayers' money is only one example.

There are many others. Our tax system has been deformed: we have shifted from income to payroll taxes, not because the payroll tax was a more just or more efficient tax, but because it could be increased under the cover of saving Social Security. And rather than raise additional revenue itself, the federal government now routinely prefers to set costly requirements for others, such as the states or private institutions. These regulatory substitutes for direct programs may keep federal spending down, but they are not necessarily good public policy. Witness the administration's effort to shift the burdens of transportation policy to the states.

Perhaps nowhere else are the ill effects of prolonged fiscal squeeze more evident than in the failure of stewardship of the nation's public wealth. That wealth consists of physical infrastructure as well as the "natural capital" of the environment. Consider the immense public inheritance that we have received from the generation that endured the Depression and fought the Second World War. The entire nation is laced with highways and bridges and dotted with schools and post offices built in that time. Those are merely the physical manifestations of a great institution-building phase in our history. Now consider the new additions to that legacy contributed in the 1980s by a much richer generation. They do not make an impressive bequest. As a proportion of public spending, public investment has been steadily declining. Between 1945 and 1952, as Robert Heilbroner has pointed out, the share of federal nonmilitary spending that went to infrastructure investment was 6.9 percent; that proportion fell to 1.5 percent in the 1970s and just 1.2 percent in the last decade. Could the federal government today even consider the contemporary equivalent of building the interstate highway system or developing the National Institutes of Health? The Strategic Defense Initiative ("Star Wars") is the closest parallel—and a reminder of the extent to which our technological and financial resources have been devoted to military defense.

Short-term financial concerns now seem to bar us from the ambitions of our predecessors. Supply-side economics was supposed to renew the well-springs of savings and investment, but it construes them to be entirely private. It has utterly neglected the public component of our capital stock, including research and education and public institutions themselves, now a technologically lagging sector. Here the failure of stewardship has been grievous, yet politically self-reinforcing. For the further public services fall behind, the more their inadequacies seem to confirm the conservative indictment against them.

Not the federal deficit itself, but the failure to provide for the future is our real fiscal ailment. Had we been resorting to deficits to pay for productive public investment and financing that expenditure out of private U.S. savings, we might have little cause for concern. But borrowing from abroad for purposes of present consumption is another matter. As a nation, we have been consuming 3 percent a year more than we are producing; the debts we have been accumulating to foreigners will have to be repaid out of future production and tax receipts. Moreover, our need of continued flows of foreign capital exposes us to the risk that for one reason or another—the proverbial "Tokyo earthquake," real or metaphorical—the flows may stop and send our economy into a tailspin.

In all this, there is an irony, a default on a promise, and a self-betrayal of conservative principle. In foreign policy, conservatives have represented themselves as the most ardent defenders of American security and sovereignty; in economic policy, they have supposedly stood for "sound finance" and the priority of investment over consumption. But administrations professing to be conservative have now presided over a decade of structural deficits, excess consumption, and casino capitalism that have compromised our strength and security. Like Lyndon Johnson's refusal to raise taxes to pay for Vietnam, Ronald Reagan's refusal to pay for the 1980s defense buildup was an historic default of leadership.

The costs of the conservative default have fallen hardest on the most vulnerable. During the last decade, income inequality has grown because of economic changes that the government has done little to soften or modify. One visible sign of that deterioration is the increased homeless population on our streets. Another indicator is the growing number of Americans without public or private health insurance coverage, up from 30 to 38 million during the 1980s. Yet a third index is the reduced real income of America's lowest fifth. These changes should not only disturb our sense of justice. As poverty grows increasingly concentrated among children and single parents, it affects the whole society's future. Children growing up without adequate education, health care, and family security make less productive citizens; those who end up unemployed or in prison become a net cost to their communities. To see the larger effects, no brilliance is necessary. But political leadership and inspiration are necessary to turn the connection between child poverty and the nation's wealth into a foundation of policy.

One reason for our failure to address these and other needs is our inability to control health care costs, which have effectively crowded out other social expenditures. In the decades immediately after World War II, health care costs rose as a percentage of national income in all advanced industrial economies. But in the 1980s health care costs in the United States far outpaced those of our major international competitors, including West Germany, France, Great Britain, and Japan. Other countries manage to provide all their citizens with health coverage and nonetheless limit the growth of health care spending. We have been unable to do either precisely because we lack the financial control that a comprehensive insurance system can provide.

Canada offers an instructive comparison. In 1971 Canada and the United States were both spending 7 percent of GNP on health care. That year Canada introduced national health insurance; in the early seventies, we also considered various plans but could not agree on any. And while health care costs in the United States now run over 11 percent of GNP, they amount in Canada to only 8.6 percent. (As it happens, the difference of two and a half percent of GNP is about the size of our trade deficit.) One recent study found that half the Canadian-American difference in health spending is explained by higher *administrative* costs for health insurance and health care in the United States. To spend more money for more clinical services would be understandable, but to pay for more administration is a deadweight loss. Many Americans suspect government of endemic inefficiency. In this case the universal public Canadian system has lower administrative costs and lower costs overall than the predominantly private and incomplete insurance system in the United States.

Whether the issue is national health insurance or the welfare of the poor, conservatives have both promoted and benefited from the pervasive distrust of governmental competence and capacities. They have played upon the pessimism, amplified and legitimated it, made it a cornerstone of the dominant public philosophy, and successfully conveyed the myth that the whole meaning of liberalism lies in its preference for more government.

American liberalism, however, is not a philosophy of omnicompetent government. Liberals, unlike socialists, did not seek to nationalize industry; they do not seek to put the economy under the command of the state but to shape the rules of the market to ensure its consistency with the values of fair opportunity, personal security, democracy, and the sustainability of the society and the natural environment. In the realm of personal choice, the commitment of liberals to individual rights is, if anything, stronger than that of conservatives. Liberals have sought strict limits on state power in the spheres of religion and moral life, free speech, and a free press.

But liberals are also mindful of the dangers of power gathered in private hands and the inequalities that spring from the market. Like an all-powerful state, the unfettered market and unrestricted private power can disrupt the security of families and prevent citizens from making real use of their political liberties. To realize in practice the full promise of a free society, we need no blind faith in the state, but a rough confidence that democratic government can work for the public advantage. To rebuild that confidence will require a renewal of democratic politics and an emphasis on policies that simultaneously advance the broad national interest while ensuring security and opportunity for the most vulnerable.

Renewing Democratic Politics

At the heart of the problem is popular contempt for politics, generated by the political system itself. Several factors have been crucial here in exacerbating long-standing tendencies in American politics.

Political campaigns in the United States have often been highly personal and lacking in substance, but never more so than in the age of political marketing. Campaigns have long been expensive and contributors have always had political influence, but the cost has now soared and the preoccupation with fund-raising has become permanent for people in public office. The problem is not simply that campaigns now revolve around the raising of money and manipulation of media images; it is that everyone knows these things, accepts them as facts of political life, and regards the entire process as corrupt. And while the forms of political competition have ceased to command respect, incumbents have gained a vast edge in resources. So all too many elections seem not to matter.

Without a fundamental reform of politics, it seems inconceivable that the public could be attracted to any positive vision of government. Campaign-finance reform is just the beginning, and it will be no beginning at all if it only pumps more money into producing thirty-second commercials. The objective of a new wave of political reforms should be not only to reduce the imperatives that now force politicians to be full-time fund-raisers and part-time public officials. We need to alter the format as well as the financing of campaigns to make them, as much as possible, occasions of debate and deliberation. Whether these objectives ought to be achieved through additional public funding or requirements for holders of broadcast licenses is a special question that ought to be decided on the merits (and not merely out of an interest in keeping down public spending). But regardless of the method, the funds or the allotted broadcast time should go, not to prepared commercials, but to genuine debates, press interviews, and spots five to ten minutes long (perhaps at the end of evening news) where candidates would be obliged to say more than they do in canned advertising.

Public funds ought also to be made available for voter registration; there is no justifiable reason why in a democracy that responsibility ought to depend on the vagaries of private funding. And the measures taken in some states like Minnesota to remove barriers to registration ought to become the basis of a national effort.

These measures would simultaneously increase popular participation, diminish the preoccupation with fund-raising, and increase confidence in the integrity of the candidates and the system. They would also diminish the advantages of incumbency. That very quality, however, impedes their adoption. The only hope, therefore, is to create a larger package of reforms that gives incumbents, including conservatives, some other things they want that also happen to advance the larger cause of political renewal.

One key additional element, it seems to me, is to reform the House of Representatives by extending terms from two years to four and limiting the number of terms to three. (By staggering the seats, half would come open every other year.) Many congressmen of both parties have long wanted four-year terms; under the present system, they never stop running. The purpose of the two-year cycle was originally to make the House more responsive than the Senate to changing public sentiment; in the early years of the Republic, it may have had that effect, as turnover in the House was enormous. But the two-year cycle no longer serves its intended purpose because the advantages and attractions of incumbency have become too great. A four-year term, while giving incumbents enough respite from reelection demands to turn their attention to legislation, would also reduce by half the number of races in any election year and thereby enable challengers to accumulate more resources and gain more attention. Contests would be less frequent but more genuine.

While a limit on the number of congressional terms has chiefly attracted Republican support, Democrats must come to see that it is their long-run interest, too. When the control of the House at some point in the future shifts to the Republicans—as it must someday—the Democrats will find themselves as locked out as the Republicans are today. Indeed, the Republicans would then add to their fund-raising edge all the advantages of incumbency that now redound to Democrats. Moreover, the electorate has become suspicious of what appears to be a permanently entrenched political class. A new system would put control of the House at genuine risk and thereby restore confidence that the House responded to the electorate's will. In addition, the reform package as a whole would free incumbents, as well as challengers, from the fund-raising practices that have cost them their collective reputation for integrity and exposed them to political scandal and even the risk of criminal indictment.

A limit on terms would also have more subtle and broader political effects. After twelve years, many congressmen would be looking to the Senate and gubernatorial chairs, thereby increasing competition throughout the system. (Indeed, this year the Republicans have an edge in key Senate contests because popular Republican congressmen are running for Senate seats, while comparable Democrats in the House have refused—another example of how the Democratic Party loses out because the House has become too comfortable a career.) Moreover, even while they remained in the House, members would necessarily have to think about interests broader than their districts, in the knowledge that they would have to appeal to wider constituencies when their twelve years were up.

I am not suggesting that these measures alone would restore the vitality to American democracy that it is now evidently missing. I mean them only to be illustrations of what ought to be a new era of reform of the political process, comparable in scale to the changes during the Progressive Era that brought us the primary and referendum. But clearly no reform of the process will matter unless there is also a change in the substance of what political leaders offer and the larger message of politics about the civic realm.

The Rehabilitation of Public Remedy

For the last decade, while national politics has largely turned on the uninspiring annual routines of the budget, the public has become increasingly disenchanted that politics can accomplish anything. The deficit is as much a metaphor for these failures as it is an objective element of them. To most people, budgetary numbers are numbingly abstract; what they do understand is that the nation's leaders apparently cannot keep their house in order. And if they cannot pay their bills, why trust them to do much else?

The general sense of futility stems partly from the deadlock between the parties that has now prevailed for eighteen of the past twenty-two years. Neither party is capable of fully imposing its will to break the deadlock (for example, by either cutting spending or raising taxes to resolve the deficit). But while undercutting the power of the parties, the deadlock promotes a diffusion of guilt. The public attributes the persistent failures to neither party and neither the executive nor legislative branch, but to government itself; and individual politicians are only too pleased to run against the system, as if they were not part of it.

In addition, as Benjamin Ginsberg and Martin Shefter have emphasized in a recent book, *Politics by Other Means*, the political stalemate at the national level has encouraged politicians to use non-electoral means in the struggle against one another. Congressional hearings aimed at members of the executive branch, ethics investigations aimed at members of Congress, probing of public figures' personal lives, criminal investigations and "stings" aimed at legislative figures—all of these have proliferated in recent years, adding to the general distrust of politics. If the rate of investigations and indictments were a true index of moral character, it would mean politicians are more dishonest than ever before. But more likely, the forms of political competition have changed in response to electoral deadlock, indirectly contributing to the sense that the politicians and system itself have no integrity.

Moreover, as Steven Kelman emphasizes (*TAP*, Summer 1990), the persistent concern with scandal and scandal-avoidance has intensified the bureaucratic maladies of public administration. Scandal begets rules and procedures, tying public managers in knots. When advocates of privatization unfavorably compare public agencies with private firms, they are often right that the public agencies are less efficient. Liberals who care about public services ought to be first to recognize these shortcomings. But instead of privatizing the services, we should think first of repairing them. We need to undo many of the excessively rigid rules that now prevent public agencies from innovating and offering employees incentives for better performance. If public agencies are to work, their managers must have more autonomy, including the ability to reward effective employees and fire ineffective ones.

On the other hand, while liberals ought to embrace the sharp criticism of public *services* and turn it to the purposes of reform, they ought to resist the more embracing criticism of public *programs*, particularly the charges that the programs of the Great Society show the futility of governmental effort. This is not the place to mount a full defense of the record of positive government, going back to what in the nineteenth century used to be called "internal improvements." However, to those who say that in War on Poverty in the 1960s and 1970s we tested public programs and they failed, at least a brief answer ought to be made.

First, where we made the greatest effort, we did reduce poverty. Increased social expenditures in the United States have primarily gone to the aged in the form of higher Social Security benefits, including Medicare. There is simply no question about the difference that this additional spending has made. As of the mid-1960s, poverty among the elderly was higher than in the population as a whole; now it is significantly lower. Moreover, measured rates of suicide, mental illness, and other indicators of distress all show a marked improvement in the well-being of the aged, far in excess of general trends in American society. Indeed, adolescents experienced worsening conditions over the same period.

Of course, when conservatives say social programs have failed, they have in mind, not the aged, but blacks. Yet for blacks, too, positive government action has made a vast difference. Civil rights law has dramatically changed America for the better. So, too, have many of the antipoverty efforts, particularly those that provided health care and education for the young. No one pretends that these measures were sufficient; their opponents—and the budgetary demands of the Vietnam War—saw to that. Today many inner-city neighborhoods are worse places to live today than they were twenty years ago. One reason is that millions of upwardly mobile blacks have moved to other neighborhoods, while new rural Southern immigrants have moved in. In the meantime, industry has moved out, and the remaining deindustrialized, partly abandoned communities have been ravaged by crack and crime. Given the economic and demographic forces at work, perhaps no set of policies could have entirely prevented the formation of a residual underclass. Nonetheless, the underclass now stands as a rebuke to all who tried to abolish poverty—and serves as a made-to-order rationalization for those who didn't.

If some social programs failed—and they did—so do many new business ventures. Neither legislators nor investors can entirely avoid mistakes, nor ought they try to. If they can learn from mistakes, the more quickly they make them the better. Some critics of the public sector say that while markets are self-correcting and eliminate inefficient firms, government fails to end ineffective programs. But a democratic government also has self-corrective mechanisms: an investigative press, social science evaluations, internal studies by agencies like the Office of Management and Budget and the General Accounting Office, congressional hearings, and other checks on performance.

These self-correcting forces have, in fact, been at work. And one thing we have learned—and should long ago have acted on—is that the most successful policies, with the greatest payback for the society, are those aimed at children and youth. That knowledge now ought to be the basis for an era of social reform that emphasizes investment in the young as part of a new social contract.

A New Deal for the Young

From separate directions, several forces are now converging to make children and young families a priority of national policy. The statistics are now all too familiar: one of every five children—one of every four children under age six, almost one of every two black children—grows up in poverty today. Even business increasingly recognizes the implications. One-third of new workers between now and the next century will come from minority groups where poverty is concentrated. Moreover, as the age structure shifts, a growing retired population will depend on relatively fewer working adults, many now struggling toward adulthood in poor families. If poor children grow up to become poor workers, the whole economy suffers. That realization is slowly producing a shift in assumptions. Instead of viewing the children of the poor as a liability and a threat, at least some Americans are coming to view them as a scarce resource that needs care, protection, and investment.

Second, the mass entry into the labor force of middle-class women, including mothers of young children, has drastically altered the politics of child care and child policy. Of all the major Western countries, the United States provides the least support to families raising small children. We do not have the family allowances, the income support and guaranteed job leave during pregnancy and immediately after childbirth, public financing of day care, or child health services that have long been common in Western Europe. The failure to provide those supports is a principal reason why the United States, of eight leading Western countries, has the highest rate of child poverty. (We are similarly distinguished in the field of infant mortality). Now middle-class families are facing the same realities that poor families have long faced—the struggle to cope with two jobs and raising children without adequate social support. In short, changing patterns of work and family life are universalizing the problems of the poor and extending the natural political base for reform.

Third, widespread reports of poor school performance have prompted alarm about our ability to stay internationally competitive. Education is now everyone's cause, and the connection between teaching deficits and trade deficits seems to be taken as virtually self-evident. Early childhood interventions seem especially promising. As a recent report from the Committee on Economic Development argues, preschool education programs can readily be justified on strict cost-benefit criteria.

These developments are helping to put child policy on the political agenda in a way not seen in the United States since the turn of the century. The social historian Michael Katz notes that in the 1890s "children became the symbol of a resurgent reform spirit, the magnet that pulled together a diverse collection of causes and their champions into a new, loose, informal—but effective coalition." A century later, the same process may be about to happen.

A child policy agenda would have several key elements.* To reduce child poverty, we need to revise federal tax policies to substitute a refundable child tax credit for the current tax exemptions and to increase the existing Earned Income Tax Credit and step up its value per child. To reduce poverty specifically among single-parent families, we need further development of guaranteed minimum support payments (advanced by a public agency authorized to collect from the absent parent). Some states have legislated job protections for parental leave; such leaves ought to be covered as paid disability. Comprehensive child health services ought to be priority; at a minimum, we ought to ensure that all children receive preventive care, including the full complement of vaccinations, which some 40 percent are currently not receiving.

A "New Deal for the Young" should be concerned not only with children but with young adults. Much evidence now shows a significant deterioration in the economic position of young workers, ages 18 to 30. A 1988 Congressional Budget Office study finds that between 1970 and 1986 adjusted family income rose 20 percent overall but fell 10 to 20 percent for families headed by people under age 25 and families without any full-time, full-year worker. But while the earnings of the young appear to have declined over the last two decades, there have been staggering increases in the costs of homeownership and higher education.

A New Deal for young adults has to be fundamentally different from the original New Deal. It cannot rely exclusively on income transfers. Unlike the elderly, the young need endowments of education and training, health, and self-discipline that will benefit them over their lifetimes. Those endowments cannot simply be redistributed; they must be created, in part by the young themselves through their own efforts. That does not mean we simply ought to abandon them to what George Gilder celebrates as "the spur of poverty." Public initiative can help the young by amplifying the rewards of effort.

Instead of simply providing benefits and entitlements, we ought to think carefully about structuring programs around the idea of *reciprocity*. Reciprocity is a theme in recent welfare reform and recent proposals for national service that ask beneficiaries to work. Superficially, the idea of reciprocity may seem to some unacceptably conservative, but it is the essence of a social contract. Programs structured around reciprocity not only have better incentives and teaching effects than pure entitlements; they are much more likely to gain stronger public support. Social Secu-

---

* Here I follow the work of Sheila Kamerman. In her article in this issue [Summer 1990], Theda Skocpol proposes much the same approach under the rubric of family security.

rity enjoys a distinctive legitimacy, not only because it is universal, but because Americans believe they earn their benefits. Even though Social Security returns to beneficiaries larger benefits than their payroll contributions strictly justify, the program rests on a simple "deal." We pay during our working years and in return receive income during retirement.

A New Deal for the Young should offer to provide more support for education and training, links to jobs, and aid to home ownership in return for work, improved school performance, or national service. The proposal for linking Social Security to aid for education and training, presented by Barry Bluestone and his colleagues in this issue, exemplifies the principal of reciprocity in two ways—first, because it calls upon the recipients to repay the awards out of later earnings; and second, because it directly links the interests of the aged and the young and emphasizes the norm of reciprocity between the generations.

Through Social Security, Americans pay for other people's retirement, and through public education, we pay for other people's children. That common interest extends to the productivity of working-age Americans. In an economic sense, other people's grown children are our own: when we retire, we depend on the income they generate. And how much they generate in the future depends on the endowments—the capital—invested in them by our society today. As Jonathan Rauch wrote not long ago in *The Atlantic*, "If boys and girls grew up to become industrial machinery instead of men and women, it would be easy to see that everybody had a stake in other people's children." To explain that stake —and to persuade Americans to act on it—is a critical task in the coming decade.

A Public Framework for Health Insurance

The task in health care is also to reconcile the nation's broader interests with those of the most vulnerable, but the answer is not to find more resources for a system that already consumes them in excess. Health care represents a major policy failure, not simply because millions of Americans lack coverage, but also because uncontrolled costs have become a growing burden on the productive sectors of the economy. The very magnitude of the problem, however, presents an historic opportunity for a liberal leadership prepared to offer the American public and American business a real alternative.

Recent public opinion surveys show great public dissatisfaction with the health care system. A Harris survey released in early 1989 asked respondents in the United States, Great Britain, and Canada identically worded questions regarding their health care. The results show dramatic differences. Americans are the most dissatisfied and Canadians the most content. For example, only 10 percent of Americans say their system works "pretty well," while 89 percent say fundamental change is needed. On the other hand, 56 percent of the Canadians say their system works pretty well. The proportion saying they are personally very satisfied with the care that they and their families receive is only 35 percent in the United States, but 67 percent among Canadians. After being given brief, neutral descriptions of the health care systems, 91 percent of Canadians say they prefer their country's health care to that of the United States. On other hand, 61 percent of Americans say they would rather have the Canadian system.

Since the United States spends much more money per person than Canada on health care, we might at least have bought more public approval. But, of course, the inability to control costs and public discontent are directly related. Many employers have responded to higher insurance premiums by reducing health coverage, adding requirements of higher deductibles and copayments and restrictions on choice of provider. The result is deep employee dissatisfaction (as last year's bitter telephone and coal strikes illustrate). In the 1940s and 1950s, the American people saw employer-provided health insurance plans being steadily expanded; now they see their benefits eroding from year to year. Employers don't like the situation much, either. Health care costs hurt their bottom line; switching from one insurance plan to another seems to offer no remedy. New accounting rules for retiree health benefits threaten to wipe out profits for many large corporations. Many executives would be perfectly delighted if the government now stepped in.

One barrier to fundamental change is the entrenched perception of national health insurance as an additional expenditure program. We need instead to think about national health insurance as a system of financial control. Currently, we lack the tools to contain health costs. When the federal government clamps down on Medicare's hospital costs, two things happen: the hospitals shift costs to private payers, and technology migrates to physicians' offices. Private sector efforts also produce more cost displacement than cost control. The American art of health care management is chiefly the art of extracting the maximum revenue from a fragmented assortment of payers. In the struggle over health care money, government agencies, employers, and insurers stand on one side attempting to impose regulatory and competitive measures to subdue rising costs. On the other side stand health care managers and physicians using their considerable skills and ingenuity to master the arcane mysteries of revenue maximization. Year after year, the game goes to the maximizers, but in the process it has created spectacular growth in administrative and marketing expenses, the single most rapidly growing category of health costs in the 1980s.

Countries that have succeeded in controlling health care costs have an institutional framework that imposes a *global budget*—so much money for the system each year, and no more. To achieve control of costs and provide coverage to all citizens, they do not need to nationalize hospitals or make doctors public employees. In both Canada and West Germany, for example, the doctors remain in private, fee-for-service practice and the hospitals continue under diverse types of ownership. The Canadian insurance system happens to be public (the plans are operated by the provinces within a framework of rules set by the national government), whereas the West German "sickness funds" are nongovernmental institutions. In both countries, the governments set limits on capital spending and hospital budgets. In Canada, the public insurance funds control fees and prohibit extra billing by doctors. In West Germany, annual negotiations between sickness funds and insurance doctors establish a total pool for physician payments; physicians then bill so many points for each service, and the monetary value of the points depends on the total points billed divided by size of the pool. If doctors as a whole bill more points, they do not create a financial crisis for the system: the points are just worth less. (Private independent practice associations in the U.S. use the same method for controlling costs.) Under these arrangements, West German and Canadian doctors do very well. So would American physicians under a globally budgeted health plan. But they and other providers would not be able to charge what the market will bear and break the Treasury.

Contrary to American intuitions, global budgets actually permit less government regulation. For once governments are able to ensure that expenditures remain under a ceiling, they are less driven to intervene in specific decisions by health care professionals and institutions. In the United States, on the other hand, the inability of both government and private health plans to control costs has led both of them to impose more regulations on providers. We have ended up, amazingly enough, with less equity, less efficiency, and less autonomy for private decision makers.

The idea of a global budget for health care, adjusted in annual negotiations, seems strange only because Americans have become used to an insurance system with no apparent limits. However, most institutions in our society have to live with budgets and limited resources. Sooner or later, so must health care institutions. When confronted with the alternative of a global budget, defenders of the current system characteristically raise alarming visions of the British National Health Service refusing to provide kidney dialysis to patients over age 65. The British, however, spend much less on health care than any other major Western nation (only 6 percent of GNP, and the British GNP per capita is much lower than ours). No one is proposing that we cut spending down to British levels. Canadian health care has some limitations, but overall it is very good, and the West Germans, who put 9 percent of GNP into health care, have a system that may well be better than ours. We also do not have to look abroad to find examples of lower rates of health care spending. Some communities in the United States, such as Seattle, Washington, and Rochester, New York, also have lower rates. The key to low costs is a conservative practice style—that is, a peer culture among physicians that encourages careful use of costly technology. Our third-party payment system has encouraged physicians to practice as if our resources were unlimited; a global budget encourages a healthy caution. Moreover, with their budgets fixed, hospital managers can apply their talents to more useful arts than milking the reimbursement system.

Historically, the path of least resistance in health policy, as in so many other areas, has been to accommodate the demands of private providers and to proceed incrementally, slowly adding new benefits and new populations. Mandatory employer-provided health insurance and Medicaid expansion are the path of least resistance today. But if we simply add to the existing system, we are certain to have steadily higher costs that ultimately erode the value of the programs, until conservatives hold them up as illustrating the hopeless cost of liberal government. Self-limiting reforms ultimately discredit our vision; we need to pursue self-reinforcing reforms that become a base for further development.

Our alternatives are two. First, we can try to seize the political opportunity created by public and employer discontent to press for a new framework of universal health insurance. That framework, like the Canadian and the West German systems, must itself be a system of cost containment. Or, if we must be content with an incremental change, we must try to make it a model for a comprehensive alternative. Universal health insurance for the young, or "kiddie-care," based on prepayment, comes closest to serving that purpose. A cost-effective program for children's health would have an exceptionally strong moral foundation and provide an especially positive model for future reform.

Getting to the Core

To recover a national majority, liberals do not need to get to the center but to get to the core—that is, core interests that Americans broadly share.

Conservatives have succeeded in persuading many people that our economic progress requires sacrificing social progress. But it is a mistake to think we can thrive economically without investing in people, particularly the young families of the poor whose children will be critical to our economy in the new century. Conservatives have promoted the illusion that we can be strong as a nation while constricting our Treasury, demoralizing our public institutions, restricting public investment, and letting the markets lead.

From Alexander Hamilton to Winston Churchill, many conservatives have known better. They have known that a nation is only as strong as its social fabric; that it cannot depend entirely on the market for investments necessary to the national interest; and that it must nurture a strong civic tradition as well as freedom for individual initiative. Liberals stand in a position today, not only to claim the legacy of the New Deal tradition that some are ready to abandon, but to inherit from conservatives the entire tradition of social stewardship and civic commitment. If conservatives want to cede their claim to that tradition, liberals should accept the opportunity to become the one party unambiguously committed to public remedy and civic obligation.

[25]

LAURENCE E. LYNN, JR.

Government Lite

Making government work better is newly fashionable. Bashing bureaucracy has been popular since Richard Nixon's presidency and has grown in popularity with voters frustrated by deficits, an uncertain economy, and "politics as usual"—and egged on by opportunistic politicians. The idea was given a positive spin in David Osborne and Ted Gaebler's *Reinventing Government.* Their upbeat principles put administrative reform on the political agenda and even in airport book shops. The reform bibliography has since lengthened, capped by *From Red Tape to Results: Creating a Government That Works Better and Costs Less,* Vice President Al Gore's report on the administration's "National Performance Review" of federal administration.

Liberals, of course, have a major stake in effective government, for government is the necessary instrument of liberal purposes. When activist government fails, conservatives can smugly say, We told you so. Achieving a humane and just state requires effective public agencies, capable leaders, and sufficient executive power to define and execute a compelling vision of economic opportunity and social justice. When welfare departments, public transit systems, and public schools fail to perform, their failures not only discredit sensible policies but also undermine faith in government and feed the urge to shrink and privatize it.

Yet liberals have been less than enthusiastic about administrative reform. Perhaps this is because recent reform agendas—the postwar Hoover commissions, Lyndon Johnson's planning-programming-budgeting system (PPBS), Nixon's management by objectives (MBO), Jimmy Carter's zero-base budgeting (ZBB), and the total quality management (TQM) movement—seem ephemeral to the ongoing challenge of creating liberal policies. Perhaps it is because government reform is so difficult

WORK DISCUSSED IN THIS ESSAY:

National Performance Review, *From Red Tape to Results: Creating a Government That Works Better and Costs Less* (The Gore Report), 1993.

and politically unrewarding. Perhaps it is out of deference to public employee unions or out of fear of executive imperialism. For too many liberals, policies are what matter, not bureaucracies.

This stance is, of course, self-defeating. As Steven Kelman has argued in these pages ("The Renewal of the Public Sector," Summer 1990), "No serious advocate of a positive role for government can any longer ignore the challenge of the renewal of the public sector." But is reinventing government the right bandwagon to jump on? Is the Gore report a plausible blueprint?

Whose Ox Is Gored?

"As our title makes clear," says Gore in his preface, "the National Performance Review is about moving from red tape to results to create a government that works better and costs less." The problems with government as we know it are several, says Gore. One is "enormous, unseen waste." A second is the ineffectiveness of the programs churned out by the legislative process "one after another, year after year," with no thought given to their design, resulting in a "performance deficit" that has alienated the public.

These are only surface manifestations of a deeper problem: reliance on "large, top-down, centralized bureaucracies to do the public's business," most of them "monopolies, with few incentives to innovate or improve." For the most part, bureaucratic accountability is about punishing mistakes. As a result, these bureaucracies have become rule-bound, with failures of control begetting more controls, producing "a culture of fear and resignation."

The solution to this deeper problem is "entrepreneurial government" based on four "bedrock principles": cutting red tape, putting customers first, empowering employees to get results, and cutting back to basics—producing better government for less. These principles are indivisible: "To create organizations that deliver value to American taxpayers, we must embrace all four." But "we need not jettison the traditional values that underlie democratic governance—values such as equal opportunity, justice, diversity, and democracy. We hold these values dear. We need to transform bureaucracies precisely *because* they have failed to nurture these values." The vice president claims that the recommendations will save $108 billion over five years. "We also expect that the reinventions we propose will allow us to reduce the size of the civilian, non-postal work force by 12 percent over the next five years [and] bring the federal work force below two million employees for the first time since 1967."

The bulk of the Gore report comprises chapters elaborating each of the four principles. First, the report offers six steps "to strip away the red tape": streamline the budget process, decentralize personnel policy, streamline procurement, reorient the inspectors general toward a focus on performance, eliminate regulations, and deregulate state and local governments. Each step is spelled out as a program of changes that range from the revolutionary (biennial budgets and appropriations) to the esoteric (end the use of full-time-equivalent personnel ceilings to control costs). Most are general and hortatory, a pattern reflected in subsequent chapters: "Dramatically simplify the current [personnel] classification system."

The aim of putting customers first, the second principle, is to "imbue the federal government—from top to bottom—with a driving sense of accountability." The idea is to end government monopolies by "transplanting some aspects of the business world into the public arena." With a bow to the quality revolution sweeping American businesses, four specific steps are proposed: giving customers a voice through regular solicitation of their views, making service organizations compete in service delivery, creating market dynamics in areas where government monopolies do serve the public interest (like air traffic control), and using market mechanisms instead of new programs to solve problems (as in pollution reduction and public housing).

Empowering employees to get results, the third principle, requires a "culture of public entrepreneurship." The idea, again obeying "the quality imperative," is "to do everything smarter, better, faster, cheaper." To accomplish the necessary transformation of employee motivations, decision making will be decentralized, replacing process compliance with accountability for clearly understood, feasible outcomes; employees will be trained in cutting-edge technologies; the quality of work life will be improved by initiating family-friendly policies and abolishing the time clock; the adversarial relationship between unions and management will be ended; and, to advance these steps, the government's top managers will assume responsibility for their implementation.

The final principle, cutting back to basics, obviously won't occur by targeting programs for extinction, Gore argues; everybody's tried that. Instead, cultural changes will create incentives to streamline programs and reduce costs. This re-engineering of government would require seeking an item veto, closing or consolidating field and regional offices, selling or eliminating programs ranging from the Alaska Power Administration to the President's Intelligence Oversight Board, raising user fees and collecting debts, authorizing the creation of innovation funds, and expanding the use of new technologies.

A concluding chapter candidly warns of the discomfort such a transformation will engender and outlines steps already under way: reinvention teams and labs in every department, performance agreements with cabinet officers, and establishment of the President's Management Council. For inspiration, the report quotes Daniel Burnham's exhortation to "make no little plans."

Reactions, Over- and Under-

Published with extraordinary fanfare, the Gore report was bound to be controversial. It is too easily dismissed as just another naive assault on the bureaucratic fortress and too easily embraced as an administration commitment to cutting the size and cost of government. Both responses trivialize the report's significance.

Pregnable Bureaucracy. The notion that ours is a top-down, unaccountable bureaucracy is a myth. Because of the inherent tensions between the branches of government, a tension designed into our Constitution, Americans were never fated to have the kinds of impenetrable and ultra-professional bureaucracies like those in Europe and Japan. Our democratic institutions lead an examined life. The need to make government work better is a leitmotif of American politics, and throughout our history the meaning of "reform" has oscillated between depoliticized professionalism and greater democratization.

The first successful reform movement was led by Jacksonians, who, contesting the elitism of the Federalists, installed the spoils system and the long ballot to bring government closer to the people. After rampant abuse of patronage by political machines, counter-reform in the 1880s instituted the civil service. Reforming spoils politics and strengthening administrative capacity were salient issues with business, professional, and middle-class urban voters who were to coalesce into the Progressive movement. With intellectual support from political scientist Woodrow Wilson, Progressives worked to separate politics from administration by creating a corps of neutral, competent civil servants efficiently organized into bureaus. The "bureaucratic paradigm," as Michael Barzelay calls it in *Breaking Through Bureaucracy*, was a hierarchical, specialized, professional, and honest public administration.

It is important to note, however, that the bureaucratic paradigm included accountability for performance. For government to be efficient, said Woodrow Wilson in *The Study of Administration*, "it must discover the simplest arrangements by which responsibility can be unmistakably fixed upon officials." The Taft Commission of 1912 advocated performance budgeting, as did the first postwar Hoover Commission in 1949.

But from the Progressive era through Nixon's New Federalism, the growth of a permanent government of proliferating bureaus staffed by tenured civil servants has been countered by moves to strengthen political control over administration through executive budgets, strong central offices staffed by patronage, authority to reorganize, and agency administration by political appointees subject to legislative confirmation.

Seen against this history, the Gore proposals are another in the succession of moves to strengthen executive command of bureaucracy. Of course, executive power has to be checked by the courts and by legislatures, which have sought to maintain the balance of political power by increasing their advisory role and their oversight and analytic capacities. The most acute analyses of policy implementation are done by agents of the Congress: the General Accounting Office and the Congressional Budget Office (CBO). As a result, America's bureaucracy, far from being an impenetrable monolith, is the most accountable in the world, and Gore's national performance review should be welcomed as another step toward constructive change rather than another quixotic tilt.

Tastes Great? Less Filling! The administration put a bullet through its own foot by equating government reinvention with cost savings. For one thing, the costs of government are notoriously difficult to project and even more difficult to control. Picking apart inflated savings estimates is easy sport for Washington's veteran budget experts in the CBO and elsewhere, and that should warn the administration off a tendency to equate success with deficit reduction. For another, government that works better in producing customer satisfaction may cost more, not less. For example, even centrist welfare reformers like Richard Nathan call for a doubling of appropriations for the JOBS program. Welfare reform, long-term health care, day care, retraining, public investment, and the rest of even the New Democrat litany will cost more, not less. Programs often do not work well, and their customers often are unhappy with them, because they are understaffed and poorly supervised. Lawsuits against welfare and mental health agencies in many states generally require more, not fewer, resources. Even if bureaucrats can be replaced by technology, government that works better is not necessarily cheaper.

Hare or Tortoise? Some critics have faulted the report as too sweeping in its goals and too impatient in its timing. Government cannot be reinvented because it was never invented, argue John J. DiIulio, Jr., Gerald Garvey, and Donald F. Kettl in *Improving Government: An Owner's Manual*. Bureaucracy evolved bit by bit, and its reform must be similarly evolutionary, experimental, and incremental. They are correct that real change will be evolutionary, but how does a process of evolutionary change toward a specific goal get started and stay focused? Here, the administration's strategy, while risky, makes sense: attract maximum attention to the cause of reform with a bold vision and clear evidence of intent to follow through. The resulting momentum is essential if directed, incremental change is to be possible at all. Indeed, the current focus on customers and quality service is already having good results, especially in federal agencies and in states and localities where the need for good management is now taken seriously. The fanfare surrounding the Gore report has emboldened change agents everywhere, an important achievement.

What Gore Reinvents

Three issues of far greater import are raised by the Gore proposals, however. They are, first, the Gore report's concept of governance, which emphasizes entrepreneurialism; second, the logic underlying its specific proposals, which emphasizes accountability through performance measurement; and, finally, its neutrality toward the substantive purposes of public programs, which tends toward an emphasis on the technical aspects of management.

Entrepreneurial or Civic? The proponents of reinvention have stressed the obsolescence of the long-reigning Wilsonian paradigm of bureaucratic professionalization. But the apparent inertia of our bureaucracy obscures an original and enduring tension between two opposing images of governance. The first image, civic or Jeffersonian, is of the town meeting in which all citizens have influence according to their willingness to participate. This image fosters inclusiveness, deliberation, and responsiveness through the dispersal of authority, multi-directional accountability, an empowered public, and the primacy of the democratic process. The second, an entrepreneurial image that evokes the centralist and businesslike approach of Hamilton, is that of an enterprise increasing its earnings and market share through successful product development, technological advances, and a productive and well-deployed work force. This image fosters toughmindedness, efficient use of scarce resources, a commitment to shareholders, a necessary concentration of executive authority, and the primacy of results.

Recent literature on administrative reform reflects this tension between the civic and entrepreneurial ideals. For example, among the civic idealists, Charles Lindblom, in *Inquiry and Change*, argues for a self-directing society featuring virtually continuous interchange between citizens and functionaries and a broad and rigorous competition of ideas until sufficient clarity and convergence are reached within the electorate to permit political authorities to act. In a similar spirit, Robert Reich, now the secretary of labor, advises managers to enter into a deliberative relationship with the public and its intermediaries. "You are not a policy entrepreneur," he writes in *Public Management in a Democratic Society*. "But neither are you a neutral and passive public servant.... You are instead a participant in an ongoing public deliberation about how problems are to be defined and understood, what the range of possible solutions might be, and who should have the responsibility for solving them." In *The Spirit of Community*, Amitai Etzioni advocates the mobilization of "under-represented majorities" to create a politics of change after the model of the Progressive movement "to shore up our values, responsibilities, institutions, and communities" and, in behalf of a genuine public interest, decimate the special interests that dominate political life.

The opposing image is executive-led government that is entrepreneurial in the style of what the Kennedy School's Alan Altshuler, in his preface to *Breaking through Bureaucracy*, calls the new business managerial vision. This image is reflected in the recent reinventing government literature. The movement's awe of business practice is carefully concealed—Osborne and Gaebler, Barzelay, and others take great pains to cite examples drawn from recent government experience and say that government isn't a business but the spirit, as the Gore report acknowledges, is the Hamiltonian one of looking to successful executives.

Thus though Osborne and Gaebler are rightly credited with giving focus to the contemporary movement for government reform, the progenitors of the movement are Tom Peters and Robert Waterman. Their *In Search of Excellence* first proclaimed the virtue of "fawning on customers" and argued for replacing the reigning rational model of hierarchy and control with an intuitive view of managerial leadership. These values are most clearly reflected in Barzelay's *Breaking Through Bureaucracy*. He, like Peters and Waterman, argues for replacing the old Wilsonian paradigm with a new, post-bureaucratic paradigm. His government agencies are "customer-driven service organizations" that empower ordinary employees to produce tangible results for citizens-as-consumers of public goods and services. Value is the imperative.

Widely credited to Osborne's inspiration, the Gore report is briskly entrepreneurial. In a curiously worded passage, the Gore report actually seems skeptical about community power. "By 'customer,' we do not mean 'citizen.' A citizen can participate in democratic decision-making, a customer receives benefits from a specific service.... In a democracy, citizens and customers both matter. But when they vote, citizens seldom have much chance to influence the behavior of public institutions.... Citizens own their government, but private businesses they do not own work much harder to cater to their needs." So, in Gore's conception, not only must government redefine citizens as customers, but citizens must redefine *themselves* as customers demanding a government "worth what [they] pay for it."

By seeking to mimic the most entrepreneurial business organizations and recast citizens as customers of the great governmental K-mart, however, the Gore blueprint glosses over the challenge that entrepreneurialism poses to the principle that government's unique role is to promote the common good and protect citizens from the arbitrary and capricious exercise of power and the abuse of fiduciary trust. There is a reason why ours is a government of laws and not of autonomous, bottom-line entrepreneurs: unmonitored power is often abused and entrepreneurial zeal is often misdirected, and citizens are the losers.

Performance Anxiety. The entrepreneurial advocates are right, however, in saying that accountability to citizens does not automatically require layers of hierarchy and truckloads of rules. *In Mandate for Change,* David Osborne's chapter argues that performance measurement is the essential ingredient in reinventing government: if you "define agencies' missions and goals, measure how well they achieve those goals, and develop budget and pay systems that reward organizations for success," public employees will become obsessive about reliable, efficient performance because they have *no choice.* Indeed, the key idea in the report seems to be that entrepreneurial government is made accountable to democratic values by performance measurement.

To obtain appropriate goals and measures, we cannot rely on the same political processes that cause the problem. Thus in an ostensibly anti-Wilsonian program we discover, ironically, the Wilsonian impulse to professionalize and depoliticize. Gore assigns to the Office of Management and Budget the role of setting up the new system. Osborne would go much further. In *Mandate for Change,* he proposed a National Information Agency to "improve the federal government's capacity to collect, analyze, and disseminate data"; a Performance Review Office insulated from political pressure to help agencies develop performance measures; a Program Design Office within OMB to "hire experts, gather and sift the relevant literature, and begin to articulate design principles that underlie success"; and a Sunset Commission to "review all programs and regulations to determine whether they should be reauthorized."

The explanation for this irony lies in different meanings of performance in the Wilsonian-bureaucratic paradigm and in the Gore approach. In the former, performance means activity—the work to be done or the service rendered—and performance measures are chosen to gauge government productivity—the measurable output achieved per unit of budgetary input. In the reinventing government lexicon, performance means results, defined in the Gore report as "measures of how government programs and policies affect their customers."

If there is fatal flaw in the performance logic, it is in the notion that performance measures can somehow short-circuit the political process and be made precise and unambiguous. To see the weakness of this logic, it will prove helpful to turn to the most politically unlikely of fields, mathematics.

Mathematicians have a notion called algorithmic complexity, the shortest set of instructions that will generate a given sequence of observed outcomes. A string of random numbers is extremely complex because its generation requires instructions as long and complex as the sequence itself. Far simpler are the laws of physics, highly compressed mathematical formulas from which vast numbers of accurate predictions concerning the natural universe can be generated. Thus complexity is equivalent to a lack of order and predictability. The goal of science is algorithmic compressibility, simpler ways to represent and predict natural phenomena.

The problem with government, in these terms, is that its outcomes are too disorderly, even random, because the instructions that generate them—the red tape—are too complex: hundreds of thousands of pages of statutes, regulations, guidelines, court rulings, job descriptions, bulletins, and so on. As Clinton and Gore showed in releasing the Gore report, it takes forklifts to hoist them. The goal of systematizers from Taft to Reagan and now Clinton and Gore has been to compress the governmental algorithm into simple executive instructions—perform or else—that will create unambiguous, efficient order and, it is presumed, greater satisfaction all around.

But neither citizens nor politicians behave like atomic particles. We cannot combine them according to logical formulas and produce predictable reactions. One need consider only the proliferation of subcommittees, interest groups, lobbyists, and special government districts to understand why there is disorder and unpredictability in government. Citizens—as employees, members of interest groups, taxpayers, investors, parents, residents of cities and neighborhoods—organize and press for special attention. And the system responds, if not voluntarily, then after being taken to court. Thus chain reactions of political activity create new molecules of political interest that add to governmental complexity and to performance ambiguity.

Even more than before, the goals of most public policies are complicated and ambiguous, the means for achieving them uncertain, the conflicts of interest intense. Choosing measures of performance and collecting relevant data sounds easy until you confront the complexities associated with virtually every area of government activity. Indeed, budget expert Allen Schick observes in the *Washington Monthly* (September 1993), "They've got so much data on performance already that they don't know what to do with it." Even a sympathetic General Accounting Office concluded recently that "performance measures have not attained sufficient credibility to influence resource allocation decisions."

If not ignored, performance measures are diluted until every zealous interest is mollified and simple order is destroyed. Why isn't a national student achievement test already turning schools into engines of high performance? Consider the Clinton administration's union-supported counterproposal to measure school delivery capacity instead of academic achievement. (You can't hold a teacher responsible for student achievement if the teacher lacks resources and autonomy and has overcrowded classrooms.) From legislators, we will begin to hear, "I don't care what the experts say; who knows better if a program is needed and how well it is performing than the citizens in my district?"

Finally, there is little genuine political pressure to allow bureaucrats to be more entrepreneurial and experimental with public funds. Instead, there is a great deal of pressure on them to cover their posteriors. Americans want their taxes to be low and used only for collective goods they value; they want the services they receive to be on time and inexpensive; they want to be heard when they are dissatisfied; they want administrators to be honest, knowledgeable, fair, and competent. Beyond these, they want to be left alone. It is unlikely that citizens with these attitudes will agree with Gore that "we must let our managers and workers fail ... we must learn to let go."

What Is Being Managed? The final significant issue raised by the Gore report is the utility of assuming neutrality toward policy. "The National Performance Review focused primarily on *how* government should work, not *what* it should do." As an exercise, this is not unreasonable. It permits identification of generic management problems and generic tools to solve them. The danger lies in overemphasizing the technocratic aspects of public management, thereby disassociating the tasks of political and administrative leadership from the technical aspects of management, a mistake I called in an earlier book (*Managing the Public's Business*) "management without managers."

Nonetheless, effective public management is ultimately measured by the success of public policies. Public policy implementation is not, in fact or even metaphorically, a business; putting customers first is not the same as putting the needs of citizens first. Fairness, just treatment, opportunity, security of person and property, participation in social deliberations, rule of law: these are the generic goals of government. They cannot be achieved solely through markets nor measured by highly compressed algorithms.

Liberal administrative reform, then, should focus on ensuring that government can deliver on the promise of economic opportunity and social justice in meeting the goals of liberal legislation. Programs that liberals endorse must perform well, whether they serve disadvantaged individuals, families, and communities—like welfare departments and public transit agencies—ensure environmental survival and prudence in national security, or protect individuals from predatory business practices and promote their legitimate rights. For the 384 recommendations in the Gore report, the right question is: will they advance liberal policy goals?

A great many of them will. Recommendations such as "allow agencies to create innovation capital funds," "clarify the goals and objectives of federal programs," and "develop an agreed-upon approach for dealing with management failures, crises, and chronic program difficulties" will simplify and refocus program activity, free up resources for better uses, and promote energetic and creative behavior by public officials. But effective public managers will recognize that the reinvention system in the form of 384 recommendations is not the solution any more than PPBS, MBO, ZBB, or TQM are the solution.

Consider the Gore report's recommendations to "eliminate at least 50 percent of all congressionally mandated reports" and "to reduce by at least 50 percent the number of internal regulations, and the number of pages of regulations, within 3 years." By themselves, they make no policy sense. They could just as easily have been endorsed by Nixon, Reagan, or Bush, and they could actually hinder liberal purposes by reducing the administration's ability to establish and enforce policy goals. So they must be measured against their impact on specific policy objectives. For example, will reducing paperwork cut Medicare and Medicaid costs without restricting access to care?

At the same time, promoting good management in large public agencies may require an occasional break with traditionally liberal power bases—public employee unions, teachers, and so on—in order to achieve efficient, mission-oriented programs. Still, it is better that system improvements be designed by people committed to liberal principles than by those for whom arbitrary results, such as fewer pages of regulations, are ends in themselves.

Finally, liberal administration is necessarily entrepreneurial in that it requires sufficient concentration of executive power to offset the particularism and favoritism of local, highly fragmented interests. As Paul Peterson argued in *City Limits*, local government is, because of competition for revenue-generating industry, biased against distributive justice. An important liberal responsibility might well be to insist on restoring Hamilton's vision (in *Federalist 70*) of energy in the political executive as "a leading character in the definition of good government." The Gore report already has been catalytic, and public administration is enlivened by a palpable new energy. Properly mobilized on behalf of good policies, the movement to reinvent government will enter the history of administrative reform as a useful step forward.

[26]

Jonathan S. Cohn

Damaged Goods: Before Reinventing Government, Clinton Needs to Repair It

The debris of Reaganism is scattered across Bill Clinton's domestic agenda: Environmentalism may be slow to take hold at the Interior Department because friends of industry have "burrowed in" to the bureaucracy. Sound industrial policy will call for better information than the Commerce Department and Federal Trade Commission have to offer. Crafting welfare reform may be more difficult because the Department of Health and Human Services keeps insufficient data to evaluate its own experimental programs. And invigorating the Environmental Protection Agency could take years because an orgy of contracting out and budget cutting has left the agency with insufficient staff to keep the private contractors honest.

After twelve years of Republican neglect and frequent Democratic complicity, perhaps it is unsurprising that the new administration has inherited a government ill-suited for activism. The toll of drastic budget cuts and the grosser casualties of deregulation have been well-chronicled; frustrated liberals realized ago that damage years in the making would take more than three months to undo.

But much of the damage to the executive branch hit below the water line. Although the conservative mandate had its limits during the 1980s, the White House's ability to undermine government did not. What Ronald Reagan and, to a lesser extent, George Bush could not accomplish through legislation or executive orders, their subordinates evidently achieved through subtle shifts in personnel and mission.

While the Reagan-Bush era campaign to eviscerate government machinery was neither illegal nor particularly illicit, it was illustrative of the right wing's extensive contempt for the public enterprise. And in the current climate of tight budgets and inflated expectations, that campaign's legacy will complicate the challenge facing resurgent liberals. Before reinventing or even reforming government, this ambitious administration will have to reconstitute it.

Invasion of the Bureaucracy-Snatchers

Although Reagan had given defenders of the welfare state plenty to fear by 1981, it was not clear at that time just how much damage his administration was capable of inflicting. After all, regulatory and social service agencies had fared well under the only other Republican administrations of recent memory, Richard Nixon's and Gerald Ford's. While that had a lot to do with Nixon's moderate attitude on domestic affairs, it also had something to do with the strength of institutional momentum.

Over the years, the independence of executive branch departments had become entrenched in statute and tradition. Although the increased regulation of the 1960s and 1970s had sparked Republican war cries of "overregulation"—cries that fueled Reagan's 1980 victory—few thought the new president capable of effecting drastic course changes in the bureaucracy, at least right away. As Susan and Martin Tolchin recount in *Dismantling America*, scholar and longtime presidential adviser Richard Neustadt warned ambitious Reaganites that taking over the government was "like steering a supertanker. You may put the wheel over hard, but it's still not going to turn on a dime."

But Reagan paid the conventional wisdom no heed, using every weapon in his arsenal to reign in the bureaucracy. When Congress was determined to defend regulatory agencies, he cut the agency budgets. And when Congress would not approve the budget cuts, he put the agencies in the hands of people determined as he was to see them fail.

The quintessential victim of these tactics was antitrust law. To disciples of the ultra-conservative "Chicago School" (named for the University of Chicago, where the movement was born), antitrust law was largely unnecessary. Reasoning that the market automatically protects competition by encouraging opportunistic firms to undercut price-gougers, Robert Bork and the rest of the "law and economics" fraternity argued that erecting laws against corporate mergers and other potential sources of noncompetitive behavior was an unfair burden on business.

Even many Republicans found the Chicago School's theories specious. Antitrust enforcement had a long history of bipartisan support—it prospered during the Nixon-Ford era and conservatives had generally accepted it as an instrument to assure that consumers get the free choice promised by market economics. But Reagan was a true believer in the Chicago School, and he imposed it on the two agencies jointly responsible for antitrust law, the Federal Trade Commission and the Justice Department's antitrust division. The result was an effective neutering of antitrust enforcement that reminded some observers of the early 1900s —the years when rampant corporate manipulation of consumers first spurred progressive clamoring for antitrust protection.

At the Justice Department, Reagan's appointees slashed the antitrust unit's staff in half and cut the real budget by more than 30 percent in eight years. The average number of annual investigations dropped from around 300 under Carter to a little more than 200 under Reagan, and most of those were filed against small businesses. Justice did keep up its practice of filing amicus briefs in private suits, but even that activity betrayed the new party line: Attorney General Ed Meese directed the unit to file briefs *supporting* companies accused of restraining trade. "You can imagine how demoralizing it was for government attorneys to be filing briefs on behalf of corporate defendants," says one antitrust scholar. "If they had wanted to do that, they could have gotten jobs with the companies in the first place."

At the Federal Trade Commission, the process was a bit more subtle. Carter's FTC director, Michael Pertschuk, had made many enemies in Washington, landing the FTC atop the Republican hit list. When Pertschuk left in 1981 (FTC commissioners serve staggered terms), Reagan quickly handed the agency over to James Miller, a Chicago School economist who had been directing Reagan's slash-and-burn campaign at the Office of Management and Budget. Miller brought a pro-business sensibility to the government's consumer protection agency, and he institutionalized it in the guise of restructuring—namely, he subordinated the agency's two investigative divisions, the Bureau of Competition and the Bureau of Consumer Protection, to its analytical unit, the Bureau of Economics. Miller also presided over substantial downsizing, cutting the staff by more than one-third through attrition.

With Justice's lawyers at the mercy of Meese and the FTC's lawyers at the mercy of conservative microeconomists, antitrust enforcement virtually vanished. The political appointees routinely refused to pursue investigations put forth by the career attorneys, and a Wall Street free-for-all ensued. Both agencies stayed silent while Northwest Airlines swallowed up Republic, a top rival in the Midwest, and General Motors began joint ventures with Toyota, its largest foreign competitor. The government backed off other high-profile investigations too, refusing to scrutinize a string of oil industry mergers and dropping altogether a Carter-era initiative to break up IBM.

With Northwest in a tailspin, IBM tumbling from the pantheon, and GM reporting record losses, today the purported economic rewards of the Meese-Miller strategy seem dubious. (In a recent *New Yorker* article, James Stewart made a convincing case that IBM, at least, would have benefited from the kind of breakup the government forced at AT&T, stimulating the competitive energies of that protected behemoth.) As for the agencies, their misfortune is a bit more certain: they lost a generation of would-be crusaders to corporate law. "There were a lot of people sitting around reading the newspaper," recalls one refugee who fled the FTC for a corporate firm in 1985. "Frankly, I was bored."

For the most part, the carnage at Justice and FTC—emblematic of what happened to almost every regulatory agency during the Reagan years—ended in 1989, since George Bush had less stomach for fighting wars with the bureaucracy. (His limited passion was reserved for wars elsewhere.) With more moderate conservatives in charge, the budget cuts slowed and the ideological war ceased. Bush even appointed a few legitimate regulators—that is, people who believed in the agencies they were appointed to direct—giving defenders of the regulatory state cause for a small sigh of relief. (David Kessler, who will continue to head the Food and Drug Administration under Clinton, comes quickly to mind.)

But declaring a truce and clearing the battlefield are two different things. Bureaucratic negligence inflicted lasting damage on everything from the American economy to the global environment—damage the Bush administration was in no rush to undo. Bush in many cases appointed activists to the political posts only to deny them the funds they needed to make repairs. Clinton can do better by not only appointing the right people but also by appropriating the necessary money. Unfortunately, in some cases that will not be enough.

Lethargy as a Legacy

Not since the days of Lyndon Johnson have career government servants enjoyed the support of an enthusiastic public. Nixon and Ford were actively apathetic about government workers, and Carter's run against the government served mainly to heighten public anger at the bureaucracy—anger that subsequently helped force him from office.

But nobody ever despised the civil service quite like Ronald Reagan and his band of ideologues did. To conservative intellectuals like Howard Phillips, now president of the Conservative Caucus Foundation, the welfare state seemed to subsidize left-wing activists intent on using the government as a means of social revolution. Though that view was far from universally shared, most conservatives at least agreed that the civil service had become something of a permanent left-wing constituency within the executive branch.

The claims were not wholly without foundation: After all, who else but liberals would shirk Wall Street to toil away at the Justice Department? (Actually, quite a few conservatives, hoping to build resumes for lobbying careers.) But even at the height of conservative power in the 1980s, Reagan could not always squeeze the liberals out. When White House strategists realized that budget cuts could accomplish only so much, they settled on the next best alternative: they sought to infiltrate the career bureaucracy by installing like-minded ideologues.

Getting old civil servants out was surprisingly easy. Often, it meant simply shuffling departments and priorities, thus promoting or—in some cases—forcing the attrition of career staff. At the Environmental Protection Agency, Reagan pushed a plan to force 5,000 of the department's 1980 staffers out within two years (there were only 5,400 in the first place). Although the initiative met with last-second opposition from Congress, the message got through: by the fall of 1981, EPA was losing staff at a rate of nearly 3 percent a month.

Filling those positions with conservatives was a tad more complicated, since the prohibition of political cronyism was precisely the reason the civil service was founded in the first place. But clever administrators usually found a way around the letter—if not the spirit—of the law.

One popular scheme took advantage of the Ramspeck Act, which allows staffers on Capitol Hill to bypass the usual civil service application process. Under the law, competitive reviews are expedited and six-month probation periods are waived for staffers seeking career posts in federal agencies. The law's intent was to keep the staff of lame-duck legislators from fleeing public service, and in fact it only applied to staffers with at least three years of Hill experience. But in practice the law was interpreted loosely, and the result was to provide conservative ideologues with a way to "burrow in" to the bureaucracy. Currently, at least seven cases of possible Ramspeck violations are under investigation at the Interior Department, where transition officials found former political appointees had burrowed in to the bureaucracy after working on the Hill for as little as a week.

Of course, infiltration of the bureaucracy did not always involve such deception, nor did it always involve a political agenda. But whatever the motives, conservative foot soldiers are now entrenched throughout the federal government. Some may leave on their own, and some may fall in line out of a commitment to professionalism. But those who do not could prove a troublesome nuisance—if not an outright obstacle—for an administration looking to undertake an expansion of the activist state. Warns one aide who worked on the transition team: "We can kid ourselves into thinking the political appointees have all the power, but in truth they are the steerers, not the rowers. And those rowers can really slow things down."

Interior may be in the most trouble. Carter had prepared the department for a renaissance of sorts, expanding the staff at key divisions such as the Bureau of Land Management and the Bureau of Reclamation. But Carter never had time to fill the posts he worked so hard to create, an opportunity Interior Secretary James Watt was quick to seize in 1981. With Reagan's strong support, Watt packed the agency with opponents of environmental protection, and during the last decade this group, dubbed "the rip-and-run set" by environmentalists, presided over a massive sell-off of federal lands to industry and developers.

Given the extensive damage, even Bruce Babbitt, known for his administrative skills, may have trouble righting the ship. The sell-off has deprived the department of several billion dollars in annual revenue, creating a serious fiscal drain. The Government Accounting Office predicts new legislation and proper collection of current fees could boost department revenues and savings by $4.5 billion over the next four years, but in practice mid-level officials hostile to these objectives could be responsible for implementing the plans.

Unfortunately, changing the crew at Interior will not be easy. Al Appleton, New York City's Commissioner of Environmental Protection, predicts it could take as long as five years to clean house, since Congress has unusually extensive oversight at Interior and many legislators are protective of the Reagan-era staffers: "It's going to be very intricate work. They're going to have to go through an entire culture change."

Time bombs are also ticking in other agencies, and officials have started to notice. At the EPA, Administrator Carol Browner has warned Congress about a "total lack of management, accountability, and discipline" within the agency. She also worries that Reagan-era moves to contract out more than $1 billion in work every year—the agency's total budget is only $7 billion—could compromise the integrity of EPA studies. At the Department of Housing and Urban Development, a confidential report obtained by the *Washington Post* said the scandal-ridden department may still be wasting hundreds of millions of dollars, because former secretary Jack Kemp's focus on ideologically charged issues deflected attention away from mid- and low-level management issues.

In principle, contracting-out can save the government money. But that outcome depends on competitive bidding, performance reviews, and careful audits. In practice, under Reagan and Bush the ranks of public officials necessary to supervise contractors have been so thinned that the putative gains of contracting out have evaporated. Agencies have been left with the worst of both worlds—demoralized and disorganized public officials and unaccountable private contractors.

Ignorance as Republican Bliss

In some cases, the private sector has stepped in to profit from what the government is failing to do. Consulting firms make millions each year by taking recently released Commerce Department data, updating it with better analysis, and selling it back to American businesses. Meanwhile, the Japanese government employs more economists to study input/output statistics for American industries than the American government does, and the city of Cleveland, tired of insufficient information from Washington, now gets its cross-border trade statistics from the Canadian government in Ottawa.

Such poor standards for information gathering and analysis are not unique to the economic sphere. Indeed, the campaign to undermine research programs was a trademark of the Reagan era. Although the professed rationale for these cuts was downsizing and a desire to privatize government functions, the strategy's main impact was to deprive the bureaucracy of the intellectual foundation it needs to function and develop new initiatives. Now that damage threatens to compromise some of Clinton's most highly touted campaign proposals—namely, his plans to revive the economy and revamp social welfare programs.

The campaign against government information began with David Stockman, Reagan's director of the Office of Management and Budget. Like many conservatives, Stockman saw in the government information apparatus tremendous waste and duplication. He also knew that information companies were eager to provide for fees what the government had always provided for free. Although privatization would squeeze out noncorporate consumers—namely small businesses and academics—and although information gathering was widely considered a public function, Stockman forged ahead and called for maximum privatization of government information services.

While the duplication and disorganization Stockman perceived was not illusory (unlike most developed nations, the U.S. divides information gathering functions among 70 agencies and subagencies), the budget impact was. Statistical research accounts for less than one-tenth of 1 percent of government spending. But Stockman could make his ideas stick: he was responsible for approving all department budget proposals, and information programs rarely had strong constituencies anyway.

The impact of the Stockman crusade was a real cut in research and statistical funding for practically every department except defense. (Stockman wanted to cut there too, but Reagan forbade it.) Agencies coped by cutting corners—using smaller statistical samples and skipping all but major recalculations—but the product inevitably suffered. As predicted, a private information industry quickly sprung to life, offering a product geared exclusively for corporate clients and priced accordingly.

By the late 1980s, the potential harm to government—which depends on reliable information—was so apparent that even Michael

Boskin, Bush's very conservative chairman of the Council of Economic Advisers, called for a massive reconstruction. But those efforts ended in 1991, and today a wide range of federal statistics remain insufficient or out-of-date. The agencies simply have too little information or too few people to analyze it, and the consumers are beginning to take notice. "There's a steady erosion in the confidence of numbers," says one congressional aide. "This affects everybody. It causes mistakes."

Such mistakes could well begin with economic policy making. Data from the Commerce Department's Bureau of Economic Analysis, including the trade deficit and the gross national product, is essential for an informed policy debate, particularly when tariffs and targeted tax-breaks are on the table. But since that same information is crucial for economic regulation too, the unit was a target of Reagan-era cutbacks and today can barely keep up with the times. When the bureau released this year's tables on input and output of American industry, it based the analysis on industry relationships from 1982.

At the FTC, the erosion of information could do more to thwart Clinton's attempts to forge an industrial policy. In the 1970s the FTC launched the Line of Business Reporting program, which required corporations to file information on annual revenues, costs, and investments in research and development. Such data is important for targeting public investment, since it provides information on industry concentration and competitiveness. But Reagan and Miller killed the program in 1982, and it could take five to ten years to get it going again. "Hundreds of hours were spent on that program under Ford and Carter," says Eleanor Fox, an antitrust expert at New York University. "Now they're probably going to have to start from scratch."

But if there is a potential poster-child for the victims of Reagan- and Bush-era abuse, it is the Department of Health and Human Services. HHS will be responsible for enacting at least one and probably two of Clinton's most high-profile proposals—welfare reform and a comprehensive national health care system. But twelve years of fiscal and political abuse have crippled the department's intellectual base, and today it has barely enough information to allow the proper administration of existing programs, let alone the implementation of new initiatives.

Consider the department's most well-known program, social security. Reagan cut the national staff of the Social Security Administration (a division of HHS) from 80,000 to 60,000, eliminating field jobs that ensured effective administration in less populated areas. He also dismantled the Office of Research and Statistics, which collected information on poverty and pensions used throughout the government.

The cuts produced a sharp decline in the quality of services. Many disability recipients now wait months for their checks, with some 800,000 claims pending. Retired people with routine questions about their pensions or recipient status wait on hold for hours and conclude the government cannot do anything right. Thanks to Reagan, social security—once the government's most popular and successful program—has become an easy target for government critics. (Leading the charge during the 1980s was Dorcas Hardy, Reagan's SSA director, who eventually published a book warning people not to have faith in social security because it was doomed to failure.)

As for the ability of HHS to carry out Clinton's expanded agenda, the outlook is equally bleak. According to the GAO, HHS has not kept adequate data on the Jobs Opportunities and Basic Skills Training (JOBS) initiative, a potential model for welfare reform. As a result, HHS is ill-equipped to judge whether JOBS is helping speed the transition from welfare dependency to self-sufficiency—the very kind of information architects of a new welfare system will need to make reform work.

Rebuilding the government's statistical base at places like HHS will not take much money. It will, however, take political chips—chips that nobody has to spare. "During the Reagan years, nobody in the administration was going to expend political capital on behalf of statistics," says one congressional staffer. "Given the big-league baseball that is being played with the budget this year, I think it is unlikely that anybody will expend political capital on behalf of statistics right now."

Getting the Last Laugh

Could something have been done to avoid this mess? Not much, aside from reversing the last two or three presidential elections. For all the talk about the bureaucracy's neutrality, agencies and cabinet departments are still part of the executive branch. As Reagan demonstrated, these departments are explicitly political.

But the state of affairs in the bureaucracy does offer one valuable—if somewhat belated—insight on the Republican legacy. As many of Reagan's critics long suspected, one reason government did not work during the last decade was that the officials running it were often determined to see it fail. Underfunding and understaffing the bureaucracy did not always cut waste, as the Republicans promised; in many cases, it increased it.

Policymakers would do well to keep that lesson in mind during the coming months. While every agency has fat, the trimming must be done with care. The Clinton administration and Congress might be surprised to learn how effective the HHS or EPA can be under the direction of true believers. At the very least, the administration needs to know that the success of new initiatives depends on the ability of the government to carry out basic functions it is now ill equipped to handle.

Rebuilding the foundation of activist government will not grab many headlines, and it holds out no promise of grass-roots appeal. But such unglamorous work lurks behind every politically potent proposal now on Bill Clinton's agenda.

Disbelief in government could still be a self-fulfilling ideology. Four years later, Ronald Reagan could still have the last laugh.

[27]

CASS R. SUNSTEIN

Constitutional Politics and the Conservative Court

Ever since 1969, when President Nixon appointed Warren Burger to replace Earl Warren as Chief Justice, observers have been anticipating the emergence of a conservative Supreme Court and the end of an era of expanding civil rights and civil liberties. For years, the predictions turned out to be premature. It was the Burger Court, after all, that in the 1970s recognized a constitutional right to reproductive freedom and first concluded that discrimination on the basis of sex would receive careful constitutional scrutiny.

But now there can be no mistaking the reality: the Supreme Court has finally taken a sharply conservative turn. In the last few years the Court has opened the way toward greater government controls on reproductive choice and authorized the states to forbid homosexual relations. It has invalidated affirmative action plans and, at almost every turn, interpreted civil rights laws unfavorably to blacks and women.

For liberals and others concerned about these decisions, a conservative Court is obviously nothing to celebrate, but neither is it a reason to go into mourning or slip into nostalgia for the Warren era. While the Warren Court achieved historic advances, it also helped to generate a conservative political reaction and raised serious questions about the legitimate role of the judiciary in a democracy. Paradoxically, a conservative Supreme Court may fuel wider engagement in democratic politics, and that renewed engagement may produce more lasting, legitimate, and fundamental change than a liberal Court could have achieved. We may already be seeing that pattern today on the issues of abortion and women's rights, but the phenomenon is far more general—or so, at least, I shall suggest.

The Death of the Warren Court

The period was extraordinary, probably unprecedented in the history of democratic government. Beginning in the early 1950s, a Supreme Court composed of rather elderly lawyers with life tenure, nearly all of them wealthy, white, and male, attempted to bring about serious social change in the interest of civil rights and civil liberties.

To recall the great cases of the Warren and Burger Courts today is like reading off the heroic battles of a war still fresh in living memory. Beginning with *Brown v. Board of Education*, the Court invalidated racial segregation in schools, public transportation, even golf courses. In *Baker v. Carr* and *Reynolds v. Simms*, it called for reapportionment of state legislatures in line with the principle of one person, one vote. In *Harper v. Board of Elections*, it struck down the poll tax. In *Mapp v. Ohio* and *Miranda v. Arizona*, among many cases, it granted a multitude of new rights to criminal defendants. In *Griswold v. Connecticut* and *Roe v. Wade*, it recognized rights of sexual and reproductive privacy, including the right to obtain an abortion. In other cases, only slightly less well known, it banished prayer from the public schools, struck down many laws as impermissible sex discrimination, gave nonmarital children and aliens the right to be free from official discrimination, and offered extraordinarily broad protection to speech, including advocacy of crime, false statements about public officials, commercial advertising, and pornography.

Many of the rights affirmed by the Court, though actually quite new, are now taken for granted, as if they had always been part of our constitutional heritage. Americans today understand the very concept of "rights" to include protection against discrimination on the basis of race and sex. Similarly, few doubt that their constitutional rights include broad protection of free expression and the vote. And as Judge Bork discovered to his dismay during his confirmation hearings, a generalized right of privacy is now firmly established in public belief. The Court's role in defining such rights was especially surprising in view of the framers' original understanding that the judiciary was to be "the least dangerous branch" (that is, the least radical). Similarly, the Court's own history, particularly during the New Deal period, gave no reason to anticipate that it would assume a leading role in reform. Indeed, the Supreme Court was for decades a principal target of progressive criticism on the theory, then widely accepted, that national policy ought not to be set by nine lawyers purporting to interpret an ambiguous document of the eighteenth century.

The Warren Court's rulings had many salutary effects, but they also preempted political solutions, raised troubling questions about the limits of judicial power, and galvanized opposition. In 1972 and 1980 successful Republican presidential candidates made the liberal Court a major issue.

President Nixon's four appointments (Chief Justice Burger and Justices Powell, Blackmun, and Rehnquist) had a significant impact on the Court's decisions, but there was no wholesale departure from the Warren era. In the 1980s President Reagan and Attorney General Edwin Meese launched a broadside attack on the Warren and Burger Courts. Meese contended that the Court's decisions did not follow from the "original intentions" of the Constitution's framers and could not plausibly count as constitutional interpretation or even law. These decisions were inconsistent, Meese and other conservatives now said, with the premise of democratic self-government and often amounted to bad social policy as well. This was the line of thought that guided Reagan's selections of nominees to the Court—not only the unsuccessful Bork nomination, but also the elevation of Justice Rehnquist to Chief Justice and the appointments of Justices O'Connor, Scalia, and Kennedy. By 1989 the predictions of a conservative majority had been fulfilled in decisions regarding civil rights, if not civil liberties.

Civil rights. The most recent developments were presaged by the important decision in *Bowers v. Hardwick* (1988). A five-to-four majority rejected the argument that the Court's privacy cases should be taken to protect the right of consensual homosexual sodomy. The decision itself was not surprising, but few would have expected the contemptuous tone. Speaking for the majority, Justice White dismissed as "facetious" the claim that a right to engage in homosexual practices is "deeply rooted" in American history and tradition. Chief Justice Burger's concurrence quoted Blackstone's *Commentaries* (1765) for the startling proposition that consensual homosexual behavior is "an offense of 'deeper malignity' than rape."

By the end of 1988 term, the pattern was unmistakable. In the Webster case, which has drawn the most attention, four justices said that they would restrict Roe and allow regulation of abortion to protect fetal life during the first and second trimesters. The fate of Roe now appears to lie in Justice O'Connor's hands, and while her vote is uncertain, we should expect, at the very least, more restrictions on the practice of abortion.

Ranking in importance with Webster was the Court's decision in *City of Richmond v. Croson* to invalidate an affirmative action program adopted by the former seat of the Confederacy. *Croson's* precise reach is unclear, but it reveals that the Court will regard affirmative action programs with great skepticism and refuse to accept past social discrimination as sufficient justification. In general, the Court seems likely to allow affirmative action only if it is a narrowly tailored response to actual discrimination by the particular institution providing the remedy.

Webster and *Croson* were the Court's most visible rulings, but the most revealing were a series of decisions interpreting, not the Constitution, but civil rights statutes enacted by Congress. Time and again, the Court ruled against civil rights plaintiffs in seemingly technical but important cases. In *Wards Cove*, the most far-reaching of these decisions, the Court severely restricted its earlier, unanimous ruling in *Griggs v. Duke Power*. In the *Griggs* decision, written by Chief Justice Burger in 1972, the Court had held that once a civil rights plaintiff showed a practice to have a disparate racial impact, the burden would shift to the defendant to demonstrate that "business necessity" justified the practice. In *Wards Cove*, by contrast, the Court held that even after the plaintiff showed a disparate impact, the burden remained with the plaintiff to show "an absence of legitimate justification." This striking departure from previous law will make it difficult for plaintiffs to win discrimination suits.

Remarkably, no black, female, handicapped, or other civil rights plaintiff achieved a significant victory in the past year. It is hard to point to more than a handful of significant victories by any such group in the past several years. (White plaintiffs have won affirmative action cases, but these are not exactly an exception.) The Court has not merely failed to interpret ambiguous precedents in favor of disadvantaged groups. On many occasions, it has restricted or abandoned, sometimes without saying so, well-established law. The Court's overriding theme is that the social status quo—existing distributions of wealth and power—should not be disturbed by either constitutional law or statute.

With increasingly firm insistence, the majority on the Court claims that the Constitution creates only "negative" rights, not "positive" ones, that is, only rights against state power, not rights to state assistance to prevent private acts of violence or to guarantee even minimal living conditions. In the past decade, the Court has often said that the Constitution does not create any rights of protection against starvation, hopelessness, or indigence. The Court has even said that discrimination among groups of people receiving government benefits will receive only the most superficial scrutiny. To be sure, defining a more aggressive judicial role in guaranteeing positive rights would be extremely difficult. But it was still surprising to read the Court's ruling in *DeShaney* that the Constitution had no bearing on a social welfare agency's refusal to protect a two-year old child from severe beatings by his father—after the service had received repeated warnings, from the child's mother, of imminent danger.

Civil Liberties. In the area of civil liberties, the picture is more cloudy. The Court has been generally unreceptive to claims of right on the part of criminal defendants. Indeed, it has partly repealed the exclusionary rule, which had barred from trial any evidence obtained by police in violation of the Fourth Amendment's protection against unreasonable searches and seizures. Under the Court's revised rule, evidence is admissible if the officers act in "good faith." The Court has also given greater scope to government to impose the death penalty, even on teen-agers and the mentally retarded.

On the other hand, the celebrated (and mostly symbolic) flag-burn-ing decision, combined with the (questionable) ruling that the First Amendment protects dial-a-porn, indicates that the Rehnquist Court will rarely permit governmental regulation of speech on the basis of its con-tent. But the Court's aggressive posture here may actually lead in unfor-tunate directions. The Court seems unlikely to allow any regulation of the speech "market" to reduce disparities of wealth and media access. Here, as elsewhere, the Court is skeptical of redistributions of wealth and power.

Two examples will illustrate the point. The first is the fairness doc-trine, designed to ensure broad debate on the airways about public is-sues and upheld by the Warren Court on the ground that it promoted rather than undermined the purposes of the First Amendment. This Court might well find the fairness doctrine to violate freedom of speech. A second example is campaign-finance regulation. The Court has been reluctant to permit campaign regulation that includes ceilings on indi-vidual and group contributions. Such regulation, now routine in Western Europe, might promote the goal of a well-functioning system of free ex-pression, but it would require a different vision of our political life, as a deliberative process among political equals rather than a mere "political marketplace." In cases of this sort, invocation of the First Amendment to protect current distributions of speech "wealth" is destructive of demo-cratic self-government.

This, then, is the picture that emerges from the recent decisions: a Court skeptical of privacy rights or general liberty interests, extremely reluctant to interpret the Constitution or federal statutes to protect crimi-nal defendants or disadvantaged groups, broadly content with the status quo governing the distribution of wealth and freedom of speech, and generally unlikely to be at all adventurous in using the Constitution to go beyond the work of its predecessors.

The Constitution's Judicial Future

What might we expect from the Rehnquist Court in the near future? It is important to distinguish here between civil liberties and civil rights. No dramatic shift seems likely in civil liberties, particularly freedom of speech. Governments may have marginally greater power to impose the death penalty and to engage in searches and seizures. The Court may also permit more public funding of religious organizations, at least when they perform secular functions. But major departures in these areas would be surprising.

The Court is likely, however, to restrict the use of the Fourteenth Amendment's due process clause to protect general interests in liberty. The due process clause ("nor shall any state deprive any person of life, liberty, or property, without due process of law") is the basic source of judicial protection of privacy rights. *Roe v. Wade* will in all likelihood be restricted or even overruled. The Court may also restrain the powers of Congress in the name of state autonomy and occasionally invalidate congressional restrictions on the executive branch (though here the signals have been mixed, with the most recent cases indicating a limited judicial role). One might also expect a greater willingness to protect rights of contract and property against government regulation.

By far the most important developments will continue to take place in civil rights. Affirmative action is under severe strain. The Court will not find discrimination on the basis of race and sex to violate the Constitution unless the relevant law draws an explicit race or sex line or is clearly based on a discriminatory motivation. The Court's work here reflects a theory of "formal equality," as it is sometimes called. On this theory, a law will not be invalidated even if it has severe discriminatory effects; race or sex discrimination must be overt. The consequences are clear. If measures are taken to be discriminatory only when there is a "smoking gun," very few measures will be invalidated. The Court's hostility to affirmative action and deference to covert discrimination are united by a belief that there is nothing wrong with the current distribution of benefits and burdens between the sexes and the races.

The Court will also continue to be unwilling to use the Fourteenth Amendment's guarantee of "equal protection of the laws" to bar discrimination on the basis of handicap, sexual orientation, poverty, and age. The equal protection clause undergirded much of the work of the Warren and Burger Courts. Here, unquestionably, is where the Rehnquist Court differs most sharply from its predecessors.

Does the Court have a theory guiding its decisions? The answer is an emphatic "No." The rhetoric of "judicial restraint" has provided a popular rallying cry for some of the Warren Court's critics, but the term is notoriously difficult to define. Under almost any definition this Court is not consistently committed to judicial restraint. Judicial restraint is sometimes understood to mean respect for precedent, but in that respect the current Court is extremely adventurous. If "restraint" refers instead to an unwillingness to overturn acts of the legislature and executive, this Court's commitment is only selective. For example, the Court is more aggressive than its predecessors in striking down governmentally adopted affirmative action programs and regulations affecting rights of private property.

The Court's varying posture is most evident in the views of the Justice in some quarters most closely associated with judicial restraint—the influential, creative, and extremely able Justice Scalia. Justice Scalia would invoke the Constitution to invalidate numerous congressional efforts in the area of separation of powers. For example, he voted to strike down the independent counsel act, which provides that someone not under the President's direct control must undertake prosecution of high-level presidential appointees. On the other hand, in his opinion in *Webster*, Justice Scalia argued that the Court in *Roe* had tried to resolve a politically divisive issue that should be dealt with democratically. But on affirmative action, where he favors overturning race-conscious programs through judicial action, Justice Scalia himself will not permit an equally divisive issue to be dealt with democratically. Here the Court's lack of restraint is especially disturbing, since it forecloses a political corrective.

It is not easy to identify any general set of ideas that would account for the results favored by Justice Scalia or the majority of the Court. The most fashionable theory, more extreme than the majority's view, finds dramatic expression in Robert Bork's *The Tempting of America*. Bork claims that the decisive factor is not majority will but the "original understanding" of the Constitution, which supposedly provides plain answers to most hard questions of constitutional law. On this view, the judge's personal opinions are irrelevant. The good judge simply says what the law is, and lets the chips fall where they may.

Without accepting Bork's theory, one might readily acknowledge that the text of the Constitution is binding and the ratifiers' understanding highly relevant. The "original understanding," however, is often ambiguous. The number of people ratifying constitutional provisions was large, and often their multiple views were inconsistent and imprecisely formed. The problem is compounded by the difficulty of deciding the breadth of constitutional principles. Was the equal protection clause —written in broad terms—meant to prevent discrimination only against blacks or against all racial groups? Against groups defined in terms of race and nationality? Race, nationality, and sex? Politically and socially disadvantaged groups in general? The historical record provides no clear answer.

The problem goes even deeper. The framers themselves may have intended to put in the Constitution, not their particular views, but general principles capable of change over time. If so, exclusive reliance on the original understanding is self-contradictory. The text self-consciously invites its interpreters to look elsewhere.

In view of these difficulties, the original understanding cannot account for the current trends in the Court or supply a complete theory of the appropriate judicial role. For all the window-dressing, "originalism" is merely the latest version of formalism in the law: the pretense that one can decide hard legal questions by reference to someone else's value judgments. Here, as elsewhere, formalism is a dismal failure. It is no coincidence that the constitutional positions of the conservative members of the Court generally line up with the conservative wing of the Republican Party: greater constraints on government to adopt affirmative action programs but fewer restrictions on governmental power to aid religion; greater constraints on federal power but fewer intrusions on presidential power; no abortion rights but greater protection of property rights.

Because the Constitution does not contain instructions for its own interpretation, judges need independent interpretive principles to make sense of constitutional law. Probably the best start on such an approach, traced by John Hart Ely in *Democracy and Distrust*, views the role of a constitutional court through the lens of democratic theory. Our system is republican, not majoritarian; it contains a range of protections of rights and groups likely to be undervalued by majorities. Judicial intrusions, from this perspective, are necessary where the political process is least likely to be self-policing. Such an approach calls on the Court to be especially solicitous of rights of free expression and political representation, and it asks the Court to be especially protective of groups, such as racial minorities, women, the disabled, and perhaps the poor, who are likely to be politically mistreated. Of course, no general theory of the Court's role is a substitute for detailed inquiry into a plaintiff's claims and the specific constitutional provisions at issue. But Ely's approach is helpful in deciding where judicial review is likely to be most justifiable. The current Court, however, shows little interest in ideas of this sort.

A Hypothetical Court Agenda

No doubt some of the legacy of the Burger and Warren Courts is in considerable jeopardy. But even more important, we can now expect little help from the Court on the contemporary equivalents of the great issues that came before the Court in the past several decades.

To obtain some perspective on the Rehnquist Court, we might ask what the Court's agenda might have looked like in the 1990s if it had continued on the path the Warren Court set. In the Warren era, practices that earlier were widely accepted came to be seen as constitutionally abhorrent. What are the new candidates today? Theories recently proposed by lawyers, judges, and academics well-disposed toward the Warren Court suggest a number of possibilities. In describing these theories, I do not mean to endorse them all or to suggest precisely how each area should be treated. I wish only to emphasize, by a hypothetical contrast, the consequences of the current Court for democratic politics, and to see whether there might not be advantages in the shift from legal to political arenas.

As the Warren Court pioneered the effort to break down the barriers of racial discrimination, so its hypothetical successor might now be pioneering the effort to break down sex discrimination. Such a Court might approach reproductive freedom, not only as a matter of privacy but also as one of sexual equality, with very different consequences. Public financing of abortion, for example, might well be required, at least if public programs cover obstetric care.

There are many other examples. Our criminal justice system deals inadequately with domestic violence, sexual harassment, rape, and abuses in the production and use of pornography. It would not be difficult at all to imagine a constitutional attack, rooted in the principle of equal "protection" of the law, on police practices that fail to protect women against domestic violence and other forms of sexual violence. Consider as well current rules of family law, which ensure that after divorce the welfare of most men will increase dramatically, while the welfare of most women will decrease correspondingly. (In California, for example, a man's standard of living increases by 42 percent after divorce, while a woman's falls by 73 percent.) The rules do not reward but rather punish women for their contributions to child care and housework.

Such a Court might also want to scrutinize the methods and assumptions used in Social Security to compute benefits. Current rules favor people the more closely they come to traditional male career paths. The Court might demand changes in workplaces that continue to be structured on the basis of male norms and expectations; it might specifically require private firms to improve half-hearted child care policies. It might insist that companies stop excluding women who are fertile but not pregnant from jobs that involve hazards to fetuses. Without much imagination, all these problems could be seen as raising issues of sex discrimination.

A successor to the Warren Court might have extended rights against discrimination to other groups. As currently interpreted, the Constitution has little or nothing to offer to the handicapped, even when fenced out by innumerable practices made by and for the world of the able-bodied. The sexual privacy of gays and lesbians, let alone their right to marry or to raise children, is also unprotected. Probably the best current guess is that the Rehnquist Court would find discrimination on the basis of sexual orientation, including wholesale exclusions from government employment, to be unobjectionable as far as the Constitution is concerned. A different Court would have taken this issue more seriously.

People who are homeless, poor, or starving have nothing to gain from the Constitution, as the Rehnquist Court interprets it. Another

Court would have made at least some inroads on the distinction between positive and negative liberties, furnishing a degree of protection to the destitute. At a minimum, a different Court would have said that selective exclusions from funding programs need persuasive justification.

These issues are only examples of the impressive set of proposals for constitutional reform that might have arisen in a second Warren era. They would have created the same sorts of pressures, dilemmas, and opportunities that the Warren Court faced beginning in the 1950s. If the agenda seems overly ambitious, perhaps we might remember how much more ambitious were the changes that the Court introduced between 1950 and 1980.

But would a second Warren Court have been desirable? Some of the preceding proposals, such as using the equal protection clause to ensure better protection against domestic violence, would not have strained the Court's remedial competence or been likely to cause a political backlash. Some decisions, such as reducing discrimination in family law, would have been relatively easy to implement. But others, such as an active judicial posture in restructuring Social Security or protecting rights to food and shelter, would have strained the boundaries of constitutional interpretation, called for complex trade-offs not readily made in court, and perhaps generated so much opposition as to be self-defeating. Such decisions would not necessarily have produced consensual, durable policy changes. Recent history suggests that some judicial victories stimulate complementary political energies. Others mainly stimulate a tide of reaction that swamps the effect of the court rulings.

In any event, because of the Court's current orientation, these issues will now be resolved through representative politics rather than the judiciary. If the Court plays any role, it most likely will become an obstacle to change, not an ally or a catalyst of it.

Judicial Defects, Democratic Possibilities

With the Court's conservative turn, what have we lost? We will have constitutional conflicts, just as before, but now the setting for resolving those conflicts will shift increasingly to the political arena.

For supporters of a progressive constitutional agenda, the most important concern about this institutional shift is that majoritarian politics might block progress. A large purpose of constitutionalism is to protect rights that are at risk in politics. Some argue that if it were not for the courts, we would not have had school desegregation, the one-person one-vote decision, and many of the civil rights advances of the Warren era. And while the argument would have to be quite elaborate, the same considerations might justify, in at least some cases, an aggressive role for a new liberal Court.

But a liberal Court is not now a political possibility. Besides, there may be significant advantages to the institutional shift. We ought to recall that during the Progressive Era and the New Deal, the Supreme Court was mostly hostile to reform but it was unable to stop it, and its very hostility may have been a stimulant. In the third great wave of reform in this century—the environmental, consumer, and antidiscrimination movements of the 1960s and 1970s—by far the most important changes, of both degree and kind, came from Congress. The courts played a subsidiary role. There are several lessons here.

Efficacy. Judicial decisions are of limited efficacy in bringing about social change. Study after study has reached this basic conclusion.[1] Brown itself is usually taken as a counterexample, but as Gerald Rosenberg demonstrates in his *The Hollow Hope*, it is the most conspicuous confirmation of the point. Ten years after the decision, no more than about two percent of black children in the South attended desegregated schools. Not until 1964, as the Congress and executive branch became involved, did widespread desegregation actually occur. Complex social changes pose difficulties that Courts are usually ineffective in surmounting.

Roe v. Wade may be another illustration of the illusions of court-ordered progress, though the picture here is mixed. Undoubtedly, the decision dramatically increased women's access to safe abortions and helped to give legitimacy to the practice. Surprisingly, however, it did not dramatically increase the actual number and rate of abortions, as Hyman Rodman, Betty Sarvis, and Joy Walker Bonar have shown in their study, *The Abortion Question*. Moreover, *Roe* may have had harmful political effects. First, by withdrawing the abortion issue from representative political institutions, it prevented the achievement of political compromises. And, second, by spurring opposition and demobilizing supporters, it helped to shift the political momentum to the anti-abortion movement.

The extraordinary public reaction to the *Webster* decision and the ensuing political mobilization of pro-choice groups provides support for this view. The Court's partial retreat from *Roe* is awakening the women's movement in a way that will probably have more favorable and fundamental long-term consequences for sexual equality than any liberal Court ruling could have produced. I am not suggesting that *Roe* was necessarily wrong, either as a matter of constitutional interpretation or as a mat-

---

1. See Donald Horowitz, *The Courts and Social Policy* (Washington, D.C.: Brookings, 1979); R. Shepherd Melnick, *Regulation and the Court: The Case of the Clean Air Act* (Washington, D.C.: Brookings, 1983); and Gerald Rosenberg, *The Hollow Hope* (Chicago: University of Chicago Press, 1990).

ter of principle. But I am saying that its effectiveness has been limited, largely because of its judicial source.

Of course, judicial review has sometimes accomplished considerable good and introduced important changes into American society. We might distinguish here between two kinds of decisions. If the Court issues a simple "No"—forbidding, for example, minimum wage laws, government censorship, or affirmative action—it is likely to be quite effective. But if the Court asks some institution to undertake large-scale social reform—to desegregate the schools, to improve conditions in mental asylums, to provide shelter and food, to reapportion state legislatures— its effectiveness will usually be limited. Here judicial action may be necessary, but it is not sufficient; the court needs help from others. For example, the reapportionment decision was successful, but this was largely because there was enough political will to bring about change.[2] It is important to remember that liberal democracies without judicial review, such as Great Britain and until recently Canada, have also achieved many of the civil rights and civil liberties protections that we have in the United States. The post-Warren Court focus on the rulings of the Supreme Court has often been myopic. The fate of civil rights and civil liberties in a democracy depends far more fundamentally on the character of our political and social life than on the nine justices.

Democracy and citizenship. Reliance on the courts diverts political energies and resources from democratic channels. The substitution of litigation for politics has large costs. Citizen mobilization is a public good, inculcating political commitments, broader understanding, and the practice of citizenship. Martin Luther King may well have been a more important source of constitutional change than all of the Warren Court's race decisions.

In any case, political channels are often a better channel for sensible and effective reform. Individual preferences and their intensities can more easily be reflected in mutually advantageous compromises. Furthermore, the shift of constitutional politics out of the courts may have the healthy effect of requiring Congress, the President, and the states to deliberate on the important questions of self-government and carry out their own obligations of fidelity to the founding document.

The narrowing focus of adjudication. When confronting complex social problems, courts are rarely expert in the areas at hand, and the focus on the litigated case makes it hard for judges to understand the complex systemic effects of legal intervention. A decision to require expenditures on school busing, for example, might divert resources from services with an equal or greater claim to the public purse. Legal thinking and

---

2. In this connection, see Gerald Rosenberg's *The Hollow Hope.*

legal procedures are most comfortable with ideas inherited from the tradition of compensatory justice. On the compensatory model, A injures B,
and B must make A whole by making payment. But this model is ill-
suited to many issues. Consider the many examples of pollution that
harm numerous people to a small degree. Here the purpose of legal controls is not to ensure compensation but to manage and reduce risks. The
inevitability of complex trade-offs makes a rights-based approach highly
unrealistic. Similarly, discrimination is usually not the commission of acts
of discrimination by identifiable actors to identifiable victims. The more
basic problem is that systems of subordination need to be reformed. Adjudication is ill-adapted to undertaking the necessary changes.

These criticisms of the judiciary are hardly novel. Though voiced
principally by conservatives in the last decades, analogous complaints
played a major role during the New Deal. It would have seemed peculiar
then to suggest that social reform on behalf of the disadvantaged should
come from the courts. Indeed, the rise of modern regulatory agencies reflected a belief that the judiciary lacked the will, the means, and the democratic mandate to bring about social reform on its own. The period that
we are entering will see a similar constellation of ideas.

Above all, we need to recognize that the Supreme Court is not the
only governmental institution charged with fidelity to the Constitution.
Crabbed understandings from the Court are nothing to be pleased about,
but if other institutions can pick up the slack, the shift from the court-
house to the statehouse will have many advantages. Legislators, executive officials, and even citizens are also responsible for upholding constitutional principles. If the Court interprets the Constitution too narrowly,
this responsibility becomes all the more insistent.

If we are to pursue constitutionally grounded social reform outside
of the courts, on what institutions might we rely? There are many possibilities. In the past decade, states and localities have shown great initiative and imagination, going well beyond the Supreme Court and Congress to enact aggressive measures forbidding discrimination on the
basis of disability, sex, and sexual orientation. Nationally, the principal
civil rights gains have occurred through legislative action to bar discrimination on the basis of sex, disability, age, and race.

The major sources of national legislative power here are the commerce clause—granting Congress authority to regulate all actions having
a significant effect on interstate commerce—and, perhaps most notably,
the great underused provision of the Constitution, section 5 of the Fourteenth Amendment. The Fourteenth Amendment, of course, has been the
source of the overwhelming majority of the important Supreme Court
civil rights and civil liberties decisions, including the application of the
Bill of Rights to the states, *Roe v. Wade*, and all discrimination cases. The

amendment's last sentence says that "Congress shall have power to enforce, by appropriate legislation, the provisions of this article." Congress has rarely taken up the invitation. Indeed, the judicial rather than legislative enforcement of the Fourteenth Amendment may qualify as the most profound irony in the history of American constitutionalism.

The Supreme Court itself, however, has concluded that congressional power under section 5 is extraordinarily broad. Indeed, the Court has permitted Congress to invoke section 5 to proscribe practices that the Court has upheld. In permitting Congress to invalidate literacy tests, for example, the Court explicitly ruled that under section 5 Congress could strike down practices the Court would permit.

This conclusion turns out to be no puzzle if we recognize that the Court's decisions reflect not only substantive theory but also institutional constraint. Precisely because it lacks a democratic pedigree, the Court is sometimes unwilling to enforce the Constitution as vigorously as it would if it were elected. Congress faces no such constraints. Ironically, the Court might well find that Congress acted within its constitutional authority to overturn the Court's own restrictive readings of the Constitution.

We are now seeing important efforts in this direction. Bills recently introduced in Congress would reject the Supreme Court's interpretation of federal civil rights statutes and to some extent the Court's reading of the Constitution itself. If enacted, these measures might well go beyond anything that liberal judges could have produced.

In many respects, the current position of the Supreme Court is akin to that of its predecessor in the New Deal. As then, constitutional politics through the judiciary is unlikely to advance liberal causes. But neither should a conservative Court arrest their progress. The Court's shift in direction might be taken above all as an opportunity—an opportunity to bring constitutional politics out of the judiciary into the democratic arena, where a more generous understanding of freedom and equality may prevail.

[28a]

Gene B. Sperling

Does the Supreme Court Matter?

How important is the Supreme Court to the advancement of individual rights? Very important, many would contend, when the people whose rights are being advanced lack political power. Our constitutional democracy rests, after all, on the notion that people disdained and disfavored by the majority can still find justice before an independent Supreme Court.

Some critics and historians, however, have always downplayed the Court's role. They argue that progress apparently flowing from Court decisions would have come eventually, or even sooner, through the political process, and that reform might been more effective or better crafted if the elected branches had brought it about.

Much of this criticism has come from those on the right who condemn the Supreme Court protections of individual rights as "judicial activism." In a different vein, some on the left see the Court as an elitist institution and view grass-roots politics as the true source of social progress.

In "Constitutional Politics and a Conservative Court" (*TAP*, Spring 1990), constitutional scholar Cass Sunstein offers a new rationale for downplaying the Supreme Court's role in advancing individual rights: optimism. Although the Court is currently narrowing the scope of individual rights, Sunstein counsels supporters of civil rights against despair. History teaches us, in Sunstein's view, that the Supreme Court's role is not only unnecessary but often counterproductive because it "stimulates the tide of reaction that swamps the [positive] effect of the rulings."

In support of his thesis, Sunstein points to *Brown v. Board of Education*, the landmark 1954 school desegregation case in which the Court declared that laws relegating African Americans to second-class citizenship violated the equal protection clause of the Fourteenth Amendment. While clearly an admirer of the *Brown* decision, Sunstein contends that it had little practical impact, because a decade later, in 1964, only 2 percent of Southern schools were integrated; he credits the progress we have made solely to the political action and organizing that led to the Civil Rights Act of 1964 and the Voting Rights Act of 1965. "Martin Luther King," Sunstein writes, "may well have been a more important source of constitutional change than all of the Warren Court's race decisions."

Yet to ask whether the Supreme Court or Martin Luther King had a greater impact on civil rights is to ask the wrong question. The Court's decisions and the civil rights movement energized each other. While *Brown v. Board of Education* would have led to little progress without a mobilized popular movement, the successes of that movement equally depended on the Court.

Sunstein misses this critical point by focusing only on the Court's shortcomings in providing an immediately effective judicial remedy to school segregation. He ignores the tremendous power of the *Brown* Court's declaration of rights in creating a political and moral climate that enabled the civil rights movement to flourish. For while the judicial remedy of school segregation in the decade after *Brown* was nearly a total failure, the rights and constitutional values proclaimed in *Brown* provided the basis for crucial political victories, as the Supreme Court struck down segregation in public facilities, transportation, and courtrooms. Two years after *Brown II*, Congress passed the 1957 Civil Rights Act, creating the Civil Rights Division in the Justice Department, and laying the administrative groundwork for future executive enforcement. In *Simple Justice*, Richard Kluger noted that "the mass movement sparked by *Brown* was unmistakably thriving as soon as six months after the Court handed down the implementation decree."

The most poignant illustration of the interplay between the right declared in *Brown* and the success of political action is the event that many, including King himself, considered the critical moment in the nonviolent, civil rights movement: the Montgomery bus boycott.

In his first address to the Montgomery Improvement Association, only days after Rosa Parks's arrest, King inspired the potential boycotters with the moral force of *Brown*: "If we are wrong, the Supreme Court is wrong. If we are wrong, the Constitution of the United States is wrong."

Eleven months later, on the very day that a distraught King thought the historic citizen boycott was about to be broken by obstructionist maneuvers, the Supreme Court, relying on *Brown*, declared Montgomery's bus segregation policy unconstitutional. "The darkest hour of our struggle," wrote King, "had indeed proved to be the finest hour of victory." The Montgomery bus boycott thus presaged the truth of King's later words: "Direct action is not a substitute for work in the courts and the halls of government.... Indeed, direct action and legal action complement one another; when skillfully employed, each becomes more effective."

Although massive resistance could prevent the Supreme Court from turning its words into remedies, the Court's interpretation of constitutional rights forced many Americans to confront the discrepancy between our constitutional ideals and racist social practices. The Court's ruling against racial exclusion compelled white America to acknowledge the hypocrisy of this rights-reality gap and created a positive tension pressuring other institutions to respond. King played on this tension like a maestro. Like other civil rights leaders, he did not try to convince Americans to change their values. Rather, he used the promise of *Brown* as he did the promise of equality in the Declaration of Independence to stir dissonance in America, showing white Americans that only by changing their treatment of blacks could they stay true to their country's ideals.

Thus, it is pointless to speculate about the relative importance of *Brown* and the legislative victories of 1964 and 1965, because *Brown* itself was an integral part of the prelude to those legislative achievements. Judge Jay Harvey Wilkinson wrote in *From Brown to Bakke* that "Brown was the catalyst that ... culminated in the two major civil rights acts." Without *Brown*, the very protest against segregation would have seemed to many to be a battle between law-breaking protesters and law-abiding segregationists. With the stroke of a pen, the Supreme Court shifted the moral weight of the Constitution—and of law generally—from those who sought to preserve the caste system to those who sought to dismantle it.

We can also see the Supreme Court's influence in the arrested development of rights that have not advanced, and have even been set back. Consider the litigation in the 1970s over racial segregation in Northern inner cities. Minority plaintiffs claimed that racial ghettoization in Northern cities stemmed from an interlocking network of discriminatory governmental and private actions that were as unconstitutional as the Jim Crow laws that had required segregation in much of the South. The Court chose not even to give these claims a full hearing.

Many would contend the Court was correct to resist such claims because the judiciary lacked the power to remedy pervasive segregation single-handedly. The Court did not, however, simply acknowledge its limited remedial power; it developed a series of evidentiary hurdles that made it nearly impossible for minority plaintiffs to demonstrate how interlocking patterns of housing, school, real estate, and employment discrimination produced unconstitutional racial segregation. While *Brown* triggered political progress, the Court's decisions in the 1970s put a stamp of constitutional legitimacy on inner-city segregation.

Had the Court of the 1970s recognized the constitutional infirmity of Northern segregation, it at least would have forced the majority to see inner-city segregation as a by-product of governmental policies. Today's civil rights and political leaders would have been empowered by the Court's declaration of constitutional rights and wrongs, just as the tension created by a rights-reality gap empowered Dr. King following *Brown.*

The Supreme Court's decision in *Bowers v. Hardwick* (where it approved a Georgia statute that defines private homosexual acts between consenting adults as a crime) is another example of how the Court's recent inaction has hurt the cause of civil rights. In an unusual admission, Justice Lewis Powell, who provided the crucial fifth vote for the Court's majority, recently admitted that his vote was a mistake. But Powell also sought to play down the significance of his vote on the grounds that no one was sent to jail.

Yet, the Supreme Court's legitimation of bigotry toward homosexuals is felt every day in the public and private lives of millions of Americans. Due to Justice Powell's fifth vote, any act of bigotry toward homosexual employees or tenants may be defended in states with draconian "antisodomy" laws as arising not from discrimination, but from criminal homosexual activities. Furthermore, according to the Alliance for Justice, more than 100 cases alleging violations of civil liberties have been denied on the basis of *Hardwick.*

Worst of all, by putting its constitutional stamp of approval on laws targeting homosexuals, the Supreme Court told Americans that they need not question whether their private prejudice or public opposition to gay rights laws could be squared with their respect for the Constitution and the ideals of individual liberty. The Court's decision in *Bowers v. Hardwick* told gay Americans who had suffered the physical and emotional scars of discrimination, that the pain inflicted upon them did not implicate our constitutional values.

Sunstein takes his argument one further step. He says that particularly strong Supreme Court opinions protecting individual rights can have a long-term negative political impact. Here his example is the aftermath of *Roe v. Wade.* In his view—which I will call the "If Not For *Roe*" myth—pro-choice forces would actually have emerged stronger in the long run if the Court had not taken the initiative in legalizing abortion in *Roe.*

Sunstein makes three arguments as to why *Roe* may be further proof of the "illusions of court-ordered progress." First, he points out that while *Roe* increased the availability and safety of abortion, it did not increase the number of abortions. Yet, this statistic only highlights the importance of the right to choose abortion, not *Roe's* lack of efficacy. If women had roughly the same number of abortions when abortion was illegal as they did after *Roe*, that only shows how serious a decision abortion has always been for women, and that, contrary to anti-abortion advocates, *Roe* did not lead to indiscriminate abortions for "convenience." The goal of the pro-choice movement has never been to increase abortions, but rather to allow women who choose to have abortions to do so in a safe and legal way. True, after *Roe* abortion remained, and still remains, inaccessible in many rural areas. But *Roe* gave Planned Parenthood the ability to organize services on a national level and thereby gave a major boost to nationwide accessibility.

Sunstein argues that *Roe* may have "prevented the achievement of political compromises" and that "it helped shift the political momentum to the anti-abortion movement." What political compromises? As Walter Dellinger explained so powerfully in these pages ("Should We Compromise on Abortion?" *TAP*, Summer 1990), every so-called compromise would deny access to many of the poorest and most vulnerable of women. The most sensible abortion compromise yet is the one in *Roe* itself, which millions of Americans find most reasonable: As a fetus becomes viable and capable of independent life, the state should have increased power to ban abortions.

Finally, Sunstein's third, and key, point is the notion that pro-choice forces were on their way to nationwide, political victory when *Roe* came down, simultaneously energizing the pro-life movement and sapping the strength of pro-choice forces. *Roe* did spur tremendous reaction on the anti-abortion side (especially from the Catholic Church), but a close look at the relevant history refutes the notion that *Roe* hurt abortion rights in the long run.

Although a handful of states had liberalized their criminal laws regarding abortion by the time the Court decided *Roe*, New York was the only state where a widespread political movement had led to legalized abortion. And legalization had passed in 1970 only by a one-vote margin achieved when a legislator switched his vote at the last minute. Yet, even in New York, the legislature voted to repeal the law only two years later in 1972, the year before *Roe*. Only a veto by Governor Nelson Rockefeller saved the right to choose abortion. This was the shaky state of the emerging pro-choice movement prior to *Roe*.

Many, including Sunstein, seek to buffer their "If Not For *Roe*" arguments by arguing that, since the pro-choice movement has been vigorous since *Webster*, it could have been equally successful politically without the help of the Supreme Court.

Yet, like Sunstein's analysis of *Brown*, or Justice Powell's "no harm done" comments about *Hardwick*, the argument that pro-choice political power would have been the same without *Roe* ignores the transformative effect of *Roe* itself on the personal and political perceptions of millions of Americans. *Roe* spurred the pro-choice movement. Prior to *Roe*, access to abortion was limited and stigmatized. The barriers particularly hurt the least powerful women: those who were poor, young, in abusive relationships, or in danger of jeopardizing their economic or social well-being if they had to go through with an unwanted pregnancy. Prior to *Roe*, Americans did not think of the decision to bear or not to bear a child as a matter of constitutionally protected privacy.

Through *Roe*, the Court said to women, that the decisions affecting your liberty in the most profound ways are relevant to the "liberty" specified in the Fourteenth Amendment. By defining women's privacy as a liberty interest deserving constitutional protection, the Court read women's liberty into the Constitution and provided women with both the platform and legitimacy to argue that their concerns were a proper matter for public and political action. Thus, rather than impede the pro-choice movement, *Roe* helped to empower millions of women to see their private decisions, as Laurence Tribe writes in his recent book *The Clash of Absolutes*, not as a "dirty secret," but as a "right" worth fighting for.

Even if this political consciousness could have been created without *Roe*, what would have happened politically without *Roe?* Since *Roe*, women in every state have had substantial protection of the right to choose. How would a world without *Roe* have made things better? One of the major defeats pro-choice advocates have suffered since *Roe* involves Medicaid funding. It seems highly unlikely there would be Medicaid funds for abortions if *Roe* had never been decided. In fact, some of the states that do pay for Medicaid abortions do so on the grounds that the right to choose abortion is a protected constitutional right poor women cannot be denied. Even under the most optimistic "If Not for *Roe*" scenario, at least ten to fifteen states would continue to ban abortion, and many others would have likely imposed restrictions that hurt the most vulnerable women.

Sunstein's position might have appeared more tenable if a pro-choice majority had failed to awaken after *Webster* because supporters of the right to abortion had become so sleepily reliant on the courts. But the powerful pro-choice mobilization after *Webster* shows that the courts did not undermine the pro-choice movement. In fact, *Roe* had a profoundly positive effect on the long-term political support for the right to choose.

I should emphasize that I am not trying to replace Sunstein's optimism (we can still make progress on civil rights even with a bad Supreme Court) with my own pessimism (we can make no progress on civil rights with a bad Supreme Court). But we mislead ourselves if we do not fully appreciate how and why the Supreme Court has been essential to advancing civil rights. If the Supreme Court has been vital to political progress for disfavored groups by forcing institutions and individuals to reconsider discriminatory social habits, what will be the source of that moral leadership in the future? Recognizing the deep void now left by today's conservative Court tells us what we must demand of others—the President, powerful members of Congress, state supreme courts, governors, and civic leaders. Several state supreme courts have, for example, almost singlehandedly kept school financing on the national agenda through their interpretations of state constitutions.

I should also stress that I am not advocating that the Supreme Court should declare rights for the purpose of promoting political action. The Supreme Court's job is to interpret the Constitution—nothing more and nothing less. But neither the Court nor those who observe it should feel that a proper constitutional decision on behalf of individual rights is worthless or meaningless simply because the Supreme Court does not have the weapons to turn its words into instant reality.

One way or another, what the Court says and does has a broad effect on the values and long-term direction of our society. The Supreme Court has a special power to rise above the PACs, soundbites, and mean-spirited stereotypes and declare what America would have to be to adhere to the highest ideals expressed in our Constitution. Sometimes, through a multitude of pressures, tensions, and political and private acts, noble words spoken by the Court can move us toward a more free and just society.

[28b]

CASS R. SUNSTEIN

Cass R. Sunstein Responds

What is the appropriate role of the Supreme Court in producing social reform? For those interested in such reform—in areas including environmental controls, the social security system, civil rights, and criminal justice—how much reliance should be placed on the judiciary? At least in part, these are empirical questions rather than ones of value and policy. We need to know whether an aggressive judicial role actually accomplishes its intended purposes; whether it might mobilize opposition or demobilize support; whether it has harmful consequences for democracy and the practice of citizenship. These questions depend on the facts, not only on our aspirations.

For too long, those who study the Supreme Court have let their aspirations cloud their approach to the facts. This problem is especially serious for those who believe that the role for the Court charted out in Brown and Roe deserves to be repeated frequently in the next generation. Let there be, they are saying, one, two, three, a thousand *Browns*.

Gene Sperling's thoughtful comment contains many empirical claims about the real-world effects of Supreme Court decisions. He says, for example, that the successes of the civil rights movement depended on *Brown*; that "the *Brown* Court's declaration of rights" had "tremendous power" in creating the political and moral climate for that movement; that *Brown* "compelled white Americans to acknowledge the hypocrisy of" the "rights-reality gap and created a positive tension pressuring other institutions to respond"; that *Brown* "provided the basis for critical political victories"; that *Bowers v. Hardwick* significantly contributed to antihomosexual feelings; that *Roe* had a "transformative effect" on the "personal and political perceptions of millions of Americans"; indeed, that *Roe* "spurred the pro-choice movement."

These claims, and Sperling's others about the consequences of Supreme Court decisions, may actually be true. But I do not know whether they are. I wonder what makes Sperling so confident about them.

We might begin with *Brown*. The only extended study of Sperling's

385

claims strongly suggests that they are wrong. I cannot do justice to the detailed analysis of Gerald Rosenberg's forthcoming *The Hollow Hope*, but I can explain how Rosenberg casts doubt on the view that *Brown* paved the way for the civil rights movement. Above all, Rosenberg reveals that Sperling's claims that *Brown* indirectly caused and helped legitimate the civil rights movement, and that it exerted moral pressure and produced attitudinal changes on the part of whites, have little or no empirical support.

Rosenberg reveals, among other things, that the public civil rights pronouncements of Presidents Eisenhower, Kennedy, and Johnson did not refer to court decisions at all; that the Montgomery bus boycott was not attributable in any way to *Brown*, and indeed that black protests, there and elsewhere, were not directly or indirectly spurred by *Brown*; that there was no increase in media coverage of civil rights issues in the years following *Brown*; that there is no serious evidence that *Brown* inspired or even especially influenced Martin Luther King, Jr., and other civil rights leaders; that the number of civil rights bills introduced into Congress actually dropped in the years immediately following *Brown*; that Southern disapproval of desegregation immediately after *Brown*, and seven years after *Brown*, was about the same, thus weakening the suggestion that *Brown* exerted moral pressure on white Americans (a suggestion that incidentally cannot find support in opinion surveys or any other measures of white opinion); and that there is little evidence that *Brown* contributed to the civil rights acts of the 1960s especially in view of the fact that there were few references to the decision in the many thousands of pages of congressional debate.

It is relevant here that Martin Luther King himself argued, both by his example and in public speeches, against excessive reliance on the judiciary. According to King, "[W]e want to avoid court cases in this integration struggle," and an emphasis on litigation was "hampering progress to this day." For King, blacks "must not get involved in legalism," since in litigation "the ordinary Negro was involved [only] as a passive spectator." For King, Montgomery demonstrated that blacks themselves could act to advance civil rights, "rather than relying exclusively on lawyers and litigation to win incremental legal gains."

All this does not mean that Sperling is necessarily wrong. It is exceedingly difficult to ascertain what the world would look like if a seemingly important event—like *Brown*, or *Roe*, or World War II—had not happened. But the available evidence does suggest that Sperling's claims about the influence of the *Brown* Court may be articles of faith.

The same, I think, is true for his claims about *Roe* and *Hardwick*. Of course, *Roe* increased women's access to safe abortions, and that was extremely important; and the *Hardwick* Court's decision to allow sodomy prosecutions was important insofar as it has been taken to permit state officials to discharge gay people from employment. It is even possible that *Roe* created a political consciousness for women seeking an abortion right and that it helped fuel the pro-choice movement. But about both *Roe* and *Hardwick*, I do not think that one can say anything much more confident than this. Many of Sperling's claims here strike me as quite speculative.

What does seem clear is that the overall consequences of the *Roe* decision for sexual equality in the United States are ambiguous. That decision did, after all, help create the Moral Majority, elect officials hostile to the women's movement, defeat the Equal Rights Amendment, and demobilize potential support. What seems unproved and even doubtful is the view that *Roe* had a transformative effect in increasing the perceived legitimacy of the practice of abortion, and that *Hardwick* legitimated homophobia. Indeed, the opposite claims may well be true. In many places, the ultimate consequence of *Roe* may well have been to decrease and to stigmatize the legitimacy of abortion. And the large public outcry that followed *Hardwick* may have played some role in spurring gay rights groups and forcing Americans to confront and perhaps to change discriminatory beliefs and practices. Sperling's suggestions about the legitimating power of Supreme Court decisions seem to me insufficiently grounded in evidence.

My own claims about the consequences of Supreme Court decisions, here and in my original essay, are quite modest. I do not doubt that Supreme Court decisions often have important effects. I do not deny that the Court has often introduced valuable changes into American society. I do not believe that an independent judiciary is a marginal or irrelevant part of American institutions. I do not believe that *Brown, Roe,* and *Hardwick* have not mattered. I am not even certain that Sperling's claims about the consequences of these decisions are false. I suggest only that because of its institutional position, the Court is considerably less effective than is usually thought. Whether a Supreme Court decision will be effective in producing social reform depends on a wide range of complex factors difficult to assess, especially in advance. Those reformers who face up to the often-surprising facts may want, therefore, to hesitate before using the Court as their institution of choice.

My strong hunch is that Sperling's views may stem partly from the following strategic concern. Those who question the efficacy of Supreme Court decisions may be helping to legitimate the Supreme Court's narrow, cautious view of civil rights. That strategic concern will seem especially pressing to Americans who, reared on the Warren Court, see the judiciary as the best hope for rights and politically disfavored groups. But that strategic concern should not deflect us from a patient, dispassionate, and clear-eyed view of facts. If the case for effective social reform through the judiciary is weak, surely that is an important thing to know.

In any event, the era of the Warren Court has long been over. While a modern-day successor to that Court might have been able to accomplish considerable good, current reformers clearly cannot rely on the federal judiciary for social change in the interest of the causes Sperling appears to favor.

More fundamentally, people interested in social reform, understood broadly, ought to be interested in the process of government as much as the outcome. For all the advances that it spurred, the Warren Court period was a historical aberration, and it should hardly be thought to represent the inevitable or even the best state of constitutional democracy in America. One of the most important lessons of the last generation is that the substitution of adjudicative for democratic processes is often an ambiguous good from the standpoint of both process and result. The next generation might do well to attend more closely to Martin Luther King's words, and example, on these questions.

[29]

RANDALL KENNEDY

The Political Court

President Clinton will likely have the opportunity to fill several vacancies on the Supreme Court. How should he go about doing it? Although the president should look to a variety of considerations, by far the most important is a prospect's substantive political commitments. By substantive political commitments, I mean a prospect's stance toward the central, inescapable, politically significant controversies of our time. In the 1850s, a president should definitely have wanted to know where a prospect stood on the slavery question; in the 1930s, where a prospect stood on the New Deal; in the 1960s, where a prospect stood with respect to the civil rights revolution. Today President Clinton should acquire knowledge that will let him know in detail and with confidence where a prospective nominee stands on all of the most vexing issues that trouble our society including reproductive freedom, race relations, freedom of expression, and the status of religion in a secular society. To acquire this information, the president (and the Senate) should directly ask prospects about their political beliefs. If a person declines to answer, the president should probably draw a negative inference, strike that prospect from the list of candidates, and move on to consider others who will allow the president access to his or her thinking.

One thing the president should not do is place a powerful branch of government in the hands of individuals whose political commitments are unknown to him. That would be folly. Yet, remarkably, that is what some observers urge.

Consider, for instance, the argument of Professor Stephen Carter of the Yale Law School. In an op-ed piece in the *New York Times*, Carter claims that the Reagan and Bush administrations "systematically eroded federal courts' independence" by applying "litmus tests to insure that those who became Judges—particularly Supreme Court Justices—could be relied on to vote the way the conservatives preferred." He portrays "quizzing nominees about their views on controversial cases" as a politically depraved exercise of power heretofore practiced mainly by discredited politicos on the right.

According to Carter, "When William Brennan was badgered by Senator Joseph McCarthy about loyalty-security cases and Thurgood Marshall was interrogated by several segregationist senators about civil rights and criminal procedure cases, liberals were properly outraged that a nominee would be asked, even indirectly, about his likely votes." Carter rails against searching for information that will allow the president to predict confidently how a nominee will vote as a justice. "Certainly it is true," he concedes, "that information is usually available from which it is possible to make educated guesses about how potential justices might vote. But to emphasize those predispositions as a prerequisite for appointment politicizes the Court." The president, Carter concludes, "should forgo litmus tests and turn to one of the many experienced federal or state appellate judges whose skills are respected across the political spectrum." Otherwise, Carter warns darkly, the cycle of judicial politicization will never end and "[t]here will be less and less reason to treat the 'opinions' of the courts as authoritative and no reason at all to grant the judges —and justices—life tenure."

Carter's argument reflects much of the confusion, mysticism, and sentimentality that commonly stymies realistic understandings of the judiciary. He objects that the course I advocate would "politicize" the Court. It would be helpful if he would point to a moment in our history in which the selection process was unpoliticized—a point at which a president was blithely indifferent to the political associations and ideological predispositions of a prospective nominee and considered only "skill." He will be unable to make such a showing because, unsurprisingly, this moment has never existed. How could it? Members of the Supreme Court occupy seats with life tenure within a bureaucracy that wields considerable power. A president would be a fool or, worse, politically amoral to elevate to such an office anyone whose politics suggested a proclivity toward policies with which the president strongly disagreed.

Carter's references to the Reagan and Bush administrations' ideological screening of potential nominees and his allusions to the difficulties that William Brennan and Thurgood Marshall received as nominees at the hands of McCarthyists and segregationists should scare no one. There was, and is, nothing wrong with politicians of any ideological stripe demanding to know where prospective justices stand on political issues that are likely to be implicated in cases arising before the Court.

What was wrong in the instances to which Carter alludes was not the questioning but an environment in which straightforward progressive responses to the inquiries posed a danger to candidates. Instead of seeking to insulate nominees from questions, liberals and the left should seek to persuade the public of the attractiveness of progressive answers.

Carter claims that insisting upon knowing the political predispositions of nominees—or, in his lingo, imposing a litmus test—erodes the independence of the judiciary. But how so? Judicial independence means placing individuals beyond the usual means of political discipline *after* that person has been elevated to judicial office. That insulation is attended to by constitutional provisions that explicitly mention two mechanisms that afford ample protection to the judiciary against interference from the other branches of government. One is life tenure: once appointed and confirmed, judges can be removed only pursuant to impeachment by the House of Representatives and conviction by the Senate—a costly, cumbersome process that has never been successfully invoked to oust a recalcitrant justice.

The second is income protection: the Constitution forbids Congress from decreasing the salaries paid to members of the federal judiciary. Neither Carter nor anyone else has set forth a convincing or even plausible explanation of why judicial independence—the autonomy of sitting justices—is eroded by subjecting a person to inquiries designed to inform a president of the political virtues of one candidate as opposed to another. After all once a person is seated as a justice, the mechanisms protecting judicial independence ensure that person can change his or her mind without fear of losing office.

Moreover, contrary to what Carter suggests, it is precisely because justices are so fully insulated from the normal rigors of political discipline (that is, periodically standing for election) that it is especially important and appropriate for those responsible for elevating them to determine as fully as possible their political character. If the electorate makes a political mistake in selecting a president or a member of the House or Senate, the electorate must wait only two, four, or six years before rectifying that mistake. If the president makes a political mistake in the selection of a justice, only the indefinite and often painfully slow process of aging can remedy it.

Why is it important to know the political character of justices? Because their interpretation of statutes and determinations of the constitutionality of laws is inevitably influenced by that character. Expertise alone is an insufficient guide by which to determine who, from the point of view of a president, would best give meaning to the ambiguous, open-ended clauses that comprise the most important and controversial parts of our written constitution: due process, equal protection of the laws, freedom of speech. "Skill" of various sorts is important. A president should certainly insist on choosing someone who will be sufficiently adept, knowledgeable, and confident to persuade colleagues, isolate adversaries, and educate the public. But juristic skill is merely a tool; it does not guarantee that a justice will reach good results. For that to happen, expertise must be guided by a good political vision. It stands to reason that the president and the Senate should avail themselves of means by which to determine a prospect's political vision. Doing so shows no disrespect for the Court. Rather, it reflects a laudable determination to avoid putting the future of the federal judiciary into the hands of persons whose political commitments are unknown.

Carter and others claim that seeking to know in detail the political views of nominees or potential nominees is bad because it suggests a desire to select persons who are close-minded. "[A]ppointing justices who make up their minds before, not after, hearing arguments threatens judicial integrity," Carter writes, "and interferes with the Court's proper functioning. It was wrong for the Republicans to do it; it would be wrong if the Democrats do it." The specter Carter invokes is a straw man. Those with whom he argues do not advocate appointing justices who are closed to argument. Rather, they maintain that any person worthy of serious consideration has *already* considered arguments, that such a person has likely reached conclusions (that are possibly changeable in light of additional consideration), and that whatever conclusions he or she has reached should be accessible to a president. The idea that knowing a prospect's current views somehow taints the integrity of the selection process is hard to fathom, given that many of the best people any president is likely to consider for a justiceship are people with public careers whose stances on heated topics are already known.

Pleas to de-politicize the selection and confirmation process, to cherish unpredictability in the future course of nominees, to purposefully keep ourselves ignorant about the beliefs of people we empower represent a quasi-religious yearning to make the Court into a shrine above the messiness of politics. But what the process of selection and confirmation needs is *more* rather than less "politics"—more widely available knowledge about nominees, more debate, more participation by the governed, more presidential accountability for nominees, and more common sense. Neither the president nor the public should be asked to accept a pig in a poke. To know fully the political character of those he is considering selecting, the president must ask pointed questions—and demand clear answers.

The Contributors

Bruce Ackerman is the Sterling Professor of Law and Political Science at Yale University. He is the author of *The Future of Liberal Revolution*.

Benjamin R. Barber is Walt Whitman Professor of Political Science and director of the Walt Whitman Center for the Culture and Politics of Democracy at Rutgers, The State University of New Jersey.

Walter Dean Burnham holds the Frank C. Erwin, Jr., Chair in government at the University of Texas at Austin and is author of *The Current Crisis in American Politics*.

Jonathan S. Cohn is managing editor of *The American Prospect*.

Walter Dellinger is on leave from the Duke University School of Law as the Assistant Attorney General for the Office of Legal Counsel.

Leslie Epstein directs the creative writing program at Boston University. He is the author of *King of the Jews* and *Pinto and Sons*.

Jeff Faux is president of the Economic Policy Institute and co-author of *Rebuilding America*.

James S. Fishkin is professor of government, law, and philosophy and chair of the department of government at the University of Texas at Austin. He is the author of *Democracy and Deliberation: New Directions for Democratic Reform*.

Marshall Ganz is a doctoral candidate in sociology at Harvard University and teaches organizing at Harvard's Kennedy School of Government.

Stanley B. Greenberg is chairman and chief executive officer of Greenberg Research, Inc. He is now pollster to the president and an adviser to the Democratic National Committee.

Stephen Holmes is professor of political science and law at the University of Chicago. He is the author of *Anatomy of Antiliberalism*.

John B. Judis is Washington correspondent for *In These Times,* a contributing editor of *The New Republic,* and the author of *Grand Illusion: Critics and Champions of the American Century.*

Randall Kennedy is a professor at Harvard Law School and editor of *Reconstruction* magazine.

Robert Kuttner is an editor of *The American Prospect* and a syndicated columnist.

Laurence E. Lynn, Jr., is professor of social service administration and of public policy studies at the University of Chicago.

Will Marshall is president of the Progressive Policy Institute and co-editor of *Mandate for Change.*

Richard E. Neustadt is the Douglas Dillon Professor of Government, Emeritus, at the Kennedy School of Government at Harvard University and author of *Presidential Power.*

Karen Paget is a political scientist and co-author of *Running as a Woman.*

Nelson W. Polsby is director of the Institute of Governmental Studies and professor of political science at the University of California at Berkeley.

Robert D. Putnam is Dillon Professor of International Affairs and director of the Center for International Studies at Harvard University.

Gene B. Sperling is deputy assistant to the president for economic policy.

Paul Starr is an editor of *The American Prospect* and professor of sociology at Princeton University.

Deborah A. Stone, senior editor of *The American Prospect,* is a professor at the Heller School of Social Work, Brandeis University.

Cass R. Sunstein is Karl Llewellyn Professor of Jurisprudence at the University of Chicago Law School and department of political science.

Richard M. Valelly is an associate professor of political science at Swarthmore College.